David Lockwood is an associate professor in History at Flinders University in South Australia. He teaches Russian, Chinese and Indian history together with broad topics in world history. He is especially interested in the role of the bourgeoisie in historical development. He combines this with work in the broad areas of the role of the state in economic development; the transition from state-controlled to market economies; and the effects of globalisation on national states. His most recent book was a monograph on the bourgeois revolution in Russia.

THE INDIAN BOURGEOISIE

A Political History of the Indian Capitalist Class in the Early Twentieth Century

DAVID LOCKWOOD

BLOOMSBURY
NEW DELHI • LONDON • OXFORD • NEW YORK • SYDNEY

BLOOMSBURY INDIA
Bloomsbury Publishing India Pvt. Ltd
Second Floor, LSC Building No. 4, DDA Complex, Pocket C–6&7,
Vasant Kunj, New Delhi 110070

BLOOMSBURY, Bloomsbury Academic India and the Diana
logo are trademarks of Bloomsbury Publishing Plc

First published in India 2022
Published in 2012 by I.B.Tauris & Co Ltd
Distributed in the United States and Canada Exclusively by Palgrave Macmillan
175 Fifth Avenue, New York NY 10010

A catalog record for this book is available from the Library of Congress.
A catalogue record for this book is available from the British Library.

ISBN: 978-93-56400-96-2
For sale in the Indian subcontinent only

Exclusively distributed in the Indian subcontinent by
Manohar Publishers & Distributors
4753/23, Ansari Road
Darya Ganj, New Delhi 110002
Tel.: 23284848, 23289100
Email: sales@manoharbooks.com, manoharbooks@gmail.com

Typeset by Newgen Publishers, Chennai
Printed and bound in India by Replika Press Pvt. Ltd.

To find out more about our authors and books visit
www.bloomsbury.com and sign up for our newsletters.

CONTENTS

Acknowledgements vi

Introduction 1

Chapter One: Industry and Industrialists before 1914 8

Chapter Two: The Great War 30

Chapter Three: Industrialisation Abandoned 52

Chapter Four: Empire 73

Chapter Five: Protection and Development: State and Bourgeoisie in the Inter-War Period 93

Chapter Six: Congress and the Bourgeoisie: Inter-War Politics 126

Chapter Seven: The Second World War 149

Chapter Eight: Planning and Partition 174

Conclusion 195

Notes 199

Bibliography 292

Index 310

ACKNOWLEDGEMENTS

I would like to acknowledge my intellectual debt to Nigel Harris and to Aditya Mukherjee in establishing the theoretical foundations of this book. I would like to thank my wife Sue and my son Karl, Graham Willett, my parents and my colleagues at Flinders University for their abiding support. Thanks should also go to the hard working staff in the Manuscripts Section of the Nehru Memorial Museum and Library in Delhi and at the Tata Central Archive in Pune.

Swaraj is not a question of sentiment, it is a question of bread. The prosperity of the country depends entirely on the amount of political freedom which we get and I think that not only in the interests of the country but in the interests of the capitalists, the employers and the industrialists we should try to fight and strengthen the hands of those who are fighting for Swaraj.

– Ghanshyamdas Birla, speaking at the Annual Meeting of the Federation of Indian Chambers of Commerce and Industry (FICCI), 16 February 1930.

INTRODUCTION

In 1970, the choice of car for well-heeled citizens of India was limited to three: the Hindustan Ambassador, the Premier Padmini or the Standard Gazel. For each model, availability was limited and the waiting lists sometimes stretched out for years. Even when new, the cars seemed old-fashioned and outdated. The car market was stagnating. The Indian Government decided to act. But it did not loosen the restrictions that had confined car production to three companies since Independence and it did not encourage private enterprise to take up the challenge. Instead, having decided in 1971 to produce a 'People's Car', the Government of Indira Gandhi awarded an exclusive contract for its design, development and manufacture to her trusted son, Sanjay. Criticism of this decision was soon drowned out by the war to liberate Bangladesh, which began shortly afterwards. Thus was born the 'Maruti' car – or, rather, not yet born, since no cars were actually produced by the time of Sanjay's death in 1980. In India, in the 1970s, the Sanjay/Maruti story fitted into a pattern of state economic arrogance, corruption and failure.

In July 1991, the Indian Government announced a series of economic reforms that started to ease the formidable control that the Indian state exercised over the economy. The reforms started a process of gradual privatisation in the public sector, the dismantling of the state industrial licensing system and the opening up of India to foreign investment. These reforms were initiated at a time when the world was coming to regard such things as commonplace. China, Eastern Europe, Vietnam, the Soviet Union and South Africa had all set about (consciously or otherwise) dismantling their state-run economies.[1] The Indian reforms were designed to open up the Indian economy to market forces and global competition.[2]

There is no evidence to suggest that the Indian reforms resulted from the demands of Indian capitalists. In fact, quite the contrary was the case. The reforms were initiated by state decree as the result of an economic crisis, a consequent balance of payments failure and the rippling effects of the first Gulf War.[3] As with almost everything else that had been done to the Indian economy since 1947, the execution of these reforms was a state-run operation.

Since Independence in 1947, the Indian state had managed to create a state-controlled and regulated economy. It was centrally planned. Industry was dominated by over 200 state-owned enterprises. The private sector was held down by a complex system of regulations, which the state could either rigidly enforce or relax at will. Ostensibly, these were designed to check the rise of monopolies. In fact, they gave the state control over business expansion. Eventually, the state would bar large business groups from key sectors of the economy. The era was known as the 'licence-permit-quota' raj.[4]

The severe effects of such a system were not confined to economic structures alone. Under it, there was an ongoing 'statification' of the Indian capitalist class, as it was pressed into a role that the state considered suitable. Since the state controlled the economy and enforced regulations as it saw fit, business had to continually approach and persuade state officials at all levels to obtain permits or circumvent regulations. Many capitalist concerns set up 'industrial embassies' in Delhi to carry out this lobbying on a permanent basis. Business had to establish and maintain high-level contact with ruling politicians. The easiest way to do this was by doing their bidding – whether that was by obeying the rules, ensuring jobs for their relatives or offering substantial bribes.[5]

This left little room for innovative entrepreneurship. Over 40 years, the Indian bourgeoisie simply decayed as a capitalist class. Dwijendra Tripathi tells us (concentrating on the period of Indira Gandhi's prime ministership) that prominent business houses 'concentrated on nursing what they already had instead of launching new ventures'. The period had 'an adverse impact on business confidence' and was 'marked by the lack of any significant development in the realm of structure and strategy'.[6] A weakening bourgeoisie was consequently unable to stop the steady expansion of the state sector, periodic nationalisations and popular campaigns against capitalists.[7]

New industries did emerge under Gandhi. But it appears that they only did so because they were *more* subservient to the state than the old ones.[8] As a result, they did not encourage innovation and technological advance; 'with the luxury of a vast domestic market largely protected against external competition, they paid less than necessary attention to the quality of their products as well as research and development'.[9]

By the late 1980s, then, one analyst could claim with some accuracy that the Indian bourgeoisie 'is not a clearly articulated business class and is neither capable of acting as a unified lobby nor of pursuing a long term policy to achieve well defined objectives'. Instead, it had become 'a rent-seeking, highly dependent, inward-looking, mercantilist-oriented business elite'.[10]

It was not always thus.

This book is about an Indian bourgeoisie that, from 1900 to 1947, cohered into a powerful, though frustrated, industrial class – a class that became, precisely because of that frustration, a political force as well. The industrial development of India, and therefore of the bourgeoisie, was twice conjured up by Britain and twice dampened down by them. For the advance of India's productive forces, industrialisation was necessary. Its advance was blocked by the interests of the British Empire in India. Those interests refused to provide the state support for industrialisation, which the bourgeoisie knew was necessary. The bourgeoisie was thus pushed into political opposition to Britain. It could not hope to take on the Raj alone. For that, it needed mass support (which it could only obtain by fusing its aims with those of the national anti-colonial movement) and political representation (which would be provided by the Indian National Congress). In this way, during the inter-war period in particular, the Indian bourgeoisie became the kind of class – articulate, unified, with definite objectives – that Stanley Kochanek (the analyst quoted above) says it was not in 1987.

Planted within the development of the bourgeoisie along these lines, however, there was a slow, but ticking, time bomb. The bourgeoisie wanted state economic intervention; so did the Congress. The capitalists were prepared to accept state planning and state control. In independent India, state economic intervention was turned into the heavily state-regulated economy described above.

The purpose of this book is to explain why the Indian capitalist class voluntarily submitted itself to the beginnings of this process in 1947.

The study is guided by the twin concepts of historical materialism and the bourgeois revolution. In terms of historical materialism, the account is based on three premises. The first is that the level of development of the productive forces provides the basis for the existence of a particular set of production relations (the economic structure), which in turn gives rise to a legal and political superstructure.[11] The economic structure exists *because* it has the ability to advance productive power – that is, to promote the tendency of the productive forces to develop. On the relationship between the forces and relations of production, Karl Marx wrote that '[a]t a certain stage of development, the material productive forces of society come into conflict with the existing relations of production'. The latter restrict (or 'fetter') the development of the former.[12] Historical advance, then, is a continuing process of productive force development, production relation fettering and eventual change in the latter forced through by the former. In India, the development of the productive forces, represented by industrialisation, came into conflict with the production relations enforced by the British state. One or the other had to give way.

The second premise is a development in the theory of historical materialism: the argument that the state, rather than being a part of the legal and political superstructure (as most Marxists assume), is in fact a production relation itself.[13] So, in a set of production relations that makes up an economic structure, it is possible that the state production relation can dominate. And were that to be the case (as it has been – and, in a very few cases, still is), that economic structure and the society it gives rise to would be dominated by the priorities of the state: defence, military preparedness, the making of war and the mobilisation of the population to those ends. The importance of this in the Indian context lies in the fact that India was, under the

British, a society dominated by the state production relation. In the context of the anti-colonial struggle, the bourgeoisie was willing to remain dominated by the same production relation, but by a different state. In both phases, the state dominated capital – until the reforms of 1991.

The third premise is that, historically, where state-dominated production relations have existed, they are eventually forced, through military competition with other states, to develop the forces of production. This was why, in two world wars, the British state appeared to be willing to develop and nurture industry in India. But on each occasion, it was frightened by the forces that it might unleash – and therefore withdrew instead into an 'imperial economic union', in which India could only play a subservient, agrarian role. The development of India's forces of production, then, depended on the existence of an Indian state.

The events and developments covered in this study represented the initial stages of the bourgeois revolution in India. Is this a plausible view, considering the size and strength of the bourgeoisie at the time and its dependence on Congress?

A study of bourgeois revolutions, of both the 'classical' variety (England, America and France) and those 'from above' (German and Italian unification, the Meiji Restoration),[14] reveals that the foundations of the bourgeois revolution and for a capitalist economy are not laid by the bourgeoisie itself. The bourgeoisie may not be fully formed before the bourgeois revolution and may not emerge immediately in its wake. In the advanced countries, it took the bourgeoisie a considerable historical period to develop. For Marx and Frederick Engels, it was 'the product of a long course of development, of a series of revolutions in the modes of production and exchange'.[15] Engels describes 'the long fight of the bourgeoisie against feudalism' in Britain as proceeding from the Reformation, through Calvinism and the English Revolution, encompassing the 'Glorious Revolution', inspired by the French Revolution, right up to the 1832 Reform Act – a period of some 300 years.[16] Bourgeois revolutions, then, are 'not . . . revolutions consciously made by capitalists, but . . . revolutions which promote capitalism'.[17]

The emergence of the first shoots of capitalism was a by-product of the need of states 'to maximise both their military investments and the efficiency of those investments'.[18] In fact, by the late nineteenth century, the state-sponsored revolution from above had become the usual form of the bourgeois revolution. Engels described it as part of 'the new age of revolution from above'.[19] The state's revolution from above, pursued for military ends, became a much more common historical phenomenon than revolution of the English, American or French type. States were, of course, generally either unconscious of the forces that they were unleashing or confident of their ability to control them.[20] The British state in India, however, for reasons touched on above and examined in detail in the book, did not consistently encourage widespread industrialisation. Its economic and political structures therefore became a fetter on the development of India's productive forces. For the forces to develop, those fetters had to be broken – the first stage of the bourgeois revolution in India. That it was carried through by a rival or putative state (the Congress) in alliance with the bourgeoisie should not obscure the fact that the final aim of the bourgeois revolution is to ensure the domination of capital as a production relation rather than the state. The aims of the state and capital are, in the long run, different.

The study is framed by two world wars. This illustrates the importance of the state in this account, since war (and defence-related issues) is the business of states and, by the twentieth century, the British state's relationship with India was primarily a military one. In the first of these wars, the Indian bourgeoisie received a boost from the British, which it hoped would continue. It did not. In the second, the bourgeoisie finally shed its hopes for British state-sponsored industrial development and confirmed its alliance with the Congress. The period in between these wars saw economic necessity push the Indian capitalists steadily closer to the movement for freedom.

Chapter one examines indigenous Indian industry and industrialists as well as the attitude of the British authorities towards them before 1914. Chapter two covers the significant development of Indian industry during the First World War. It outlines the encouragement given to Indian industrialists by both the Government of India and the

British Government, producing hopes of a rosy future under British rule amongst the capitalists. Such hopes had to be abandoned when the British state withdrew its support after the war, covered in chapter three. To fully explain why this occurred, chapter four involves a lengthy excursus into the nature of colonialism and Britain's attitude to India in the post-war world. Chapters five and six consider the economic pressures that pushed the bourgeoisie towards the Congress and the political manifestations of this emerging alliance. Chapter six also considers economic policies of the Congress and suggests some reasons for them. The Second World War is dealt with in chapter seven – India's position in British imperial strategy and its effect on the war economy are examined. What was needed for the defence of Empire is contrasted with the needs of the defence of India. The seeds of partition are also considered. In the final chapter, we see the cohering of a state-run economy out of the war. The eventual acquiescence of the bourgeoisie to partition is explained. The conclusion considers the position of the Indian bourgeoisie at the start of Indian Independence.

CHAPTER ONE

INDUSTRY AND INDUSTRIALISTS BEFORE 1914

Indian industry

The development of industry in India was not originally a priority of either British capital or the British state. Even less of a preoccupation was the development of industry owned and operated by Indians. British commercial interests focussed on the extraction of raw materials for export and the construction of the infrastructure essential for this purpose. The British state regarded India as a great strategic asset – a base for prosecuting the interests of the British Empire in the East. But the equipment for that prosecution would come, as far as possible, from Britain.[1]

Yet industry did develop in India, at first in the hands of British manufacturing entrepreneurs, and then through the efforts of an emerging Indian bourgeoisie.[2] The foundations of capitalism were laid down by the British (as Marx had suggested they would be[3]), through and around their great trading ports. Indians also built on these foundations. Scottish and English businessmen established jute and tea industries in the latter half of the nineteenth century, while Indians pioneered the cotton textile industry, especially in Bombay.[4] The latter were helped considerably by the capital accumulated as a consequence of the cotton boom resulting from the American Civil War.[5]

The origins of the early Indian capitalists lay among trading communities. Shiva Chandra Jha suggests that Indians taking up commercial or industrial activities were either those whose caste status permitted such an occupation, or those outside the caste structure. From the first category came Gujarati trading castes and Marwari moneylenders, followed by Chettis (moneylenders) and Naidus (cotton traders) from South India. From the second category came primarily the Parsee community of Bombay.[6]

From 1900, Indian industrialists moved into coal mining, especially in Bengal. By 1914, some four dozen mines were together producing over fifteen million tons of coal annually, making India a net coal exporter.[7] Attempts were also being made by Indians to initiate the production of iron and steel (see below). Amartya Kumar Sen notes that 'the two manufacturing industries that provided the basis of the British industrial revolution, namely cotton textiles and iron and steel, were both developed mainly by Indian and not British enterprises'.[8] Taking Indian and British industry together, Morris estimates that by 1914 India had one of the world's five largest cotton textiles industries, one of the two largest jute industries and the third largest railway network.[9]

In terms of industrial development, however, India had a number of weaknesses. There was little heavy industry (except that associated with railways) and even less capacity in 'new' industries – chemicals or heavy electricals, for example. Industry was concentrated in three areas: Bombay, Calcutta and the western Bengal/Bihar coal mining region. And the capacities of Indian industrialists were dwarfed by those of British stock.

Further development, especially of Indian-owned industry, required some kind of external stimulus. The obvious candidate for this role was the state, whether in the form of the British Government or the Government of India. As we shall see, government policy was somewhat erratic on this question, until its hand was forced by war. Generally speaking however, Morris is correct to conclude that 'the basic nineteenth-century policies of the government [of India] had produced by World War I about all the benefits that they could automatically yield'.[10]

Indian industrialists

'The Indian *bourgeoisie*,' says Sen, 'was not a decaying, but a rising class in 1914.'[11] Indian industrialists were conscious of their interests and organised to defend them – most especially to pressure the Government of India to initiate, advance and protect Indian industries. Annual industrial conferences were held together with industrial exhibitions, beginning in Benares in 1905 and after that meeting in tandem with the annual sessions of the Indian National Congress.

Indigenous enterprise was inspired and supported by the Swadeshi movement from 1905 onwards. Originating in the campaign against the partition of Bengal (executed in October 1905), Swadeshi was, according to *The Leader* in Allahabad,

> the promotion of indigenous industries, the use of articles of indigenous manufactures. It is essentially and almost wholly a movement of an industrial revival, destitute of all political significance, and only patriotic so far as the love of indigenous industries is concerned.[12]

Accordingly, the campaign established Swadeshi enterprises 'for the manufacture of piece goods, soap, matches, pencils and cutlery, and of stores where the products of these factories were to be sold'.[13] On occasion, larger manufacturers took up the Swadeshi theme. A number of Indian cigarette manufacturers were established in Calcutta and East Bengal.[14] The Swadeshi Steam Navigation Company advertised as follows:

> Do you want mother India to ascend her ancient throne and lead the world's nations? Then help at once . . . this pioneer shipping industry financed, managed and run by Indians on purely *national* lines.[15]

The other part of the Swadeshi movement was a boycott of foreign goods. On this count, major sections of Indian business were not so keen.[16] They were at pains to portray Swadeshi as an economic movement, not a political one. The president of the 4th Industrial Conference, held in Madras in 1908, declared that Swadeshi 'is not combative and aggressive, but merely demands from the people support and protection for the nascent industries of this country, in the keen competition they have to meet from the established ones of foreign lands'.[17] Yet in an autocratic system, the views and demands of the industrialists, however modestly economic they may have appeared, inevitably became questions of policy and politics. The industrial conferences themselves, according to the Montagu-Chelmsford Report in 1919, 'had the effect of linking the movement towards industrial independence more closely with politics'.[18] M.B. Dadabhoy told the seventh industrial conference in 1911: 'Political power is the handmaid to industrial success ... Political servitude follows commercial and industrial servitude as sure as night the day.'[19] Opening the United Provinces Industrial Exhibition in December 1910, the Lieutenant Governor, Sir John Hewett, emphasised the importance of economic development, for 'in India political questions are as nothing compared to economical ones'. Two days later, *The Leader* replied:

> His Honour would have carried opinion entirely with him if there were no relationship between the two. In point of fact, industrial development in India is greatly dependent upon Government action, and political reform which will facilitate economic progress cannot be made light of.[20]

Many of the Swadeshi enterprises eventually failed. Despite the industrialists' protestations, Swadeshi was essentially a political movement rather than an exercise in viable economics. Its aims concerning the advance of indigenous industry coincided with those of the Indian capitalists. In the wake of the movement's decline and the failure of the Swadeshi enterprises, the bourgeoisie drew two political conclusions. The first, according to Montagu and Chelmsford, was that '[t]he people have recognised their inability to carry out their own programme without the help and guidance of Government'.[21] The second, as expressed by D.E. Warcha, a prominent spokesman for Indian mill owners at the 1901 Congress session, was that:

> the fundamental notion of Swadeshi, that of self-help was wrong. There would be no industrial development unless the government could be persuaded to change its policies. Political work to this end, and not self-help, must be the main line of nationalist activity.[22]

State intervention was necessary for Indian industry to develop. To bring it about, there had to be a change in the Government of India's non-interventionist (and at times anti-interventionist) stance.

Demands on the state

The bourgeoisie and its representatives therefore increasingly directed its demands to the British state. In 1892, the judge and social reformer Mahadev Govind Ranade, speaking at the Deccan College in Poona, had suggested that 'the pioneering of new enterprises is a duty which the Government might . . . systematically undertake with advantage'.[23] Over the next few years, the Indian capitalist programme manifested itself through industrial conferences at both provincial and national levels. A general stand was established in favour of state intervention for industrial development.[24] At the 1st Industrial Conference in 1905, Lala Baij Nath was confident that the Government of India would respond positively.[25] Three years later, the Conference president was a little more critical:

> In a country situated as India is, a special responsibility lies on the Government to promote the expansion of commerce, the revival of old industries and the establishment of new ones . . . But little has been done to give support or encouragement to the manufacturing industries.[26]

The Conference called for the appointment of a Director of Industries in each province and a state industrial plan. During this period, the state's policy on this question lacked any consistency, as we shall see presently. In the absence of government action, the industrialists' level of criticism rose. 'A benevolent activity' could not be expected from the government, R.N. Mukherji told the Allahabad Conference in 1910. Nevertheless, he demanded: 'Nothing short of definite, and fully authorised assurances of support, confirmed, if necessary by legislative enactment.'[27] *The Leader* suggested that if the government would not help, industrialists should consider moving their operations into the princely states, where they might receive more aid.[28] A call was also made for the provision of technical and industrial education by the state to train future industrial leaders. As early as 1887, the Indian National Congress session had called on the government 'to elaborate a system of Technical Education, suitable to the condition of the country, to encourage indigenous manufactures ... in regard to utilizing such manufactures for State purposes'.[29]

The experience of other countries and the activities of their governments were often held up as an example for the Government of India to follow. This ranged from broad categories like 'the West' to the more specific examples of France and Germany.[30] But the experience most often cited was that of Japan. 'How sadly the attitude of the Indian Government towards Indian industries contrasts with that of the Japanese Government towards Japan's industries', editorialised *The Leader* on 9 March 1910. The Indian Industrial Commission noted some years later: 'the success of Japanese industries, brought home forcibly to India by a very large increase of Japanese imports, was cited as an instance of what a previously backward eastern nation could accomplish with Government encouragement'.[31]

Indian industrialists also demanded of the state protection of Indian industries against foreign (including British) competition. Lala Baij Nath pointed out that 'there never was any free trade before the advent of British rule, nor is it suited to the circumstances of the country'.[32] This question, said the president of the 1908 Conference, 'must be pressed again and again'.[33] And it was. Syed Hasan Imam told a Provincial Industrial Conference in Bihar that 'no infant industry can be expected to stand the tug of war with industries in their manhood ... Protection of home industries ... should be the concern of the individual and the state alike'.[34] R.N. Mukherji exhorted the industrial representatives in 1910 that 'not only this Conference but every man of this country should continue to constitutionally agitate, until Government affords Protection, in some shape or other, to local manufacturers'.[35]

These demands met with some sympathy in the administration of the Government of India. The British Trade Commissioner Thomas Ainscough had described Swadeshi as 'an earnest desire among both Indians and Europeans, industrialists, merchants and officials alike, to render India as far as possible self supporting'. According to the Montagu-Chelmsford Report, 'Government officials were allowed and even encouraged to assist the [industrial] conferences'. No less a person than Sir Guilford Molesworth, an engineer and a senior railways adviser to the government, told the 1st Industrial Conference, 'India requires protection from England as well [as] from foreign countries'. He declared that the Government of India should govern India '*in the interests of India alone*'.[36] At even greater heights, the Viceroy Lord Minto wrote to the Secretary of State for India, Lord Morley, in 1910: 'I have long thought that the great battle of future Indian policy will be fought over tariffs. The natural desire to foster Indian industries must be in opposition to any favouritism of imports from home.'[37]

Possibly encouraged by sentiments such as these, Indian capitalists before 1914 appear to have been brightly optimistic about the prospects of changing government policy on industrial development. Nath said in 1905: '[T]he Government of India ... has always taken the initiative in fostering new industries or reviving decaying ones.'[38] The following year Sassoon David told the Bombay Millowners Association: '[C]hallenged though my views may be in some quarters I earnestly believe that the Government of India are most sincere in their desire to help local industries.'[39]

The 1908 Conference was assured that 'further State aid will be forthcoming as soon as we have proved our fitness to take full advantage of it'.[40] Vishnawath Prasad Marta told the Bihar provincial conference in 1910 that 'the Government is always ready to foster and encourage the infant industries of the country'.[41] In the years before the First World War, these hopes of state intervention were repeatedly to be raised – and dashed.

The Government of India and industry

The Government of India was not deaf to the demands of Indian industrialists and politicians. Its response to those demands resulted from a combination of its own interests, those of the British Government, its problems with revenue, the political situation in India and the strategic interests of the Empire.[42]

The government undertook infrastructural development that was necessary to British trade and British strategy – railways, docks, ports and harbours. But in the latter half of the nineteenth century, the government's industrial development policy, according to the Indian Industrial Commission, consisted only of 'a very imperfect provision of technical and industrial education, and the collection and dissemination of commercial and industrial information'.[43] As noted above, sections of the administration saw no problem with state intervention in the economy. The Madras Agriculture Committee declared in 1888 that 'active intervention to lead and assist agricultural progress' was 'absolutely necessary'.[44] The Superintendent of the Government Gun-Carriage Factory in Madras, Captain Collingwood Townsend, suggested establishing a local iron and steel industry and *ordering* the state railways, the military and the Public Works Department to use its products.[45] But attempts to use state intervention to develop Indian industries were generally met with grim-visaged laissez-faire condemnation from London. When the Government of India imposed duties on manufactured cotton imports (for reasons of revenue rather than protection), the House of Commons unanimously resolved in July 1877 that the duties, 'being protective in their nature, are contrary to sound commercial policy and ought to be replaced without delay'.[46]

The prospects brightened somewhat under the Viceroyalty of Lord Curzon, from 1899 to 1905. Curzon believed that India would become 'the greatest partner in the Empire' – that is, not just an adjunct to Britain – and that it should be ruled from India in the interests of

India.[47] To that end, India should be developed into 'a great industrial and manufacturing country'. In 1904 he told the Legislative Council that the Government of India 'have done all in their power to develop the Commerce and Industries of this country'. The following year he told them:

> The days are gone when Government can dissociate itself from the encouragement of commercial enterprise ... the whole air is alive with movement, rivalry, competition ... we desire to push our products, our manufactures, and our industries upon the attention of the whole world.[48]

Advances were made. The rules for the purchase of government stores were altered and industrial and technical instruction facilities were extended. A central Department of Commerce and Industry was set up in March 1905. Curzon made it clear that this was not to be 'an agency for the promotion of British commerce alone'; the new Department was concerned 'only with the development of the country'.[49] Some assistance was given to the iron and steel industry (see below). Government experiments with different strains of tobacco were carried out in aid of the fledgling cigarette industry.[50] Curzon's administration opposed protection, however, since 'protective measures would necessarily seriously affect imports from the United Kingdom'.[51] On the other hand, it also rejected schemes of 'imperial preference' (privileging imports from the Empire) when this was raised by the British Government in 1903.[52]

The Tata experience

Jamsetji Tata was one of the Bombay cotton industrialists whose attempts at accumulating capital were aided by the American Civil War and the Second Abyssinian War of 1868. He used it to advantage in the textile industry before attempting to expand into iron and steel. According to his biographer, this was with patriotic motives in mind:

> [H]e saw that under the exploitation of colonial rule his country was being bypassed by the industrial revolution which was

> rapidly transforming Europe and America ... he decided, almost single-handed, to launch India on the path of modern science and industry and to risk his future in the process.[53]

Patriotism, however, did not rule out an appeal to the Government of India for support. Initially, this seemed to be forthcoming. In 1882, the Viceroy Lord Ripon proposed that iron and steel production should be initiated in India. This would, he suggested, reduce the cost of railway construction, reduce the Government of India's Home Charges, create non-agricultural employment and create areas for capital investment.[54] The Government of India's Finance Department declared in August 1882:

> The Government of India have, for some time past, had under special consideration the importance of developing the iron and steel industry. The advantages which such a development would afford to both the State and the public ... are too well-known to require exposition.[55]

Ripon's administration therefore proposed that the government should aid prospective iron and steel producers. The Government of India 'have offered the patronage of the State to any company which will pioneer the new industry', wrote *The Economist* India correspondent in November 1882.[56]

But the proposal was rejected in London. The Secretary of State, Lord Hartington, told Parliament a few days later that prospective iron producers in India should stand on their own feet, without government aid – and that the Government of India had been made aware of Britain's serious objections to the scheme.[57]

Attitudes towards the Indian iron and steel industry were to change – and quite rapidly. The prospect of government aid was resurrected by Curzon after he became Viceroy in 1899. Curzon was, as we know, fired by 'the strategic vision of India as a second base of British power east of Suez' – for which military industry was required.[58] To this end, his administration reformed the mining rules, encouraged British capitalists to invest and subsidised the Bengal Iron and Steel

Company.[59] That the British Government allowed him to do this might say something about the force of Curzon's personality, but it was also due to what the British saw as looming commercial and strategic threats. Belgian steel had made an appearance on the Indian market and although, according to the Government of India, inferior to the British product, it was cheaper – and therefore, along with German steel, was displacing it.[60]

Tata's efforts, initially buoyed by Ripon's proposals, had thus far been held back by lack of state assistance. The Curzon administration, by contrast, seemed likely to aid Tata in his plans for iron and steel production. Perhaps in order to ensure that this positive approach was not blocked again, in 1900 Tata travelled to London. He met the new Secretary of State, Lord Hamilton, who 'promised to authorize the Government of India to give him all possible help. The promise was faithfully fulfilled'.[61] Tata and Sons informed the Industry and Commerce member of the Government of India:

> we proceed with our Scheme in express reliance on the assurance given by Lord G. Hamilton and the Government of Lord Curzon ... that we shall receive at the hands of the Government the same treatment as any other manufacturer of Iron, Steel and Railway Material in India.[62]

As far as Tata and Sons were concerned, that treatment included large amounts of state aid. In the same letter they requested extra railway lines to the iron and steel works, concessional freight rates and some guarantee that the railways would purchase rails from Tata Iron and Steel. They asked the government to 'instruct the Railways that it is Government policy to encourage the consumption by Railways of articles made in the country'.

In pursuit of a state-constructed railway line for the transport of ore to the proposed steel works, Tata Iron and Steel met with the managing director of the Bengal-Nagpur Railway Company, Robert Miller, in 1904–5. In Miller, the Tata representatives were confronted with a curious combination of state intervention and commercial indifference. He told them: 'We are an executive agency on behalf of the Government of India. The railway is the property of the Government of India.' He admitted that '[w]hen Mr Tata first came to this country, he was wet-blanketed and told to take his proposal away'. Yet despite the Government of India's new policy, when the Tata representatives put their proposals in terms of national development, he insisted:

> This Railway Company ... is a commercial undertaking, and must not be actuated by anything like patriotic or philanthropic motives: it must only be actuated by commercial motives. We must not consider the advantages to India; and, figuratively, we do not care a snap of the fingers about the advantages to India. What we have to think of is the interests of this Company as a commercial concern.[63]

Nevertheless, state aid was forthcoming. W.L. Harvey, secretary to the Government of India, wrote to Tata in August 1905 that 'the Government of India are desirous of rendering you all reasonable assistance'. A reduction in freight rates was promised, as was the guaranteed annual purchase by the government of 20,000 tons of steel rails. Harvey was confident that 'railway companies will readily follow the lead given by the Government'. Approval for the construction of a railway to the works was promised by Harvey and confirmed by the Secretary of State in July 1906.[64]

Government support in the provinces

Curzon's policies allowed the Provincial Government of Madras to commence a programme of state intervention in Indian industry. The leading figure here was Alfred Chatterton, who would become the Madras Director of Industrial and Technical Inquiries (in 1906) and then the Director of Industries (in 1908). In a memorandum to the Provincial Government in January 1901, Chatterton set out a scheme of general import substitution, which included regaining the local market in cotton fabrics for Indian producers. He urged the government to use locally manufactured goods and to provide help for new industries.[65] Later he wrote that if this scheme were followed, 'Indians will gradually acquire a commanding position in the mercantile and manufacturing industries of the Presidency. This, I submit, is eminently desirable'.[66]

Through the government-run Madras School of Arts, Chatterton initiated state manufacturing in aluminium, leather tanning and weaving. These efforts were praised by Indian industrialists – for example at the Industrial Conference held in Madras in 1908.[67] But they produced a predictable outcry from the European business community, which, according to the Indian Industrial Commission, 'interpreted them as a serious menace to private enterprise and an unwarrantable intervention on the part of the State in matters beyond the sphere of Government. On the other hand, the Indian public approved of the policy which had been pursued.'[68]

Chatterton seemed as interested in pursuing state interests as in fostering Indian enterprise. In response to European objections, he pointed out that if the School of Arts had not started manufacturing aluminium goods, they would have to be imported – from Germany. In the leather industry, he circularised the local regimental commanders, advertising the benefits of state-produced leather for marching boots.[69]

Despite European objections, the attitude of both central and provincial governments to Indian industrialisation was clearly a positive one. *The Leader* noted on 20 December 1909 that 'sympathy with the efforts of the people to make an advance in the establishment of manufacturing industries' was expressed by 'exalted personages' from the Governor of the Punjab (Sir Louis Dane) to the Viceroy.[70] The Governor of Bombay announced an industrial survey in January 1910 'to ascertain the obstacles with which the various local industries contend, and to devise measures for their removal'.[71] Local officials helped in the organisation of provincial industrial conferences.[72] The Lieutenant Governor of the United Provinces, Sir John Hewett, convened an industrial conference at Naini Tal in May 1907. The conference requested the appointment of a Director of Industries, the stimulation of existing industries and the introduction of new ones – as well as government loans and grants to that end.[73] Sir John endorsed these proposals.[74]

The following year, the Governor of Madras, Sir Arthur Lawley, convened an industrial conference in Ootacamund to review Chatterton's work and endorse his position of Director of Industries. The recommendations of this conference were, in turn, put forward by the Government of India's Finance Department to the Secretary of State. Given what Chatterton had already done, the tone of these proposals was circumspect, to say the least. Introducing the conference papers, the secretary to the provincial government, A.G. Cardew, wrote:

> The work to be done by the Department of Industrial and Technical Inquiries is purely pioneer work. It is intended to be merely in aid and encouragement of the introduction of private capital and enterprise. The Government have no intention whatever of embarking on commercial undertakings and are at all times ready to withdraw from any experiment as soon as private enterprise will take it up.[75]

Nevertheless, British capitalists expressed their objections to government intervention at considerable length.[76] Following the conference, three of their members (A.J Yorke, E.W. Orr and C.B. Simpson) published a note of dissent, denouncing Chatterton as having

> so clear a bias ... towards State Industrialisation that, in the absence of any express and official disclaimer on the part of the Government against such a tendency, we can not shut our eyes to a danger of its being allowed to creep in and develop.[77]

British dissent was taken on at the conference by a number of Indian participants – and Chatterton himself was bold enough to conclude that 'the views put forward [by the Europeans] are diametrically opposed to the policy which is now pursued in this Presidency and which it is not unlikely will be adopted in other parts of India'.[78]

But Chatterton's prediction turned out to be wrong.

Morley and after

The enthusiasm for state aid within India was not long reflected in London. The Secretary of State from 1905, Lord Morley, did not favour state economic intervention in India, or anywhere else. He was increasingly displeased by the stream of helpful suggestions on state economic policy pouring forth from Indian industrial conferences, apparently endorsed by the provincial and central governments.[79] He rejected the recommendations of the Ootacamund Industrial Conference – and they seem to have provoked him into action to halt the trend once and for all. In a despatch to the Viceroy in July 1910, he signalled an end to state aid and state industry:

> The policy which I am prepared to sanction is that State funds may be expended upon familiarising the people with such improvements in the methods of production as modern science and the practice of European countries can suggest; further than this the State should not go and it must be left to private enterprise to demonstrate that these improvements could be adopted with commercial advantage.[80]

Chatterton's enterprises were shut down, his post abolished and the Madras Department of Industries ceased to exist. Lord Morley's objections were made known to all the Indian governments. The secretary to the Government of India's Department of Commerce and Industries told the Supreme Legislative Council that although the state had made industrialising efforts:

> in consequence of strong protests received from the commercial public on the ground of possible competition with private enterprise and in pursuance of the policy laid down by the Secretary of State regarding State assistance to industrial progress, the Government of India are not now prepared to undertake experiments in this direction.[81]

Indian businessmen and politicians protested against Morley's new rules. The 6th Industrial Conference at Allahabad in December 1910 expressed 'deep regret' at the Secretary of State's decision and lodged 'a protest against the policy laid down by him that the State should not pioneer new industries as unduly limiting State help in industrial development'.[82] The Indians were not alone. In the Madras Legislative Council, a motion was moved in February 1911 requesting the Secretary of State to reconsider his decisions regarding the Department of Industries. It was carried 21:3. All the official members of the Council abstained.[83]

After Morley's departure in 1910, his restrictions on government intervention were somewhat modified by his successor, Lord Crewe. In early 1912, he informed the Viceroy that state aid did not have to be confined to industrial schools alone. Pioneer factories could, in some circumstances, be justified. Two years later, he authorised the reinstatement of the Madras Director and Department of Industries. But now, the Indian Industrial Conference reported:

> the Government of India seemed to be in doubt as to how far they would be justified in sanctioning proposals for demonstration plants, financial assistance and other forms of direct aid to industries. Their desire to move in these matters ... had received a decided set-back.[84]

Confusion

Confusion reigned in the Government of India's industrial policy, from the departure of Curzon until the outbreak of war. This resulted not merely from changing opinions emanating from the India Office, but from a basic conflict of interest between the British Government and the Government of India. This conflict partly concerned the emphasis that the two governments placed on imperial and Indian interests. London's priority in India was an Empire that paid for itself, that provided military resources for imperial operations and that functioned as a source and destination for British imports and exports. The problem for the Government of India was that financial self-sufficiency was coming into conflict with its obligations to British industry.

For most of its existence, the Government of India's revenue had come from land taxes and sales of opium. From 1870, land revenue from most provinces was declining and scope for its revival was limited. Opium sales were being phased out.[85] Budget deficits inevitably followed. Raising state revenues demanded either higher duties on imports or the encouragement of industrial development. The British Government opposed the former as an obstruction to British exports. Rejecting a Government of India request to raise duty on imported tobacco, the financial secretary at the India Office, Lionel Abrahams, explained that such a rise would be 'likely to protect the Indian tobacco growing and tobacco manufacturing industries ... the growth and manufacture of tobacco in India might be developed on new lines if very high duties, such as the Government of India recommend, are suddenly imposed'.[86]

As to industrial development, London was wary, firstly with regard to potential competition with British industry, and secondly with an eye to the drain on an already severely drained budget that state intervention might entail. Lethbridge commented in 1913: '[W]e have rigorously insisted ... that all taxation must be for revenue purposes only, and none for the purpose of encouraging Indian industries ... the results ... have been disastrous both to Indian and to British industry'.[87]

Indian industrialists were loudly in favour of both import duties and state industrialisation, and this brought them periodically into alliance with the Government of India.

While the Government of India benignly observed the Madras experiments, aided the embryonic iron and steel industry, encouraged the industrial conferences and pressed their requests on the British Government – the latter was increasingly suspicious of the local authority's role.[88] Thomas Holderness, under-secretary in the revenue and statistics department of the India Office, believed that the Government of India had a plan to promote India's industries 'through protectionism by stages, which is not the present policy of the U.K. government'.[89] Disturbed by the trend of opinion within the Government of India, the British Government sought to ensure that sound people on these questions were appointed to Indian posts.

When the future Viceroy, Lord Hardinge, met the Secretary of State at Windsor in 1910, he noted: 'What struck me as curious at the time was that the only question he put to me was whether I was a free-trader and I was honestly able to say that I was then and always had been a free trader.'[90]

The strategic question

But free trade was not a universal principle. There was one area in which neither the British Government nor the Government of India were in any doubt as to the virtues of state economic intervention – and that was the area of military preparedness.

The strategic importance of India to the British Empire is well known.[91] India was seen as the base for the defence of British interests in the East – near, middle and far. Captain D.I. Macauley spoke for many when he told the Central Asian Society in November 1909 that 'India is the pivot of world strategic interest east of Suez and Indian defence is the key to the defence of all our territory touching the Pacific and Indian Oceans'.[92]

India's role in this respect had a major impact on its economy and on the place of the state in that economy. Curzon had 'envisaged the building up of India as a source of manpower and munitions, as a second centre of British power that would take on increasingly the strategic burden east of Suez'.[93] The most stringent free-traders, in Britain and India alike, were prepared to allow and even encourage state activities in the military sector of the economy to this end.[94]

The military policy of imperialism was essentially a state project. The state therefore had to construct the means to carry it out. Thus, the Government of India, fully supported by London, was prepared to ignore free market orthodoxies and involve itself in strategically important industrial projects: railways, ports and docks, administrative buildings and many kinds of military works (harness and saddlery, ordnance, barracks buildings and so on). Defence expenditure took up a large part of the Government of India's total spending, rarely falling below 25 per cent of the total between 1857 and 1893. According to Purshotamdas Thakkurdas, net military expenditure rose from £29.34

million in 1911–12, to £66.72 million in 1918–19.[95] Justifying such expenditure, Lord Roberts told the Committee of Imperial Defence in June 1891: 'India is well worth a capital expenditure of many millions, if by such expenditure we can compensate in some measure for our deficiency in British soldiers'.[96]

Not everyone was convinced. Congress sessions regularly protested at the level of and increases in military spending – they were 'unnecessary' (1885) and better spent 'in promoting the welfare and the progress of the people' (1897). The Benares Congress session in 1905 correctly pointed out that 'the Military expenditure of this country is determined not by its own Military needs and requirements alone but also by the exigencies of British supremacy and British policy in the East'. It suggested, therefore, that the Empire as a whole should pay for it.[97] Even when the Government of India itself proposed reductions in military expenditure in 1911, it was opposed by the British Chief of the General Staff (General Haig) and the Army Department, who, according to the Viceroy, 'fought hard against any reduction whatever'.[98]

The greatest strategic industry of the Indian Empire was the railways. The railway network clearly had important commercial features, but its military role was the priority. Without it, it is doubtful that the Government of India would have pursued the project with such vigour.[99] In the expectation of war with Russia through Afghanistan, Lord Roberts proposed further extensions to the railway network to the Committee of Imperial Defence in 1891. These consisted of

> the extension of our railway system to the principal points we should admittedly be obliged to occupy in the event of war. The construction of trans-frontier railways would, I firmly believe, produce political and military results, the value and importance of which can scarcely be exaggerated.[100]

A sub-committee, appointed to consider the military defence of India, recommended in 1901 a considerable extension of railways around the North West Frontier Province, Dacca, Sind and Bombay.[101]

Such was the scale of a strategic railway network that it was necessary for the state to initiate the project. The Government of India provided substantial aid for the railway companies, beginning in 1849 – a minimum rate of return (usually 4.5–5 per cent) for 99 years and provision of land free. On this basis, the major ports – Calcutta, Bombay and Madras – were connected with Delhi and the Ganges Plain.[102] The government turned to state construction in 1869 but returned to the private companies in 1882, though the state still constructed the strategically important lines and reserved the right to purchase the railways from the companies once their 25-year contracts were up. In this way, 'the bulk of the railways had become the property of the State in the first decade of the twentieth century'.[103]

The building of railways edged the Government of India along the path of state industry. It began exploring the possibilities of manufacturing railway requirements itself – and thus followed railway workshops and its forays into iron and steel.[104] The latter were encouraged by a report on the manufacture of iron and steel in India in 1899, delivered by Major R.H. Mahon, the Deputy Director General of Ordnance. State ordnance factories were established to manufacture defence goods. The government also set up a number of enterprises to manufacture goods ranging from building materials to stationery. Dockyards in Bombay and Calcutta as well as workshops of the Public Works Department were also areas of state economic activity.[105]

State industry in India moved all of industry forward in matters of training and technique, introducing modern machinery and advancing production processes. According to the Indian Industrial Commission, 'by far the most important development of mechanical engineering in India is represented by the numerous locomotive and carriage building shops which are an essential adjunct to the railway system'. They became 'the main training ground for engineering artisans of every class', along with the ordnance factories.[106]

One of the reasons that state industry could play this path-breaking role was that profit was not its main concern. This was particularly the case in industries considered to be strategic, like the railways. It can also be demonstrated in the development of the oil industry in Burma. There, due to the Royal Navy's need for oil and the scarcity of the resource within the Empire, G.G. Jones argues that '[t]he authorities' concern ... was for the development of the Burmese oil industry and not for the financial success or failure of the British companies operating there'. The Government of India eventually excluded 'foreign' oil companies (specifically, Standard Oil), to the benefit of the British company, Burmah Oil. But they were 'once again acting in what they considered to be the best interests of the oil industry [as an imperial priority] and not as agents of British capital'. Their policy was 'no longer underpinned by a rational economic argument'.[107]

Conclusion

With no immediate interest in industrial development in India, British economic policy was dominated for most of the nineteenth century by *laissez-faire* doctrines, which meshed nicely with the main British commercial interests.

Change came, partly due to the need for internal pacification but largely as a result of India's strategic position within the Empire. Both factors brought pressure to bear for the development of modern defence industries. From Curzon onwards, Indian governments became increasingly aware that, for India to play the strategic role assigned to it within the British Empire, industrialisation was required – and that the state would have to play a major part in its creation and protection. There were elements in the British Government coming to the same conclusion, but progress there was derailed by the Morley-Crewe interlude and the confusion that followed.

A combination of Indian entrepreneurial effort, plus the Government of India's exploration of industrial possibilities, together with the stimulus of war elsewhere, brought an Indian bourgeoisie into existence, regardless of British disinterest. It put forward a strong case for state aid and for protection of Indian industries. These demands found an echo in the national movement. As the bourgeoisie developed, the Government of India's position changed, enabling it (especially at the Provincial level) to welcome and encourage Indian industry and industrialists. London, however, remained distrustful and reined in Indian Government attempts to aid industry.

Before 1914, then, British policy on industrial development in India was inconsistent, to say the least. Here, one finds the Madras

Government outlining a plan for state-led industrialisation. There, one finds a Secretary of State condemning any kind of state intervention. Here is Curzon calling for an industrial India to defend the Empire. There, are a group of British manufacturers in India demanding that their monopolies should be unmolested.

War and the needs of the state during war are an important catalyst to economic development, not least to industrialisation and the development of the bourgeoisie. Neil Charlesworth suggests that British domination of South Asia by the late nineteenth century and the absence of threat to British rule meant that there was no 'political and military drive to compete effectively with neighbouring rivals'.[108] Industrial capacity in India, then, did not seem a matter of great urgency to the British Government – and may have created more problems than it solved. Such complacency was destined not to last. At the beginning of the twentieth century, a military threat – not to India but to Britain itself – was not long in coming.

Chapter Two

The Great War

The demands made by the Empire on India's resources for the duration of the war, in terms of soldiers, equipment and cash, were enormous. At the outbreak, the Government of India dispatched an expeditionary force to France, seven brigades to Egypt, a further brigade to the Persian Gulf and troops to East Africa. The Viceroy, Lord Hardinge, was able to report to the Imperial Legislative Council in September 1914: 'I was able to offer to his Majesty the finest and largest military force of British and Indian troops that has ever left the shores of India.'[1] In addition to the troops, India also sent 70 million rounds of ammunition, 60,000 rifles and 550 guns to the main theatres of the war.[2] As trench warfare set in on the Western Front, there was 'an enormous demand for sandbags', for which India supplied the jute, while '[u]nlimited quantities of hides were required' for boots, which India also supplied.[3] During the course of the war, the size of the Indian Army more than tripled (from 155,000 to 573,000).[4]

The burdens of the Government of India were eased somewhat by the fact that the Indian elite was strongly in favour of the war. 'The spirit and temper of the princes and the people of India', editorialised *The Leader* in Allahabad, 'is indisputably one of whole-hearted support of England'.[5] On 8 September 1914, Sir Gangadar Chitnavis (a non-official member) moved in the Imperial Legislative Council not only to demonstrate loyalty, but urging the government 'to take into consideration the wish of the people of India to share in the heavy financial burden imposed upon the United Kingdom by the war'.[6] That wish was granted in full measure. India's financial contribution was substantial. Over £140 million had been made available to Britain by 1920.[7] The desperate need of the British Government for this money can be seen in the fact that in 1916, the Government of India agreed to supply the required amount (at that time a 'war gift' of £100 million) only if it were permitted to raise the duty on cotton imports (from 3½ to 7½ per cent). The British Government agreed, despite outraged pressure from the domestic cotton industry.[8] Considering the situation in late 1914, Hardinge later concluded that 'India had by that time been bled white by the War Office'.[9]

Despite the Government of India's attempts to keep up with expanding imperial war needs, India as a whole was ill-fitted to meet the demands of industrialised warfare. As the official account put it, 'India found itself, on the outbreak of war, not only ill-provided with the necessary machinery, but without the technically trained personnel required for her industrial expansion'.[10]

The Indian Army itself was woefully under-equipped for the task at hand. This was largely due to the pre-war assumption that the Indian Army would primarily be for internal and frontier use – and to the 'strong and continuous pressure in the direction of economy [that] was exercised' as a result of that assumption.[11]

Early war measures

Given the weaknesses in the economy and in the defence forces, the Government of India rapidly discovered what all the belligerent governments discovered: that reliance on private enterprise and the market economy could not meet the needs of prolonged industrialised warfare.[12] The economy had to be directed by the state towards those demands. There was therefore a dramatic shift towards state economic intervention and an increase in the powers of the state.[13]

The *Defence of India Act (1915)* gave the government the right to regulate, relocate, confiscate and destroy private property – industrial enterprises, factories, workshops, mines and land – in order to facilitate the war effort.[14] The government took up its new and expanding responsibilities, rarely having to employ the Act's punitive clauses. The export of munitions and material for munitions and the export of cattle, horses, mules, sheep, goats, hides, lead and surgery stores were swiftly forbidden, while a general ban on trade with Germany was introduced.[15] Restrictions were imposed on 'the export of foodstuffs and articles capable of being turned to warlike uses'.[16] Exports of raw wool were restricted and eventually the state took control of all wool produced in or entering India. In the initial stages of the war, all six woollen mills in British India (plus one in Mysore) were given over entirely to war-related production.[17] Coal was requisitioned, its distribution rationed and a Coal Controller appointed. Subsequently, 'the whole output of first class coal and coke in India was under requisition and was distributed by the Coal Controller'.[18] Wheat purchases had been placed under state control by early 1915.[19] By the end of 1916, a Jute Control Scheme was under consideration and the export of all steel goods had been prohibited.[20]

Remnants of pre-Morley thinking on state industrial intervention began to reappear, at least at the provincial level. In August 1914, the United Provinces government resolved to establish a Board and a Director of Industries. They were charged with undertaking a survey of industries in the province – 'to study the indigenous industries, large and small, and advise the Government on their encouragement and development and on the extension of markets for them'.[21]

But in India, it was not just a question of establishing state power over existing industries. Such were the demands of the war that the state itself had to attempt to fill the gaps in the industrial economy that the war had revealed. In this attempt, it was encouraged by the British Government.[22] The Morley restrictions were rolled back. The Secretary of State for India telegraphed the Viceroy in January 1916:

> I am willing that you should instruct Local Governments that in cases in which they desire to help particular industries they may do so, subject to your approval, and to financial exigencies, without being unduly restricted by my predecessor's rulings.[23]

The Controller of Munitions and Director of Industries in Bengal wrote approvingly in 1919, 'Military necessity drove the State into the great markets ... The old theory that private industry should be left to look after itself is dying. In war time, industry cannot look after itself.'[24]

If the Government of India was hesitant on this score, there was plenty of Indian opinion to stiffen its resolve. The restrictions on German traders in India were heartily supported by Indian business, which called for their extension.[25] *The Leader* ran a vociferous campaign during the war, calling for the state to take advantage of the opportunities afforded by the hostilities to develop India's industries. The war had revealed India's fundamental weakness, the newspaper declared: 'The economic evil of a great country depending on the export of raw produce without converting it into manufactured goods is forcibly brought out today more than ever it was.'[26]

The Government of India should imitate the British state, replacing German imports with indigenous industries, 'thereby hitting Germany so hard as no war can permanently do'. To this end, 'the Government ... should not hesitate to pioneer and subsidise promising new industries until they take root'.[27] If the government did not take this sort of initiative, then German and Austrian goods would soon be replaced with those from the USA and Japan.[28] The newspaper further editorialised: 'industrial development in India on any considerable scale is possible only if the Government come forward with liberal pecuniary offers ... what we plead for is *support* – practical support – substantial support'.[29]

The 1914 Industrial Conference, held in Madras in December, resolved that India should exercise fiscal autonomy in regard to import and export duties and that 'the state should aid the starting and pioneering of new industries through the establishment of a department of Government for the purpose'. Speaking in support of the resolution, 'Mr. Yakoob Hossain ... said that the war could prove a blessing in disguise if only the people knew how to make the misfortune serve a useful purpose'.[30]

There were indeed opportunities opening up for Indian industries at this time. Raw materials required for the prosecution of the war have already been mentioned. In addition, the disruption of global trade occasioned by the war led to price rises in India's main imports – and therefore to the possibility of import substitution. Indian efforts in iron and steel, cement, sugar engineering and chemicals began to expand.[31]

The Indian Industrial Commission

In 1915, the Government of India requested permission 'to examine the whole question [of state aid for industrialisation] *ab initio* with the help of a specially selected Committee'. Such a committee should be 'permitted to consider... all questions of direct State-aid to industries, which do not involve a modification of our existing fiscal policy'. The proposal was a cautious one – New Delhi suggested that it would 'in all probability be impossible for the Committee to begin its work till after the close of the war'.[32] The British Government gave its approval. The Government of India subsequently decided that the committee should be appointed at once in order that action could be taken on its recommendations as soon as the war ended.[33] Thus was born the Indian Industrial Commission (IIC).[34]

The exclusion of considerations that might 'involve a modification of our existing fiscal policy' was official code for the fact that the Commission was forbidden from examining the question of protection for Indian industry. The majority of the British Government was of the opinion that such questions could only be examined after the war, in an Empire-wide context.[35] But the upper reaches of the British Government were split on the issue. Lord Islington (the Under-Secretary of State for India) and T.W. Holderness (the permanent Under-Secretary) championed 'free trade', while the Secretary of State, Austen Chamberlain, the Viceroy, Lord Hardinge, and some members of the Viceroy's Council (C.H.A. Hall, R.H. Craddock and Sankaran Nair) were prepared to accede to some kind of protection.[36] L.J. Kershaw at the India Office suggested that if the Commission was precluded from considering or even taking evidence on protection, 'it may at the outset fail to enlist confidence, and suspicion may possibly be caused'.[37] 'Free Trade', however, won the day and the question was specifically excluded from the Commission's remit.

It began its proceedings in May 1916, but not before some minor skirmishes about its composition. Its president, Sir Thomas Holland, felt that the 'majority of those suggested seem already to be committed rather to the view that it is the abiding duty and should be the constant practice of Government to assist industries by direct financial support'. Despite the fact that 'this may perhaps be regarded as a foregone conclusion', he felt that the opposing view should be represented.[38] Hardinge objected to the participation of Edward Hopkinson, 'as connected with Manchester and its textile and free trade interests', who was likely to be 'very unacceptable to Indian opinion'.[39] Three Indian businessmen sat on the Commission (Dorab Tata, R.N. Mukherjee and Fazilbhoy Currimbhoy).[40] They were joined by the nationalist politician Madan Mohan Malaviya – a man mildly described by Holland as 'our only Colleague who has had no practical experience of business,' and rather more boisterously by the Finance Member, William Meyer as 'a rabid protectionist'. The Viceroy felt that he was 'of doubtful loyalty'.[41]

The Commission was officially charged with examining 'whether and, if so, in what manner, Government can usefully give direct encouragement to industrial development'. Hitherto, it reported, industrial investment had taken place 'only [in] those industries . . . which appeared to offer safe and easy profits'. For the right kind of industrial development (which may not be immediately profitable), it was necessary 'to devise proposals which will bring the State into far more intimate relations with industrial enterprise than the policy of the Government or public opinion has hitherto permitted'.[42] The Commission's report urged 'a policy of energetic intervention in industrial affairs'. It declared: 'in future Government must play an active part in the industrial development of the country with the aim of making India more self-contained in respect of men and material'.[43] It proposed central and provincial departments of industries to see the project through.[44]

In all of its deliberations, the Commission had much more on its mind than simple economic development. The strategic importance of India's economy was prominent in its proposals. India's industrial deficiencies 'threaten national safety'. This was 'brought into prominent notice by the interference with industrial supplies from overseas during the war'. Consequently, '[i]t is vital, therefore, for Government to ensure the establishment in India of those industries whose absence exposes us to grave danger in event of war'.[45]

The report also suggested that the Government of India should give direct assistance to new industries of strategic importance. That there would be plenty of those was indicated by the Commission's opinion that 'the requirements of modern civil and especially industrial life largely coincide with the list of essential munitions of war'. The Commission's whole programme of industrial development was designed 'in particular, to meet military needs'.[46]

After the Commission had submitted its report, Chamberlain replied in September 1919, accepting the two principles underlying its recommendations: state intervention in industrial development and the establishment of an administrative structure to bring this about.[47] The Under-Secretary, Lord Islington, had said in the House of Lords in March 1919 that the 'past record of the Government of India in this connection cannot, I think, be characterised as progressive, and I hope that the result of this Report will give a very strong stimulus in the direction of industrial enterprise'.[48] The Government of India moved in the Legislative Assembly in December 1919 to establish a committee to put the IIC recommendations into practice.[49]

The Indian Munitions Board

The relentless pressure of the war, however, made it imperative that more immediate action was taken. Even as the Industrial Commission was deliberating, the Commander in Chief in India had initiated (in December 1916) an inquiry 'as to whether more could not be done to develop Indian resources for war purposes'. He suggested the creation of an organisation like the British Ministry of Munitions.[50] Endorsing this, Hardinge wrote to Chamberlain early in the following year:

> It has become apparent to us for some time past that all the articles you mention besides many others for Army use might be produced locally if the resources and industries of India were

> controlled and developed with special reference to needs created by the War . . . it is necessary to create a special organisation under a first class businessman possessing the necessary technical knowledge besides ability and driving power.[51]

The formation of the Indian Munitions Board was duly sanctioned on 16 February 1917 and Sir Thomas Holland was summoned to Delhi from his duties at the IIC to organise it.[52] The Industrial Commission commented later that the Munitions Board 'became, in effect, an experiment on a large scale designed to test the value of many of our conclusions'.[53] By the end of the war, the Munitions Board was controlling significant sections of the Indian economy. It controlled all government ordnance, clothing, hide and leather factories; the production of woollen and worsted goods for the military; the shipment of raw and tanned hides; and the production of railway track and rolling stock. The Board had set up a tent factory and purchased the entire output of the jute industry. It had established a river craft branch, controlled the export of timber to the Eastern theatres of war and controlled the steel and pig iron production of the Tata works (of which, more below). It also took over the entire output of the cement industry.[54]

Later war measures

As the war proceeded, the new conditions of international trade, together with domestic war demands, encouraged both state intervention and Indian industrialisation.[55] A War Conference in Delhi in April 1918 was told by no less an authority than the King-Emperor himself that '[t]he need of the Empire is India's opportunity'. The conference concluded that 'considerable development is possible in the local production of war materials and other munitions'.[56]

Indian industries were both protected and increasingly controlled. In 1917, duty on imported cotton goods was increased. The excise on domestically produced cotton goods was not. The import of foreign cloth was later halted altogether. As a result, some 40 new Indian cotton mills were established by the end of hostilities, together with eight woollen mills.[57] The Government of India purchased a large part of the tea industry's products in order to ensure its survival.[58]

Control was the obverse side of the protective coin. In the salt industry, once imports were restricted, the price rose. To prevent speculation, '[p]ower was taken by Government to regulate, restrict or prohibit, the use of salt from the salt sources under its control'. The government also had the power to control salt sales and impose maximum prices.[59] Government 'Controllers' were appointed for food, internal transport and coal.[60] In the latter case, the Coal Controller was also expected to stimulate the production of a better product.[61] The measures taken to this end were gladly accepted by the coal producers.[62] In Bombay, a Controller of Prices was appointed. He was urged on in his work by the Rice Merchants' Association in February 1918:

> [W]e consider the food supply of the poor should be given as much prominence as it deserves and that the Government should see that the quantity available in the market should be sufficient for the requirements . . . if necessary by commandeering ships.[63]

Ships were, in fact, already being commandeered for war purposes. By the end of 1917, 57 steamers and 32 flats and barges from the Indian shipping industry had been pressed into service.[64] The government also set up Boards to control manpower, resources, recruitment, publicity, communications, foodstuffs, transport, employment and labour.

But perhaps the most extensive area of state intervention and control was the cotton industry. A Cloth Control Committee was appointed in March 1918 to investigate whether it was possible or desirable to regulate the price of cotton cloth. The Bombay Millowners' Association told the Committee in June that 'the time had arrived when the cotton market should be regulated on a healthy basis and all outside influences to its detriment should be eliminated'.[65] In September the *Cotton Cloth Act 1918* was passed 'to take powers for the cheap supply of cotton cloth to the poorer classes of the community'. Under the Act, the Cotton Controller was empowered to direct and regulate the manufacture, transport, distribution, sale and purchase of cotton cloth, in order to maintain supply at reasonable rates to the poor.[66] The Controller eventually directed cloth manufacturers to produce 'standard cloth' for sale at regulated prices.[67] This was welcomed by Indian manufacturers but denounced by their British counterparts.[68] One of the most prominent Indian industrialists (and a member of the Cloth Control Committee in Bombay), Purshotamdas Thakurdas, suggested both price controls and the establishment of state cloth shops for the distribution of standard cloth at fixed prices.[69]

At the provincial level, the Government of Bombay appointed controllers and control committees for grain, household necessities, salt and development (housing and road construction proposals) as well as a central committee to co-ordinate the others. Beneath these were Ward committees, which were expected to establish state shops for grain, household necessities and cloth and to report infringements of wartime regulations to the appropriate controller.[70]

State intervention: an ongoing policy

The new ideas on state intervention were not confined to wartime exigencies. Indian industrialists and nationalists, the Government of India and the British Government all regarded them as the policy of the future.

(a) The Indian view

On the Indian side, the war increased the demands for state-led industrial development and projected them well beyond the period of hostilities. This was evident as early as December 1914, when newspaper editorials, the Madras Industrial Conference and the Congress session, held in the same city, raised a chorus of demands for the government to take the industrial initiative.[71] The Congress session resolved that 'this Congress urges that immediate measures be taken by Government to organise and develop Indian industries'.[72] The following year's Bombay session further demanded 'that complete fiscal freedom in special reference to import, export and excise duties should now be conceded to the Government of India'.[73]

The Government of India's Commerce and Industries Department noted in 1915 that '[m]anufacturers, politicians, and the literate public have for long been pressing their demands for a definite and accepted policy of State aid to Indian industries'.[74] As part of this pressure, Sir Ibrahim Rahimtoola moved in the Legislative Council in March 1916 to appoint a Committee of Official and Non-Official members to consider measures for the growth and development of Indian industries.[75] This was noted by Hardinge, who reported to Chamberlain: 'Much public interest is being taken in the matter, and the Government of India are generally taxed with inertness'.[76]

Indian business leaders remained supremely confident in eventual government action. The twelfth Industrial Conference (Lucknow, 1916) was told by its president:

> Government aid is needed for enabling struggling Indian Industries to stand on their own legs and for the establishment of new industries...the Government of India have grasped the essential needs of the situation and we hope we shall strive together in perfect accord towards the attainment of the ideal before us.[77]

V.P. Madhava Rao, writing for the Sons of India, declared that 'there is no doubt whatever that the British Government will do their best to develop Industrial India to her utmost capacity'.[78]

The demands of Indian capitalists and nationalists were not contingent on an end to the war. They were in fact increasingly focussed on India's development – both as a nation and as an economy – after the war had ceased. This was evident at the Lucknow Congress of 1916. Jagat Narain told the session that India had not simply demonstrated her loyalty during the war: 'She has, so to say, found herself. She has acquired a new spirit of self-reliance and dignity, and realised her own worth by coming to Britain's help at a critical juncture.' That being the case, he continued:

> India now demands that after the War things shall not revert to their original condition, but that she shall occupy a position

> worthy of herself as a member of the Imperial family ... It is also essential that in any scheme of Imperial Federation India should occupy the same position as the self-Governing Dominions.[79]

The war, its demands and India's response became a vehicle through which to assert the national interests of India. For Indian nationalists, it was preferable that such interests should be exercised and safeguarded through a national (that is, Indian) government.[80] But there was at least a hint that the Government of India could be won over to Indian interests. Presciently, A.C. Mazumdar told the Lucknow Congress in 1916, 'We are looking forward to a time when the Government will become national if not in its "personnel" at least in its aims and purposes.'[81] Satyendra P. Sinha told the Bombay Congress in 1915 (over which he was presiding) that the government had to abandon the policy of *laissez-faire* – despite the fact that if it did 'it will test, as no other question has done, the altruism of English statesmanship, for in promoting and protecting Indian industries it may become necessary – it *will* become necessary – to sacrifice the interests even of English manufacturers'.[82]

The question of protection became a critical industrial and national demand. The war had taken away what had been rapidly developing central European markets for India's raw materials and had restricted imports.[83] Before the war, goods from the central powers were finding buyers in India. Thomas Ainscough complained:

> Any article gaudily and brightly finished will sell better [in the bazaar] than one not so attractive, even though in use the badly finished one proves to be better. The German and Austrian manufacturers worked on these lines much to their benefit.[84]

Apparently despite this, both domestic markets and exports increased, and, as we have seen, new industries opened up.[85] But now those industries were threatened by imports from Japan and the USA. As *The Madras Times* succinctly put it: 'as far as the development of industries in India is concerned, the longer the war lasts the better. As soon as it is over, the flood of foreign goods will revive'.[86] India's national interests demanded that the industries set up as a result of the war should be protected when the war was over.

The Indian bourgeoisie participated enthusiastically in the work of the Indian Industrial Commission and endorsed its recommendations for future state intervention. The Delhi Congress session of December 1918 welcomed the commission's recommendations and strongly endorsed the call for the government to play an active part in India's industrial development.[87]

(b) The Tata experience

As we noted in chapter one, the Government of India had eventually given much-needed aid and concessions to the struggling Tata Company even before the war.[88] The war brought their relationship much closer. The Industrial Commission Report said that, while the government had agreed to purchase 20,000 tons of steel rails a year, 'on account of the heavy demands of the war, much larger quantities have been taken'.[89] The Tata Iron and Steel Company (TISCO) was the only steel producer in the British Empire east of Suez and therefore vital to the Empire's war effort as hostilities spread beyond Europe.[90] Thus Dorabji Tata was able to tell the TISCO Board in October 1917 that the war has 'stopped imports of steel into this country, and has thrown the Government of India solely into the arms of the Company for its supply of rails'.[91] By September 1917, Tata was selling 78 per cent of its steel output to the government, rising to 98 per cent a year later.[92] Sir Thomas Holland told the TISCO Board that 'the entire output of steel at Sakchi [the Tata steelworks] at present was required by Government for rails and accessories for military and strategic purposes'.[93] During the war, the company supplied the government with 1500 miles of rails and 300,000 tons of steel. These materials were essential for the campaigns in Mesopotamia, Egypt, Salonika and East Africa, as well as for the Indian railways and military and civil departments of government.[94]

Like other Indian companies, Tata willingly accepted government direction during the war years. According to the official account, Tata agreed to 'complete control over the distribution of the output of steel . . . without having recourse to compulsion under the Defence of India rules'.[95] Dorabji Tata told the board that Tata 'allowed itself to be controlled so as to be able to meet war requirements first and foremost'. On the other hand, he pointed out that 'Government have, on their part given us every possible help'.[96]

The Tata men believed that they had not only been reliable suppliers to the state, but that they had done so in the national interest – and at considerable cost. Steel taken by the government was bought at controlled prices. As the proportion going to the state rose ever higher, TISCO had less to sell at a profit on the open market. The company had been required to purchase highly priced machinery to fulfil the government's war production needs.[97]

The government, though, was fulsome in its praise and gratitude. The Viceroy Lord Chelmsford visited the Tata Steel Works on 2 January 1919 and told the assembled dignitaries:

> I have come here today in the first place to see this fine example of Indian industry. As you know, it is the policy of my Government to encourage all industries in India so far as is possible to do so . . . In the second place I wanted to come here to express my appreciation of the great work which has been done by the Tata Company during the past four years of this War. I can hardly imagine what we should have done during these four years if the Tata Company had not been able to give us steel rails, which have been provided for us not only for Mesopotamia, but for Egypt, Palestine and East Africa.[98]

The town of Sakchi was renamed Jamshedpur, in honour of the company's founder, while the local railway station of Kalimati was transformed into Tatanagar.

Tata Steel then was a confident Indian company during the war – confident not only in its wartime capacity, but also that government support and its own expansion would continue after the war was over. Dorabji Tata, the TISCO chairman, described the foundations of the company's confidence to shareholders in December 1916: 'Bumper earnings; production 30 per cent up over original design; cost lower than before . . . Ready and willing markets; capable of yet more expansion . . . Order book full to bursting.'[99]

On this basis he, together with Burjorji Padshah and Charles Perin, proposed the 'Greater Extension Programme' – new blast furnaces, coke ovens, machine shops and foundries – aimed at raising the company's steel capacity five times and eventually supplying India's total steel requirements.[100] Discussed and approved by a board meeting on 30 March 1916, the estimated cost was 20 million rupees. This was revised upwards to 80 million by the beginning of 1918, and again to nearly 125 million in July of the same year.[101] Tata had good reason to believe that it had state support in its expansionary endeavours, since the Government of India had approached the company to include a 96-inch Plate Mill in the expansion plans, which it regarded as vital for the war effort. The TISCO Board declared in September 1917:

> If Government required the [Plate] Mill to be installed as an urgent War measure, the Board requested that Government should pay the entire extra cost . . . which may be necessary for putting up the plant at the present high prices.[102]

The government appears to have agreed to this (although there is some confusion on this point in the TISCO Board minutes).[103] Both the Plate Mill and the Greater Extensions Plan were, however, destined to run into difficulties at the end of the war. Holland told the TISCO Board in August 1918 that, although it had been the Government of India's intention to help with the Plate Mill, 'the war situation had undergone a radical change since then, and unexpected conditions had come into existence'. With the prospect of hostilities ending and the international steel trade resuming, 'manufacture of the same articles in India was of secondary importance'.[104] As for the extension programme, international competition and a fall in the price of steel ensured that its progress slowed dramatically.[105]

Nevertheless, during the war years, with help from the state, Tata boomed. Padshah told the TISCO Board, 'Government orders and Government custom could always be safely depended upon . . . There was an almost endless variety of uses to which the steel output of the Company can be put on the market.'[106] It was rumoured (and duly reported to the TISCO Board) that the Munitions Board would establish two Indian shipyards, using TISCO ship plate.[107] The board was also told that the government was going to establish an Arsenal near Jamshedpur and put up defensive works 'as the Tata Steel Works were becoming an institution of national importance'.[108] When the British Ministry of Munitions proposed the establishment of a glycerine plant to the Government of India, Tata offered to come forward with the capital. Padshah wrote to Kershaw at the India Office: 'You can easily understand that the proposition was made entirely in the interests of success for the War... as a proposition of service to the State in an emergency.'[109]

By the end of the war, Tata saw itself as an example to the nation and as the embodiment of a new national spirit, working for India in tandem with the government. Dorabji Tata told the board:

> The war has taught us all a great and terrible lesson. It brought home to us our utter helplessness and dependence on foreign machinery and foreign goods, particularly in its early stages... [we need] a new India built up on the foundations of industrial sufficiency... Is it not time to stir ourselves, to wake up to the great opportunity and the stern duty before us, the task of India's industrial regeneration? And is it not a task that calls for the earnest endeavours, both of Government and people, and for the closest co-operation and association on all sides?[110]

The main point about Tata's war experience was this. The company expected (as I suspect did the Government of India) that the wartime policy of state intervention and guidance would continue. It was on that basis that it launched its expansion plans, confident that, in alliance with the state, it would see them through and that its example would be followed by others.

(c) The Government of India

The Government of India gave every impression of wanting to continue the programme of Indian industrialisation in the post-war period. In his 1915 memorandum on *Questions Likely to Arise in India at the End of the War*, the Viceroy, Lord Hardinge, wrote that Indian efforts would be 'fruitless' unless the government led and guided them. Brushing aside *laissez faire* (a policy which 'has collapsed even in Great Britain where State-aid and even State-aided industry have become tenets of the new political creed'), he acknowledged Indian demands for 'a more energetic industrial policy in the future under the aegis of the Government of India, and it would be as well that this demand should be forestalled'.[111] Further, he called for the abolition of the excise duty on cotton goods (the tax on cotton goods produced and sold in India), which he described as a policy 'forced on herself in deference to the interests of a single English interest'.[112] The Government of India's Commerce and Industries Department told the Secretary of State in 1915 that 'a definite and self-conscious policy of improving the industrial capabilities of India will have to be pursued after the war' – otherwise she would become a 'dumping ground' for foreign manufactures.[113]

The Industrial Commission urged the continuation of state assistance to industries 'of which the scope is not in every case limited by the possible duration of the present war'. It suggested that the Indian Munitions Board – or at least those features of it 'as are properly adaptable to peace conditions' should be preserved.[114] In the absence of state intervention after the war, the commission concluded, 'India cannot possibly become strong and self supporting, and cannot possibly fulfil her duty to herself and to the Empire'.[115]

In correspondence with the Secretary of State, Hardinge's successor, Lord Chelmsford pressed the case for post-war state industrialisation. He envisaged replacing the munitions board with a development board 'for the purpose of expediting the industrial development of the country and carrying out the recommendations of the Industrial Commission'. He saw wartime organisation as a prototype for the future: 'the war in this sense has proved a not unmixed evil'.[116] A variety of official sources predicted the continuation and expansion of state intervention after 1918. Sir Thomas Ainscough, the Senior Trade Commissioner, wrote in 1919 that '[t]he task of stimulating indigenous industries by Government cannot, however, be allowed to be even temporarily suspended'. State intervention, he continued, was now widely accepted and a future imperial industries board in India would be even more powerful than the munitions board.[117] The official account of India's role in the war stated that 'the policy of State participation in industrial development . . . is likely to produce results stretching far into the future'.[118] A 'Prefatory Note' addressed to the third conference of (provincial) departments of industries in 1921 even suggested that state intervention was 'in part glimpsing the eventual approach of state socialism'.[119]

As we have seen in the IIC Report, the future of Indian industry was not only an economic question. Its importance was a strategic one, to be extended to future wars, which were confidently expected. Holland wrote that 'the duty of equipping the armies in the field brings the department of Government that is directly responsible for this duty into immediate touch with the industrial life of the country'.[120] According to Ainscough, the war had revealed that 'practically every industry in the country was dependent on overseas supplies' while the IIC warned that Indian industry would grind to a halt in a future conflict that blocked sea transport. These weaknesses were to be rectified.[121] As Rajnarayan Chandravarkar puts it, the lesson learned was that 'it was well to add an ordnance base to the oriental barrack'.[122]

In future conflicts, India would have to be far more self-sufficient – and building up that self-sufficiency was the job of the Government of India. This was a part, said Ainscough, of 'the new Imperial policy of stimulating the development of all local resources for the benefit of the Empire as a whole'.[123] Chelmsford suggested to the Secretary of State that, in order 'to expand India's production to meet military requirements', an attempt should be made to 'come to a clear understanding with the War Office as to the direction in which India can best give assistance to the Empire'.[124]

An example of the Government of India's concept of industry as a strategic tool can be seen once again in Burma. In the last chapter, we noted the efforts of the government to exclude non-British companies from Burma's oil industry, primarily for strategic rather than economically rational reasons. From 1917, the same effort was made with regard to Burma's deposits of lead and zinc – and to the sulphuric acid that zinc smelting produced. The Government of India wanted to take control of the Burma Corporation and the Smelting Company (dealing with lead and zinc respectively). In June 1917 they declared:

> Local prodn {sic} zinc and sulphuric acid is essential part of the programme for making India self-sufficient in war time... Both on political grounds, and in order to ensure adequacy of our control we consider it essential condition of Government assistance that the smelting works should be located in India, and further, that the Company also be domiciled in India, with Indian capital and management in India.[125]

The following day, 'permanent British control' over the companies was demanded, on the grounds that, without it, shares could be sold to foreign interests.[126] It was, they said, 'really vital to our programme for making India a self-sufficing entity that sulphuric acid should be produced in India.'[127]

Later that year, Thomas Holderness, at the India Office, confirmed: 'the lead and zinc ores of Burma... are essential for the future industrial development of India, and the Indian Government will insist on being masters of their own raw materials'.[128]

Finally, there was a political dimension to the Government of India's enthusiasm for state industrialisation. In *Questions Likely to Arise*, Hardinge associated the new attitude towards the Indian economy with the need for increased autonomy, both for the Government of India and for Indians. On the first, he advocated a 'relaxation of the far too stringent control exercised by the Secretary of State over the Government of India': 'Surely in all questions, except those of high policy, it is reasonable to expect that the views of the Government of India should prevail, and that their hands should be free.'[129]

On the second, he pointed out that educated Indians were generally confined to employment in clerical positions or government work:

> It is largely among the proletariat of ill-paid but busy-brained clerks, school-masters and their like, the "intelligenzia" of India,

> that political discontent has its origin... Industry and responsible political participation are bound to contribute in an increasing degree to political solidity and personal contentment.[130]

The Lieutenant Governor of the United Provinces, Sir James Meston, agreed, warning that at war's end:

> India will be flooded with soldiers – not all of them reticent or modest – who have fought white men and beaten them, who have met with great attention in England, and whose attitude to the English in India must in consequence be altered from the old traditions of the classes to which they belong.[131]

(d) The British Government

The British Government joined the chorus in favour of state-led industrialisation. The Montagu-Chelmsford Report of 1919 (the main purpose of which was political reform) came out in favour of industrialisation for many of the same reasons as the Government of India. It would give India economic stability and satisfy the aspirations of her people. It would provide an outlet for the young, mobilise unproductive capital and curb 'the too speculative and literary tendencies of Indian thought'. It was necessary then 'that the Government must admit and shoulder its responsibility for furthering the development of the country'. The report endorsed the creation of a central department of industries and urged action 'in respect of which considerations of military security, political expediency, and economic advantage are coincident, and are in agreement also with the interests of the Empire as a whole'.[132]

It was those latter interests that concerned the British most of all. For the British Government, Indian industrialisation was a matter of imperial military strategy. It was necessary as a result of the changes in that strategy that the war and its aftermath dictated. Lloyd George argued that India had to be equipped 'to be the bulwark which will save Asia from the tide of oppression and disorder which it is the object of the enemy to achieve.'[133] In May 1916, the Secretary of State for the

Colonies, Bonar Law, suggested a conference of Britain, the Dominions and India on the post-war imperial economy. It would consider the industries necessary for economic security; the steps needed to recover lost trade; the development of self-sufficiency; and the prevention of sources of supply falling to foreign control.[134] Thus, an Empire-wide strategy of militarily oriented economies was envisaged – and India would be part of that strategy.[135] The Montagu-Chelmsford Report contained a section (number 337) devoted to the 'Military value of economic development'. It stated:

> the war has thrown a strong light on the military importance of economic development . . . the possibility of sea communications being temporarily interrupted forces us to rely on India as an ordnance base for protective operations in Eastern theatres of war . . . the development of India's resources becomes a matter of almost military necessity.[136]

Imperial military strategy was the concern of the state. Since this was the British Government's priority, they tended to place an even greater emphasis on the role of the state than their subordinates in India. They endorsed the Government of India's activities in this regard during the war years and urged them on to greater efforts.[137] When the prospect of shellac exports arose, London accepted a recommendation from the Imperial Institute 'that one or two large scale Government factories be started, to put the manufacture on a thoroughly efficient basis and safeguard the interests of India and the Empire'.[138] Further, they informed the Government of India that, after the war, they should take steps to increase production of oil-producing nuts and seeds; increase production of cotton; carry out experiments in growing flax in India; take control of the jute industry; and conserve 'the Imperial supplies of ores containing tungsten'.[139]

The beginnings of a different approach to Indian industrialisation on the part of the British and Indian governments can be discerned here. To be sure, the Government of India was, as states tend to be, interested in the military build up of India and the role that industrialisation could play in that endeavour. But their aim was to develop

India (as a military force, which necessitated an industrial economy) – not to fit it into a pre-arranged imperial grand strategy (in which, after all, India might still only play the role of a raw materials supplier).[140]

The merest shadow of this difference could be detected in the cotton industry during the war. As we have seen, state intervention in the industry was extensive. From the side of the Indian industrialists and the Government of India, that intervention, as well as keeping up military supplies, was 'for the purpose of maintaining the supply, at reasonable rates, to the poorer classes of the community, of cotton cloth manufactured in this country'.[141] The British Government, on the other hand, was primarily in favour of state control over the industry because it regarded cotton as a strategic good. A Board of Trade memorandum to the Economic Offensive Committee of the British cabinet in May 1918 said that the Allies would have to have 'complete control of exports of important raw materials during the period immediately succeeding the war'. The Government of India therefore should consider export prohibition and price fixing in the cotton industry. This would constitute 'a bargaining asset for the purposes of negotiating with our enemies'.[142]

We will consider the differences between the Government of India and the British Government further in chapter four.

By the end of the war however, a clear consensus had emerged around the notion of state aid and guidance for the purposes of Indian industrialisation as a thoroughly good thing. But this consensus did not hold together for very long. For reasons that will be explained in the next two chapters, the British Government lost interest in Indian industrialisation. The Government of India could not push it forward in the face of London's disinterest. The Indian bourgeoisie meanwhile had discovered the potency of a state – and most particularly a state at war – for industrial development. Faced with the eventual indifference of the British state, they began looking for an alternative.

Chapter Three

Industrialisation Abandoned

The bold plans for state-led industrialisation of the Indian economy faded away in the inter-war period. They were abandoned first in London and then, more slowly, by the Government of India. Indian capitalists drew their own conclusions and, deserted by the British state, began looking at the state of the future.

A number of explanations have been offered for why state industrialisation languished. The sudden absence of the project's main architect, the end of hostilities, the post-war financial situation and political reform have all been suggested as likely culprits. However, each of these factors appears to be a symptom rather than a cause. Given the clear indication on all sides by war's end that state-directed industrialisation was a continuing priority, we need to ask why that priority faded? For it was this which in turn allowed its principle architect to be released, its military importance to be downgraded, its cost to be regarded as too great and for it to be sacrificed in the process of political decentralisation.

The simplest explanation put forward was the departure of Sir Thomas Holland. In 1919, the Indian Munitions Board (of which, we will recall, Holland was the president) was transformed into the Department of Munitions and Industries. Holland became the department's member on the Viceroy's Council. In 1921, he was also made the Member for Commerce.[1] However, '[a]t the end of 1921 a difference with the Viceroy (Lord Reading) on the withdrawal of a munitions prosecution in Calcutta led to Holland's resignation'.[2] Holland left India four years earlier than he had planned. The author of his obituary in late 1948 declared, 'This premature retirement of Sir Thomas Holland was an economic disaster for India'. He continued:

> Although there has been some growth of industries in India since the issue of the Report of the Indian Industrial Commission, how much greater would this advance not have been if the chief architect of this report had remained in India to implement its recommendations![3]

Holland in fact remained an active proponent of industry for three years after the war. But it was evident even during those years that the tide was turning against him. Talented though he undoubtedly was, it is unlikely that he could have stood against it, even if he had stayed at his post.

A more serious explanation is that, in the absence of war, the state reverted to a *laissez-faire* approach, leaving capital to prosper or not as best it could.[4] Trade Commissioner Ainscough argued as early as 1919 that in the 'totally different' conditions after the war, the state would no longer be able to manipulate economic conditions in India, with the result that Indian industries would be left unprotected.[5] Tomlinson adds: 'Once the need to further the imperial war effort in all possible ways ceased to be the British policy towards India, the case for the new industrial policy was weakened considerably.'[6] But did it cease to be? In all the British documents around the subject at the time, from the IIC Report to the Montagu-Chelmsford reforms, the pressing military need for Indian industrialisation was solemnly asserted and re-asserted. India remained a crucial factor in imperial military strategy, with 180,000 troops scattered around the Empire in 1918. No sooner was the war over than the Indian military was required to fight the Third Afghan War (1919) and to put down a rebellion in Mesopotamia (1920). Later, Indian forces were sent to quell unrest in what had become Iraq (1925–6) and Shanghai (1927), as well as being stationed in Singapore (from the late 1920s to the early 1930s). During the inter-war period there was a constant imperial demand for military resources raised, trained, equipped and sent from India. Industrialisation had always been seen in part as a way of more easily meeting this demand. It seems unlikely then that the 'end' of hostilities in 1918 occasioned the end of industrialisation (though a change in imperial military strategy may have, as we shall see).

It has also been suggested that an economic slump in India following the war and the need to cut government spending in its wake caused the state to abandon aid for industries. Vera Anstey wrote in 1929 that 'the financial situation made it impossible for Government to adopt all the recommendations of the Industrial Commission'. Those that were (partially) implemented, such as the central and provincial Departments of Industries, had disappointing results, 'primarily owing to the policy of [financial] retrenchment'.[7] Indeed, a Retrenchment Committee for India was set up in 1922 '[t]o make recommendations to the Government of India for effecting forthwith all possible reductions in the expenditure of the Central Government, having regard especially to the present financial position and outlook'.[8] Clive Dewey argues that, as a result of financial cutbacks, '[t]he wartime predilection for intervention receded', and the committee 'reduced the Indian industries departments to a skeleton of what the Industrial Commission had hoped they would become'.[9]

Again, however, this begs the question of *why* industrialisation – and the administrative structures to carry it through – were now not important enough to escape the cost-cutters' knives, when only a few years before they had been regarded as vital for India and the Empire?

Finally, it is argued that the decentralisation of government that took place as a result of the Montagu-Chelmsford reforms of 1919 (in which the British ceded some power to Indians at the provincial level, while holding on to most of it at the centre) devolved industrial policy to the provinces – where it languished and died, starved of co-ordination, resources and cash.[10] This can only be a partial explanation. As Partha Sarathi Gupta says, decentralisation of industrial policy 'did not necessarily rule out some degree of all-India co-ordination and pooling of experience'.[11] In fact, the

Government of India attempted just that kind of central co-ordination for some years, though its determination to do so steadily weakened. The question remains, why was the *political decision* taken to lower the priority of industrialisation – to make it of less importance than constitutional reform?

It is the purpose of this chapter and the next to readdress these questions in order to provide a satisfactory explanation why industrialisation was abandoned and why the views of the two governments, in London and New Delhi, diverged on the matter.

Mesopotamia

This will take us back to the role of India as a strategic asset to the British Empire. The war in Europe had staggered into trenches and stalemate on the Western front by September 1914. The warring powers looked for opportunities to break out of this stalemate, either by sheer force across the trenches or by attacking their enemies outside the European theatre. When the Ottoman Empire entered the war in late November 1914, it presented the Allies with a number of potential non-European targets. One of these was Mesopotamia.

In order to smite the Central Powers outside Europe, it was decided to attack the Turks at the extremity of their Empire in Mesopotamia, from the Persian Gulf. Before the war, it had been broadly agreed that the base of imperial military operations in the East would be India. As the war approached, responsibility for such operations became more finely tuned. The Mesopotamia Commission (convened to investigate the affair) revealed later:

> Asia was divided between the Imperial and Indian War Intelligence Departments . . . a line was drawn through Arabia from Akaba to Basra, all north of that line belonging to Whitehall, all south to Simla . . . the areas so defined for the purposes of information [intelligence gathering] would, in the event of their becoming theatres for warlike operations, be under the control of the organisation which had previously collected the information.

This division left Mesopotamia in an ambiguous position, since the 'line' passed through it:

> Basra [a major city in southern Mesopotamia] was thus given to India, Mesopotamia to Great Britain – a somewhat confused division of responsibility, inasmuch as Basra must inevitably become the base of any operations in Mesopotamia from the Persian Gulf.[12]

Initially, the conduct of the operation was given to the Government of India. The British Government directed them to dispatch troops to the head of the Persian Gulf. Indian Expeditionary Force D (Forces A, B and C having gone to Europe and East Africa) was duly dispatched and the Mesopotamia campaign began. After bombarding the fort at Fao in November 1914, Force D captured it and advanced on Basra.[13]

The operation's horizons expanded. An advance on Kut (further up the river Tigris) was thought possible and perhaps even an attack on Baghdad. In April 1915, General Sir John Nixon was put in command by the Government of India. Together with Nixon, the Government of India remained firmly in control of the operation.[14]

Having taken Kut, Force D moved on but then had to retreat back to Kut in early December 1915. Kut was surrounded by Turkish troops, besieged and finally forced to surrender in April 1916. By this time, the British Government had relieved the Government of India of responsibility for the operation (in February 1916) and placed it under the control of the War Office.[15]

The Government of India's attitude to the Mesopotamian campaign was, from the beginning, ambivalent to say the least. Pointing to the thousands of troops already sent abroad, they felt that insufficient troops remained to defend India itself.[16] Described by the commission as 'lukewarm' about the plan, in the end 'it was only under compulsion of a most imperative order from Whitehall' that the necessary forces were sent.[17]

New Delhi displayed a distressing tendency throughout to put Indian (rather than imperial) interests first. When the time came to send reinforcements, 'the Indian Government adopted the attitude that, having already denuded India of troops by overseas expeditions, it was impossible to send reinforcements from India to Mesopotamia', according to the commission.[18] On the medical side, Sir William Babtie (until June 1915 Director of Medical Services in India and then Surgeon-General in Mesopotamia) told the commission 'it was necessary to economise in Mesopotamia in order to provide for the medical needs of forces mobilised in India for internal defence'.[19] When further reinforcements were requested from India for an advance on Baghdad, the Government of India evidently attempted to hide its available forces from the British Government. The Indian Commander-in-Chief's military secretary wrote to the military secretary of the Viceroy:

> It is clear that the Home Government are very anxious that Baghdad should be taken and they will send us the required force if we hold out [i.e. supply no reinforcements], but they will give us nothing if the least sign of willingness to find reinforcements is shown by us, and we shall have to do it all by ourselves, and be so weak everywhere that both in India and in Mesopotamia we shall be in danger.[20]

The Government of India's approach, the commission concluded, 'was not the attitude of an Englishman but of an Indian Rajah'.[21]

But a mere outline of the operations in Mesopotamia and the Government of India's reluctance to commit themselves fully does not convey the strategic debacle, logistical collapse and medical horror that were involved. The fact was that practically every aspect of supply for the campaign broke down. The reserve system of the Indian army collapsed. Essential infrastructure for the advance of troops, especially river transport and railways, was not built.[22] Provisions for the troops failed to materialise. Lord Hardinge wrote to Thomas Holderness at the India Office: 'When some weeks ago I enquired of the Commander-in-Chief whether proper provisions had been made for warm clothing for the troops, he told me that he was relying on private charity for this.'[23] Consequently, conditions for the most vulnerable – the sick and wounded – were appalling.[24] Having inspected the military base at Basra, Sir George Buchanan (Director General of Port Administration) declared, 'I came to the conclusion that I had never before in my life seen such a hopeless mess and muddle'.[25]

Who was responsible? The Mesopotamia Commission was quite clear on this. In its report, critical remarks are made about various aspects of the British Government and its military commanders – in particular, General Nixon.[26] But page after page of the report condemns the Government of India root and branch: '[I]t is impossible to refrain from serious censure of the Indian Government for the lack of knowledge and foresight shown in the inadequacy of their preparations and for the lack of readiness to recognize and supply deficiencies.'[27]

Criticism zeroed in on the autocratic structure of the Government of India and specifically on the role of the Viceroy and the Commander-in-Chief. Josiah Wedgwood (a Labour MP, whose minority report is appended to that of the commission) argued that 'even the Viceroy's Executive Council was passed over, and the Viceroy and Commander-in-Chief governed and thought alone'.[28] The Viceroy had too much power and so did the Commander-in-Chief. And that power was exercised from, of all places, Simla.

> Its remoteness from great towns and great cantonments of India and its inaccessibility render it singularly unsuitable for the residence, during the greater part of the year, of the one high official [the Commander-in-Chief] who has to discharge this unique mass of military responsibilities.[29]

General Sir Harry 'Beauchamp' Duff and his advisers were 'specially responsible for not realising more completely that the medical provisions intended for the North-West Frontier could not be sufficient or suitable for a campaign on the Tigris'. Indeed, Duff was accused of 'a dereliction of duty'.[30]

The critique broadened out to encompass a quite remarkable indictment of the Government of India and its attitude to the war. The report asserted:

> [A]s the dimensions of the war grew and the character of its issues became more and more apparent, the Indian Government do not appear to us to have fully risen to the situation . . . Neither as regards compulsory service for Europeans, not in the organisation of industrial resources for purposes of war, nor in general finance was sufficient alacrity shown during the first year and a half of the war.[31]

Wedgwood went further with the extraordinary accusation that the Viceroy and the Commander-in-Chief 'have shown little desire to help and some desire actually to obstruct the energetic prosecution of the war'.[32]

When the scale of the disaster in Mesopotamia was realised in Britain and India, the outcry was tremendous. Newspaper editors, politicians and military figures were at one in trenchant criticism, mostly of the hapless Government of India. As early as March 1916 (that is, before the surrender at Kut), *The Times* revealed that it was receiving 'bitter complaints' from the forces in Mesopotamia, which 'seem to point to something like a breakdown of the medical arrangements'. The article concluded darkly: '[F]ar too little has been made public about the trials of the Mesopotamia Expeditionary Force.'[33] In October of the same year, *The Morning Post* accused the Government of India of trying to remain neutral in the war:

> It merely does not want to be bothered about a distant and disagreeable conflict . . . In the meantime we are informed that the dances and picnics for which Simla is justly famous go on as usual. With soldiers dying in neglected hospitals our Indian officials still continue to maintain their gaiety.[34]

In Parliament, as we have seen, a Special Commission was established in August 1916 to enquire into the affair. It reported in May 1917. The commission passed severe censure on the Viceroy, the Commander in Chief, the Surgeon General, the Director of Medical Services and the Commanding Officer in Mesopotamia. A judicial tribunal was appointed to look into possible charges arising from the commission's report. The Viceroy reportedly offered his resignation to the British Government no less than three times.[35] The Secretary of State, Austen Chamberlain, did resign.[36] Generals Duff and Nixon, together with Surgeons General Hathaway and MacNeece, were placed on half pay. At the same time, 'a large number of generals . . . have been removed by the War Office from their commands in Mesopotamia'.[37]

Before resigning, Chamberlain wrote to the Viceroy, pointing out that

> public confidence in the Government of India is profoundly shaken, and . . . we cannot count, in dealing with the urgent problems that beset us, upon the same measure of confidence which in other circumstances would have been accorded to us.[38]

The Viceroy replied, lamenting the Mesopotamia Commission Report's 'disastrous effect upon the position and prestige of the Government of India'.[39]

In its own defence, the Government of India could say that before the war, its strategic position in imperial schemes was woefully under-supported by the British Government. The Indian army, it was agreed, had two tasks before 1914: to defend India's North-West Frontier and to maintain internal security. The Mesopotamia Commission admitted that '[w]hatever preparations were made in England for a European war before August, 1914, no preparations were made in India'.[40] Given the Indian army's prescribed tasks, it was not surprising that, in the opinion of the Commander-in-Chief, it was only prepared for 'semi-savage fighting', it did not have the equipment for overseas expeditions and it was 'backward in every particular'.[41]

Furthermore, confined to a domestic role, the army was continually subject to cost-cutting, as the Government of India attempted to save money.[42] As late as 1913, the Nicolson Commission, set up to study Indian finances, recommended (in March 1914) that the Indian military not finance any preparations for overseas expeditions.[43] This meant that when things broke down in Mesopotamia, 'India was not herself in a position to supply some of the lacking material, such, for example, as heavy guns'.[44]

For the Government of India, this illustrated the folly of neglecting India's industrial potential and strengthened its resolve to carry through an industrialisation programme.

The British reaction

The British Government drew quite different conclusions from the Mesopotamia affair. In its opinion, the failure of India militarily was too abject to be blamed on a lack of industry. It indicated to London a failure of the entire system of government in India.[45] And a failure on such a scale as to necessitate a root and branch overhaul of that system.

Political reform of the Government of India was taken up by a host of speakers in the parliamentary debates on the Mesopotamia Commission's Report in July 1917. Lord Sydenham told the House of Lords:

> The whole system of government which has grown up in recent years must be completely overhauled. It is not only on the military side that this system has shown grave defects which are plain to all who have served in India within the last ten years.[46]

The Mesopotamia Commission itself had recommended that the Secretary of State's India Council and the Viceroy's Executive Council should be dispossessed of their old powers and that there should be 'a devolution of responsibilities and duties from the over-centralised bureaucracy of the Supreme Government at Simla'.[47] In his minority report, Wedgwood extended this, recommending that Indians should be allowed 'a large share in the government of their own country and in the control of that Bureaucracy which in this war, uncontrolled by public opinion, has failed to rise to British standards'.[48] Reform and decentralisation were enthusiastically endorsed by the former Under-Secretary of State and Minister for Munitions, Edwin Montagu, the man who would succeed Chamberlain as Secretary of State after his resignation over this affair.[49] Montagu added his voice to those who wanted to decentralise, from London to New Delhi, and from the Government of India to the provinces. 'Really', he told the Commons, 'the whole system has got to be explored in the light of the Mesopotamia Commission. It has proved to be of too much rigidity'.[50] Most famously, he declared:

> The Government of India is too wooden, too iron, too inelastic, too antediluvian, to be any use for the modern purposes we have in view. I do not believe that anybody could ever support the Government of India from the point of view of modern requirements. But . . . it required a crisis to direct attention to the fact that the Indian Government is an indefensible system of government . . . What I am saying now is, in the light of these revelations of this inelasticity of Indian government . . . the time has now come to alter them.[51]

In that speech lay the beginnings of a new British attitude to its Empire in India. For while the reforms envisaged were partly a concession to respectable Indian nationalism and partly an exercise in holding on to central power while conceding it at the edges, they were also part of a reappraisal of India's military role ('the modern purposes we have in view') in future conflicts. Montagu said (now addressing himself to the Government of India):

> [Y]our great claim to continue the illogical system of government by which you have governed India in the past is that it was efficient. It has been proved not to be efficient. It has been proved to be not sufficiently elastic to express the will of the Indian people; to make them into a warring nation as they wanted to be.[52]

Wedgwood accused the Indian military command of 'belonging to an old type . . . deprived by long residence among European subjects of that energy, wider patriotism and education which is essential for the successful prosecution of a long war'.[53]

The implications of Mesopotamia for India's imperial role and their effects on Indian industry and Indian industrialists will be more closely examined in the next chapter.

Given its own preference for economic development rather than political reform, the Government of India was lukewarm in its reaction to London's new enthusiasm for the latter. In this, they were at one with the now fading Secretary of State, Austen Chamberlain, who tried to persuade the Commons not to 'make the discussion of the Report of the Mesopotamia Commission ... the text for a great Debate upon the future of the Indian Empire'.[54] The Viceroy told the Imperial War Conference in New Delhi the following April, 'The liberty of the world must be won before our aspirations for the liberalising of Indian political institutions can acquire any tangible meaning'.[55] In 1916, the Lieutenant Governor of Bihar and Orissa, Sir Edward Gait, had suggested to the Viceroy that fiscal independence for India would be the most effective way of meeting Indian aspirations.[56] Echoing government opinion, the pro-British Bengali statesman, Sir Syed Shams ul Huda, told the Governor of Bengal that:

> The extension of India's trade and commerce and the protection and development of her industries are the most important means of securing India's prosperity and the happiness of her people and are much more important than any of the three questions [self government, employment of Indians in administration, Provincial Councils] discussed in the [Viceroy's] Memorandum [of 20 July 1916].[57]

Political reform

'I cannot leave the Government of India untouched', wrote Edwin Montagu in his *Indian Diary*:

> because I felt it was bad. I felt it before I came out; I feel it more so now I am here. The dead hand of the Government of India is over everything, blighting it. It is worse than anything, except the Government of Madras.[58]

An over-centralised and unnecessarily unrepresentative government had produced the Mesopotamia disaster and was feeding the nationalist fire. That government had to be decentralised and given at least the appearance of increasing representation. Montagu, the new Secretary of State and Lord Chelmsford, the new Viceroy, eventually produced in 1918 a report that attempted to tackle these two questions. The essence of the Montagu-Chelmsford reforms was to devolve some of the powers of the Government of India to the provincial level. Their report stated:

> The provinces are the domain in which the earlier steps towards the progressive realization of responsible government should be taken... This involves at once giving the provinces the largest measure of independence, legislative, administrative and financial of the Government of India which is compatible with the due discharge by the latter of its own responsibilities.[59]

Eventually, these provinces would be part of 'a sisterhood of States, self-governing in all matters of purely local or provincial interest' under the Central Government of India. Starting with the provinces, each level of government would be 'increasingly representative of and responsible to the people of all of them'.[60]

On the face of it, the Government of India seemed to concur wholeheartedly with the spirit of the reforms (though, as we shall see, there was considerable disquiet beneath the surface). Chelmsford's predecessor, Lord Hardinge, had broached the subject of reform back in 1915. He wrote then of the 'unnecessary and really useless interference by the Government of India with the Provincial Governments' as a result of British strictures. He was prepared to accept more power at the provincial level, since this could be monitored by the central legislature and the Viceroy's veto, 'by which provincial legislation can always be modified or negatived'.[61] A few months after taking up the viceregal position, Chelmsford sent a circular letter to the provincial rulers. This endorsed the British goal, 'to endow India, as an integral part of the British Empire, with the largest measure of Self-Government compatible with the maintenance of the supremacy of British rule'.

Even the Indian National Congress seemed in tune with the initial thrust of the reforms, having resolved at its December 1915 session in favour of '[t]he introduction of Provisional Autonomy, including financial independence'.[62]

For Indian industrialists, the Montagu-Chelmsford report seemed to hold out the prospect of continuing state intervention to bring about industrial development. It declared, 'if the resources of the country are to be developed the Government must take action;' and further on, 'the Government must admit and shoulder its responsibility for furthering the industrial development of the country'.[63] The report contained the obligatory military justification for industrialisation:

> We know that the possibility of sea communications being temporarily interrupted forces us to rely on India as an ordnance base for protective operations in Eastern theatres of war . . . the development of India's natural resources becomes a matter of almost military necessity.[64]

India's industrial development was therefore 'a matter in which considerations of military security, political expediency, and economic advantage are coincident, and are in agreement also with the interests of the Empire as a whole'.[65]

This certainly sounded convincing enough – and the Indian Industrial Commission was one body that was convinced. The commission's report had gone to the printers before the reform scheme was announced, but the commission was confident enough to state: 'It is evident, however, that our scheme is in general accord with the administrative changes proposed by His Excellency the Viceroy and the Secretary of State.'[66] The industrial commitment of the reforms was sufficiently strong to alarm the Indo-British Association, which declared that they were aimed at 'a wide system of State-aid [to Indian industry]'. Further, 'the [Indian] politician clamours for complete control of the trade of India; and Mr Montagu and Lord Chelmsford are doing their best to give him that control by the transfer of political and economic powers to his hands'.[67]

But the optimism of the Industrial Commission and the misgivings of the Indo-British Association were both entirely misplaced. For, whatever the conscious intentions of the reforms' proponents, the reform scheme itself dealt a serious blow to the prospects of state-led industrialisation. The scheme envisaged that, henceforward, government should be divided between the Central Government of India and new governments in the provinces. The Government of India would hold on to important imperial concerns – 'matters adjudged by [the Government of India] to be essential in the discharge of its responsibilities for peace, order and good government' – such as defence, foreign policy, tariffs and shipping, which would be known as Central or Imperial Subjects.[68] The rest would go to the provinces, where they would be once again divided between 'reserved' subjects (for the governor and his council) and 'transferred' subjects (for the new provincial governments and the new, partially elected, provincial assemblies).[69]

The question of industrial development found itself cast out of the list of Central Subjects that concerned the Government of India. Furthermore, at the provincial level, it was placed in the 'transferred' category, under the control of Indian provincial governments.[70] Now, while the idea of state industrial development being in Indian hands may have appealed to Indian nationalism, the fact that it was consigned to the provinces fatally weakened the state's intervention in this area. State development is necessarily a centralised project. It requires central planning to avoid duplication of effort and to construct an integrated national economy. India's industrial resources may have been just strong enough to set out on this path on a national scale under a national plan. At the provincial level, it was out of the question.[71] Provincial efforts in this regard would, under the reforms scheme, also be hampered by lack of funds; 'the provinces were assigned inadequate and non-expanding sources of revenue to carry out these development functions'.[72]

The prospects of state industrialisation received a further series of blows from the 1922–23 Indian Retrenchment Committee, set up to prune the Government of India's expenditure. The committee's report pointed out (several times) that, in the aftermath of the reforms, the Government of India was only supposed to take up industrial development in cases declared by the Governor-General in Council to be in the public interest – and that no such declaration had to that point been made.[73] It noted the anomaly that, just as the Central Department of

Industries was being created, the Central Government was losing its powers in this area.[74]

The committee then turned its attention to the central industrial institutions that still maintained a tenuous existence. The Industrial Intelligence Section and the Labour Bureau, the committee thought, 'could be discontinued without serious inconvenience'.[75] The functions of the Departments of Commerce, Industries, Revenue and Agriculture, Education and Health and Public Works should be combined into three departments: of Commerce, Communications and 'General'. The construction of a proposed central School of Mines and Geology should be postponed for three years. The Indian Stores Department, set up by the Government of India to encourage the use of Indian goods rather than importing them from Britain, should not be expanded.[76] The committee concluded: 'In reviewing the expenditure of the commercial and *quasi*-commercial departments and manufacturing establishments of Government we have had occasion to observe that in many cases these are not conducted on commercial lines' – which of course was the whole point of state intervention.[77]

Not even the Government of India's military expenditure was safe from the committee's axe – a fact that further weakened the government's main motive for encouraging industrial development. In the committee's view, India simply could not afford its current spending on the armed forces. In peace conditions, 'the first essential is for India to balance her budget . . . by a very substantial reduction in the military estimates'. It was, according to the committee, 'fortuitous' that, in the 1922–23 military budget, 'the strength of the army was under establishment' and that 'inadequate provision was made for the maintenance of the R.A.F'. The Royal Indian Marine should be 'drastically curtailed'. The committee also recommended abandoning 'a forward policy of military domination' in Waziristan and 'reductions in the cost of frontier defence' in the North West Frontier Province.[78]

Initially, the Government of India attempted to resist the pressures towards decentralisation and away from industrialisation represented by the reforms. Despite its eventual (and perhaps ostensible) agreement with provincial government, the Government of India was reluctant in its acceptance. In July 1916, Chelmsford had pointed out that provincial autonomy was a Congress demand and that London should be 'very wary' before conceding it. He advised that it was 'most desirable to pause for the present before effecting any material expansion of the constitutional powers of the [Provincial] Councils'.[79] His Council resolved in September that '[t]here should be no change in the *powers* of the Councils'.[80] In Despatch Number 17 of 1916, the Government of India told the British Government

> We do not recommend any immediate expansion of these powers [of provincial councils] in the direction which a number of 'progressive' politicians desire. We have no wish to develop the councils as *quasi*-parliaments. Nor are we prepared to give them anything in the nature of direct financial or administrative control; this may we think come at some later stage of their political evolution.[81]

Little wonder then that neither the India Office nor the Secretary of State was impressed with the Government of India's attitude to the reforms by the end of 1916.[82] The Viceroy told Montagu in May 1917 that enlarging the powers of the councils 'would be tantamount to transferring to these bodies the control of the whole of the internal administration of India'. Such a policy would have 'disastrous results'.[83] In his *Indian Diary* Montagu complained that

> [the Government of India] does not concede provincial autonomy, or begin to concede provincial autonomy. At every stage the Government of India keeps its control, and it does not go nearly far enough in giving responsibility to the Legislative Councils.[84]

As we have seen, however, the Government of India did accommodate itself to the version of provincial autonomy that appeared in the Montagu-Chelmsford Report.

Its recalcitrance on the question of industrialisation was much more prolonged – though whether this was recalcitrance, or simply blundering ahead having failed to notice that industrial development had been taken out of its hands (as the Indian Retrenchment Committee believed) remains an open question. It is possible that the Government of India realised that the imperial tasks that India was still being exhorted to undertake towards the end of the war were impossible to fulfil in the absence of state-led industrialisation.[85] In the negotiations over the workings of the Montagu-Chelmsford reforms, the Government of India had requested that industrial development (and higher education) should be retained as reserved subjects – to no avail.[86]

The changing fortunes of centrally directed industrial development can be tracked in the *Statement exhibiting the Moral and Material Progress and Condition*, produced annually by the India Office in these years. The 1920 edition was still castigating pre-war *laissez-faire* policies ('attempts to encourage Indian industries . . . were effectively discouraged from Whitehall') and rejoicing in the fact that '[f]ortunately experience gained in the war has effectually demonstrated the necessity of Government playing an active part in the industrial development of India'.[87] These sentiments were repeated more or less word for word in the 1921, 1922–23 and 1923–24 editions.[88] Both the 1920 and 1921 editions noted that, under the reforms, industrial direction had gone to the provinces, but both also pointed to the existence of the new Central Department of Industries. The 1921 *Statement* noted that the Central Government could take control 'when it considers such a course to be necessary' and gave several instances where this might be the case.[89] By the 1925–26 edition, however, the reassuring words on 'Government playing an active part' had disappeared. There only remained a defensive comment that India 'must become industrialized to some extent, and it is therefore premature to condemn the present policy of the Indian Government with regard to the protection and development of Indian industries'.[90] Subsequently, all comment on central industrial policy ceased.

Post-war industry policy was also revealed through the annual conferences of the directors of industries (central and provincial). These were initially presided over by Sir Thomas Holland of the Industrial Commission and the Munitions Board – now the Government Member for Munitions and Industries. During his trip to India in 1918, Montagu had met with Holland who informed him that the 'aim ought to be, after the War, to make India self-supporting in five years' – but that this would be a mammoth task.[91] Holland convened the first conference of Industries Directors in April 1920. He emphasised the important co-ordinating role of the Central Department.[92] The secretary to the Department of Munitions and Industries, F.R. Rudman, noted that 'in the very rare instances when a certain policy might jeopardise India's interests as a whole', the Central Department might intervene.[93] Holland also raised the question of an All-India Industrial Service, as recommended by the Indian Industrial Commission.[94]

At the second conference in November, Holland claimed, in his opening remarks, to be using the Indian Industrial Commission Report as a 'textbook'.[95] He raised once again the All-India Industrial Service, though he now assured his listeners that the service would not trespass on 'the rights of the new ministers'. The directors were still of the opinion that there would be 'work connected with the development of industries that will devolve on the Government of India under the Reform Scheme'.[96] But the future of industrial development was beginning to look a little bleaker. While the new system would 'impose no restrictions at all upon the powers of local Governments to spend money in this connection', there was little money there to be had. Where there was money – at the centre – the Munitions and Industries Departmental representative told the conference 'that under the new financial scheme the Government of India could embark on such expenditure only in cases affecting the national safety.[97]

The next conference, in May 1921, found Holland still claiming that 'the most important product of the Reformed Constitution' was 'the development of Indian industries by, and especially for, Indians with a view of making the country self-supporting'. For this, it was necessary to artificially modify India's 'natural tendency' to trade in raw materials in order to make her 'as quickly as possible self-contained in the production of material for defence'.[98] The necessity of central direction was here unstated but clear. Such a policy, said Holland, now obviously with an eye to the dangers of provincialisation, would 'bind the provinces into one nation ... with a view especially of uniting the country into one unit for purposes of defence'.[99]

But the directors, now joined by their provincial ministers, were accommodating themselves to the changes in British attitudes much more rapidly than was Holland. They decided to postpone consideration of the All-India Industrial Service and the All-India Chemical Service yet again – and with obvious frustration: 'The President [Holland] . . . suggested that members might find time to read Chapter IX of the Industrial Commission's Report.'[100]

Holland's single-minded concentration on the importance of munitions may have been one reason that he did not get a lot of support from the Indian politicians now gathered around the table. The Punjabi Minister for Industry, Lala Harkishen Lal, pointed out that Holland's constant emphasis on defence industries might not be in the best interests of the Indian people: 'The Government of India would naturally incline first towards munitions, while the people would incline first towards textiles, food, etc.'[101] The All-India Industrial Service and the All-India Chemical Service were decisively rejected by the Indian ministers at the fourth conference in April 1922.[102]

The Government of India also produced some mild resistance to the swingeing recommendations of the Indian Retrenchment Committee. In line with those recommendations, the Industrial Intelligence Bureau and the Labour Bureau were shut down and the peacetime establishment of the armed forces and the Royal Indian Marine was reduced.[103] But on frontier defence, the Government of India maintained that '[t]he position on the frontier is still unstabilised' and agreed only to cut rations rather than men.[104] On collapsing five departments into three, they reported 'Government have not adopted the exact line suggested by the Committee' – instead starting three new departments which included one of Industries and Labour.[105] Despite the committee's recommendation to postpone, funds for the School of Mines and Geology 'were voted by the Assembly for 1924–25 and 1925–26 and the school is now under construction'.[106] Finally, the government did not accept the committee's injunction to stop further expansion of the Indian Stores Department.[107]

In the end though, the Government of India's resistance or recalcitrance was futile, for the underlying drivers of industrialisation, in an imperial sense, had ceased to function.

In this chapter I have discussed some of the immediate mechanisms through which the Indian state's programme of industrial development was abandoned. It is clear that the decentralisation of the Montagu-Chelmsford reforms and the attacks of the Indian Retrenchment Committee were the most important of these. The more significant issue, however, concerns why the context had changed so dramatically. Why was industrial development now no longer important enough to survive administrative reform and cost-cutting? The reason lay in the fact that after the war, Britain's attitude to her Indian Empire changed fundamentally – a development that will be addressed in the next chapter.

Chapter Four

Empire

The purpose of this chapter is to place the abandonment of state-directed industrialisation in India in a wider context – that of the Empire and of colonialism. By the end of the First World War, the interests of Britain's rulers with regard to the Empire had changed. India's perceived role within the Empire therefore changed as well. From this point, India was regarded primarily as a strategic asset, from which men and materials could be drawn. Questions of industrial development wilted under the pressure of strategic priority. In order to demonstrate why and how this occurred, a general framework in which to consider empires and colonialism is needed.

I shall argue that modern European expansion was generally motivated by two forces. One was the expansion of capital, extending the boundaries of international trade. The other was the expansion and consolidation of national power. The former process was identified with trade, plunder or exploitation (and usually with all three). The latter was identified with colonisation. It is this process that I shall refer to as colonialism.[1] The distinction between 'informal' and 'formal' empire is a representation of these two forces. The general move from the former to the latter in the late nineteenth century can be seen as the strengthening of one at the expense of the other.

The origin of one of these forces, capital, is clear to us. What was the origin of the other? Eighteenth-century capitalist opponents of empire, like Richard Cobden and John Bright, believed it came from the landed oligarchy:

> Both formal and informal imperialism supported the armed forces; the armed forces supported the aristocracy; the aristocracy supported the empire, and with it bellicosity, war, waste, outdoor relief for its cadets and clients, and a steadfast opposition to free trade.[2]

Joseph Schumpeter's explanation was somewhat similar. Writing in 1919, he certainly saw two systems in play: 'The social pyramid of the present age has been formed, not by the substance and laws of capitalism alone, but by two different social substances, and by the laws of two different epochs.'[3]

The other 'social substance' was a throwback, a surviving remnant of a previous age, when 'the vital needs of situations . . . molded peoples and classes into warriors – if they wanted to avoid extinction'.[4] Colonialism then (the extension of territory and, by extension, war) was 'atavistic . . . an element that stems from the living conditions not of the present, but of the past'. The past that it came from specifically was feudalism in its absolutist phase.[5] The surviving social remnants of this period – for example in the aristocracy and the professional armed forces – still exercised considerable influence in the imperialist countries. They were alien to the spirit of modern capitalism.[6]

Karl Kautsky, the most prominent Marxist theorist after the death of Frederick Engels in 1895, also found the origins of imperialism in ancient warrior societies.[7] For him too, imperialism was linked to precapitalist remnants. It did not arise from the needs of capitalist industrial development, but from 'classes whose interests are opposed to the requirements of economic development'.[8]

More recently, Ronald Robinson and John Gallagher examined the state officials who increasingly supported colonialism in distinctly Schumpeterian terms:

> The aristocrat by right, the official by *expertise*, both felt socially superior and functionally detached from those who pushed trade

> and built empires. It was their high calling to mediate between jarring and selfish interests and to keep the state from being used as the tool of any of them . . . Those who governed still thought of themselves as arbiters above the tumult, slightly contemptuous of the short-sighted businessman, the impractical philanthropist and the ignorant populace alike.[9]

The problem with seeing colonialism in these terms was that these atavistic elements, feudal remnants and aspects of warrior societies were, during the course of the nineteenth century, gradually dying out. Their influence was declining. As Schumpeter himself put it, 'in the end the climate of the modern world must destroy them'. Therefore, '[s]ince the vital needs that created it [colonialism] have passed away for good, it too must gradually disappear'.[10] This was clearly not the case. In the transition from informal to formal empire, from influence to direct rule, from trading posts to the 'Scramble for Africa' – the colonialist element was growing stronger.[11]

An alternative set of explanations for the evolution of colonialism links together the two forces that I have distinguished: capitalism and imperialism.[12] According to these arguments, there are forces inherent in the capitalist system that drive the economic and military subjugation of the more backward economies by the more advanced. Lenin, for example, argues that while capitalist cartels proceed with an economic division of the world, 'parallel and in connection with [that process]', states carve out colonies and spheres of influence. A little further on, he suggests that 'capitalism's transition to the stage of monopoly capitalism . . . is connected with the intensification of the struggle for the partitioning of the world'.[13] But the lines of causality seem to run in both directions at once. If imperialism resulted from the contemporary stage of capitalist development, it was necessary to show how the former was caused by the latter. Yet Lenin makes it quite clear that, while the empires were convenient for the monopolies, they preceded (and therefore did not result from) capitalism as it then was.[14] In fact, no such direct identification was possible. Capital, which originated in an imperial nation, did not restrict its overseas investments to the boundaries of empire.[15]

Capitalists were in fact often opposed to the expense and waste of colonial adventures and the wars that they engendered.[16] As we have seen, both Schumpeter and Kautsky argued strongly against the notion that colonialism was in some way a natural development (Lenin's 'Highest Stage') of capitalism.[17] Fieldhouse suggests:

> Formal ownership of territory was seldom essential or even relevant to economic activity and in some places might have positively inconvenient consequences for traders, planters, land speculators and others. Conversely the official mind of Europe for long assumed that economic interests could and should look after themselves without direct interference by the state.[18]

The origin and driving force of modern colonialism – the promotion of formal empire – was neither feudal remnants nor industrial capitalism. It was the national state.[19] This is why there is more than a kernel of truth in Schumpeter's and Kautsky's arguments. But the national state was not a throwback, a dying avatar. It was (and thus far remains) a real force, with real interests and by the end of the nineteenth century, it was, in its most advanced forms, on the march.

States at first emerge primarily as territorial units.[20] They therefore rapidly (if not simultaneously) become military units as well. The young state needs its own military forces to protect its territory, its trade and to compete with other emerging states.[21] The state brings with it (into a capitalist economic structure, for example) a deal of historical baggage – a territorial basis, a war-making capacity and a drive to competition deriving from its existence in a system of similar states. In economic structures that are dominated by the state it is these phenomena that tend to dominate the economics, politics and even culture of the society in question.

Capital and state are not two faces of the same beast – they are two different beasts. While capital is constantly driven to internationalise – to seek the largest markets and achieve the largest concentration of capital – the state is wedded to a national territory.[22] While capitalists compete, in the main, commercially, states are able to compete with each other by means of physical power. War and territorial conquest are the prerogatives of states.

In the imperial context, a contingent link between the interests of capital and national states was created when trading activities or investments were threatened, either by rival capitalists or rival states.[23] Imperialism – the expansion of formal empire – became a twin project, but not an identical one. That is why, for example, Lenin (and others) could see that colonial expansion and capital export took place (very roughly) concurrently – but had difficulty in demonstrating any causal link between the two. Empire and capital seemed to move together. So closely were they entwined that it appeared they had fused.[24] It was not so. A contingent linking of interests took place, not a fusion.[25] Even during imperialism's heyday, divisions could be seen. The colonial state in the Gold Coast 'clearly perceived the divergence of its interests from those of the [gold] mining capitalists', according to John Sender and Sheila Smith. A Colonial Office official declared in 1911 that '[t]he total failure of the mining industry would cause . . . no more than a temporary setback to the revenue of the Government'.[26] Manali Chakrabarti cites the case of the Upper India Chamber of Commerce in Kanpur – a predominantly European organisation – which, 'because of the peculiar nature of its business, found its economic interests in congruence with those of Indian big business and consequently also with those rallied for by the Congress'. One of its members, Mr Briscoe of the Elgin Mills, was thus able to conclude that 'India as a trading nation would be equally as glad to do business with Germany and Italy as with England or Scotland'.[27]

Nation states entered into the world of international trade and investment, at first to protect it, but gradually in pursuit of interests of their own. Those interests could be discerned in the impeccably state-oriented forms through which state intervention took place: the extension of military power, formal annexation of territory and the establishment of colonies that were extensions of the national state itself.[28] The real division between the informal and formal empires of the earlier and later nineteenth century lay in the extent to which state intervention was involved. Once the state came in and colonialism proper began, the interests of the national state tended to eclipse all others – a process that can be traced from the conduct of trade with India through to the 'Scramble for Africa'. As to the latter, Robinson and Gallagher point out:

> The British colonies and protectorates in tropical Africa had not been claimed originally because they were needed as colonial estates. Rather, they had been claimed for strategic reasons, and they had to be developed as colonial estates to pay the costs of their administration. Their economic development was more a consequence than a motive of the 'Scramble'.[29]

The state received a tremendous boost to its power from the First World War. It now began to shoulder aside the power of capital on a world scale.[30] In India, we have already examined the strengthening of state power as a result of the war. The resurgence of the state meant that by the end of the First World War, the economic imperative (the interest of capital) for the Empire in India was permanently shifted to a lower priority than India's strategic importance (the interest of the British state). This was to have a profound impact on India's place in the Empire and on her economic development.

India and Empire

When the European powers turned their attention towards India, their interest was clearly in trade. The East India Company, pushed out of the East Indies by their Dutch counterparts, petitioned the Mughal Empire for the right to trade and by 1700 the company had established itself in the future presidencies of Madras, Bombay and Calcutta. Two factors soon impinged on their status as traders. The first was the disintegration of the Mughal Empire by the 1660s, which disrupted the company's relations with Indian authorities and left them vulnerable to the aggression of the Mughal successor states.[31] The company took measures in its own defence.[32] From 1675, it drilled its European employees in order to resist attacks on its 'factories'. Thus, a military dimension was added to the company's trading priorities. Nevertheless, the company directors maintained in 1681, 'All war is so contrary to our interest... that we cannot too often inculcate to you our aversion thereunto'.[33]

The second factor that affected the company's trader status was the intervention of the British state. The defence of its trade had necessitated the enlargement of the territory that the company occupied. This brought it up against the trading interests of commercial rivals, most notably those from Holland and France. This attracted the attention of the British Government. When aggressive commercial competition 'assumed the character of national rivalry, then, of course, the British Government commenced meddling with the affairs of the East India Company, and the double government of India sprung up in fact if not in name'.[34] This took place in the context of Britain's emerging global military contest with France.

The British state's increased interest in India as a strategic asset can be seen in the contrasting experiences of the War of the Spanish Succession (1701–1714) and the War of the Austrian Succession (1740–1748). The first left India relatively unscathed since the East India Company and the Compagnie des Indes were able to agree a neutrality pact. In the second, the French Governor of Pondicherry, François Dupleix, offered another neutrality pact to the East India Company in Madras: 'The Company played for time, but offshore the Royal Navy raided the Compagnie's shipping. Hostilities had begun.' Thus, 'the British state propelled the two companies into open hostilities'.[35] From this point, the British state regarded India as a player (under its control) in the global struggle against its imperial rivals. British forces were sent to reinforce the company's armies, while at the same time, those armies came to be regarded 'as an important supplement to national strength in the struggles against France, Spain, and the Dutch'.[36]

There is some evidence that company directors and officers tried to resist the statification of the company's operations – by opposing the unification of the regular army with those of the company, for example.[37] But while successful on that score, the company was thoroughly statified by the late 1700s. 'The events of the Seven Years' War [1756–1763]', wrote Marx, 'transformed the East India Company from a commercial into a military and territorial power'.[38] The company's armies increased from 18,000 men in 1763 to 154,500 in 1805 and war became its major preoccupation. 'Instead of merchants and traders, a succession of soldiers and aristocrats ruled the Company's possessions, accentuating the burgeoning militarisation of its operations in India.'[39]

The finishing touches to the process were put in place after 1857 when it became clear, under the blows of the Indian uprising, that indirect rule through a once commercial company would no longer suffice to maintain either the British state's strategic interests in India or British capital's commercial ones. The change to direct British rule was brought about by the Government of India Act, passed in response to the uprising in August 1858. British India was now under the control of a Viceroy, a Secretary of State and ultimately the British Government. The British state would now determine India's role within the Empire – and that role would increasingly be a strategic one.

India as a strategic asset

The defence of India and the routes to India and beyond became synonymous with the defence of the Empire. And although 'the defence of India was itself a heavy strategic burden upon the British Empire', the British state had come to regard it as a worthwhile investment.[40]

The jewel at the centre of the Jewel in the Crown was the Indian army. This was a force which was originally raised as a by-product of British commercial activity in India.[41] India now paid for its own army and for units of the British army stationed in India itself.[42] India became a means to finance and support the British armies in India. David Washbrook points out:

> Nearly half of all Indian government revenues were spent directly on the army's maintenance and its interests lay behind most (of the few) infrastructural development policies – from railways to medical services to industrial planning – which the Raj ever pursued.[43]

India became the launching pad for the extension and consolidation of British influence into the Middle and Far East.[44] Major E. Peach of Military Intelligence told the War Office in 1901 (by which time this process was well under way) that India should 'be made strong enough not only to look after herself but to be a radiating centre of force'.[45] Robinson and Gallagher observe:

> The Indian army provided the means of over-awing and, in the last resort, of crushing the resistance of Asiatic rulers who obstructed British influence and trade . . . Control of India meant the control of an army and of an almost inexhaustible reserve.[46]

It followed that the military policies of the Empire, including those of India, should be controlled by the British state.[47] Various moves to bring this about proceeded as war threatened in the early twentieth century. In 1905, Lord Kitchener argued that the military policy of India should in the future be controlled by the British Committee of Imperial Defence instead of the Government of India.[48] Prime Minister Asquith told the committee in 1909 that, in the event of war, both its reason and its locations would be common to the whole Empire: 'A homogenous organisation for Imperial Defence and a single direction was therefore necessary, and this he believed would be recognised more and more in the future.'[49] At the military session of the Imperial Conference in the same year, it was recommended that the armed forces of the Empire should be 'standardized' so that it would be possible 'to mobilize and use them for the defence of the empire as a whole'.[50] Before the Imperial Conference of 1911, the Dominions were asked 'whether they would now be prepared to undertake certain defence responsibilities in connection with the defence of the Empire as a whole'.[51]

Post-war reorganisation

The strains and experience of the First World War increased the pressure for an imperial defence policy and for the integration of India into that policy. At the same time, Britain's post-war economic situation necessitated a reintegration of the Empire as an economic unit. These problems were manifested in British proposals for political, economic and military reorganisation of imperial structures.

During the war, Lord Milner raised (or revived) the idea of a single government for the Empire – an Imperial Cabinet leading 'a single

British State embodying all the scattered portions of our race throughout the world'.[52] Despite making the Dominions nervous for their autonomy, Lloyd George himself proposed a version of the scheme to Parliament in May 1917. His Imperial Cabinet was 'to determine by consultation together the policy of the Empire in its most vital aspects without infringing in any degree the autonomy, which its parts at present enjoy'. It would include the British Prime Minister, British ministers concerned with imperial affairs and the Prime Minister of each Dominion. To this point, discussions of imperial co-ordination had really only included the Dominions. Such had been India's role in the war, however, that Lloyd George's scheme would also include 'a representative of the Indian people to be appointed by the Government of India'.[53] The Imperial War Conference of 1917 resolved that there should be a special Imperial Conference following the war to consider 'the readjustment of the constitutional relations of the component parts of the Empire'.[54] Any increased co-ordination and/or control over the Empire meant, for India, an increase in the control of the British state – and a consequent reinforcement of her strategic, rather than economic, role in imperial fortunes.

As we have seen, during the war years, the Government of India displayed considerable leadership in the progress of India's industrial development – and was encouraged in its endeavours by London. In the war's aftermath, however, the idea of the economic development of each part of the Empire gave way to the idea of the development of the Empire as an economic unit, within which a clear division of labour would exist between industrial and agricultural areas.[55]

In December 1915, the French Government suggested 'a conference in Paris between the Allies to discuss economic questions arising out of the war'.[56] Shortly before that, the British Government called together an Imperial Council of Commerce (comprising Britain, the Dominions and India) to consider the Empire's post-war economic security requirements, the prevention of sources of supply falling to foreign control and the development of imperial self-sufficiency: 'To what extent and by what means the resources of the Empire should and can be developed so as to render it independent of foreign supplies.'[57] The French Economic Conference convened in Paris in June 1916, particularly concerned with the threat the Central Powers might still pose when the war was over. There was no conception, on the Allies' part, that in just over two years, Germany and her allies would collapse quite as comprehensively as they did. Instead, it was believed, the end of military hostilities would simply signal the commencement of economic ones. The conference resolved that Germany and her allies 'are today preparing . . . for a contest on the economic plane, which will not only survive the re-establishment of peace, but will at that moment attain its full scope and intensity'. The British Government's Reconstruction Committee declared:

> the present rulers of Germany have a definite economic policy in view for the post-war period . . . of regarding commerce, industry and agriculture as instruments for the promotion of aggressively political ends . . . as a leverage for increasing the influence and the striking force of Germany in competition and conflict with other States.[58]

The Allies resolved 'to take the necessary steps without delay to render themselves independent of the enemy countries insofar as regards the raw materials and manufactured articles essential to the normal development of their economic activities'. This might mean sanctioning 'enterprises subsidised, directed or controlled by the Governments themselves'.[59] Chamberlain commented that the Conference's Transitory Measures 'would appear to amount to a continuation, in a modified form, of some of the measures adopted during the war'.[60]

The difference was that the British Empire attended the conference and agreed to the resolutions as a bloc. Post-war self-sufficiency was something for the Empire as a whole. India was not represented at the conference. When the Government of India raised the question of representation it was told:

> it should be borne in mind that India is permanently represented in His Majesty's Government, that the Secretary of State for India is the natural channel by which the separate special

> interests of India are brought under consideration, and that he is in daily communication with you.[61]

A year later, an Imperial War Conference convened to further consolidate Britain's imperial post-war economic position. It declared:

> The Conference agrees that it is necessary to secure for the British Empire and the belligerent Allies the command of certain essential raw materials... The Conference is of the opinion that the Governments of the British Empire should make such arrangements amongst themselves as will ensure that essential raw materials produced in the Empire shall be available for the above purposes.[62]

The Government of India was particularly anxious about the conference's intention, on behalf of the Empire, to restrict trade with Germany and her allies after the war. Its concerns were voiced in Parliament by Sir John Simons:

> I do not know at all what the view of the [British] Government is as to the future trade of India if restrictions of this sort are made. The greater part of India's cotton crop went before the War and in the ordinary sense would go again after the War, to Germany or Austria. What are you going to do about that?[63]

But these concerns were swept aside in the desire for an autarchic Empire. In October 1917, the Government of India asked the India Office whether it wanted New Delhi's views on the recent conference's resolutions. Within the India Office, Thomas Holderness' note on the file to L.J. Kershaw reveals a great deal:

> Only if it is part of the British Empire policy as a whole? India in such a matter cannot act independently of the policy which H.M.'s Govt, considering the position in which it finds itself when peace is concluded, decide to pursue?[64]

The British state intended to shape the Empire into a single economic unit. It was to be, as far as possible, self-sufficient – which meant that the existing division of labour within the Empire should remain. Given the post-war economic situation in Britain and rising competition from the USA and Japan, the idea was 'to seek some means of disengaging from the international system while taking a large enough slice of it to ensure supplies of food and raw materials on the one hand and markets for manufactures on the other'.[65]

To this end, in the complex negotiations on trade after the war, it was strongly felt that the Empire should act as a united force. Lord Cecil (Under-Secretary of State for Foreign Affairs) told the Imperial War Conference in June 1918, 'If we speak as an Empire, we have a far better chance of bargaining successfully than if we speak each of ourselves'.[66] The Empire was to strive for self-sufficiency. The Imperial War Cabinet resolved in April 1917: 'The time has arrived when all possible encouragement should be given to the development of Imperial resources, and especially to making the Empire independent of other countries in respect of food supplies, raw materials, and other essential industries.'[67]

The government's Committee on Commercial and Industrial Policy (set up in June 1916 under Lord Balfour) resolved in early 1917 that 'special steps must be taken to stimulate the production of food-stuffs, raw materials and manufactured articles within the Empire... for the safety and welfare of the Empire as a whole'.[68] At its first meeting, Balfour had explained what Empire development meant: 'the intention was imperial self-sufficiency, although that phrase had been omitted from the published terms of reference so as to prevent unnecessary anxiety on the part of countries allied to Britain in the war'.[69] For the Balfour Committee, a self-sufficient Empire implied a system of imperial preferential trade.[70] The Imperial War Cabinet agreed, resolving in 1917 'that each part of the Empire, having due regard to the interests of our Allies, shall give specially favourable treatment and facilities to the produce and manufactures of other parts of the Empire'.[71]

It was not the aim of the imperial economy, however, to develop each of its parts to the same level. It would instead function on the basis of a division of labour within it. R.F. Holland suggests that this was part of its attraction to Britain's rulers – it prevented the development of rival industrial centres within the Empire that might compete with British industry. The Imperial economy 'was based on the assumption of complementary specialisations among Commonwealth partners'.[72] But it was already too late to prevent or retard industrial growth in the Dominions. That left the non-industrialised parts of the Empire, including India. Their position within the imperial economy was made clear in a 1923 Colonial Office Memorandum:

> Inasmuch as both the physical and social conditions of the Colonies and Protectorates make it unlikely that they will generally be able to carry on manufacturing industries, except of an elementary nature, on any considerable scale for many years to come, if at all, their economic programme is bound up with the development of their natural resources... The potentialities of the Colonies and Protectorates as producers of foodstuffs and raw materials and as markets for manufactured goods are of the greatest interest and importance to the mothercountry, and to all the other States of the Empire.[73]

The response of the Government of India to these imperial schemes was not a positive one.[74] New Delhi had made clear during the war its desire to develop Indian industry and to protect it against foreign competition.[75] Kershaw of the India Office noted to the Foreign Office that 'India's interests are not identical with those of the United Kingdom and other parts of the Empire'. But he opined that 'no surrender of the right to protect indigenous industries is involved, should this in the future be found necessary' – when in fact it was precisely this 'right' that Britain wanted India (and the other non-industrial parts of the Empire) to abandon.[76] The Government of India stuck to its position in the immediate post-war years. With an eye to the forthcoming Imperial Economic Conference, the Commerce Department told the Secretary of State in December 1922:

> Any proposals which might bear the construction that they were intended to base the future commercial intercourse between

> India and the United Kingdom on an increase in the export of raw materials from India to England, and the import of manufactured articles from England to India, would probably be regarded with great disfavour.[77]

As late as 1930, Sir Geoffrey Corbett told the Imperial Conference on behalf of the Indian delegation that India's Legislative Assembly had 'accepted the principle that our fiscal policy might legitimately be directed towards fostering the development of industries in India'. That being the case, India 'would approach this question of [imperial] economic co-operation with some reserve'.[78]

Military matters

The end of the war induced in the British Government an optimistic outlook on imperial defence, rapidly followed by a pessimistic one. Both attitudes gave rise to an increasing burden on India's human resources. The sharp increase in the power of states that the war had occasioned accrued in particular to the British state and was translated into an extension of the Empire, especially in the Near and Middle East.[79] Jeffery writes that after the war 'the empire included larger stretches of territory held by military force than at any other time in its history'. According to Gallagher, this added 'a great new spur of control . . . from Egypt to Arabia, to Baghdad and to Tehran, linking at the eastern frontiers of Persia with the westernmost bounds of India'.[80] Security for these new territories had to be sought at the Peace Conference and, just as importantly, defended on the ground.[81] The burden of that defence would fall on India. And since this was now the defence of territory, rather than of British superiority on the high seas, it meant most directly the demand for troops.[82] India's military responsibility within the Empire was now to supply it with those troops – not to create a self-sufficient war economy through state-driven industrialisation.

During the war and in the making of peace, the Empire had acted as a single unit, with the Dominions in particular being consulted on imperial policy. Lloyd George told the Imperial Conference in 1921 that '[t]he War demonstrated... to the world, including ourselves, that the British Empire was not an abstraction but a living force to be reckoned with'. Field Marshal Haig believed that the war had already created an 'imperial army'.[83] By the early 1920s, however, it was already becoming clear that the Empire had over-reached itself. The military was now advising that if British interests in Ireland, Egypt and India (all under attack) were to be protected, the army had to pull back in Persia, Arabia and Mesopotamia. Field Marshal Wilson (Chief of the Imperial General Staff, 1918–22) declared that between 100,000 and 200,000 men were needed to hold Ireland alone.[84]

Given its perilous post-war economic situation, Britain could not shoulder this burden alone. Imperial defence then became an all-Empire task. According to the War Office (writing to the India Office in June 1920), 'the only sound and economical method of imperial defence is to regard the forces of any portion of the Empire as being available for use in any other'.[85] This was a move away from autonomous centres of industrial development and towards a division of labour within the Empire in which Britain (and perhaps parts of the Dominions) would supply the munitions, while India and the colonies would supply the men.

But all-Empire schemes of defence foundered quite rapidly after the war on a number of obstacles. Inside Britain, the electorate was none too keen on imperial adventures, even if the rest of the Empire played their part.[86] Electoral pressure manifested itself in defence-spending cuts. The 'Ten Year Rule' was set down in August 1919, in which the armed services were required to request spending 'on the assumption that the British Empire would not be engaged in any great war during the next ten years and no Expeditionary Force is required for the purpose'.[87]

Neither were the Dominions enthused by the idea of imperial defence – and they had said so at the 1917 Imperial War Conference.[88] They did not want the British Government supervising their defence policies (or any other policies for that matter) and maintained and strengthened this attitude in the post-war world. By 1920, the leader of the British Conservative party had to tell the House of Commons that the Imperial Cabinet was not functioning: 'The reason is that the

Ministries of the Dominions have not thought it suitable to have a representative.'[89] A further attempt was made to bind the Dominions closer to Britain in matters of imperial defence around the 1930 Imperial Conference, but once again the Dominions declined.[90]

With cuts at home and Dominion reluctance abroad, the gaze of Britain's rulers settled on the one place that could at least partially fulfil the imperial scheme and that would have difficulty in resisting it: India.

The British Government's Committee on the Army in India was set up under Lord Esher in July 1919 to review the organisation of the Indian Army 'and of the part allocated to it in any general scheme of Imperial defence'. It arose out of the disastrous events in Mesopotamia.[91] The committee's deliberations were overshadowed by the view of the War Office 'that the administration of the Indian Army should be handed over to them and controlled from Whitehall'.[92] Nevertheless, the committee set to work, preparing a report on the Army in India, 'including its relations with the War Office and the India Office'.[93] It was told by Haig that there should be an Imperial General Staff.[94] The committee believed that 'the Commander-in-Chief in India should be more directly in touch with the Chief of the Imperial General Staff... so as to develop the military resources of India in a manner suited to Imperial necessities'. It eventually recommended that the Indian army be placed directly under the British Government and that the Commander-in-Chief in India should act on the advice of the Chief of the Imperial General Staff.[95]

These ideas were confronted by solid opposition both from British and Indian India. Neither the India Office nor the Government of India endorsed the views of the British state. The India Office regarded Esher's ideas as unrealistic, given that India was in the midst of nationalist challenge, political reform and economic downturn. The Secretary of State told the Cabinet on Christmas Eve 1920 that the idea of India becoming 'the base for vast military operations in the Middle and Far East must be definitely abandoned'. Furthermore, 'we must definitely get out of our heads the vague idea... that India is an inexhaustible reservoir from which men and money can be drawn towards the support of Imperial resources or in pursuance of Imperial strategy'.[96]

The India Office publication, *Statement Exhibiting the Moral and Material Progress and Condition of India during the Year 1920*, put their position with remarkable frankness. The Esher Committee's recommendations, it said, 'excited a storm of reprobation':

> [C]ritics discovered in the detailed recommendations...an attempt to deprive India of control of her own forces and to make them a tool for Imperial aggression in Central Asia...the phraseology of certain parts of the Report...was such as to lend these suspicions an air of verisimilitude.[97]

The Government of India was similarly put out.[98] Their objections partly concerned cost – the constant friction with London as to who should pay for Indian soldiers on imperial service outside India. But not cost alone. In the course of its deliberations, the committee had met with the Viceroy in New Delhi. The Viceroy told them that Esher's initial recommendations (which had already been circulated) would take the command of the Indian armed forces away from the Government of India. They would, he suggested, give the Chief of the Imperial General Staff

> such a say in Indian military policy as to make the statutory control of the Governor General in Council merely nominal...the nominees...of the Chief of the Imperial General Staff will have all the power and the Governor General in Council will have no say in the military policy of the Government of India.[99]

He complained that the rot had already set in with regard to the 180,000 Indian troops still overseas: 'The Chief of the Imperial General Staff had these troops under his control and the Government of India could do nothing to get them back.'[100] As Keith Jeffery points out, 'the Indian government displayed a marked reluctance to slip easily in with London's plans for the imperial disposition of the Indian Army'.[101] The Viceroy also warned the committee that the new political structures (under the Montagu-Chelmsford reforms) would allow Indian politicians 'to take more interest in questions of this sort' – 'the new Legislative Assembly... might well take exception, for instance, to Indian troops being used to garrison Egypt'.[102]

He was proved quite correct. Within a month of its convocation, the Legislative Assembly debated the question of Indian troops serving outside India and rejected the Esher recommendations.[103] The Nagpur Congress session in 1920 had declared that 'the Esher Committee and its report... is calculated to increase the sub-servience and impotence of India'.[104]

It seemed that the British Government was caught in a contradiction here between its insistence on political reform (which came about partly for military reasons) and its insistence on military centralisation in the Empire. The latter was able to take priority, however, as even the reformed Indian political structure was designed so that the British Government could ignore the views of the Legislative Assembly. Thus 'the Indian government found itself pushed inexorably into the orbit of increasing imperial defence commitments'.[105]

The British position was restated by the Simon Commission, reporting in 1930. India was expected to provide troops 'for service in other fields' who would be paid for by Britain. The defence of India itself was an imperial question: 'Imperial foreign policy, Empire communications, Empire trade, the general position of Britain in the East, may be vitally affected.' As such, it could not be handed over to an Indian government. It had to be controlled by 'an Imperial agency' – in the first instance, 'the Viceroy acting in concert with the Commander-in-Chief' (both of whom were controlled by the British Government).[106] The British position remained that there should be an imperial defence strategy. India was a part of that strategy and its most important role was to supply troops for it. It was in this military context that industrial development was at first allowed to lapse – and was then positively discouraged.

State conflict

Britain's post-war position on the Empire emphasised imperial defence (primarily the provision of troops) and an imperial economic unit (based, as far as possible, on the existing division of labour). The

Dominions' refusal to comply with this scheme led to its full force being directed at India. This undercut plans for state industrialisation in India and allowed those plans to be overwhelmed by decentralisation and retrenchment – from which they would not recover until the next world war. It also brought the British Government into conflict with the Government of India.

New Delhi was keen to build up its own military machine and to make India a centre of the Empire in the East, rather than a combined branch office and military labour exchange. Such was the opposition to this in Britain that Helmut Mejcher describes the relationship between the two governments as becoming 'intransigent and devious', producing a 'smouldering quarrel . . . over the Persian Gulf'.[107] India as an imperial centre with an independent military machine at its heart necessitated an independent industrial base – and this was the Government of India's second point of contention with London. As we have seen, New Delhi's plans for state-led industrialisation would be in tatters by the mid-1920s, though some of the rhetoric survived even after that.[108]

This was conflict between the interests of two states.[109] The interests of the British state led to its attempts to rearrange the Empire around itself in its own defence. The interests of the Indian state forced it to resist these pressures to the extent that it could. The contest was, of course, a mismatch. New Delhi could not withstand London's intentions indefinitely. Once the former's resistance had faded – and along with it, state-led industrial development – the Government of India became a fetter on the development of the productive forces in India and a fetter on the development of the Indian bourgeoisie. From that point, Indian industrialists had no choice but to turn elsewhere for assistance and support.

Chapter Five

Protection and Development: State and Bourgeoisie in the Inter-war Period

Returning to our main subject, it is appropriate to assess where stood the Indian bourgeoisie and the Indian bourgeois revolution at the beginning of the inter-war period. We have noted the emergence of the bourgeoisie before and during the First World War. In the inter-war period, its consciousness evolved from its economic position and its aims were adjusted in line with those of the nation – or at least those of the national movement. This chapter will examine that process.

Indian industry, and thus the Indian bourgeoisie, was nurtured by the state (the Government of India) during the First World War.[1] Aditya Mukherjee argues, however, that the growth of Indian industry 'occurred not as a result of colonialism but in spite of or in opposition to it'.[2] Certainly this was true with regard to its commercial rival, European industry. As we shall see in this chapter, Indian industrial efforts in cotton, jute and shipping (to name but a few) were resisted by European business interests. The same, however, could not be said for the colonial state. Bearing in mind the strategic interests of the state (as manifested in both the Government of India and the British Government), it is clear that Indian industry was encouraged during the war, when the Empire's war effort demanded it – and encouraged to believe that such an attitude would continue after hostilities ceased.

The fact that it did not – for reasons explained in the last chapter – brought Indian industrialists into conflict with the state. From this point, if Indian industry were to advance – if the level of development of the productive forces were to rise – it could only do so in conflict with the British state.[3]

The objective economic position of the Indian industrial bourgeoisie brought it together around a number of economic demands on the state, which, since for the most part they remained unsatisfied, cohered into a political position of anti-colonialism.[4] Thus, 'the Indian capitalist class constituted itself as a class . . . able to organize itself on an all-India basis as a self-conscious "class for itself"'.[5] Homi Mody, the Bombay mill owner, conveyed something of the class's view of itself when he told the Round Table Conference in November 1930 that

> they [the business classes] may not be powerful in numbers today, but they are powerful for everything else which counts in the life of a nation . . . It may be that we who represent those classes, have not at the moment the ear of our countrymen, but we shall have it tomorrow.[6]

Was the class consciousness of the Indian bourgeoisie dependent on its adherence to Indian nationalism, or did it arise from economic self-interest? Mukherjee argues that it was 'inextricably linked with the growth of the Indian national movement and the Indian "nation in the making"'.[7] Claude Markovits, on the other hand, denies that Indian capitalists 'shared a grand design, which was the industrialization of India'. He continues: 'Indian capitalists were hard-headed, calculating businessmen who launched industrial ventures if they thought there was a reasonable chance of making good profits and not out of any great ideology of national industrialization'.[8]

These positions are not necessarily mutually exclusive – certainly not if the development of consciousness is seen as a process rather than the achievement of a fixed position (either 'profit seeker' or 'nationalist'). The Indian bourgeoisie could reasonably pursue its economic interests during the war – and, for some of its sections, for some time afterwards. But then those interests met with a political obstacle: the British state (which no longer wanted Indian industrial development on any great scale). If economic interests were to be pursued from this point, the political obstacle had to be removed.[9] A political strategy was therefore economically necessary – and, as we shall see, this began with attempts to pressure the existing state for reforms and developed into the demand for a new (Indian national) state. In this way, the hard-headed pursuit of profit led to nationalist politics.[10] However, we would do well to remember that the bourgeoisie's relationship with nationalist politics (a portent of the relationship between capital and a future state) was a coincidence of interests. The bourgeoisie did not endorse nationalist politics *because* they represented the nation's good (except in individual cases) but because they furthered their own.

The political leaders of the Indian bourgeoisie became aware also of the need for a mass political organisation to fight against the existing state, as well as a new political elite to replace it. In the next chapter, we will examine their turn towards Congress politics. This, of course, did not place Indian business in the militant vanguard of the civil disobedience movement. The moderation of the bourgeoisie's anti-colonialism has often been pointed out.[11] They worked for 'a non-revolutionary pattern of anti-imperialist struggle . . . [a] stage by stage (or step by step) advance towards a bourgeois nation state and independent economic development'.[12] This was hardly surprising, given the bourgeoisie's objective class interests (what Bipan Chandra calls 'the capitalist character of the Indian capitalist class').[13] Those interests and the evolving nature of their position can account for the timidity of their initial approach, for the differences in approach between them and their preference for moderate tactics. But these factors and their unwillingness to adopt a more radical road for India ('socialism', for example) should not blind us to the bourgeoisie's support for the Indian national movement. Economic interest ensured that support. Questions of law and order did not at any stage permanently deter it.

As the leaders of the bourgeoisie were compelled to enter the world of nationalist politics, they were also compelled to express their class interests as the interests of the nation.[14] Karl Marx and Frederick Engels drew attention to this phenomenon:

> For each new class which puts itself in the place of one ruling before it, is compelled, merely in order to carry through its aim, to represent its interests as the common interest of all the members of society... it has to give its ideas the form of universality and represent them as the only rational, universally valid ones.[15]

For Marx and Engels, there is clearly an element of deception or even trickery here. The bourgeoisie (for that is whom they are discussing) is 'compelled' to 'represent', to 'give its ideas the form' of general aspirations. For this, the bourgeoisie has been, from then until now, lambasted by Marxists (and others) for entrancing their followers with false consciousness. There is, however, a period in historical development – the era in which the bourgeois revolution allows and pursues progress in society – when the interests of the progressive bourgeoisie really do coincide with the interests of society as a whole. Countering their own implied accusations in *The German Ideology*, Marx and Engels also point out that the bourgeoisie can portray its aims as universal precisely because 'its interest really is more connected with the common interest of all other non-ruling classes, because under the pressure of hitherto existing conditions its interest has not yet been able to develop as the particular interest of a particular class'.[16] At the stage of the development of India's productive forces with which we are concerned, the interests of the Indian bourgeoisie[17] actually did represent those of Indian society at large.

Protection

The most contentious and important issue that divided the Indian bourgeoisie from the Government of India during the inter-war years was that of protection – the demand that the Indian state, through measures such as tariffs and import duties, should ensure the survival of both existing and emerging industries.[18] The demand was raised well before the war and noted in the Montagu-Chelmsford Report.[19]

According to the India Office, the war 'introduced an atmosphere of economic protection in which the industries of India, both nascent and established, have flourished to an unprecedented degree'.[20] At war's end, Indian industries faced challenges from foreign competition which they expected the government to help them resist.[21] The Government of India moved from considering tariffs largely as a revenue-generating exercise to envisaging them as a means of developing Indian industry.[22] In October 1917, the Government of India's Commerce and Industries Department, in a despatch endorsed by the Viceroy's Executive Committee, emphasised that 'the necessity for the full exploitation of our own resources, not merely on economic but also on political grounds, will probably compel some measure of protection for the nascent industries specially suited to this country'.[23]

India's capitalists continued to push for tariffs in the context of a similar nation-building agenda. As state enthusiasm for new industries faded, however, the government tended to drift back to the revenue-producing aspects of tariffs. This did produce some important measures of protection in the inter-war period, mainly in terms of preserving existing industries.[24] But this was not enough for the Indian bourgeoisie. In 1933, Walchand Hirachand, the leading Bombay industrialist, told the annual meeting of the Federation of Indian Chambers of Commerce and Industry (FICCI):

> I personally hold the conviction that no country at the present day can develop her industries without following a deliberate policy of discrimination, without excluding the non-nationals in the country, without giving substantial help . . . to those nascent industries that require careful bringing up . . . It is no use mincing matters on this most important question, and the longer the right of economic self-government is delayed, the more embittered will be the feelings of the nation towards those who withhold it.[25]

The capitalists could see that protection could only be provided by a state. Since neither Britain nor the Government of India were now willing to provide it, the link between protection and the national movement was clear.

Imperial economic union

The demands of Indian business for the protection of Indian industries were continually frustrated by Britain's attempts to put together a kind of imperial economic union in the inter-war years. Looking back from 1936, FICCI pointed out that early attempts to transform the Empire into an economic bloc (from 1902) had 'failed to evoke any appreciable enthusiasm in the various self-governing units of the Empire'.[26] Despite this, the British Government continued to push in the same direction.[27] Thus, 'after the termination of the Great War, the British statesmen found it imperative to re-open the question of creating an economic block within the Empire'.[28] This they did with gusto into the 1930s. Faced once again with Dominion recalcitrance, the full force of the British effort was concentrated on India. 'The choice which lies before each of our countries', Prime Minister Baldwin told the Indian delegation to the Ottawa Imperial Economic Conference in 1932, 'is whether to participate in such an economic *bloc* or to attempt to pursue a policy of economic isolation'.[29] The Finance Member, Sir George Schuster, took up the theme in the Legislative Assembly in December, warning his listeners of

> the terrible risk of [India] standing on her own and rejecting the proffered hand ... amidst all these dangers, amid the tremors which may presage a violent earthquake, I believe that there is only one solid bit of ground in the world today and that is the ground of those territories which are working together within the British group.[30]

As far as FICCI was concerned, quite the contrary was the case. An imperial economic bloc would not safeguard India's trade and industry, but would inhibit it: 'the intense economic nationalism initiated by the United Kingdom in creating an economic block within the Empire has restricted the growth of internationalism of trade instead of encouraging it'.[31]

Throughout the inter-war period, these two sets of interests – the protection of industry for national development, on the one hand, and the integration of a largely non-industrial economy into an imperial bloc, on the other – would remain at odds. The contradiction between them was the objective basis for the Indian bourgeoisie's turn towards nationalist politics.

Finances

The period appeared to begin on an economically optimistic note for Indian business. The Joint Select Committee looking into the Montagu-Chelmsford reforms had reported:

> Nothing is more likely to endanger the good relations between India and Great Britain than a belief that India's fiscal policy is dictated from Whitehall in the interests of the trade of Great Britain. That such a belief exists at the moment there can be no doubt.[32]

The committee recommended that a convention be adopted that when the Government of India and the Legislative Council agreed on fiscal policy, the Secretary of State should not interfere. Accepted by the British Government, Indian 'fiscal autonomy' came into being in March 1921.[33] Both the Indian bourgeoisie and the Government of India were well pleased with this – but for different reasons. From the bourgeoisie's point of view, fiscal autonomy seemed to make possible their demands for industry protection. On the Government of India's part, it was seen as a method of raising government revenue rather than a strategy for economic development. And it was the government's view that tended to prevail. Fiscal autonomy was an arrangement between London and New Delhi. Indian opinion was considered but was by no means a determining factor. As Basudev Chatterji puts it, the convention 'turned out to be more a device to secure the Government of India's orthodox budgetary concerns than to serve the interests of Indian capital'.[34]

Indian agitation for protection was not assuaged by fiscal autonomy. In 1921, Sir Thomas Holland advised the Government of India to 'institute an enquiry if only to demonstrate to the public the danger of tampering with a purely revenue-earning tariff'[35]. In May, the Government of India announced the appointment of an Indian Fiscal Commission to examine tariff policy. The commission commenced its work in October and reported the following July. Three representatives of Indian business sat on the commission – Ghanshyamdas Birla of Birla Brothers in Calcutta, Narottam Morarjee of Scindia Shipping in Bombay and Ibrahim Rahimtulla, the Bombay merchant and mill owner – together with two nationalist politicians.

In its report, the commission pointed out the now familiar features of India's lack of industrial development and gave its readers to understand that such development would generally be a good thing. It suggested that 'a certain measure of industrial life and opportunity is an essential condition for building up a vigorous national character'.[36] The priority here seems to have been a military one, overriding (in the commission's view) considerations of imperial economic strategy: 'considerations of national defence may set legitimate bounds to the extension of the principle of international division of labour'.[37] The report continued: '[W]e have no hesitation in affirming the principle that any industry which is essential for purposes of national defence, and for which the conditions in India are not unfavourable, should, if necessary, be adequately protected'.[38]

Having established that some industries should exist and that strategic ones at the very least should be helped, the commission could hardly avoid a recommendation for industrial protection. In a final desperate hedging of bets, the commission added that any such protection should be applied 'with discrimination', on a case by case basis, by an Indian Tariff Board.[39] The British congratulated themselves on this outcome. C.H. Kisch (the Finance Secretary) at the India Office chortled: 'Provided that all the safeguards and qualifications . . . are rigidly insisted on, the adoption of a policy of protection with discrimination . . . is hardly more than a synonym for a policy of free trade with legitimate exceptions'.[40]

But for Indian business, let alone Indian nationalism, it would not do at all. The Fiscal Commission's three businessmen and two nationalist politicians appended a 'Minute of Dissent' to the report. While espousing the same hopes as the commission for Indian industrialisation, the dissenters understood that these could only be achieved by widespread state intervention and vigorous protection policies.[41] Protection therefore should be implemented without qualification: 'we do not think it would be right to hedge the policy in such a manner as to lead to inadequate results'.[42]

In fact, the Government of India was extremely discriminating as to which sections of the report it implemented. Industrialisation schemes for India were by this stage fading and therefore the sentiment of the report in this direction faded with them. Discriminating protection was gratefully embraced – but a permanent Tariff Board was not. The non-comprehensive nature of government protection policy was reinforced by individual tariff boards being set up, when the government thought necessary.[43]

Imperial preference

The idea of an imperial economic union was continually reiterated by the British Government through pressure on India to adopt 'imperial preference' – the application of lower tariffs on imported Empire (mainly British) goods.[44] This was raised by the Fiscal Commission, which noted that the war had given fresh impetus to 'the policy of consolidating the Empire' and to 'the whole question of the organization of the Empire as an independent economic unit'.[45] A majority of the commission therefore advocated imperial preference on the grounds of imperial patriotism:

> Imperial Preference is regarded throughout the Empire as a means of strengthening the ties which bind together its scattered units. Adhesion to the policy of Imperial Preference is thus coming to be regarded as a test of loyalty to the Empire, as a proof that the various parts of the Empire look beyond their own immediate interests and recognise their position as parts of a greater whole. From this point of view we firmly believe that India should not turn her back on the principles which have been adopted in the greater part of the Empire and are rapidly being extended to the remainder.[46]

The Government of India, however, was not easily persuaded as to the merits of such a scheme – and had been saying so for some years. In October 1917 they told the British Government, somewhat reluctantly, that if imperial preference 'is found to be to the advantage of the Empire as a whole, we shall be prepared to take our part in carrying such a scheme into effect' – provided that the Government of India's financial resources were secure and they were allowed 'a freer hand than hitherto in framing our fiscal policy'.[47] Before the Imperial Conference of 1923, the Government of India told the Secretary of State that the 'Government of India reserves all liberty of action for their representatives in regard to Imperial Preference even if necessary to the extent of their abstaining from discussion on that subject'.[48] The Indian delegation refused to commit their government to such a policy.[49]

Opposition to imperial preference was also rife amongst Indian opinion. The Minute of Dissent to the Fiscal Commission Report declared that 'India cannot accept the principle of Imperial Preference until she has attained responsible government and is able to regulate her fiscal policy by the vote of a wholly elected legislature'.[50] Somewhat more bluntly, Hirachand told the Maharashtra Chamber of Commerce in May 1929:

> So far as India is concerned there is no reason why we should discriminate between different countries. The treatment that this country is having at the hands of Britain . . . has left no enthusiasm in us for imperial interests. The country does not accept the principle of Imperial Preference in any form.[51]

The influential economist Dhananjaya Gadgil (Director of the Gokhale Institute of Politics and Economics in Poona) wrote in 1932 that, since the Empire was an artificial economic unit, 'the adoption of Imperial Preference necessarily involves a considerable deflection of trade from its present channels', which would not be in India's best interests. India's best customers were outside the Empire, so there was no economic argument for imperial preference – 'No reasons, other than purely political ones, can be found to support the policy of an Empire division of labour.'[52]

Ottawa

The Imperial Economic Conference in Ottawa in July–August 1932 was a major opportunity for Britain's rulers to lay their cards on the table regarding imperial economic union and the imperial division of labour. The previous imperial conference in 1930 had not been able to reach agreement on 'the fullest development of inter-Imperial markets' and had therefore postponed the economics to Ottawa in 1932. Britain, in the meantime, had adopted some protectionist measures of her own with the Import Duties Act of March 1932. A 10 per cent duty was imposed on non-Empire goods. Goods from the Dominions and India were only exempt from the duty until November – and after that, only if agreements had been concluded with Britain at the Ottawa Conference.[53]

FICCI had suggested to the government before the conference that a trade agreement with the UK was only really possible 'after India got effective control over her fiscal policy under the new constitution', which was then under discussion. The Government of India vetoed the participation of FICCI representatives in the Indian delegation, despite the Secretary of State's recommendation to include them. The Viceroy, Lord Willingdon, regarded FICCI as an active supporter of the current civil disobedience movement and objected in particular to Birla – 'that basically non-cooperating fellow, motivated by selfish interests'.[54] In response to its exclusion from Ottawa, the FICCI president Lal Shri Ram wrote to the Secretary of State and the Government of India:

> I have the honour to make it clear on behalf of the Federation that any commitment made at any Conference until India gets full freedom over her own affairs will not be binding on her. And Indian commerce will have no option but to take the first opportunity of repudiating any agreement made at any such Conference in contravention of this considered opinion of the Committee of this Federation.[55]

FICCI was aware of the issues on the table at Ottawa and was right to be wary of their implications for India's development. The Imperial

Economic Committee assured the conference that 'the object of [imperial economic] co-operation is not, and must not be, to arrest change, but wisely to direct and facilitate its course'. But the intended division of labour within the Empire was clear:

> It should, in the opinion of the Conference, be the object of any policy of industrial co-operation within the Commonwealth to secure the best division of industrial activities among the several parts of Commonwealth and the ordered economic development of each part, with a view to ensuring the maximum efficiency and economy of production and distribution.[56]

The Indian delegation reported that the aim was 'to leave to the less industrialised Empire country the market in certain classes of goods and to the more industrialised Empire country or countries the market in more specialised goods'.[57]

The pressure was on in Ottawa for India to accept imperial preference in an agreement with Britain. Despite India's unwillingness to do so, the Indian delegation clearly felt it had little choice. 'It was', the delegation reported, 'no longer a question of what India stood to gain, but of what she stood to lose'.[58] The UK-India Trade Agreement was signed on 20 August 1932. The Indian delegation's assurance that the agreement did not 'in any way limit India's right to shape her protective policy in accordance with her own conception of her national interests' begged the question as to who would decide what those interests were.[59] Clearly, those of the British, the Government of India and even the moderate Indian delegation to Ottawa were all slightly different. And those of the bourgeoisie, waiting impatiently for the results back in India, were dramatically different again. In any case, the whole tone of the Ottawa Conference belied the delegation's assertion that 'India retains complete freedom to shape her tariff policy in the manner she thinks best' – whether that was the India of Ottawa, New Delhi or FICCI.[60]

The reaction in India was instantaneous and prolonged – initially because the government was now saddled with the responsibility of taking the agreement to the Legislative Assembly, allowing it to be debated and, hopefully (from the government's point of view) getting it approved. FICCI campaigned against the agreement throughout. The Viceroy opined that the opposition in the assembly was 'engineered and influenced by... Indian commercial bodies led and paid for by Birla'.[61] The assembly narrowly ratified the agreement.[62] Hirachand told FICCI soon afterwards, 'the country had the misfortune to witness the tragic farce of the Legislative Assembly ratifying the Ottawa pact in spite of the unanimous verdict against it from all economists and representatives of the Indian commercial interests in the country'.[63]

The campaign continued. FICCI accused the government of refusing to consult with it over the agreement, but of being in constant contact with British capitalists. Thus, 'India was made to pay at Ottawa a premium to the British manufacturers for their inability to compete with continental manufacturers'.[64] The nature of the agreement was such that it would restrict India's trade outside the Empire and might provoke the other colonial empires into establishing economic blocs of their own.[65] FICCI's strongest argument, though, remained the political one: any such agreement 'would not work in the fullest interests of India unless and until the Government of the country came into their own and their interests were identical with those of the general public'.[66] The campaign only ceased in 1936 when the Ottawa Agreement was terminated by the Legislative Assembly.

Steel

The evolving positions of business, the Government of India and the British Empire can be observed through the fortunes of the Indian steel industry in the inter-war period. As the reader may remember, we left the foremost representative of Indian steel, the Tata Iron and Steel Company, at the end of the war-time boom. The company's vision was one of Indian industrialisation and company expansion, with both the help and the guidance of the state. The company recognised the importance of the state as its benefactor, but also regarded state aid as its right. Sir Dorab Tata told a meeting of shareholders in 1923:

> The Steel Company has been grateful all along to the Government for what Government has done to give it a start . . . [but] the services of the Steel Company have amply repaid all the favours of this intelligent policy of Government . . . and we have every right to expect that Government will continue its support.[67]

Unlike other sections of Indian business, Tatas were not especially inclined towards industrial activism and still less towards nationalist politics. Dorab Tata was among the Bombay businessmen who denounced the Non-Cooperation Movement in 1921 and, by the late 1920s, seemed more interested in fighting communism than the colonial authorities. Tata did not join FICCI when it was established. The reason for the distance maintained by the steel company from the national movement was that, up until the post-war period, the former did not need the latter for its economic advance. Nurtured and protected by the government, since it was essential for the war effort, Tata remained aloof from the industrial and political struggles raging around it.

With the war over, however, demand for steel dropped, the import of steel from Britain and Europe once again became possible and Tata's post-war problems began. Despite agreements to supply steel to the Government of India for the railways and other government projects in 1920, the company found itself in considerable financial difficulties.[68] John Peterson (Director-in-charge, 1924–31) told the government in January 1923 that if 'the present dumping of steel in this country' continued, the company 'will soon not have the money to pay wages at these rates or possibly at all'.[69] In a lengthy memorandum to the Government of India, the company warned that it was 'in danger of being extinguished for want of working capital'. Its expansion plans (see chapter two) had had to be drastically curtailed.[70] As well as the dumping of foreign steel (by Belgium, the USA and Britain), the company was afflicted by the rising standard of the steel required and rises in the costs of coal and labour. The company appealed to the government either to pay for purchases in advance or give them a substantial loan.[71] 'Our financial position is getting steadily worse', Peterson wrote to Sir Charles Innes in January 1924; 'I really do not see how the Company can carry on unless fresh money is made available to us over the next six months.' Promising 'to do the best we can', he warned 'the natural consequence will be the collapse of the whole thing'.[72] Tata turned to the Government of India for help.[73]

From the Government of India's point of view, steel was a strategic industry – necessary not only for industrialisation in general, but for national defence in particular. Given the government's needs during the war and its plans for the post-war period, it was only natural that state aid for the steel industry would be forthcoming. Despite the imperial state's disenchantment with Indian industrialisation, the Government of India stood firm on steel – at least for a few years.

While Tata, up to this point, may not have been very interested in nationalist politics, the nationalists were certainly interested in Tata. Like the government, elements in the Congress leadership could see the strategic importance of an Indian steel industry, along with its role as the foundation stone of industrialisation. They made it their business to publicly uphold Tata and demand that it be protected. In the inter-war period, Lala tells us, 'Tata Steel and the town of Jamshedpur had become a regular halt on the itinerary of many of India's key leaders and freedom fighters. While they fought for independence from Britain, the Tatas laboured for a new industrial future'.[74]

Some went further than the occasional visit. When the time came to debate protection for the steel industry (see below), Chaman Lal, N.M. Joshi (both trades union leaders) and V.J. Patel (a prominent member of the Swaraj party) advocated nationalising the industry. Patel, complaining that 'the Tata Board did not consider this question from the point of view of encouraging the steel industry in India', continued: 'I think this is the most opportune time for any national Government to task over this concern: run it as a national concern and impose not these half-hearted duties, but give real and substantial protection.'[75]

These views were too advanced for the moment. But by 1924, from their opposite corners, the Government of India and Indian nationalism had come together around the question of steel industry protection.[76]

The Government of India therefore established a Tariff Board to consider the question in 1923. Not surprisingly, the board concluded (with defence very much in mind) that the case for protection was 'overwhelmingly strong'.[77] The consequent Steel Protection Bill was supported by Indian business, Indian nationalists and the government in May–June 1924. The Bombay industrialist, Purshotamdas Thakurdas, stated that 'the introduction of this measure in the House marks a new departure in the policy of the British Government in India ever since the time of British rule in India'.[78] Supporting the Bill, and going further than either the government or the Congress, C.S. Rangu Iyer (Swaraj Party) asked, 'What is Swaraj? Swaraj is nothing but protection for Indian industries by an Indian Government, the nationalisation of industries by a national Government'.[79] Madan Mohan Malaviya, while also speaking in support, was less confident in the government's future intentions:

> I fear... that the Government of India have not made up their mind absolutely clearly on the policy they are going to pursue. I fear that they are still fighting shy of firmly and clearly saying that they think it their duty to afford protection to such Indian industries as are genuinely Indian.[80]

On the British side, Sir Basil Blackett (Finance Member) said that protection was necessary because

> it is desirable in the general interests of India to build up not merely a steel industry, which is already founded, but from that to go on to build up an industrial system in India with other industries increasingly numerous and increasingly strong, to get away from what might be called the somewhat lopsided development of the India of today.[81]

Other European speakers reminded the assembly of Tata's role in the war and predicted national calamity if the industry collapsed.[82] The Steel Industry Protection Bill was passed by a large majority on 5 June 1924. The company told its shareholders in November that, as a result of protection, it had been placed 'in an exceptional position'. There was therefore 'no doubt as to its future success'.[83] In reality, however, almost as soon as the legislation hit the statute books, Tata was petitioning for more assistance.[84] John Keenan blamed a lack of confidence in the Government of India's plans to foster industries, which 'paralyzed the normal release of fearfully withheld Indian capital'.[85] Tata argued that, due to a fall in steel prices in Europe, cheaper Continental steel was being imported into India at an alarming rate.[86] The company wanted protection against these imports in particular. The Government of India was not particularly sympathetic. A company agent cabled R.D. Tata in September 1924: 'Asked Secretary if he could not expedite decisions... He replied could promise nothing and was evidently annoyed at my suggesting that delay was fatal to us. Intimated that Government was unwilling to interfere.'[87]

Tata persisted. Its board decided that 'the first step to take is for a deputation... to wait upon the Government of India for further finance to the Company'. Further, it would tell the government 'that the Company would be willing to reconstruct its capital in a manner which would be acceptable to the Government, and that Government should help the Company with a loan of Rupees four crores'.[88] The Government of India finally agreed to an Ad Hoc Tariff Board in October 1924. Its report conceded that 'in the early months of 1924 very large quantities of steel were ordered from the Continent in anticipation of the new duties'. Furthermore, due to the difference in price, 'extensive substitution of continental for British steel... has already begun'.[89] Protection against Continental steel (as opposed to all foreign steel, including British), however, raised the question of imperial preference. Aside from the practical difficulties of differentiating between British and Continental steel (steel from Belgium was allegedly being rolled in Britain at this time, thus muddying the preferential waters), the Tariff Board did not want to become embroiled in the question. Imperial preference, it said, was 'quite as much political as economic' and should be resolved 'on its own merits' by the Government of India and the Legislative Assembly.[90]

The Government of India's lack of enthusiasm for further protection to the steel industry, in marked contrast to its attitude only a few months before, may have been the result of Tata overreaching itself. It was also a sign of things to come. When the question of protection for steel was raised again in 1927, the coalition of interests that had carried through the Steel Protection Bill of 1924 broke apart.

As we have seen, the British Government kept up constant pressure for the formation of an imperial economic union in the inter-war period. Despite its justified misgivings, the Government of India succumbed to that pressure – and this was reflected in its position on renewed protection for steel. The Tariff Board that considered the question from 1926 to 1927 recommended differential duties – a lower tariff on British than non-British steel. When the government took this to the Legislative Assembly in early 1927, it wrapped it up in the purely functional argument that British steel was of a higher quality than Continental steel. It was therefore necessary 'for all purposes connected with the industrial development of India' and should be easier to import.[91] Indians smelled a huge rat. B. Das told the assembly:

> A Conservative Government are sitting in Whitehall. The Baldwin Government want to introduce Imperial Preference all over the Empire. There is a definite policy of direction from the British Government and so we find Bills giving preference are on the anvil in the Dominions and in India.[92]

Speaker after speaker denounced the Government of India for attempting to introduce imperial preference by the back door. Some of the speakers on the British side rather let the cat out of the bag. Mr T. Gavin-Jones declared, 'I frankly believe in Imperial Preference, because I believe in the British Empire, and I believe in strengthening the bonds of the British Empire'. Arthur Moore, while conceding the need for some protection, nevertheless took up the theme:

> [I]n our isolated position in the East we cannot afford to be without a steel industry...I look forward with confidence to the time...when India will recognize that it is to her advantage to realize that she is part of one organic whole, the British Empire.[93]

But business and the nationalists would have none of it.[94] The Indian position was summarised by Jamnades M. Mehta:

> [T]he introduction of the principle of Imperial Preference in this report has burst like a bombshell on us and much as we are inclined to give protection to the Indian steel industry, we cannot reconcile ourselves to this Imperial Preference.[95]

The Bill was passed on 22 February 1927, 50 votes to 40. When steel protection was again considered by a Tariff Board in 1933–34, imperial preference (in the form of differential duties) had become an integral part of the protection package.

The steel industry, its protection and its continued existence had become inextricably linked with nationalist politics. Like it or not, the Tata company had to move closer to the nationalists to ensure its survival.

Cotton

Protection for the cotton textiles industry agitated the mill owners and the Indian bourgeoisie in general in the inter-war period. Differences over whom to protect the industry from drove the two in slightly different directions, as we shall see, but protection of the cotton industry, like that of steel, became entwined with the politics of the national movement.

The first issue for the Indian industry was the excise duty on Indian cotton goods – a tax on cotton goods produced and sold in India. This had been imposed by the Government of India since 1896 in order to offset the minor duty imposed on imported cotton goods. It had been demanded by the British cotton industry, based in Lancashire, with strong backing from the British Government.[96] By the start of the war, the Government of India was agitating for its abolition.[97] It told the British Government in 1916, 'We cannot insist too strongly upon the expediency of removing this grievance, as being the source of irritation and distrust'. In 1919 it recommended again to the Secretary of State, 'Excise duty on cotton manufactures to be removed. This is an essential part of our scheme'. The Indian Fiscal Commission 'unreservedly condemned' the excise in 1921 and urged the government to 'clear the slate'.[98] Hard economic times in Indian cotton gave the agitation a sharper edge. In late 1925, the Viceroy recommended that the excise be 'suspended', but London, afraid of a Lancashire backlash, still did not budge. There were evidently some quiet negotiations between Bombay and Lancashire over the question. The British Government finally agreed to abolition in November 1925.[99]

Like other Indian industries, cotton boomed during the war. It entered a depression in the post-war years. The cotton industrialists added their voices to the demand for abolition of the excise and petitioned the government for protection against foreign imports. Industrially and politically, the mill owners were divided between the industrial centres of Bombay and Allahabad. The latter produced finer cotton, in direct competition with the British cotton industry in Lancashire. The Bombay mill owners produced coarser cotton and found themselves in competition with Japanese mills, rather than British ones after the war. Whereas the Allahabad industrialists, competing with the British, fell in step with the Congress and Indian nationalism, their Bombay brethren, in competition with Japan, did not. 'Unmoved by the appeals of the nationalists', says Chatterji, 'the Bombay millowners stuck to their demands against "unfair" Japanese competition'.[100] Politically then, the Bombay mill owners were 'traditionally staunch moderates'. They remained outside FICCI and distanced themselves from nationalist policies.[101] Japan was their main concern and they sought to enlist Lancashire against a common enemy.[102]

The Government of India was aware of the precious loyalty of this influential section of Indian business opinion and took what care it could not to compromise it. The Bombay mill owners were not to be ignored.[103] To this end, the government could help in the abolition of the excise. But they were unwilling to do much more. When the Bombay Mill Owners' Association (BMOA) petitioned the Viceroy for further economic assistance – anti dumping legislation, duties on Japanese imports and immediate abolition of the excise – they were rebuffed. These measures, said the Viceroy, were economically too difficult (though he was to change his mind on the excise).[104] Their leader, H.P. Mody, retorted:

> [T]he [textile] industry is being crushed by heavy taxation and unfair competition from countries which exploit their labour and subsidise their industry. Government of India are, however calmly looking on as if it were no concern of theirs and say it is a matter which affects only a few industrial magnates.[105]

The government was persuaded to appoint a Tariff Board from 1926–27 to consider the state of the Indian cotton industry and recommend remedial measures. This the board duly did, suggesting that duties on all manufactured cotton imports should be raised from 11 to 15 per cent. Neither the Government of India nor the British Government were prepared to do this, arguing that 'a long established industry, such as the cotton textile industry in Bombay should need no stimulus at the cost of the general tax-payer'.[106] Both governments were keen 'to avoid accepting the [Tariff Board] majority recommendations'. There was no increase in duty and no action against Japan.[107] Mody remarked, 'The conviction is growing that the Department of Commerce and Industries exists for every purpose but that of serving the commerce and industries of India'.[108] There followed 'a strong protest by a conference of representatives of the cotton textile industry who urged the Government of India to reconsider this decision'.[109] Depression in the industry continued. Eventually the government responded with the Cotton Textile Industry (Protection) Bill in March 1930, which offered some protection for Bombay, but also slipped in preferential duties for Lancashire. While Mody (on behalf of the BMOA) accepted this, Birla (on behalf of FICCI) did not.[110] This difference set the scene for a wider split between the Bombay mill owners and mainstream business nationalism.

It was becoming more difficult for the British Government to directly interfere with Indian tariff policy. Their ability to defend the interests of the Lancashire industry consequently lessened. Lancashire was therefore advised to undertake negotiations directly with their Bombay competitors.[111] This in itself was something of a concession.

British and Indian capitalists were to negotiate as equals. As Nalini R. Sarkar (the FICCI president) said afterwards, the agreement that followed 'marked the first recognition by Lancashire of India's right to protect her industries'.[112] The Bombay mill owners responded favourably and negotiations began in Simla in September 1933; 'Mody had invited millowners and important businessmen from all over India to join the representatives of the BMOA to form the Indian delegation.'[113] But that delegation soon split apart, primarily due to Bombay's willingness to sign an agreement on the basis of imperial preference for Lancashire imports.[114] Japan was still the main enemy. Bombay and Lancashire united against Japanese cotton. The agreement, known as the Mody-Lees Pact (W. Clare Lees was the chief British negotiator), was signed on 28 October 1933.

The pact was a sectional one, reflecting the Bombay textile industry's current difficulties with Japanese imports and a temporary alliance with British textile interests to combat them. Mukherjee argues that '[t]he Pact did not have the support of the bulk of the capitalist class'. Nevertheless

> these difficulties generally did not reflect basic differences in attitude towards imperialism ... Even people like H.P. Mody ... were not necessarily 'selling out to imperialism' when they argued for certain agreements against popular opinion in general as well as within the capitalist class ... Mody, however, in his own wont, continued to try to protect national economic interests and certainly at no point could be accused of pushing British economic interests.

What made eventual conflict between Bombay and British interests inevitable were Lancashire's attempts to press home their advantage after the Mody-Lees Pact was signed. As Birla put it in a letter to Kasturbhai Lalbhai:

> The Mody-Lees pact, although concluded with good intention, was a great blunder but I think Lancashire has now tasted the human blood and they are no longer satisfied with Mody-Lees

> pact. They are asking for reduction of tariff to 11%. The fiscal autonomy is proposed to be thrown to [the] dogs.[115]

According to Birla, a Lancashire deputation had demanded of the British Government that it should 'dictate' terms, not only to the Indian textile industry but to the Government of India itself: 'it asks to abolish the fiscal autonomy convention'.[116] Lalbhai had complained to Sir Joseph Bhore (Commerce Member) that while negotiations between Lancashire and the Government of India were going on, 'the commercial community is entirely in the dark as to the nature of these negotiations'.[117] The negotiations continued, however, and brought forth the Indo-British Trade Agreement (which incorporated the Mody-Lees Pact) in January 1935.

In the assembly debate, Mody, though urging acceptance, criticised the government for not consulting Indian business and maintained that the agreement did not weaken the Government of India's right to protect Indian industry. Despite the Legislative Assembly's rejection, the Government of India put the agreement into operation, where it remained until March 1939[118] – thus institutionalising a disadvantageous situation for India's cotton industrialists. As a result, the latter were constantly edged towards a form of nationalism – though not a radical nationalism – in self-defence.[119]

The disputes over the Indian cotton industry shed some light on the different interests of British governments and those of British industry. This relates to the argument in the last chapter on the differences between state and capital and the strategic, rather than economic, importance of India to Britain. It was representatives of the Government of India (along with the Indians themselves) that championed the cause of abolishing the cotton excise, in the face of Lancastrian opposition. It was the British Government that finally let them do it. Despite the setbacks of the Mody-Lees Pact and the Indo-British Trade Agreement, during the early 1930s, the Government of India (again, with London's permission) raised the duties on imported cotton several times.[120] Had the question of profit been uppermost in the British state's mind, we would surely have expected a more vigorous pursuit (or even defence) of it. The British state (in both its forms) was, in the cotton trade and elsewhere, trying to bring about a political settlement that would allow strategic stability (for political developments see the next chapter). Birla himself seems to have recognised the difference between the interests of the British state and British capital. On behalf of FICCI, he wrote in 1929:

> There can be no question that as a rule, in regard to India, the interests of England and the interests of the British trading community in India are far from being identical. The interests of England require a free, prosperous, and friendly India as an equal member of the British Empire. The British trading community in India demand that their profits should not be impaired and their privileges and practical monopolies should be left untouched even at the sacrifice of both the vital interests of India and the political and economic interests of England.[121]

Development

In terms of India's vital interests, the bourgeoisie was now looking beyond the protection of industries that already existed towards the creation of industries that were vital to industrial development – heavy industries (for example machine building and chemicals) together with the capacity to build automobiles, aeroplanes and ships.[122] In the absence of radical land reform, the domestic market for Indian-made consumer goods was reaching its limit. The development of intermediate and capital goods industries required investment and an ability to withstand low profits that could only be supplied either by the state or by foreign capital.[123] The Indian bourgeoisie was opposed to the entry of the latter into heavy industry, preferring the intervention of the state.[124] But the state would no longer intervene. In the inter-war period, both London and New Delhi obstructed development in India. The Fiscal Commission made it clear that there would be no tariff protection for new industries. Later, discriminating protection was only on offer for existing industries.[125]

Even in defence, where, given British strategic priorities, it might have been thought that development would be encouraged, it was not.

Initially, when another war was considered a distinct possibility, the development of war industries was still receiving favourable attention from the Government of India.[126] But as we have seen, enthusiasm even for defence-related industrial development died out under the dual pressure of British imperial defence plans and retrenchment both at home and in India.

For development, the state had not only to provide initiation and protection but ongoing planning and direction as well. During the inter-war period, the Indian bourgeoisie came to accept all of these features – and to demand that the British state implement them.[127] India 'has yet to develop her industries on right lines', Hirachand told the FICCI annual meeting in 1933, 'and in these days of severe competition, they cannot be developed without the active help of the State'.[128] Sarkar devoted his presidential speech to FICCI in1934 to planning.

> [A]n economic plan should be instantly adopted by India... An economic plan is needed to develop the resources that are today lying undeveloped or are being wasted... For a comparatively weak and economically young country like India, the importance of economic planning for both defensive and developmental purposes can hardly be exaggerated.[129]

Sarkar advocated the establishment of a Supreme Economic Council or National Planning Commission at the centre, with similar bodies at the provincial level.

Indian industrialists had already shown their willingness to support state industry for developmental purposes in the case of the railways. In 1920, the Government of India had established a Railway Committee to consider whether state-owned railways should be managed by the state, by British companies or by Indian companies. Purshotamdas Thakurdas was appointed a member of the committee. 'I shall be there', he wrote to Ralph Odell in New York, 'to represent the Indian Commercial Community for the whole of India'.[130] Thakurdas was a strong supporter of state management of the railways and in this he was backed up by the bourgeoisie in general.[131] The Punjab Chamber of Commerce 'accepts without compromise the principle that the railways owned by the State should be managed by the State'.[132] The Indian Merchants' Chamber was convinced 'that no scheme for Company management . . . of Indian Railways is feasible'. A dissenting note was struck by the manager of the Empress Cotton Mills in Nagpur, who wrote to Thakurdas that state management 'is sure to prove a huge blunder'. Yet even he advocated 'a most capable and efficient State Board of Control, exercising almost autocratic powers over the Company-managed railways'. *The Hindu* editorial of 25 January 1921 declared: 'Opinion is solid and overwhelmingly strong in this country in favour of State management'.[133] The committee was evenly split between those advocating state management and those urging the case for private enterprise. The former group eventually recommended that 'in India the State should manage directly the railways which it already owns'. As for the rest, 'as and when the contracts fall in, [they should] be entrusted to the direct management of the State'.[134]

The Indian bourgeoisie realised that for development, new strategic industries had to be initiated under state guidance and protection. A case in point was shipping. Towards the end of the war, the Government of India was asked in the Legislative Council what progress had been made in forming a ship-building branch of the Indian Munitions Board to pursue the possibilities of the industry in India. Sir George Barnes replied that such a branch had been formed.[135] Some months later, it was moved in the Imperial Council 'that immediate steps be taken which would enable the Government to assist and develop the building of an Indian Mercantile Marine at as early a date as possible'.[136]

The vanguard of Indian shipping was the Scindia Steam Navigation Company, set up by Hirachand (together with Narottam Morarjee and others) in 1919 on the basis of having purchased a single steamer, the SS *Loyalty* from Maharajah Scindia of Gwalior. The company immediately ran into opposition from the dominant British India Navigation Company, led by the formidable Lord Inchcape (James L. Mackay). A gruelling rates war ensued. The Scindia Board refused to sell the company to Inchcape but was forced to confine its operations to India and its fleet to seven ships.[137]

The question of Indian shipping was linked by its proponents to India's national aspirations. During the legislative debates, shipbuilding was portrayed as part of the *swadeshi* movement.[138] Morarjee told the Scindia Company's general meeting in December 1923:

> India wants her own separate Merchant Marine to increase her national wealth by preventing the annual drainage of crores of rupees taken away by Foreign Shipping Companies. India wants a separate Merchant Marine for the proper growth of her own trade and commerce and the real protection and development of her neglected ports . . . Had India such a National Merchant Marine at the time of the great war, what a tower of strength it would have been to the Empire.[139]

National interests, then, were joined with those of the Empire. Frequent reference was made to the advantages that an Indian industry would have conferred on the imperial war effort.[140] The prospect of future wars and the necessity of an Indian navy were put forward as justifications for Indian shipping. 'If an Indian Navy is to be created', said Morarjee, 'the Indian Mercantile Marine must come into existence . . . The Indian Merchant Marine will act as a second line of defence, not only to the Indian Navy but to the British Navy also'.[141] To this end, however, Indian business did not demand the establishment of a state shipbuilding industry or a state-run shipping line. 'What we want for India', said Morarjee, 'is the direct and indirect forms of State Aid which have given such remarkable results in Japan'.[142] Subsidies, loans and bounties were what the shipping bourgeoisie wanted – together with the reservation of Indian coastal trade to Indian shipping companies.[143] Inchcape's British Indian Steam Navigation Company and British shipping interests, in general, pursued a vigorous campaign against Indian shipping. Sir William Currie told the Chamber of Shipping in 1928:

> The expropriation of British shipping rights [through coastal reservation] is only the thin end of the wedge. Unless the British Government puts its foot down now, it will only be a matter of

> time before other British interests, and all the many other industries in India, founded and managed by British merchants, will be attacked in the same way.[144]

They had strong backing from the British Government.[145] London's firmness of purpose here was in marked contrast to its attitude in the cotton industry. The reason was that Britain did not want to lose control of India's coastal shipping, nor had it any intention of creating an Indian navy.

The Government of India's position was slightly different. Right up until 1930, it was encouraging in its attitude to Indian shipping. The chairman of the Fiscal Commission told Scindia that he sympathised with the company's aspirations – only finance was a problem.[146] The secretary of the Commerce Department wrote to Scindia in December 1929 that 'they [the Government of India] are in full sympathy with the widespread desire that India should possess a merchant fleet of its own'.[147] Scindia's Abbas Ali Haji reported the same year that the company was strongly backed by the Government of India and the Viceroy.[148] The Viceroy, Lord Irwin, was particularly forthright in his support for the industry. Even when opposing the Coastal Traffic Reservation Bill (see below), he criticised British shipping's defensive manoeuvres:

> [W]hatever economic justice there may be for such developments, they make it difficult for a new company to cut in and it is not surprising, in these circumstances, that Indian capitalists should wish to invoke the aid of the Legislature . . . it is an ambition – and who shall say it is an unworthy ambition – that India should have its own Merchant Marine.[149]

The Viceroy told no less a person than Lord Inchcape himself that the Government of India was 'bound to encourage Indian Merchant Marine'.[150] His remarks at the Shipping Conference of 1930 were similarly positive. He described the development of Indian shipping as the 'development of one side of Indian nationalism'. There was, he said, 'no difference of opinion as to the desire for an Indian Merchant Marine' between the Government of India and Scindia.[151]

There were two qualifications to the Government of India's attitude towards Indian shipping. The first was that it would not (or could not) interfere in Scindia's commercial battles with the British India Navigation Company.[152] The second was that it would not support the Coastal Traffic Reservation Bill. Sir Charles Innes (Commerce and Railways Member) equated reservation with expropriation in 1929, which would eventually endanger other industries.[153]

As it turned out, under the combined pressure of the British Government and the necessity for fiscal rectitude, the Government of India did very little for Indian shipping.[154] There was much truth in C.W.S. Subrahmanayam's remark to the Legislative Assembly that when it came to industrial development:

> the Government simply stands up and says: 'I am at one with you. I have my whole-hearted support with you, and I am endeavouring night and day to do what you just now propose. Absolutely, there is no difference of opinion.'[155]

But concrete action was not forthcoming. The government appointed an Indian Merchant Marine Committee in February 1923 to look into the question, the majority of which duly recommended the eventual reservation of the coastal trade, the inauguration of state shipping lines and (under certain conditions) subsidies for the industry. Following its report, the Scindia directors noted 'the ominous silence of the Government of India'.[156] Indian assembly members introduced a bill 'to reserve the coastal traffic of India to Indian vessels'. As already noted, the Government of India refused to support it. To head it off and produce some kind of alternative, Irwin called together an Indian Shipping Conference in January 1930. Indian shipping, led by Scindia, went into the conference 'committed to the Coastal Reservation Bill as being under the existing circumstances the *"only method"* for the development of an Indian Merchant Marine'.[157] Neither the Government of India nor the British shipowners had any alternative proposals and the conference ended without result. Despite his earlier assurance that, in this event, the Government of India would take action to remove obstacles to the industry, Sir George Rainy told the Legislative Assembly after the conference, 'it became obvious that the political atmosphere had become wholly unfavourable to a settlement by agreement, and the Government of India felt that no purpose could be served by reopening the discussion'.[158]

Once again, the development of an industry was fettered by lack of help from the British state. And, once again, the development of that industry became a political question.

Economic conclusions

By the end of the inter-war period, the leading elements of the Indian bourgeoisie had evolved a series of economic demands that, in their view, were essential for India's economic progress – but which could not be satisfied within India's economic structure and political system. I will conclude the chapter by summarising them.

Development and planning

For a state to promote development, it has to have its own concept of the national interest – and that has to have some degree of acceptance by the people at large, including the bourgeoisie (unless their expropriation is part of the state programme). The Government of India had no such concept – despite its disputes with the British Government, it remained subordinate to it. As Mody told FICCI in 1930, 'our great grievance is that our government's outlook on economic matters is anything but national with the result that today the industrial and commercial community of India are among the strongest critics of the present government'.[159] The point was made repeatedly by capitalist representatives that, had India a national government (rather than a British one), it would do more and better in protecting and developing the Indian economy.[160]

For economic planning to be effective, there had to be a state that could and would plan, on the basis of such a national interest. In his speech endorsing planning in 1934, FICCI president Nalini Ranjan Sarkar noted, 'I fully realise that, in the absence of political power, it would be difficult to induce the Government to accept our proposals'.[161]

Domestic economic policy

British attempts to deal with the economic problems of the inter-war years were seen as self-serving by the Indian bourgeoisie, making the Indian situation worse. That meant that those attempts were damaging an economy that the bourgeoisie hoped to inherit. Negotiations, conferences, commissions and Government of India declarations to the contrary, Indian business was not able to exercise control over the domestic economy. Without political power, government economic policy could not be held to account. Hirachand, speaking on the drop in India's balance of trade, told FICCI in 1933:

> [I]n India, unfortunately, the administration not being in national hands, there have been no re-adjustments in either the currency or the tariff policy of the Government of India whose currency policy has always been subordinated to the interests of Great Britain.[162]

Even when, in the negotiations for a post-Ottawa trade agreement (which would become the Indo-British Trade Agreement, Mark II), the Government of India appointed the leading lights of FICCI as 'unofficial advisers', it eventually rejected their advice. The new agreement was rejected by the Legislative Assembly but put into force by the British Government.[163]

International economic policy

In the view of the Indian bourgeoisie, external economic policy was formulated by non-representatives of the nation and placed dangerous restrictions on Indian trade in order to skew it in the interests of the British Empire. Hirachand told FICCI in 1933 that 'the nation's rightful representatives' should attend the next world economic conference and 'express candidly the nation's point of view before it'. He said, 'India will have to strike out [on] an altogether different path of her own', even if this meant 'an honest clash of interests between the western nations and herself'.[164] The next FICCI president, Lalbhai, objecting to the Government of India's view that India should concentrate economically on the Empire, declared that 'India, as a substantial producer of raw materials [could] not in the long run afford to depend upon one single market – however stable – at the risk of losing her place in the other important foreign markets of the world'.[165]

FICCI therefore campaigned, eventually successfully, for the termination of the Ottawa agreement. The Legislative Assembly passed a Congress motion to this effect in March 1936. The termination of the agreement, however, did not result in proponents of India's economic interests representing India at future international gatherings, nor did it allow India to pursue an international trade policy of her own devising.

State intervention

The pivotal issue in carrying out development, initiating planning and instituting economic policies in India's national interest was the question of state intervention. The bourgeoisie, as we have seen, was well aware of this, despite its devotion to the rights of private property. By the end of this period, there was not, on the part of the bourgeoisie, a begrudging acceptance of a limited role for the state in the economy. There was instead a demand for full-scale state intervention in heavy and strategic industries, in planning and in policy.[166] The Indian bourgeoisie had before it the example of a number of state-driven war economies (the Soviet Union, Italy, Japan, Germany) that appeared to leave previous attempts at industrial development in the shade.[167] In a period in which the state in all industrialised nations moved to protect its national economy, the Indian bourgeoisie looked for state intervention – and found that it had no state. The British state (both in London and New Delhi) was intent on protecting the British Empire, industrially and strategically. It would not serve Indian purposes.

The Empire: Too much and too little

In one respect, the imposition of British policy preferences economically, politically and militarily was too much for the Indian bourgeoisie to accept by the late 1930s. It was true that, from the bourgeoisie's point of view, the British state provided a commercial and legal infrastructure, law and order, some tariff protection and some government contracts.[168] But this was no longer enough. More than that, it was an obstacle to providing those things necessary to raise the level of the productive forces in India. Engels wrote in *Anti-Duhring* that

> where . . . the internal state power of a country becomes antagonistic to its economic development, as at a certain stage occurred with almost every political power in the past, the contest always ended with the downfall of the political power. Inexorably and without exception the economic development forces its way through.[169]

For this, however, an alternative political power and a political struggle were necessary to burst the fetters holding back the forces of development.

Chapter Six

Congress and the Bourgeoisie: Inter-War Politics

The Raj had become a fetter on the development of India's forces of production. The Indian bourgeoisie, in the forefront of that development, therefore came into conflict with the British state. But they were neither strong enough to confront that state structure on their own, nor to dominate Indian society in the aftermath of colonialism. All of the bourgeoisie's interests (protection, development of new industries, planning) led back to the question of the state. Since the British state was unwilling to undertake these tasks – and in fact was moving in quite the opposite direction – a new state was needed. The leading elements of the bourgeoisie could see that state taking shape in the form of the Congress and were willing to join forces with it – even at times to subordinate their own interests to it – to unleash the further development of India's productive forces.[1]

For the bourgeoisie, the attractions of nationalist politics did not precede the quest for making profits. 'I am interested in politics', said Purshotamdas Thakurdas, 'only to the extent that politics reacts on economics'.[2] Their economic survival and progress pushed them – at different speeds and to different depths – into a political position that had, by the mid-1930s, crystallised around two elements: opposition to the Raj and (in varying degrees) and support for the Congress.[3]

Congress economics

Preoccupied with questions of political struggle, the Congress did not have a great deal to say on economic policy until the mid-1930s.[4] From 1905, the annual industrial conferences (which we considered in chapter one) were linked to the annual Congress sessions. But as *The Leader* pointed out in 1912, the industrialists were made to meet *after* the Congress: 'after three days of exciting political oratory, the matter-of-fact of the Industrial Conference are bound to fall flat'.[5] On specific economic issues (protection, the currency question, financial safeguards), the Congress tended to take its position from FICCI. Its general line on the economy, however, was clear: the future Indian state would be actively interventionist and (as the economic importance of the state increased dramatically in the inter-war period) would control, regulate and plan significant sections of the economy. As early as its third session in 1887, the Congress wanted the government 'to encourage indigenous manufactures... in regard to utilizing such manufactures for State purposes'.[6] In the 1926 elections, the Swaraj Party promised 'the pursuit of a definite economic policy against exploitation and in furtherance of national industrial development'. Its manifesto continued:

> [A]ll proposals for granting discriminating protection to vital national industries will continue to receive the sympathetic support of the party... There is no reason why such industries should not rapidly develop if a well-thought-out industrial policy is steadily followed.[7]

The Karachi Congress of 1931 started to envisage firmer control of the Indian economy. In its programme for an Indian government, it declared, 'The State shall own or control key industries and services, mineral resources, railways, waterways, shipping and other means of public transport'. The 'Swaraj government' would also protect indigenous industries against foreign competition and regulate currency and exchange.[8] Jawaharlal Nehru wrote later:

> In the Karachi resolution [the Congress] took a step, a very short step in a socialist direction by advocating nationalisation of key

> industries and services, and various other measures to lessen the burden on the poor and increase it on the rich.[9]

Gandhi himself endorsed state intervention to the extent that it was needed to protect Indian industries: 'I am an out-and-out protectionist', he declared, endorsing protection for the cotton industry and the reservation of coastal shipping for Indians.[10] But it was the Congress Left who were the most enthusiastic about state control – and in this, they were led by Nehru. At the Faizpur Congress in 1936, he advocated 'a great planned system for the whole land and dealing with all these various national activities, co-ordinating them, making each serve the larger whole and the interests of the mass of the people'.[11] Under the auspices of Nehru and the other leader of the Congress Left, Subhas Chandra Bose, the Congress set up a National Planning Committee in 1938 (on which, see chapter eight). 'The very essence of this planning', Nehru wrote, 'was a large measure of regulation and co-ordination. Thus while free enterprise was not ruled out as such, its scope was severely restricted'. Defence industries were to be state owned, while 'key industries' would be state controlled. 'Such control of these industries, however, had to be rigid.'[12] The Congress manifesto for the elections of December 1945 advocated 'social control of the mineral resources, means of transport and the principal methods of production and distribution in land, industry and in other departments of national activity', as well as 'large state farms'.[13]

The Congress trend towards a state-run economy was not just the result of economic fashion in the inter-war period, coloured in by trips to the Soviet Union (and in Bose's case, to Italy, Germany and Japan). The social position of the majority of the Congress leadership made it particularly open to the notion of a state-dominated society. Where did that leadership come from? Akshayakumar Desai tells us that, under the British

> [t]he professional classes [which he also refers to as 'the intelligentsia'] comprising modern lawyers, doctors, teachers and professionals associated with modern educational institutions, managers and clerks working in modern commercial and other

> enterprises, officials functioning in state administrative machinery, engineers, chemists, technical experts, agronomists, journalists and others formed another new social group... The new economic, social and state systems required as personnel, cadres of educated Indians, versed in modern law, technology, medicine, economics, administrative science and other subjects.[14]

The Congress leadership was dominated by these forces.[15] Of 61 Congress leaders between 1918 and 1923 surveyed by Gopal Krishna, 50 had a university education; 21 had travelled abroad; and 51 were professionals (lawyers, journalists, doctors and teachers).[16] The percentage of professionals and full-time Congress workers in the All-India Congress Committee in these years was as follows:[17]

1919	80%
1920	78%
1921	72%
1922	41%
1923	46%

As the struggle heated up, professionals abandoned their professions and became full-time Congress workers.[18] This created a stratum of Congress leaders and functionaries whose existence was bound up with the organisation and whose future prospects relied on a Congress state. Desai contends that the intelligentsia were 'the pioneer organizers and leaders of all national political movements'. Furthermore, they led it 'in all phases of development... whichever section of [the intelligentsia] led it and however different its ideology, methodology, and programme from those of other sections'.[19]

The natural benefactor of such elements was the state, which, as it expanded, could be expected to employ squads of experts, professionals, educators and technicians. The problem for the intelligentsia in India was that they were discriminated against by the British in state employment – and that, as their numbers increased (through expanding education programmes), the number of available jobs under the British did not.[20] Thus one of the earliest demands of the Indian national movement was for the 'Indianisation' of the Indian Civil Service and of the officer corps of the armed forces. On these and other issues, the intelligentsia swung into political action. Their salvation seemed to lie in an indigenous Indian state.[21]

India was not alone in experiencing this phenomenon. In fact, it was not confined to the developing countries. The First World War, engendering a huge increase in the power of the state throughout Europe and beyond, provided a tremendous boost to the influence of 'engineers, planners, technocrats, high-level administrators, architects, scientists and visionaries', empowered by state intervention and schooled in the wartime virtues of planning and efficiency.[22] For many after the war, private enterprise and capitalism were on probation. They would be retained to the extent that they served the national interest. Such elements emerged in Russia well before the Bolshevik insurrection. There, Peter Holquist tells us, '[e]ducated society came to idolize the state as an ideal in its own right and an instrument for achieving all its own fondest dreams'.[23]

In the developing countries, the intelligentsia tended to reject untrammelled private enterprise, together with imperialism, and to accept some elements of the Soviet economic model. They regarded themselves as above sectional and class interests, representing the national interest and it alone. Tony Cliff concludes (though it should be noted that he was writing primarily about China and Cuba): 'They [the "revolutionary intelligentsia"] embody the drive for industrialisation, for capital accumulation, for national resurgence . . . All this makes totalitarian state capitalism a very attractive goal for intellectuals'.[24]

The kind of large-scale economic projects that the intelligentsia's visions of a new society entailed had to be carried out by the state. They necessitated an increase in state power and the power of the state over capital. The alliance between the bourgeoisie and the Congress was not then a 'natural fit' for the bourgeoisie. It would entail subordinating the interests of capital to those of the future Congress state.

The bourgeoisie and Congress

It has been argued that the Indian bourgeoisie's attitude towards the national movement and towards the Congress was an ambiguous one. Some historians contend that the capitalists were deeply divided over the question.[25] Ghanshyamdas Birla expressed the ambiguity when he wrote to Thakurdas in 1932:

> [T]he position of the business man is rather peculiar. He is neither a Congress man nor a Government man. So he does not know where he stands. My own feeling is that during the next few years business men will have to suffer very much at the hands of the Government and of their own countrymen.[26]

There were, no doubt, all sorts of nuances in the political positions of the bourgeoisie and many differences between different groups, pursuing their own interests within the class. As we have seen, economic interests produced different degrees of opposition to the current structures and different targets at which that opposition took aim. But by the 1930s, the mainstream Indian bourgeoisie ranged itself against British colonialism because the prospects of economic development demanded that it do so.[27] For this reason, its opposition was endemic. It may have surged forward and receded – but generally it increased and deepened from the beginning of the inter-war period to its end.[28] As early as 1917, Annie Besant told the Calcutta Congress that the attitude of business was changing – that Tata, beset with economic woes, now supported the national movement.[29] Ten years later, Thakurdas was approached by a Colonel Crawford to form a political alliance with like-minded Britishers:

> I definitely told him that, that was not to be, as the political convictions of Indians and Britishers (in their present mentality) are quite wide apart . . . I said that I was quite sure that in trying to keep everything to themselves, the Europeans had done us a service and made us more active, and generally speaking better to look after ourselves.[30]

Politically therefore business gravitated towards Congress.[31] Medha Kudaisya puts forward a model of mutual understanding: the Congress supported the bourgeoisie in economic policy, while the bourgeoisie supported the Congress on political issues.[32] This was generally the case, except that (as we shall see) at important junctures business was apt to defer to the Congress in economic matters as well.[33] The bourgeoisie's political leadership was the Congress. Its class leadership became those closest to the Congress.[34] Perhaps we can see the close political relationship between the bourgeoisie and the Congress emerging in Ratan Tata's 'unfeigned admiration' for Gandhi's struggle in South Africa, which he expressed in a letter to Gokhale in November 1909. He enclosed a donation of 25,000 rupees, 'the money to be spent in relieving destitution, and in aid of the struggle generally'. A year later he sent a further 25,000 rupees, hoping that it could be publicised 'in a somewhat sensational manner' in order to encourage others 'to keep alive this struggle of our cause in South Africa'.[35] Later, John Keenan, the Tata director, said that the Tata family 'want to see India a self-governing dominion. So, feeling that eventually the Congress Party will win dominion status for India, the Tatas give the Congress a helping hand in a quiet way'.[36]

Jamnalal Bajaj, a sugar industrialist with interests in steel, was one of the first in the business community to join the Congress. He was, for 22 years, the Treasurer of the Congress Working Committee. As chair of the 1920 Nagpur Congress Reception Committee, he admonished his peers that 'they may have successfully amassed wealth under British rule, [but] it was done by making the country helpless . . . at the cost of the ever-growing poverty and impoverishment of the people'. Despite this, he appealed to their self-interest: 'Fellow businessmen, our trade, industry and commerce will flourish a hundredfold by our participation in the great national endeavour for swaraj.' Bajaj himself was an active participant in that endeavour. He was gaoled for a year in 1924 for leading a demonstration of some hundreds in Nagpur to fly the national flag. In 1931 he refused to give the local District Commissioner an assurance that his workers would not undertake anti-government activities – demanded before he could open a new sugar mill. He was arrested again for entering the princely state of Jaipur in 1939, in defiance of a ban.[37]

Birla and Thakurdas have already made their appearance in our story as spokesmen for the bourgeoisie. Neither were members of the Congress. Birla in particular, however, was politically in lockstep with it – most especially with what he called 'the Gandhi group'. His political instincts had originally been aroused by early economic difficulties. Trying to launch a jute mill, he ran into opposition from the European interests that controlled the industry, restricting his access to credit and influencing the government against him. He recalled later, 'I smarted under these insults, and this created within me a political interest which, from 1912 until today, I have fully maintained'.[38] He wrote to Sir Dorab Tata in June 1929 of his conviction that:

> Indian commerce and industry are only an integral phase of Indian nationalism, and that deprived of its inspiration in Indian nationalism, Indian commerce and industry stand reduced to mere exploitation...we are Indians first, and merchants and industrialists afterwards.[39]

Thakurdas became convinced that economic progress was dependent on political progress – and the latter was represented by the Congress and the national movement.[40] He disagreed with the Congress on a number of issues around the civil disobedience movement launched in April 1930, advocating a more conciliatory attitude towards the British and participation in the Round Table Conference. Despite these disagreements, he resigned his seat in the Legislative Assembly in May 1930.[41] This earned him the praise of Motilal Nehru, who added: 'I hope this is only an earnest of greater co-operation with the Congress in the near future'.[42] Thakurdas wrote back – with the civil disobedience movement now in full swing:

> [W]e are anxious to prevent the Congress from having a set-back and to ensure to the country the full benefit of the sacrifice made by the Congress people...In short the question is whether you can give us any indication of the lines on which to work...our anxiety is to ensure the Congress the success that its activities have earned.[43]

The institutions of the bourgeoisie were increasingly influenced by the Congress' political leadership. Thakurdas told the FICCI session in 1928:

> Indian commerce and industry are intimately associated with, and are, indeed part of the national movement – growing with its growth and strengthening with its strength . . . The ideal of the national movement in the political sphere, namely to make the Indian nation united, prosperous and progressive, is also the ideal of Indian commerce and industry in the economic sphere.[44]

Business opposed both the Public Safety Bill of 1928 (aimed at deporting radicals) and the Trades Disputes Bill of 1929 (aimed at suppressing strikes), following the Congress' lead on civil liberties grounds.[45] In 1929, Birla, Motilal Nehru and Madan Mohan Malaviya had considered a Congress/FICCI alliance to contest the forthcoming elections.[46] FICCI accepted direct Congress leadership at the Second Round Table Conference in late 1931 and would not participate in the reformed Constitution of 1935 without Congress approval.[47]

It has been argued that the Congress/business relationship was firmly sealed only after the end of the civil disobedience movement and during the period of the Congress provincial ministries from 1937 to 1939.[48] We will discuss the bourgeoisie's attitude to the civil disobedience movement and towards constitutionalism below, but there is no doubt that the 1937–39 period of 'peaceful construction' had a beneficial effect on its relationship with the Congress and ensured that the two forces went into the Second World War united.

It would be absolutely wrong to conclude (as the Left tended to do – see below) that the Congress was simply a 'tool' of the Indian bourgeoisie. In fact, for much of the time, quite the contrary was the case. When crossed by the bourgeoisie, the Congress was strong in its rebuke. After a disappointing attempt to raise funds from the mill owners for the Swaraj party in 1928, Motilal Nehru wrote:

> An alliance between the Congress and capitalists who are bent on profiting by the sufferings of the nation is an impossible

> one...Mahatmaji never believed in such an alliance with the latter, and I have now told him that he was right and I was wrong.[49]

On the Bombay mill owners he went further: 'they are a mean and selfish lot and should, in my opinion, be taught a lesson they are not likely to forget'.[50] At the Second Round Table Conference (September–December 1931), Birla and Thakurdas argued, on behalf of FICCI, for discrimination in favour of Indian industries at the expense of their British competitors. Gandhi, however, promised the Lancashire lobby that there would be no commercial discrimination on racial lines. Birla and Thakurdas fell into line with Gandhi's position, despite blistering criticism from FICCI on their return. They were accused of being too close to the Congress. They responded that business had to remain with the national movement: 'Do those who insist on racial discrimination as such seriously believe that they have any chance of success in a fight in which the weight of the Congress is against them?' they asked.[51] Once again, during the negotiations for a new trade agreement in 1937–39, the capitalist representatives wanted to support some concessions to Lancashire. The Congress (through Gandhi and Patel) said no – and thenceforward the capitalists opposed concessions on political (rather than economic) grounds.[52]

Radical constitutionalism

In October 1929, the Viceroy Lord Irwin issued a statement that declared that Britain's ultimate goal for India was Dominion status and that a Round Table Conference would be convened to devise a constitution for it. The reaction of the bourgeoisie to the 'Irwin Declaration' wavered somewhat, and in this, it reflected the reaction of the Congress itself. At first, it was met with some relief, as providing a possible break in the political turmoil consequent on the Simon Commission. Thakurdas in particular was of this view. 'India', he said, 'has had quite enough strain put on her during the last ten years, and it is necessary that we should now have a little peace in the political sphere'.[53] He joined with prominent Indian Liberals in publicly welcoming the declaration. For this he was roundly criticised by Birla and Ambalal Sarabhai, who both felt he should have waited for the Congress word on the subject.[54]

The Congress, however, had problems of its own in regard to its response. At first, it indicated support for the Round Table Conference – as long as its purpose was to frame a Dominion constitution and not to discuss Dominion status. But in December, the Congress session rejected the Irwin Declaration and prepared to launch civil disobedience. Thakurdas considered that this was 'a dire misfortune for the country'.[55] But despite any private misgivings, once the Congress line became clear, FICCI declared that if the Congress boycotted the Round Table Conference, it would follow suit. Thakurdas tried to convince the British that, unless they conceded 'complete self-government to us in all domestic matters', a Round Table Conference without Congress would be fruitless.[56] FICCI's Executive Committee resolved:

> no Conference (of the nature of the Round Table Conference) convened for the purpose of discussing the problem of Indian constitutional advance can come to a solution of the present political difficulty which will be acceptable to the country, unless such a Conference is attended by Mahatma Gandhi, as a free man, or has at least his approval.[57]

During 1930, FICCI represented its views on the political situation in a submission to the Viceroy (subsequently published as a pamphlet). Now in the midst of civil disobedience, it accused the Viceroy of running a 'regime...more befitting the rule of a reactionary ruler'. It complained that the function of the Round Table Conference was still unclear – 'And this even at the time when the one man who alone can *deliver the goods* is cast behind iron bars!!' On the civil disobedience, it declared: '[T]here seems to be no alternative. Government have made it impossible for even the most moderate minded people to help the former...The situation has simply gone from bad to worse'.[58]

When the civil disobedience movement was brought to an end by the Gandhi-Irwin Pact in March 1931, the way was open for both business and the Congress to attend the Second Round Table Conference from September to December of that year.[59] The business agenda was straightforward: that the new constitution should ensure that Indian finances were in Indian hands (without burdensome 'safeguards' giving control to the Viceroy) and that there should be discrimination in favour of Indian industry (dropped at Gandhi's insistence). They were disappointed at the British refusal to discuss the devaluation of the rupee. Both FICCI and the Congress rejected the eventual British offer of provincial autonomy first, central power later. As noted above, the FICCI representatives were criticised by their fellow business leaders for returning with so little.

Despite their disappointment, the leaders of the bourgeoisie took up the struggle once again. They maintained their insistence on the participation of Gandhi and the Congress in any constitutional discussion. Birla demanded 'a constitution introduced with the direct or indirect co-operation and approval of the Congress, without which there is no chance of a smooth working of the new constitution'.[60] Business leaders also protested against the Government of India's policy of steadily rising repression. The Bengal National Chamber of Commerce and the Indian Chamber of Commerce in Calcutta wrote to the Governor of Bengal, denouncing the Emergency Powers Act, which was partly aimed at suppressing propaganda by the business community in favour of indigenous manufacturing. The Chambers pointed out that '[t]he Ordinances are so wide in their scope and so ambiguous in their nature that the ordinary citizen feels that he could be hauled up on mere suspicion of pro-Congress sympathy on the part of a police officer'.[61]

The Indian Merchants' Chamber in Bombay protested against the government's Press Ordnance, which had 'shaken the confidence of the Indian commercial community in Government'.[62] FICCI resolved in April 1933 'that in its opinion the repressive policy of the Government has failed' and demanded once again that Gandhi and other political prisoners be released.[63]

It should be clear that the bourgeoisie did not enjoy failed negotiations, rising civil disobedience (see below) or the consequent government repression. This was not the way, in its view, that Indian political reform would advance. Much more in tune with its radical constitutional approach were the moves and counter-moves around the 1935 Government of India Act.

On the basis of the Round Table Conferences, the British Government issued a White Paper in 1933 setting out proposals for constitutional reform, which culminated in the 1935 Government of India Act. The proposals envisaged, in the first instance, a transfer of power at the provincial level (provincial governments responsible to provincial Legislative Assemblies). The Viceroy would continue to 'direct and control' defence and external affairs (and, incidentally Ecclesiastical Affairs). At a later stage, power would be transferred at the centre to an Indian Federation of the provinces of British India together with the Princely States.[64]

At first, FICCI was severely critical of these proposals. In a commentary on the Government White Paper, they were described as 'entirely unacceptable to the Indian mercantile community'. The proposals 'breathe complete distrust of Indians in the management of their own affairs'. The reserved powers to the Viceroy 'can only mean a powerful domination by British interests'. Furthermore, the promise of Dominion status had now disappeared.[65] FICCI resolved that the proposals 'fall far short of even the modest aspirations of the country and make the conferment of Dominion Status recede into a remote future'. Nalini R. Sarkar told the annual meeting in 1933, 'the little that India had, has been taken away, and to the much which Britain enjoyed in India, more has been added'.[66]

Despite these public pronouncements, the bourgeoisie saw the 1933 proposals as a major step forward along the constitutional path to freedom. Birla in particular was active around the Congress Right and Gandhi, urging them to contest the elections (to be held after the Act had passed) and accept office in the provincial ministries.[67] Eventually he and his co-thinkers were successful. Despite remaining fiercely critical of the reforms, the Lucknow Congress of 1936 agreed to contest the elections. It shelved the question of whether to accept office, leaving it to the All-India Congress Committee (AICC).[68] Once the Congress victories in the 1937 election were clear, the AICC resolved that Congress representatives should accept office. This, wrote the Viceroy to the Governors, 'unquestionably represents a victory for the rightwing of Congress'.[69]

For business, this was the way forward – despite some misgivings regarding the speed of Congress reforms in the provinces.[70] The system would develop into a central federation and from there to freedom. Birla wrote of 'the bright prospect that lay before us'. But it was not to be. Happy ideas of power transfer from the 1937 elections were, as Birla put it, 'only to be shattered so tragically two years later by the impact of the World War'. He wrote later: '[W]hen war came the Viceroy [Linlithgow] instead of pushing Federation through, hastily scrapped the whole plan. Had he not done so, the whole history of India would have been very different, and partition need never have come upon us'.[71]

Moderate civil disobedience

But when the constitutional path showed signs of failure during this period, the bourgeoisie was confronted with the national movement's radical tactics of non-co-operation and civil disobedience. The movements based on those tactics were big, unruly, mobilised realities that could not be ignored. The bourgeoisie preferred constitutionalism. But that did not call into question its even stronger preference for an Indian national state – or its general support for the Congress which would take it there.[72]

The bourgeoisie's position on radical tactics was not a fixed one, either temporally or geographically. There was, for example, a good deal more support for civil disobedience in early 1930 than there had been for non-cooperation ten years previously. The attitude of the bourgeoisie did not change primarily because of this or that Congress tactic. Rather, their increasing frustration with the British over the economic grievances detailed in the last chapter – which brought about the realisation that only a new state would bring development – encouraged a progressive endorsement of increasingly radical tactics.

At the beginning of the century, the industrialists were in favour of the national *swadeshi* campaign but were against the boycott of foreign goods. Their support was, at best, 'lukewarm', according to Sarkar.[73] Many of them remained, however, politically active (as we have seen), in an effort to have the state build up indigenous industry. Business was even less supportive of Gandhi's first mass non-cooperation campaign, which began in 1920. Thakurdas wrote to Thomas Holland that the campaign was 'more likely than not to put back India by a good deal'. He went on, 'the classes that have no stake in the country are mustering strong roundabout Gandhi'.[74] Thakurdas felt so strongly on the matter that he, together with several other prominent Bombay businessmen, formed an 'Anti-Non-Cooperation Association' in 1920.[75] Over in Calcutta, Birla's newspaper, *New Empire*, editorialised against the Non-Cooperation Movement, which, it said, was doomed to failure. His other paper, *The Bengalee*, was praised by the European press for its stand against the campaign.[76] But opposition to the movement was not uniform amongst the bourgeoisie. Due to merchant (rather than industrialist) support, Bombay was nevertheless 'the stronghold of the boycott movement. The merchants dealing in Lancashire piece-goods joined the movement in large numbers'.[77] And the Congress received substantial funding from business for the campaign.[78] It should also be noted that those industrialists opposed to the campaign were simply adopting the same stance as many moderate nationalists at the time.

Business attitudes on the kind of tactics needed to press the nationalist cause were already changing. When the British Government appointed the all-British Simon Commission to examine the Government of India in 1927, business leaders fully endorsed the Congress' call for a boycott of the commission and all its works. 'About the Statutory Commission', wrote Birla in November, 'I cannot suppress my indignation... It should be entirely boycotted'.[79] As the campaign continued into 1928, Thakurdas wrote to Motilal Nehru:

> I do not think we should, under any circumstances, give up our opposition to the Simon Commission. I admit that things are not going well. But our cause is so just, and our opposition so correct, that I expect help from unexpected quarters.[80]

The Viceroy Lord Irwin made his declaration on Dominion Status and the Round Table Conference at the end of October 1929. The Lahore Congress resolved on a new campaign of civil disobedience in December. The details were left to the Congress Working Committee, and ultimately to Gandhi himself. In early March, he warned the Viceroy of the approaching campaign and a few days later began the famous Salt March to Dandi. When he arrived there and made salt on 6 April, the mass civil disobedience movement was unleashed.

As the mass campaign approached, prominent capitalists were apprehensive, to say the least. Birla attempted to dissuade Gandhi from action, urging him to attend the Round Table Conference.[81] Continuing economic difficulties with the British meant that business still stood firmly behind the Congress in its political objectives. It was the mass nature of the campaign that made them hesitate. Pressure built up to take some sort of stand inside and outside the business community. Gandhi, after all, had included in his 'Eleven Points' (served on the Government of India on 30 January 1930) measures of particular interest to the bourgeoisie: the reduction of military spending by at least 50 per cent; a protective tariff on foreign cloth; and the passage of the Coastal Traffic Reservation Bill. Lalji Naranji, the usually moderate representative of the Indian Merchants' Chamber, wrote to Thakurdas in late March:

> [B]efore the 6th of April . . . it is very necessary that the mercantile community should express very clearly that the situation, created by the British Government in withholding from India the Constitution acceptable to them [i.e. to Indians], which will give them real control of the course of the country, is very serious and that it will be the only solution that will save India from going into further troubles. Political and economic matters are so much inter-mingled that you cannot get one without the other.[82]

For the bourgeoisie, then, the ball was in the Government of India's court. When it was dropped and then ignored, business swung its support behind the campaign. According to the *Times of India* in May, 'The pure negation for which Mr Gandhi's policy stands has obviously spread to the Indian commercial community and the mass is sweeping along with it even those men who are capable of seeing what is being done to India'.[83]

Homi Mody, the Bombay mill owner, told the Round Table Conference in November (while breaking the Congress/FICCI boycott of the conference) that:

> the commercial classes . . . have come to the conclusion that unless India is politically free she cannot be economically healthy, and she cannot build up her trade and industries as she would want to. That conviction is at the root of the movement we all deplore, and which largely derives its sustenance from the commercial classes.[84]

According to British Intelligence, Birla alone donated somewhere between 100,000 and 500,000 rupees to the movement. In support of the boycott of foreign cloth, he opened a number of shops selling *khadi* materials.[85] In the midst of the campaign, FICCI formed a *Swadeshi Sabha* sub-committee to promote the *swadeshi* campaign.[86] Thakurdas commented that '[t]he agitation started by Mahatma Gandhi has taken root and has found an extraordinarily good field for it in the deep distress prevalent amongst the masses and the middle class'.[87]

The support of the bourgeoisie was not unanimous. A.D.D. Gordon argues that the attitude of the Bombay industrialists was similar to that towards the Non-Cooperation Movement in 1920–22.[88] Bombay merchants, on the other hand, 'formed the backbone of Congress' civil disobedience campaigns of boycott and hartal' and became more radical as the movement went on.[89] The British were not as convinced of the Bombay industrialists' anti-civil disobedience stand. Sir Frederick Sykes, Governor of Bombay, told the Viceroy 'that in Bombay the mercantile community has already given to Gandhi a measure of support which it refused him until the later stages of the Non-Cooperation Movement of 1921–22'.[90] The Government of India pointed out that:

> it must be recognized that the commercial community of Bombay has in pursuit of political power been lending its support, both moral and material, to a movement in defiance of the law, which

> might have been expected to have no attraction for those whose interests depend on stable and peaceful conditions.[91]

There is little doubt though, that the bourgeoisie's enthusiasm for the campaign was waning by the latter half of 1930. Clearly, the severe economic disruption that the campaign brought in its wake had much to do with this.[92] They were also disturbed by the drubbing governmental authority in general was receiving at the hands of the movement – and the implications this had for a new state. 'I notice', wrote Naranji, 'that this dis-regard for authority will have very disastrous after-effects which no Government of Swaraj will be able to recover and bring the country back to normal conditions'.[93] Thakurdas concurred, telling Sarabhai in November that the movement (which he claimed, rather dubiously, to have opposed 'since last March') 'might teach the people an extremely dangerous lesson, which may greatly inconvenience even a Swaraj Government'.[94]

With these concerns in mind, which became greater the bigger the movement became and the longer it went on, the bourgeoisie tried from the beginning to keep open the possibility of negotiations with the British authorities. Thakurdas was particularly active in this respect.[95] It should be noted, though, that his approaches to the government were always designed to convince them that they had to give the Congress some substantial concessions if there was a chance for the movement to be called off.

It is clear that in late 1930, much of the leadership of the bourgeoisie felt that a change of tactic – not a change of objective – was required.[96] Birla said that at that stage he had two objectives:

> One is that we should jump in at the most opportune time for a reconciliation and the other is that we should not do anything which might weaken the hands of those through whose efforts we have arrived at this stage.[97]

The British would not play the game. Neither negotiations nor concessions were forthcoming. The bourgeois leaders requested permission to visit Gandhi in gaol in September 1930, 'to bring home to Mahatma

Gandhi the present position as some of us see it'. The Viceroy refused, suggesting instead that if the capitalists 'were prepared to make it publicly plain that they were no longer willing to stand the enforcement of the policy dictated by Congress', then this would 'bring Congress and its leaders to a more reasonable frame of mind'.[98] This the capitalists would not do. As late as January 1931, Birla was declaring that 'the present movement should not be allowed to slacken'.[99]

But, as is well known, the movement did slacken. Congress brought it to an end with the Gandhi-Irwin Pact of March 1931. The final reckoning was something of a draw: Congress stopped civil disobedience, but entered the Round Table Conference process. It has been suggested that business had a hand in bringing the sides together and bringing the Pact about.[100] FICCI certainly gave the Pact a warm welcome: 'a pact that every member of the commercial community in India will be grateful for'.[101] Once again, there was nothing particularly surprising either in business moves (if such there were) to bring it about, or in their reaction to it. The bourgeoisie had gone along with – and in some cases actively supported – a radical civil disobedience movement for as long as it considered it necessary to demonstrate the movement's power and to show the British of what the movement was capable. With the Gandhi-Irwin Pact, the bourgeoisie put aside for the moment its moderate civil disobedience stance and took up again radical constitutionalism – its preferred *modus operandi*. This did not mean that more radical tactics were permanently abandoned. When Congress resumed civil disobedience in early 1932, FICCI's member bodies were in favour of breaking off all negotiations with the British.[102] Once Congress had decided to accept office on the basis of the 1935 Act, Birla told Lord Halifax that if the new system did not work to India's satisfaction and did not advance towards India's goal, 'the Congress would again be compelled to resort to direct action'.[103]

The Left

In moving closer to the Congress, the bourgeoisie also had to cope with the emergence of a strong Leftwing in the freedom movement during the inter-war period. This evolved under the leadership of Jawaharlal Nehru, Subhas Chandra Bose and Jayaprakash Narayan. Later, Jayaprakash Narayan was instrumental in forming the Congress Socialist Party (within the Congress) in October 1934, with the dual aim of strengthening the movement while transforming it in a socialist direction. The key spokesman for the Left at this time, however, given his position in the Congress leadership, was Nehru.

Nehru made no secret of his views. In his presidential address to the Lahore Congress in 1929, he embraced socialism and republicanism and denounced 'the order which produces the modern kings of industry, who have greater power over the lives and fortunes of men than even the kings of old'.[104] In *Whither India?* (1933), he argued that 'the national struggle for political freedom is becoming a social struggle for economic freedom. Independence and the Socialist State become the objectives'.[105] As Congress president again at Lucknow in 1936, he told the session that socialism – 'in the scientific, economic sense' – was the solution to the world's and India's problems. 'That means the ending of private property, except in a restricted sense, and the replacement of the present profit system by a higher ideal of co-operative service.'[106] In his *Autobiography*, published the same year, he endorsed 'the establishment of a socialist order... with a controlled production and distribution of wealth for the public good'.[107] A book on Nehru's socialism, published in 1943, declared: 'He has been called the "Red Star of the East" because of his deep faith in the doctrines of socialism and communism and due to his immense work for [the] socialist movement in India and abroad'.[108]

The bulk of the Congress leadership (that is, the Right) did its best to combat leftist enthusiasm. In June 1934, the Congress Working Committee criticised 'loose talk about confiscation of private property and necessity of class war' and reminded the Congress members (particularly those in the Congress Socialist Party) that Congress policy embraced neither phenomenon. Nevertheless, the committee was obliged to acknowledge that 'the Congress does contemplate wiser and juster use of private property so as to prevent the exploitation of the landless poor, and also contemplates a healthier relationship between capital and labour'.[109]

As the political situation intensified, the Left's strength – and its volume – increased. The *Bombay Congress Bulletin*, an illegal publication during the resumed civil disobedience of 1932, spent several issues roundly denouncing the capitalists, taking particular aim at Thakurdas: 'His faith in Swadeshi is strictly proportionate to the profit it brings.' A later article, 'Are They Traitors or Not?' renewed the attack on the bourgeoisie. 'Such men do not, in their hearts, care a rap as to what happens to the country as long as they can do what they like.'[110]

The reaction of some elements of the bourgeoisie to the rise of the Left was in the nature of a frontal attack. In 1929, Dorabji Tata (together with Cowasji Jehangir and Ibrahim Rahimtoola), in reaction to the strike movement in Bombay, wanted to form a 'Capitalist Party' to take on the Left politically.[111] Even Birla (whose more considered approach will be examined below) said in June 1932, 'The Indian merchants will find great difficulties in dealing with Jawaharlal [Nehru]'.[112] He also denounced the formation of the Congress Socialist Party in 1934, claiming that the Congress Socialists depicted the Indian businessman 'as a blood sucker who has joined the vested interests of the Britishers for the exploitation of the masses'.[113] Nehru's speech at the Lucknow Congress in 1936 stampeded 21 Bombay businessmen (including Thakurdas, Jehangir, Walchand Hirachand, Mody and A.D. Shroff) into publishing a lengthy denunciation in *The Times of India* in May 1936. They were 'unequivocally opposed' to Nehru's socialism – all the more so since economic distress made it popular in 'the mind of the unthinking millions'. Business supported 'the national movement for the achievement of political freedom'. The Left divided and therefore obstructed it.[114] Mody told the paper some weeks later:

> His [Nehru's] meaning is clear and the programme is fairly definite. First, political independence, and the Socialist State, in which vested interests, property rights and the motives of profit will have no place at all. Let those whose minds are running in the direction of intermediate stages and pleasant halting places not forget that they are really buying a through ticket to Moscow.[115]

Birla, however, advocated a different approach – which eventually became the dominant one. He strongly discouraged Bombay's 'Capitalist Party'. He told Thakurdas that such an organisation would be 'the last body to put up an effective fight against communism'. Instead, 'we capitalists' should try to remove the causes of communism and bring into being a national government. 'The salvation of the capitalist does not lie in joining hands with the reactionary element.' He hoped 'the new association must come to grief eventually'.[116] When the Bombay manifesto appeared, he severely rebuked Thakurdas and Hirachand for signing it.[117] As against the direct assault, Birla argued for a strategy against the Left *within* the Congress – strengthening the Right and rallying around Gandhi.[118] Gandhi, he wrote to the Secretary of State, was 'alone ... responsible for keeping the leftwing in India in check'.[119] With the support of an enlightened business community, he could continue to do so.

The political collaboration of the Indian bourgeoisie with the Congress was made easier by the fact that there existed considerable areas of agreement in economic policy – even with the Left.[120] It has been made clear more than once that the bourgeoisie approved of state intervention and even of state ownership in the new Indian economy. In the extensive notes he made on the Swaraj government programme (adopted by the Karachi Congress in 1931), Sarabhai wrote that it was the duty of the state to develop industries – and government control should be exercised 'with a view to prevent misuse of power or inefficiency'. He went on:

> It must be admitted that the present order of things is wrong. When thousands have to toil on starvation wages or earning for the benefit of the few, a new order of things is necessary. The Measures proposed by the Congress, if they are successful, will constitute a Government on Russian model and will have to follow similar programme. In the interest solely of India, right of private property and ownership should continue to be recognised; but in order to provide funds to maintain a fair standard of living for all, those who get more than a particular amount, should, to the extent necessary, be taxed even if it means taking away the entire surplus in income.

In common with the Left, he advocated the abolition of the 'large landlord class which ... lives on the labour of the cultivators'. The state 'should buy over the properties of landlords ... and sell them to ... the actual cultivators'.[121] Even Mody conceded that '[t]he Capitalist system had much to answer for in its early stages'. Society had to adjust to meet changing conditions – and 'it must be admitted that the pace requires to be accelerated', as long as that did not mean the destruction of the system.[122]

Due to these overlaps, business was not continually at daggers drawn with the Left. In fact, some business representatives had links with some of its leaders. The Tata Iron and Steel Company, for example, was happy to accept Bose's attempts to mediate in the 1928 strike. The company chairman wrote to Bose that 'nobody appreciates more than me the work you have done for the Tata Iron and Steel Company Ltd ... Between us, we can and must make the industry prosperous'.[123] Birla found Bose 'friendly and amiable' (according to Rahimtoola). Birla went on:

> Mr Bose ... appreciates the necessity of co-operation with reasonable and advanced type of capitalists ... He is one of those who think industrialisation in many directions a quintessence of modern civilisation and therefore is ready to help the industries by protection and other methods.[124]

Chapter Seven

The Second World War

At the outbreak of war, the Viceroy Lord Linlithgow told India:

> Confronted with the demand that she should accept the dictation of a foreign power in relation to her own territory and her own subjects, Poland has elected to stand firm ... Nowhere do these great principles mean more than in India. There is no country that values them more highly than India, and none that has at all times been more concerned to safeguard them.[1]

The irony contained in Linlithgow's sentiments would not have been lost on the Indian political leadership.

The mounting international crisis of the late 1930s and the outbreak of war in Europe in September 1939 caused the British to bring to a halt the process, begun by the 1935 Government of India Act, towards a semi-independent Indian Federation. It was a process, as we have seen, in which the Indian bourgeoisie had invested a great deal of hope. The war now took precedence over everything else – and political obstacles to the war effort (including the working of the 1935 reforms) were swept aside.[2] The fact that war threw everyone off the path that they thought they were traversing serves once again to emphasise the continuing (and increasing) importance of state decisions in the inter-war period, culminating in the ultimate expression of state power – the war itself.

The defence of Empire

We would do well at this point to review India's strategic position from the imperial point of view, since this is what determined the British state's attitude to the political situation in India. It has been suggested that India's strategic importance had lessened somewhat by the late 1920s.[3] Bisheshwar Prasad, however, makes a strong case for its continuing role as a vital part of the Empire's defence. Just after the Legislative Assembly had declared that India's obligations in this regard should be no greater than the Dominions', India had 'to ear-mark portions of her armed forces for service outside her frontiers and largely in the interest of the British Empire'. By the late 1920s, he continues, 'it was evident ... that any major war would lead to a call on the Indian Army for guarding British interests in the East'.[4] There is no doubt that the late 1930s crisis turned an important strategic need into an absolutely crucial one. Now faced with the prospect of war with Germany, Italy and Japan, the British once again turned to India as their strategic hub in the East. In such a global conflict, India's role could not be confined (as it had been after the last war) to the provision of troops. Once again, the development of military industry in India became a question of strategic importance.[5]

There was a major difference this time around. During the 1914–18 conflict, industrialisation helped to develop India's productive forces, despite it being in concert with the Empire's war aims. During the Second World War, what was good for the Empire was no longer necessarily good for India. The development of industries needed by the Empire and fitted into an imperial division of labour did not represent development for India. The defence of the Empire and the defence of India were no longer the same thing (if they ever had been), which meant that, when representatives of the bourgeoisie declared themselves for the defence of India *and* in sympathy with Britain's war aims, they were straddling something of a contradiction.

But back to imperial strategy. The Garran Tribunal was set up by the British Government in 1933 to consider the perennial question of who should pay for the imperial obligations of the Indian army. It declared that 'the Army in India is a force ... which is specially available for immediate use in the East and which has on occasion been so used'.[6] Furthermore, it expressed the willingness of the government to pay £1.5 million per year for the pleasure. Under these arrangements, Indian troops were deployed over the next four years in Perak, Singapore, the Anglo-Iranian oil fields, Somaliland, Aden, Palestine, Hong Kong and Burma.[7]

As international tension increased, so too did the number of government committees stressing India's strategic importance. The Pownall Sub-Committee (of the Cabinet Committee on the Defence of India) made similar recommendations on the deployment of Indian troops outside India and also urged self-sufficiency in 'supplies of warlike material'.[8] The same year, an Indian military committee under General Auchinleck (Deputy Chief of the General Staff in India) urged that India's current capacity to manufacture munitions and weapons should be modernised.[9]

Finally in 1939, the Indian Defence Committee under Admiral Lord Chatfield reaffirmed that Indian forces were not merely for local defence but also for use against external threats. Indeed, external deployment was 'no longer a contract to perform something outside the sphere of their normal duties; it becomes an integral part of those duties'. Closer collaboration with imperial forces was needed, as well as 'making India as far as possible self-sufficient in the more essential munitions both in peace and war'.[10] This was to be undertaken despite the fact that 'Indian public opinion has lagged far behind' the pressures that the international crisis was exerting on the Empire.[11]

Given these extensive preparations, it is not surprising that India was swept straight into the war in 1939. Protestations against the lack of consultation from the Congress and the bourgeoisie indicated a lack of comprehension of India's now vital position in the imperial game plan. Of course, the British offered some recompense for this unseemly haste: Dominion status as an ultimate aim, after the war; and in the meantime, a consultative committee to advise the Viceroy.[12] This was, as we shall see, a long way short of satisfying India's political demands at this time. The gulf between what had seemed to be on offer under the 1935 Act and what was offered now illustrated the extent to which the war shouldered aside other considerations.

Meanwhile the British war effort, translated onto Indian soil, took its usual toll. The size of both the armed forces and defence spending rocketed upwards. Government controls and regulations expanded rapidly. In March 1945 the Government of India reported to London that India had given up to the war economy all mill-produced woollen textiles; all factory production of footwear and leatherwear; all of its timber output; 75 per cent of both steel and cement production; and over one-sixth of all mill-produced cotton textiles.[13]

Yet in the midst of the war economy, what was not taking place – despite hints in this direction by Garran, Pownall and Chatfield – was industrialisation. In fact, a careful reading of the Chatfield Report made this quite clear. The committee had reported not only 'an almost complete absence of any armament industry in India', but as well (with 'the possible exception of Tata's steel works'), no potential for creating one. Munitions production in India, then, relied on 'the expansion of the existing Ordnance Factories'. The report went on: 'The Indian Ordnance Factories are, and are intended to remain, free from any control by the Provincial [i.e. Indian] authorities. This point may be of some importance in political conditions as they may develop in the next few years.'

Just in case industrialisation did show signs of spreading beyond the existing factories and beyond the government's control, the committee recommended 'the co-ordination of these proposals with any similar plans that are contemplated in other parts of the Empire' – the imperial division of labour once again.[14] That division remained designed to ensure that Indian industries that might prove inconvenient competitors at war's end were not to be encouraged.[15] FICCI certainly felt that this was the British position. At its annual session in 1942, according to *The Statesman*, '[t]here were veiled suggestions by other speakers that ... the post-war trade interests of Britain and the USA were still influencing official policy'.[16]

The Government of India's attitude to war-time industrialisation was, for the most part, obstructive. The Secretary of State, Leo Amery, declared that it was 'impossible' to produce internal combustion engines in India. When, nevertheless, Indian plans were put forward for an automobile factory, the British Government blocked it on the grounds that it would take away skilled labour from war work.[17] When a skilled labour shortage appeared anyway, rather than training Indians, the Commander in Chief (Wavell) suggested importing militarised American labour ('soldiers, under military discipline') – 17 companies of them, to work on railways and docks.[18]

India's place in imperial strategy was made plain by a number of initiatives from the Government of India during the war:

The Eastern Group Conference

This conference was convened in New Delhi in October 1940 to co-ordinate the war effort of the British Dominions and possessions south and east of Suez.[19] The Viceroy opened the conference with the following remarks:

> All or almost all the countries represented here are producers of raw materials; some are fortunate in possessing more or less highly organised industries; and some are able to manufacture munitions of war on a fairly large scale... You may find when you come to consider the establishment of new manufactures, that it is convenient that one or more countries within the group, should concentrate upon particular items and that some general allocation of industrial responsibility will be inevitable.[20]

The conference threw Indian business into a frenzy of suspicion, exacerbated by the fact that no representatives of the Indian bourgeoisie were invited to attend. They were further unsettled by the more unguarded remarks of the Australia delegate who flatly declared that new war industries should not be started when they already existed in other parts of the Empire.[21] To the bourgeoisie, the Eastern Group Conference seemed to be another instance of the British arranging India's place in an imperial economy – not just for the duration of the war, but for the post-war world as well. As M.C. Ghia told the Indian Merchants' Chamber in April 1941, '[w]hile such an arrangement would suit admirably the interests of some of the advanced countries within the Group, it is very sinister as far as India is concerned'.[22]

The implications were pointed out by Chunilal Mehta: 'when certain articles are produced in say countries like Australia or South Africa, India may be asked not to attempt production of such articles and to rest satisfied with the other Empire countries producing those articles'.[23]

This did not augur well for Indian industrialisation. According to FICCI, it was strategically mistaken in the war context: 'it would not be prudent for one country to rely for several essential supplies or armaments . . . on another distant territory, even though it might be a part of the same Commonwealth'. FICCI demanded that the Government of India not enter into any agreements 'which in any way, would preclude India from establishing and developing her own key defence industries or which would check India's industrial development which is essential in war as in peace'.[24]

The Missions

While the Eastern Group continued its (secret) deliberations, a mission arrived from the British Ministry of Supply, led by Sir Alexander Roger. Its purpose was to boost the Indian war effort. Once again, no consultation with Indian industrialists took place. The mission recommended various ordnance factory expansions, the expansion of production in government workshops and railways, as well as several new ordnance factories (one of which was to produce Bren guns). But these limited and British-controlled initiatives remained unimplemented.[25] Small wonder when one considers the remarks of Guy Locock, a member of the Roger Mission and Director of the British Federation of Industry: 'in his report on the Mission's work, [he] expressed satisfaction at the fact that nothing was done by the Mission which would impair the post-war interests of British industry'.[26]

In March 1942 came the American Technical Mission (sometimes known as the Grady Mission) to examine the possibilities of defence production. Once again, FICCI was suspicious. 'It was apprehended', reported the Executive Committee, 'that American industrial interests were exercising an indirect but powerful influence on the war economy of India and there were plans for Anglo-American collaboration during and after the war'.[27] In fact, the Mission had more to do with Anglo-American competition after the war. It was not in the interests of the USA to encourage India's place in Britain's imperial schemes.[28] Instead – and just as worrying for the Indian bourgeoisie – the Americans appeared to want to integrate the Indian war economy into 'a general programme for the United Nations'.[29] Martin Wainwright says that while at first the Mission appeared neutral, 'it soon allowed the United States to be identified with Britain as a power willing to exploit India for its own ends'.[30]

Scorched Earth

Perhaps the most dramatic illustration of Britain's attitude to the defence of India's economy during the war was over the question of the 'Scorched Earth' policy – the wholesale destruction of economic assets at the last unction in order to deny them to the invader. Reports of wanton destruction of property by British forces prior to the withdrawal from Rangoon were enough to raise the question in India. The Government of India indicated that such a policy would be invoked if the Japanese invaded. This and the fact that they took several weeks to clarify their stand fanned the flames of disquiet. A scorched earth policy revealed a willingness to make a total sacrifice of the Indian economy in order to impede the progress of an enemy of the British Empire. Indian business reacted predictably. Time and again, the point was made that the state did not own most of the economic assets in question (unlike in the Soviet Union, where such a policy had been carried out). In India, Purshotamdas Thakurdas told FICCI:

> [W]here factories are put up by private capital and private enterprise I would like to put it very bluntly – do the Government expect that the masses and the classes both will contentedly look on when factories are being converted into scorched earth?[31]

The National Herald (a Congress paper) declared that '[o]ur industries owe very little to the Government who have no moral right to lay their violent hands on them for any reason whatsoever'.[32] Furthermore, as an unrepresentative government, the Government of India had no right to take such a decision.[33] Business protests were not universally taken at face value. *The Statesman* in Calcutta campaigned vigorously against the industrialists on this point.

> Recent speeches by prominent industrialists are shocking and shameful. The argument . . . that in India industrial property belongs to private persons and not to the State, is bound to seem to any truly patriotic man an argument why such a state of affairs is wrong. Courage Mr Birla! Revive Sir Pushottamdas! Think again, Official Spokesman! Play the man.

The newspaper went on to accuse the industrialists of defeatism, while one of its readers suggested they were fifth-columnists, on whom 'anti-Fascists' should keep a close watch.[34] To counter this, FICCI was at pains to present the issue as 'a question which concerns the people as a whole and not merely the industrialists or the propertied classes'.[35]

Eventually in April, the Governor of Bengal, Sir John Herbert, stated that, while stocks of rice and means of transport would be removed in the event of a Japanese invasion, 'there is no intention of indulging in wanton destruction of industrial wealth or civil necessities'.[36] Despite this, the question had been raised of what an unrepresentative and uncontrollable state, on a war-footing, *might* do if an invasion took place. For Indian capitalists it was one more argument – and an urgent one – for a state of their own.

From Britain's strategic imperatives flowed the Government of India's political strategy. That strategy now revolved around the absolute necessity of maintaining British control over India's defence and foreign policies. The vague promises of 1935–37, the half-glimpsed prospect of a loose Federation, the attempts to enlist Indian support to this end, all vanished under the blow-torch of wartime necessity.[37] The Chatfield Committee had proceeded on 'the principle that responsibility for the defence of India rests through the Governor-General and the Secretary of State for India, with the British Government and with no one else'.[38]

This was why the British Government's various constitutional suggestions during the war appeared so half-hearted. For the British state, they were a mere side-show to the main game, which was winning the war and preserving British power.[39] Having taken India into the war, bypassing both the Provincial Governments and Indian political opinion in general, it was clear Linlithgow's offer of concessions would be rejected as woefully inadequate. The Viceroy's second foray was the 'August Offer' of 1940, which proposed an expansion of his Executive Council, the establishment of a National Defence Council and, after the war, a body to devise a new constitution for India as a Dominion.[40]

Britain's offers were now hedged around with so many qualifications regarding the rights of (among others) minorities, princes and Europeans, it was hard to see how they could be implemented. Ghanshyamdas Birla wrote to the Viceroy, explaining the view of 'the man in the street':

> Since the achievement [of Dominion status] depends on the consent of at least princes, Muslims, Scheduled castes and British interests, for all practical purposes Dominion Status may never be achieved . . . On the other hand, the Act of 1935 has . . . been scrapped.[41]

As to the expansion of the Executive Council, this was 'a damp squib,' Ghia told the Indian Merchants' Chamber in July 1941. Those added were 'not representative of any large and influential section of public opinion'. Business, he said, wanted 'the real representative political parties in the country' in power at the centre.[42]

The Cripps Mission, in 1942, proposed a weak central government for India – made weaker by giving provinces the opportunity to opt out of Indian political structures. Sensing the danger in this, the Indian Merchants' Chamber wired the Congress that the option of provinces hiving off as separate and sovereign states 'will destroy fundamental central unity of the country and will result into causing perpetual internal conflict of interest'. The Chamber continued:

> Both from [a] military and economic point of view such divisions will tend to weaken India's position . . . Economically[,] proposed divisions will cramp India's capacity to develop her vast mineral resources . . . as independent States will naturally try attainment of economic self-sufficiency for themselves.[43]

What had become by this stage a British obsession with minority rights (especially of those willing to support the war effort) and a refusal to assume the unity of India, represented, at least in part, the desire for a weak central government that would allow the British to go on organising India's strategic role in the British scheme of world power. Fundamentally, both the August offer and the Cripps Mission failed 'because the British were not prepared to relax executive control over the Indian war effort'.[44]

The war simplified politics in India, at least from the British point of view. Once the Congress looked as though it would declare less than total support for the war effort, the Government of India was able to regress to a kind of pre-1935 Act position of unremitting hostility to Indian nationalism. This was a welcome return for some. Francis Hutchins suggests that '[t]he war, and Congress resignation of office in protest to it, provided the Indian Government with a welcome opportunity to stem the Congress tide'.[45] With Winston Churchill in power, they seemed to have a prime minister who would back them in this. The objective appeared to be – once again with British strategic interests in mind – to prevent both Congress disruption and a post-war handover (if it had to come) to a strong, Congress-dominated central government, which would have its own ideas about defence and industrial development. The Government of India therefore prepared itself, in the event of a new civil disobedience movement that could impede the war effort, for the total elimination of the Congress. This would include 'economic warfare' on Congress' wealthy supporters.[46]

In fact, British hostility towards the Congress now extended to what the Government of India called 'Big Business' as well. They regarded the two, correctly, as inextricably entwined.[47] In 1943, the Governor of Bengal wrote to the Viceroy that 'the greatest danger now lies in the insidious activities of the big financial and commercial interests behind Congress'.[48] The Governor of the Central Provinces and Berar enlarged on the theme:

> I have always regarded it as virtually axiomatic that the Congress could rely for ample financial support on a number of prominent industrialists. The reasons for this support are probably mixed – partly pure nationalism, partly a feeling that a national government will provide opportunities for Indian 'Big Business' to become even bigger, and partly a desire to 'insure' with a rising political party more or less as the German industrialists found it expedient to insure with the National Socialist Party.[49]

The Governor of Assam attributed Birla's support to 'the almost hypnotic influence which Gandhi exercises upon him and by a deep-seated religious Hinduism'.[50] The Viceroy's private secretary confided to his opposite number with the Secretary of State that, at the commencement of the Quit India movement, it was a matter of regret 'that the Birla brothers were not put away with the rest of the Congress leaders' as punishment for 'their crooked and always anti-British activities and the financial support which they gave again and again to subversive movements'.[51]

Relations between the Government of India were further damaged by the introduction of the Excess Profits Tax in early 1940. Premised on the notion that the war had 'created opportunities for the earning by companies and persons engaged in business of abnormally large profits', the tax sought 'to secure for the Government a considerable portion of the additional business profits', primarily by taxing profits in excess of those earned in the 'standard' year of 1935–36.[52] The industrialists protested vehemently. The Indian Chamber of Commerce in Calcutta cabled the Government of India's Finance Member: 'Proposed measure has created serious apprehension amounting to panic in commercial circles.'[53] The tax was seen as yet another indication of (at best) British indifference or (at worst) British hostility towards Indian industries. The Indian Merchants' Chamber declared that 'the present proposal... would act as hammer blows on all the dreams and visions of the commercial and industrial community and... would definitely put a stop to any scheme being set afloat for new industries'.[54] FICCI set up an 'E.P.T. Bill Sub-Committee', which co-ordinated protest letters, public meetings and deputations against the Bill.[55] But the Government of India remained intransigent. In fact, ignoring the protests, it not only pushed the tax through, it raised it in the following year's budget.[56]

The hostility of the British spawned two further ideas in their ranks. The first was that the Indian bourgeoisie not only strongly supported the Congress, but in fact, controlled it (in this, the British were in peculiar agreement with some sections of the Indian Left).[57] As was hopefully demonstrated in the previous chapter, such a notion represented a complete misjudgement of the relationship between the industrialists and the Congress. The bourgeoisie had allied themselves with the Congress, as a state coming into being. As will continue to be clear, it was an alliance in which the bourgeoisie were – and were willing to be – the subordinate partner.

The second idea emerged as Britain was harder and harder pressed by the Japanese. For its non-cooperation, Congress was routinely painted by the British as pro-Japanese. This came from the highest levels of the British Government. Churchill himself had declared that the Congress' 'Quit India' resolution (on which, more below) would be welcome in Tokyo. 'It may well be', he told Parliament darkly, 'that these activities by the Congress Party have been aided by Japanese fifth-column work on a widely extended scale and with special direction to strategic points'.[58]

Business was now regarded in the same light. At the very least, India's industrialists were thought likely to adopt a 'Pétainist' attitude to the war – that is, they would prefer capitulation to the economic loss involved in resistance.[59] No less a person than the Viceroy sent a 'Most Secret and Personal' letter to the Provincial Governors in November 1942 along these lines.[60] The Viceroy judged that the bourgeoisie's support for Quit India (see below) seemed odd – 'it is therefore necessary to look for ulterior motives'. Since business feared destruction of their property in a Japanese invasion, they wanted a government that would either be friendly to Japan or would be willing to make terms with them. A 'clique of financiers' was using Congress to this end, so that business could 'establish for themselves a position of financial domination in India comparable to that obtained by the "Big Four" in Japan'. If that were the case, 'it may well be . . . that "Big Business" is the *fons et origo* of the recent disturbances and the real link between the Congress and Japan'.[61] The fact that the Viceroy – and he was not alone – saw things in these terms was symptomatic of Britain's desperate situation in the East at this time. It also made any conciliation between British interests and those of the Indian bourgeoisie highly unlikely.

The defence of India

We have noted that by 1935, the preferred position of the bourgeoisie was to work through the Government of India Act, initially in the provincial governments, then to a Federation and finally, on to independence. Given this scheme, the bourgeoisie increasingly came to regard the contemporary Indian economy as theirs – or rather, as something they would share with the new state. The economic structure had therefore to be defended, both against external enemies and against those (governments or foreign investors, for example) who would undermine it from within. The bourgeoisie's careful political strategy was shattered by the outbreak of war. British plans for India's crucial role in the imperial war effort swung into action, stalling the progress towards Federation – and sending both business and the Congress back into militant opposition to British rule. It was true that most of the industrialists were prepared to co-operate with the war effort. Birla cabled the support of 'most of us who belong to the Gandhi school of thought' to Churchill.[62] Lala Shri Ram told FICCI in May 1940, 'We must at this stage give full cooperation to the British Government if not for anything else then for India's selfish interests'.[63]

Politically, however, the war marked a parting of the ways, which widened as the war continued. Linlithgow's statement, sweeping India, with unseemly haste, into a European war in September 1939 'ended the experiment of co-operating with the British in governing India, which Birla had believed could ultimately lead to the complete devolution of power into India hands'.[64] The fact that Britain had called a halt to that process was highlighted by Churchill's famous statement in November 1942 that he had 'not become the King's first Minister to preside over the liquidation of the British Empire'.[65] This was a clear indication, as the FICCI president G.L. Mehta pointed out, that 'no fundamental change was contemplated in the position of the Empire'.[66]

While they were willing to co-operate with the war effort (especially after Japan's entry into the war in December 1941), the capitalists had their own views on how that effort should be expended. They had a precise set of demands without which, they believed, the nation could not be mobilised and could not be properly defended.

The first of these was the demand for a national government. A FICCI manifesto, drafted by Birla in August 1939, stated that '[u]nless the democratic principles for whose vindication Britain claims that she is to fight are effectively translated into practice in India... India's willing co-operation would not be possible'.[67] But the issue was not simply one of democratic consistency. Without a national government (that is, one solely responsible to the Indian people) FICCI said, in the midst of the Quit India campaign, 'there can be no fully effective mobilisation of all the forces for the Defence of India or an adequate solution of the existing turmoil'. The Federation suggested that '[t]he vital importance of the co-operation of the people, as a whole, and of the industrial front in a modern war is not adequately realised by the authorities'.[68]

The second demand was for industrialisation. Thakurdas placed this in an imperial context at a town hall meeting called by the Governor of Bombay in June 1940: '[T]he equipment of India and [of] the Indian people to play their adequate part under an emergency like the present one was a duty of Great Britain towards the British Empire as a whole, let alone [towards] India itself.'[69]

But Indian industrialists were distinctly dissatisfied with the role allotted to India in imperial schemes. They would not agree simply to send 'battalions of Indian sepoys to the West'. They were unwilling for India to remain 'the hewer of wood and the drawer of water'.[70] Thakurdas was concerned that Britain wanted India 'to continue as a Dependency to be sent for at Great Britain's will and necessity'.[71] The industrialists pointed to India's lack of industrial preparation for the war situation – a lack brought about by various decisions of the British Government in the inter-war years. 'When the present war started', Chunilal B. Mehta told the Indian Merchants' Chamber in June 1941, 'India stood as unprepared as she stood in 1914'.[72] FICCI pointed to 'the helpless condition of this country in the supply of important war materials necessary for its defence'.[73] Business wanted defence and heavy industries established in India – and it wanted the state to establish them: 'The initiative for any planned programme should necessarily come from Government and it should be the anxiety of the authorities to push through such a programme.'[74]

The bourgeoisie's demand for industrialisation was not confined to defence industries or to the duration of the war. FICCI's position was that the development of industries was necessary 'for achieving a strong and self reliant national economy as well as making India an arsenal of the East'.[75] What was needed was an industrialisation plan – something which the Government of India assiduously refused to supply.[76]

The third issue for the bourgeoisie was the question of defence spending – how much was being spent, on what and by whom. This related back to the capitalists' concerns about the direction of India's economy, the question of national sovereignty and the prospects for industrial development. The FICCI Executive Committee noted with alarm the 'heavy and increasing scale of expenditure on Defence' in 1941. They concluded that 'it is imperative for the Indian public to have the fullest assurance that whatever additional expenditure is being incurred, is strictly for the defence of India and for the protection of India's interests' – something which was, of course, a long way short of the truth. The committee pointed out in the same communiqué that, despite the amount spent on defence, it was not having a particularly favourable effect on India's economy.[77] As far as Homi Mody was concerned, defence money was being spent on the wrong things. India, he told the Bombay Rotary Club, could not afford a Western-style army. It needed a small, highly mechanised army – 'together with a network of basic industries so that at a pitch the country could undertake the manufacture of planes, warships, tanks and guns'.[78] Mody's advice was directly contrary to the policy that the British were carrying out – precisely because it represented Indian needs rather than imperial ones. In 1944, FICCI, while acknowledging that 'the demands of the war must take precedence in war-time budgets', was still questioning 'whether the allocation of defence expenditure that has to be incurred by India . . . is really equitable and in her best interests'.[79] The solution was 'to establish popular control over the raising and spending of the expenditure necessitated by the war'.[80]

The British Governments would not accede to these demands. While Indian business saw them as crucial to the very war effort that the British were trying to promote, the British regarded them as contrary to their long-term imperial interests. In response to the demand for a national government, the Government of India was only prepared to expand (twice) the Viceroy's Executive Council. On the second of these occasions, the Indian Merchants' Chamber responded:

> The chief objective of the Government, at such a juncture should have been . . . to form a National Government at the Centre. The Council now formed cannot by any means be called 'National', and in certain respects may even be regarded as anti-national.[81]

As for industrialisation, the British had set the idea aside in the years leading up to the war and did not take it up again while the war raged.[82] The Commerce Member in the Government of India, A. Ramaswami Mudaliar, warned against further industrialisation. He was reported as saying 'it was not a wise policy for a country to aim at economic self-sufficiency', nor to aim at producing 'every kind of manufactured goods that we can think of'.[83] The Government of India obstructed attempts to set up automobile, air craft and shipbuilding ventures – even though they were clearly related to the war effort. The FICCI Executive regretted 'that so far as vital industries are concerned . . . Government have taken no action to encourage such enterprises even as part of the War effort'.[84] Nor would the government protect Indian war industries. 'Already', Birla told Thakurdas in June 1940, 'I have heard, that aeroplanes and motor cars may be manufactured, but perhaps not by Indians but by Englishmen'.[85] *The Hindu* speculated that 'foreign vested interests who see in the building up of new Indian industries the rearing of a potential trade rival' lay behind government obstruction. 'Now and then', mused the editor of *The Hindustan Standard*, 'one is afflicted with a doubt as to whether the policy of the Government in relation to India's industries, unsatisfactory as it is, is more backward than it was in the past'.[86]

Faced with the rejection of its demands, the bourgeoisie took its political stand by the side of the Congress leaders. Their support for Congress civil disobedience campaigns had perhaps wavered in the pre-war period, when it was thought that a constitutional path to freedom was opening up. With that path blocked, business support for the Congress was based on two elements. The first was that, as FICCI put it, 'without the attainment of political freedom, economic advancement of the country is not feasible, and to this end [business leaders] have always identified themselves with all endeavours to attain complete liberty for the country'.[87] The second was, in Thakurdas' words, the sense of 'a definite tendency on the part of the British element in India, both commerce and Government servants, trying to look ahead – according to their lights – and make sure of British influence here being supreme'.[88]

These two elements drove business back to the Congress – and to the acceptance of civil disobedience as well. The president of the Indian Merchants' Chamber reminded his members that although business wanted law, order and defence, it also wanted Dominion status as soon as the war was over – and therefore 'it must be understood that the business community cannot stand away from the people in general and from the national policy which India has accepted'.[89]

The British were keenly aware of the bonds between the bourgeoisie and the Congress leadership. The Governor of Bengal told the Viceroy in March 1943, 'That certain leading Indian financiers (e.g. Birla) are in the thick of Congress Councils and are providing the sinews of war for Congress is, of course, an open secret'.[90] The Intelligence Bureau provided the Viceroy with a list of businesses, businessmen and business organisations (seven were named) providing 'large-scale, all-India support for the Congress'.[91] When Churchill openly accused Indian business of being behind the Congress, the FICCI president, G.L. Mehta, responded that:

> Indian commercial organisations did not feel apologetic about the fact that they were an integral part of the national movement and were fully in accord with the essentials of the Congress demand for freedom and transfer of power . . . without the achievement of complete self-government, economic advancement of the people was not possible.[92]

Quit India

The Congress Working Committee decided in principle on a mass civil disobedience campaign in July 1942. The campaign would be launched under Gandhi's command. In early August the All-India Congress Committee passed the 'Quit India' resolution that signalled the beginning of the movement. The following day, the Congress leadership was arrested.

The bourgeoisie, despite some misgivings that we will examine in a moment, did not refuse to support the campaign – contrary to the Diwan of Travancore's opinion (expressed to the Viceroy) that 'they are making too much money now to participate fully in a campaign which is bound to affect them most prejudicially'.[93] Nor did they attempt to undermine it, which was the fear of the Left and the view of even moderate nationalists like Chakravarti Rajagopalachari, who wrote, 'Indian industrialists, while shedding copious tears for nationalism, are making their pile by quiet and uninterrupted services at the call of a bureaucratic Government'.[94]

On the other hand, the movement was not the brainchild of the capitalist class and they did not dominate it, as the British tended to suppose.[95] In fact, the bourgeoisie's approach to the onset of civil disobedience was characteristically cautious and its support was not immediate. Birla had expressed misgivings to Gandhi when the Congress approved a campaign of limited *satyagraha* in March 1940.[96] Later in the year, however, he wrote to Thakurdas that '[t]he Congress is . . . left with no other alternative than to launch non-co-operation . . . It does not want to fight, but what else can it do'.[97]

But his letter makes clear that he was expecting a limited, rather than a mass, campaign. By late 1942, Thakurdas was still of the opinion that his preferred strategy – 'a slow and steady process of exposing the motives of Great Britain' – was 'impossible with the policy adopted by the Congress'.[98] Likewise, the president of the Indian Merchants' Chamber opined that 'the country should now adopt, to a large extent, again, the parliamentary programme'.[99] FICCI's Nalini Sarkar was urging a reconsideration of the Cripps proposals as a way out of the constitutional dilemma.[100]

Such moderation was undermined by a combination of Britain sweeping India into the war, the abandonment of British interest in constitutional reform, British hostility to the Congress (exacerbated by Nehru's gaol sentence in 1940) and the war danger from Japan.[101] By 1941 Birla, at any rate, was prepared to endorse Gandhi's next move – including mass civil disobedience if necessary.[102] Two days before the Congress adopted the Quit India resolution, Thakurdas, J.R.D. Tata and Birla wrote to the Viceroy, acknowledging that '[i]f the movement is started, it must have grave results'. They went on: 'We have reason to believe that Gandhiji has no desire to create the very serious situation in India which is bound to be in consequence of starting Non-Co-Operation Movement.'

But power had to be transferred to India – and that, according to the businessmen, was the way to mobilise the population for war against the Japanese.[103] Birla and the others, together with the bulk of FICCI, swung their support behind the Quit India movement. The Intelligence Bureau reported that there was 'no room for doubt that the Congress movement, both overt and underground, has received substantial support from Indian "Big Business"'.[104] As this suggests, that support took various forms. Numerous public declarations of support were made. A joint conference of industrial and commercial concerns in Calcutta in August 1942 called on the Government of India to reverse its policies and open negotiations with the Congress.[105] G.L. Mehta, the FICCI president, condemned the arrest of the Congress leadership and declared that 'no amount of repression could reconcile Indians to continuance of the present unrepresentative system of Government or enthuse them for war efforts'.[106] As the campaign continued and repression mounted – 'unsurpassed in the history of British administration', according to FICCI – the Federation said it led to a 'growing conviction that Britain did not desire to give up her imperialistic domination over India'.[107]

An important measure of business support was its financial aid to the campaign. Before the campaign began, the Congress leader Vallbhabhai Patel solicited funds from businessmen for the struggle to come. The Intelligence Bureau noted Birla and 'the Ahmedabad Millowners generally' for their 'large scale financial support'.[108]

The bourgeoisie, however, were disturbed by the militancy of the campaign. This entirely predictable reaction by men of property was expressed by the FICCI Executive Committee in September 1942. The committee 'looked with horror upon the tendency to acts of violence and sabotage which would ultimately recoil on the country itself and bring in its train a vicious circle of repression and violence'.[109] Pursuing the same theme, Ram wrote to Thakurdas:

> I am afraid that this sabotage may one day start of private property also. Once the Goondas know this trick, any Government, whether Congress of Muslim League, will find it difficult to control it. Today Mahatma Gandhi may be able to stop it, but later on it may go out of their hands also.[110]

But these fears did not cause the bourgeoisie to stop supporting the campaign. Indeed, the militancy of elements of the bourgeoisie may have deepened as the campaign went on. The Intelligence Bureau was convinced that some industrialists – including the Ahmedabad and Calcutta mill owners, the Birla brothers and Tata – were financing strikes by their own workers in support of Quit India.[111] It was also widely rumoured that, when sections of the movement were driven underground by British repression, the bourgeoisie supported them in continuing the struggle.[112]

Business support for the movement and opposition to the government reached its height in February 1943 when Gandhi began a fast in protest against British repression. The fast was to last 21 days, but given Gandhi's state of health in gaol, there were real doubts as to whether he would survive it. This immediately became the new focus of the movement – and a new way for the Congress to illustrate British indifference. FICCI took up the issue at once, calling on the Viceroy to release Gandhi.[113] In a press communiqué the Federation expressed its 'grave concern' and also the 'widespread and deep-rooted distrust of British promises and intentions with regard to India's freedom'.[114] A meeting of business leaders organised by FICCI in Delhi called for Gandhi's release, as did one in Bombay.[115] As Gandhi's state of health slipped dangerously lower, the most dramatic response came from the business leaders on the Viceroy's Executive Council – Mody, Sarkar and their nationalist colleague M.S. Aney. Mody wrote later (in 1944) that, while the three had originally agreed with Gandhi's arrest, '[w]ith the starting of a fast by Gandhi, the position changed'. They told the Viceroy, 'it would be nothing short of a disaster for the country if the Mahatma were allowed to die in detention'. The British Government remained intransigent. The three Executive Council members therefore resigned their positions.[116]

During the Second World War, three elements cemented the bourgeoisie by the side of the Congress. Firstly, British losses to Japan and the approach of the war to India's borders seemed to indicate that the British state could no longer defend India's economic structure. Secondly, there emerged Britain's apparent preference for retreat and destruction of the economic structure rather than mobilising the nation through a political settlement with the Congress. Finally, there were increasing signs that Britain planned to do all it could to frustrate industrialisation in India in order to fit it into a post-war imperial economy. For the capitalists, the way forward was clear. Since they were comfortable with an interventionist state and not particularly disturbed by the leftwing rhetoric of some in the Congress, they would cast their lot with the Congress leadership and proceed, in the post-war world, to a free India.

There was, however, a problem.

Seeds of Partition

Tensions between the Hindu and Muslim communities had been evident since well before the war. It could be asked why they have not been addressed in this account until now. The short answer is that they were simply not relevant to the Indian bourgeoisie before the war. Even as communalism became more and more of a problem during the war years, it was not until the emergence of plans to partition India and form the state (or states) of Pakistan that the question touched on the bourgeoisie's material interests.

Bipan Chandra argues that 'the grouping of Indian capitalists as Hindu or Muslim had, till the late 1930s, no objective validity'. Muslim capitalists had no common interests as Muslims. Furthermore, if Hindu or Parsi capitalists (the vast majority) 'turned communal', their Muslim brethren would have been the losers.[117] The reason that, by this stage, the majority of capitalists were of Hindu or Parsi background was not because of their religion. Chandra says 'while colonial history guaranteed the growth and economic domination of the merchants and moneylenders, medieval history had guaranteed that they would be mostly Hindus'.[118] Non-Muslim capitalists did not oppress, exploit or exclude their Muslim counterparts. 'Certainly, some capitalists "ate" others up. But that is a basic feature of capitalism. There is no proof that any industrial capitalist or capitalist group was curbed or suppressed for being Muslim.'[119]

Businessmen from different religious backgrounds had common interests as businessmen – and their primary interest was 'to preserve and develop further the all-India market and to expel imperialism', not to suppress 'rival' communities. Communalism *obstructed* this aim.[120]

Thus, the support of 'Muslim' capitalists for communal aims was not strong. Until the 1940s, attempts by the Muslim League, its leader Mahomed Ali Jinnah and one of its major financial backers, Mirza Ispahani (a Karachi merchant) to establish specifically Muslim business organisations were less than successful. 'Instead', says Chandra, '[Muslim businessmen] participated fully in the secular all-India or regional business organisations'.[121] A Muslim Chamber of Commerce was set up in Calcutta in 1932 – but this was primarily to fill the seat reserved for 'Muslim Commerce' in the reformed Bengal assembly. It raised no specifically 'Muslim' issue until 1942. Up to that point, it acted in concert with FICCI.[122] The Muslim Chamber was reported as a participant in the protest against government repression during the Quit India movement.[123] Ispahani explained to Jinnah one of the obstacles to communalising the bourgeoisie in March 1944:

> A letter from Peshawar informs me that there are considerable difficulties in establishing a Muslim Chamber there. It appears that there is a Merchants' Association which is open to both Hindus and Muslims and all influential Muslim merchants are members of this Association.[124]

In fact, Ispahani himself continued to be listed as a committee member of FICCI in 1947–48 and 1948–49.[125]

The non-Muslim industrialists, for the most part, took a strong stand against communalism – even when it might have been seen as working in their interests. In the dying days of the Bombay textile workers strike of 1929, when Muslim workers were returning while Hindu workers were staying out, Birla wrote to Thakurdas that, while pleased to see the strike ending, 'I am a bit up-set by the way in which the communal tension has been utilised by the Mill-owners for ending the strike'.[126] Thakurdas himself warned against communal tensions around political reforms in 1930, urging the communities not to go forward 'on crutches of communal jealousies and bickering against imaginary wrongs'.[127] The bourgeois case on the communal question was summed up by Chunilal B. Mehta to the Indian Merchants' Chamber in May 1940:

> [S]o far as trade, business and industries are concerned up to now I have not seen any questions which affect only one community and not the other. If it is heavier taxation, all of us have to pay it; if it is any grievance or difficulty with regard to Railways or Customs, all the businessmen, whether Muslims, Hindus, Parsees, have to suffer therefrom. If India is backward

> in industrialisation, all of us suffer from the poverty of the land. Even though riots have occurred ... yet I find that as between businessmen of different communities, there is always a friendly feeling and good relations ... any movement which aims at having a cleavage between the two communities and partitioning the country in two should be strongly deprecated.[128]

Eventually, in the wake of the Muslim League's 'Pakistan Resolution' (on which more below), a national Muslim business organisation was set up, but even this was fraught with difficulty. Initially it was blighted by internecine Muslim politics.[129] However, Ispahani reported to his leader that, with factional disputes resolved and various affiliations accomplished, 'the Federation of Muslim Chambers of Commerce and Industry at Delhi has now grown into a robust and representative [body] of the Muslim merchants and industrialists of India'.[130] But Jinnah lost patience with its slow progress. He wrote to Ispahani (its main organiser) in April 1945:

> Have you been sleeping over the Federation of Muslim Chambers of Commerce and is it merely to remain a paper scheme? I am very much disappointed indeed that so much delay has been caused in holding even your first meeting ... unless you wake up and ginger up things, the business and commercial Muslim India [sic] will suffer very seriously'.[131]

The first meeting was held some ten days later. The aim of the Muslim Federation, Ispahani wrote later, was

> to co-ordinate their members' activities and make representations and demands to and from the Central Government of India at Delhi on behalf of its members and to protect and promote their interests in the field of Commerce and Industry.[132]

Through the Federation, he went on, Jinnah 'gave the Muslims one more instrument of unity and commercial and industrial strength for achieving independence'.[133]

By this stage, the question of a material base for a distinctly 'Muslim' bourgeoisie had, at least potentially, changed. At its Lahore session in March 1940, the Muslim League had passed the 'Pakistan Resolution'. This stated, in part, that 'the areas in which the Muslims were numerically in a majority as in the north-western and eastern zones of India should be grouped to constitute independent States in which the constituent units shall be autonomous and sovereign'.[134] Speaking in support of the resolution, Jinnah declared that Muslims were a 'nation' that should not be forced into a unitary government with Hindu India.[135]

Once the demand for a separate Muslim state had been made, whatever the constitutional niceties of its existence, an objective basis for specifically Muslim capitalist interests became real. If, in such a state, Muslim capitalists were privileged with the backing of the state, struggling 'Muslim' capitalists in India could identify an advantage in bringing Pakistan into being.[136]

But the formation of Pakistan would only be to their advantage 'if an exclusively Muslim state was created and its entire weight thrown behind Muslim capitalists to the exclusion of Hindu capitalists'.[137] Thus it was that the Pakistan project, once conceived as a separate state, achieved some measure of support from the Muslim (for the occasion) bourgeoisie, along with its political consequence: a non-unitary India with either a weak or non-existent central government.

For the time being, the non-Muslim bourgeoisie maintained its stand against communalism and against Pakistan. But this too was to change, as we shall see in the next chapter.

Chapter Eight

Planning and Partition

As hostilities ended in 1945, Britain was still attempting to fit India into its post-war strategic plans. In India meanwhile, the 'war state' necessitated by the conflict had led to a dramatic increase in state power – and an acceptance of that increase by capitalists, Congress and the Government of India alike. State intervention and state planning became the dominant themes of India's post-war economy. The Indian bourgeoisie gave itself over to this post-war vision, and that, in the end, determined its attitude towards partition.

Imperial strategy

By 1945 it was clear that Britain could no longer rule India in the old way.[1] In fact, most of Britain's rulers did not want to. War-time sentiment had evolved in an anti-colonial direction, manifested in the election of a Labour government in 1945. In addition, the imperial gaze itself had shifted somewhat, from India to South East Asia. Christopher Bayly and Tim Harper argue that the latter had become Britain's priority asset in the region.

> [South East Asia] exported two-thirds of the world's tin, and British Malaya alone provided half the world's production of rubber. Most of it passed through the port of Singapore. These industrial colonies were a major buttress of the sterling area.[2]

They had been regarded as vital to Britain's economic recovery before the war and remained so afterwards. Britain was also able to expand (albeit temporarily) its holdings after the war: 'the troops of the British Empire reconstituted the great crescent of land that Britain had occupied before 1941, and then fanned out beyond it'.[3] Thus, India's political and economic importance lessened. South East Asia was '[t]he region [that] was now crucial to Britain's Great Power status'.[4] Militarily, however, India's resources were still needed. South East Asia Command (the body set up by the Allies in 1943 to take charge of operations in South East Asia) wanted to deploy Indian troops in Burma, Malaya, Singapore, Thailand, French Indochina and the Dutch East Indies.[5] The British Government wanted to be able to use independent India as a military base for Eastern operations, as it was using Egypt and Iraq. To that end, both the Cabinet Mission plan (1946) and Lord Mountbatten's first plan (April 1947) envisaged military treaties between Britain and whatever successor states came into being.[6]

The war state

The Government of India strengthened and extended state economic powers and instituted a series of state controls during the war. Compulsory national service was introduced for skilled Indian technicians, as were powers to compel firms to release them for war production.[7] From May 1940, a large number of imports were controlled, and that control expanded as the war continued. 'Later in August 1941', writes Prasad, 'practically all description of import items was controlled and by January 1942, the remaining items of import were also brought within the purview of the import control system'.[8] Export controls were also introduced. The production levels, technical specifications, prices, movement and distribution of wheat, food grains, textiles, sugar and cotton were brought under state control.[9] In the coal industry, the state was empowered to take over mines and execute 'such changes as would be required for increase in quantity and quality of coal and coke'. Under the Defence of India Rules, the government could also direct companies to deliver specified quantities of coal to railway stations. In 1944, the Colliery Control Order 'exercised an effective control over the development, production, distribution and price of coal'.[10]

As in the First World War, state economic intervention was regarded as modern, equitable and efficient. These sentiments exercised a distinct pressure on economic thought during and after the war.[11] The Government of India certainly gave the impression that vigorous state economic activity would last beyond the duration of hostilities. In October 1941 it announced the appointment of a post-war reconstruction committee. In 1943 this was followed by the formation of six policy committees for reconstruction: land, roads and transport, agriculture, forestry, fisheries and education.[12] At the Reconstruction Committee's first meeting, the Finance Member, Sir Jeremy Raisman, stated that its objective was 'drawing up a co-ordinated All-India plan on broad lines and assisting in the development of Provincial plans in greater detail'.[13] According to the committee's deputy president, Jwala Prasad Srivastava, the question of state controls was 'a thorny one'. But he told the Committee that '[t]he planned development of Indian economy will necessitate a continuance for some time of economic controls and require considerable State initiative and help in the realms of tariffs, commercial policy, bulk control of imports and exports, etc.'[14]

The Reconstruction Committee's second report (October 1944) reiterated the need for state initiative and planning. It also stated that '[u]nder modern conditions a country without highly developed industries has no political future as the present war has demonstrated'. It proposed that the state should direct 'a substantial portion of the profits of [large scale] industries for further expansion'. Furthermore, the state should own and manage defence industries and control industries of 'national interest' – while leaving the rest to 'competitive, capitalist enterprise'.[15]

However, what was notably absent from the government's proposals was any programme of state-initiated industrialisation and the establishment of state industries. Industry was absent from the six policy committees, as it was from the Reconstruction Committee's second report. The Government of India was criticised by the American Technical Mission in 1942, whose report stated that 'under the emergency of war struggle, there must be unification, coordination, the restriction of initiative, the subordination of the profit incentive, and the complete concentration of the nation through its government on the defeat of the enemy'.[16] Another vociferous critic of the Government of India on this point was Sir Mokshagundam Visvesvaraya, the former Diwan of the princely state of Mysore and a prominent member of the All-India Manufacturers' Organisation. He wrote in 1944 that 'industries are conspicuous by their absence in all important announcements of the Government of India'. He went on:

> In this industrial age, it is the desire of the Government that the population of India should remain agricultural... During the war heavy industries have been kept out of the country... On the other hand there is no instance of Government having taken the initiative to start or establish any new heavy industry.[17]

He accused the government of neglecting or obstructing a long list of industries that included shipbuilding, steel, automobiles, aircraft, locomotives and machine tools.[18]

So while the Government of India seemed keen to encourage central direction and planning, it remained markedly less positive about state-initiated industrialisation.

The Congress and planning

The Congress became even more identified with a centrally planned economy during the war. In 1938, Congress premiers (in May) and Congress industry ministers (in October) had resolved to set up a National Planning Committee (NPC) for the future Indian economy. The Congress president, Subhas Chandra Bose, set the tone when he told the industry ministers that India needed 'an industrial revolution'. Would it be gradual, on British lines, or a 'forced march' as in the USSR? 'I am afraid that it has to be a forced march in this country', he said.[19] The industry ministers declared that 'the problems of poverty and unemployment, of national defence and of the economic regeneration in general cannot be solved without industrialisation'. For this, a national plan was needed.[20] The NPC started meeting in December under Jawaharlal Nehru. Its membership included Purshotamdas Thakurdas, A.D. Shroff and Walchand Hirachand from the business community.[21]

Nehru's guiding ideas are evident throughout the early activities of the NPC. In various memoranda and notes to committee members, he set out the principles that underlay his (and in general, Congress') economic thinking at this time. The first was the need for national independence ('an indispensable preliminary for taking all steps that might be found necessary for carrying out the plan') and national self-sufficiency.[22] Citing the resolutions of the 1931 Karachi Congress on state ownership and control (see chapter six), Nehru told the NPC, 'A legitimate extension of this principle would be to apply it to all large-scale enterprises...even if the State does not own such enterprises, it must regulate and control them in the public interest'.[23] He directly related the necessities of war-time state regulation to the virtues of post-war planning.

> War has compelled planning, though this planning is for the specific purpose of destruction. When the war ends, this planned economy and State control cannot be given up and there appears to be no possibility [of] a reversion to pre-war capitalism.[24]

Thus the NPC's general objective was 'a socialistic planned structure'. Nehru added: 'Private enterprise has certainly not been ruled out but it has to be strictly controlled and co-ordinated to the general plan'.[25]

It followed that the defence industries were first in line for state ownership.[26] Beyond defence, 'key industries' and public utilities were considered.[27] Nehru reported:

> Regarding Key Industries, the majority were of the opinion that they should also be State-owned, though a substantial minority considered that State control would be sufficient. It was made clear, however, that any control of such industries must be a rigid one. Public Utilities, it was also decided, should be owned by some organisation of the State.[28]

Sub-committees on the key industries continued the theme. The sub-committee on engineering industries said that they were essential for both development and defence – '[s]uch a key industry is the foundation for all Planning'. All such industries should be state-owned or controlled. In terms of new industries, such was the support on the sub-committee for central control that it advocated 'the concentration of... this heavy mechanical industry in one National Workshop situated in the coal mining area of Bihar-Bengal'. [29] Meanwhile, the sub-committee on manufacturing industries resolved that 'all monopolies which are injurious to public interests, or whose acquisition is beneficial to public interests, should be acquired by the State'.[30] The sub-committees on chemical industries, power and fuel, and currency and banking all wanted state ownership or control of the industries in their areas.[31] In addition, currency and banking wanted the state to 'prevent profiteering and control price levels', while general education proposed one year's compulsory labour service for all those between the ages of 18 and 22.[32] As Nehru wrote a little later, 'The more we thought of this planning business, the vaster it grew in its sweep and range, till it seemed to embrace almost every activity'. The process, he said, 'was inevitably leading us toward establishing some of the fundamentals of the socialist structure'.[33]

But the NPC's activities were halted by the outbreak of the war. Nehru argued in late September 1939 that '[t]here is no question of our stopping our work because of this war. Indeed our work has to be carried on with greater vigour'.[34] But the resignation of the Congress ministries 'added to our difficulties', while '[b]usinessmen were busier than ever making money out of war requirements and were not much interested in planning'. Furthermore, 'the government was not interested in our work and in fact viewed it with great disfavour'.[35] The NPC meetings of September 1940 would be its last. Nehru himself was arrested in late 1940 and the Government of the United Provinces informed the Committee that 'Government are unable to agree to his [Nehru] carrying on the work of the National Planning Committee while he is in jail'.[36]

The Congress was not alone in its promotion of state economic intervention. On the other side of what was now the communal divide in Indian politics, the Muslim League was promoting similar ideas. In March 1943, Mahomed Ali Jinnah had fulminated against 'landlords and capitalists' who presided over a 'vicious and wicked system'.[37] At the League's Karachi session in December, Jinnah was authorised to appoint a committee to prepare a five-year plan for development and industrialisation in the Pakistan zones.[38] Thus was born the All-India Muslim League Economic Planning Committee. Its chairman Ali Nawaz Jung told the first meeting that the need for 'some form of State interference' was 'increasingly evident', especially in defence, key industries, services and mineral resources. The committee's Draft Plan (submitted to Jinnah) contained much on the alleviation of poverty, a list of industries for nationalisation and the call for land reform.[39]

The activities of both the Congress and the League in this regard should be seen as part of the process of a new state (now perhaps two states) solidifying within the shell of the old. The process was much more advanced in the Congress case simply because its leaders had been at it longer – and in India, even an India minus 'Pakistan', they had the prospect of a viable industrial economic unit that could be centrally controlled and planned. We shall return to this question later in the chapter. In the last years of the British Raj, the state itself was undergoing a transformation. David Potter points out that by the end of the war, after some years of more Indian than European recruitment to the Indian Civil Service (ICS), 'Indian I.C.S. officers had moved up through steady promotion to occupy a dominant position within the colonial structure'. Worse than this for the British was 'the belief in London that the undivided loyalty of the Indian I.C.S. officers could no longer be relied on'. He concludes: 'The national movements were important as forces to which Indians in bureaucracies, both civil and military, could shift their loyalties at the point in time when they perceived that British power was weakening as a result of the war'.[40]

In the armed wing of the state, the experience of the Indian National Army (INA), the widespread military sympathy for those in the dock at the INA trials and the revolt in the Royal Indian Navy all demonstrated a shift of loyalty in the armed forces towards the national movement.[41] Not for nothing did Nehru tell the NPC, 'Now... the Congress is, to some extent identifying itself with the State'.[42]

The capitalist attitude

Not surprisingly, India's industrialists were occasionally disturbed by the more extreme statements on state ownership and socialism expressed by Nehru, the NPC and the Congress generally. They had no substantial objection to the nationalisation of defence and some key industries. This was, in their view, in the national interest. It reflected their basic agreement with the view that in India state intervention was required for industrialisation and for building a viable national economy. Beyond that, however, state ownership should be extended only on the grounds of necessity, when private capital was not forthcoming – not as a principle, as sections of the Congress and the Left argued.[43] Acknowledging that there was a disagreement between the bourgeoisie and sections of the Congress leadership here, we would do well to remember that the alliance between capital and the future Congress state was a contingent one. And as the national movement moved onto freedom, it was the future Congress state that was the dominant partner.

Business was in favour of state economic planning.[44] In his 1943 pamphlet, *Principles of Planning*, Ghanshyamdas Birla cited the experience of planning in the Soviet Union and Germany as well as in mobilisation for total war. Even under capitalism, the power of the state was expanding into new areas. Economic controls would continue after the war. Furthermore, '[u]nder the new planned economy the role of the capitalist entrepreneur will be different from what it was in the past'.[45] But, he asked, could there be planning without socialism – 'For let there be no mistake about it; socialism is totalitarian... It is bound to be dictatorial'. Birla advocated a 'middle way'. State ownership of defence industries, basic industries and some monopolies had to be tempered by democracy over the state. Meanwhile, 'private enterprise will function under definite limits subject to overall co-ordination by the planning authority'.[46] Other business leaders were advancing similar ideas.[47] FICCI was represented on the Government's Reconstruction Committee and its sub-committees. Ardeshir Shroff told the Reconstruction Committee that 'the business community was convinced that during the post-war period, it would be necessary for

Government to exercise far-reaching control in all fields of business activity – and that business would cooperate in the interests of economic development'.[48]

When the Congress set up the NPC, M.A. Master wrote to Hirachand that 'it is necessary for us to establish our contact with this committee'. He suggested that Hirachand should become a member – which he duly did, along with Shroff and Thakurdas.[49] Naturally, the business representatives were not comfortable with the demands for total nationalisation made by some of their fellow committee members. Nehru wrote that 'Big business was definitely apprehensive and critical, and probably joined up because it felt that it could look after its interests better from inside the committee than from outside'.[50] But the business representatives stuck with it – in fact, their ideas may have changed as a result. Nehru again goes on to say:

> The big business element was the biggest single group, and its outlook on many matters, especially financial and commercial, was definitely conservative... Yet the urge for rapid progress... {was} so great that all of us were forced out of our grooves and compelled to think on new lines.[51]

The Bombay Plan

Evidence of growing sympathy towards the Congress' economic philosophy can be seen in the fact that, when the NPC declined, leaders of the bourgeoisie themselves took the initiative in advancing the case for a planned economy. J.R.D. Tata proposed a meeting of major industrialists to create an 'informal Post-War Economic Development Committee'. The meeting took place in the Tata Board Room on 11 December 1942. Present were Thakurdas, Shri Ram, Birla, Kasturbhai Lalbhai, Shroff, John Mathai and Tata himself. Thakurdas was elected chairman.[52] This committee eventually produced *A Plan of Economic Development for India* – the Bombay Plan – the first part of which was published in January 1944, the second a year later. The Plan envisaged extensive state intervention. Baldev Raj Nayar comments:

> [T]here was something inherently contradictory in a group of businessmen devoted to the pursuit of private profit proposing a program of economic development on the pattern of the Bombay Plan, with its firm invitation to the government for the state regulation of the business community.[53]

Why did they do it? To answer the question, let me begin by reiterating a point made in chapter five. At this stage, the interests of the Indian bourgeoisie represented those of Indian society at large – and the leadership of the bourgeoisie was certainly fired with this idea.[54] Consequently, Indian capitalists wanted some input into independent India's economic policy. Tata said that the Plan 'started with a feeling that Indian businessmen must prepare themselves for what was to happen after the war... Businessmen and not only the Government should play a role'.[55] A further consideration was clearly a fear of state socialism which seemed to be advancing on all fronts after the war. In a memorandum for the first Post-War Economic Development Committee meeting Mathai, noting developments in Eastern Europe and China, wrote:

> The inevitability of a change in the direction of a socialist economy even in a country like India must now be recognised and leaders of industry would be well advised to take this into account and be prepared to make such adjustments as may meet all reasonable demands before the socialist movement assumes the form of a full-fledged revolution.[56]

The approach was to accommodate rather than confront socialist demands. The committee did not want to be seen as vindicating capitalism. Indeed', [t]he enquiry should begin with a study of the defects of capitalism, particularly in respect of planning and distribution'. Then it should look into 'what modifications are necessary to enable [capitalism] to render the best possible service to the country'.[57] The Plan itself argued that 'the distinction... between capitalism and socialism is somewhat overdone' and called for a 'judicious combination' of both. While continuing to defend private enterprise, it said it had to be 'enterprise which is truly enterprising and not a mere cloak for sluggish acquisitiveness'.[58] The Plan, Birla told FICCI after the release of the first part, sought 'to mobilise and harness the good will of all sections of the society, be he the leftist or the rightist, of all progressive minded citizens'.[59]

The Plan was characterised by the essential features of the bourgeois political and economic programme:

- The independence of India and the unity of the Indian economy.[60]
- Economic uplift and the reduction of inequality. The Plan recognised that the existence of the latter retarded the progress of the former. It acknowledged that private ownership had 'failed to bring about a satisfactory distribution of the national income'. It pledged to double per capita income within fifteen years while reducing inequalities of wealth and property.[61]
- Industry – and 'especially heavy industry' – as a priority. Attention had to be directed 'primarily to the creation of industries for the production of power and capital goods'. Basic industries were to be given 'priority over the other type of industries in the earlier years'. Otherwise, 'we shall naturally be at the mercy of foreign countries'.[62]
- State control.[63] The Bombay planners acknowledged that 'the State should exercise in the interests of the community a considerable measure of intervention and control'. These controls would be similar to those of the war economy – 'to which the country has become more or less accustomed; but they will be better coordinated and more systematically administered'.[64] There should be state ownership of defence industries and of new industries important to public welfare or security. Key industries should be state controlled – and here the Plan warned: '[t]he rights attaching to private property would naturally be greatly circumscribed'.[65]
- Land reform. In the *ryotwari* system, 'the State should take over the landlord's functions', paying the latter fair rent. Later, 'this

> may be commuted into a lump-sum payment and the landlord's claim finally extinguished'. This system should also be extended into the *zamindari* areas. The aim was 'the establishment of a class of peasant proprietors'. To help in this process, there should be 'a large extension of model farms'.[66]

The Plan was received with some enthusiasm in business circles and by the political elite. FICCI welcomed it as 'a remarkably constructive contribution' and endorsed its essential principles.[67] The second part of the Plan was given varying degrees of editorial approval by *The Hindustan Times* (17 January 1945), *The Bombay Chronicle* (18 January 1945), *Amrika Bazar Patrika* (19 January 1945) and *The Hindu* (21 January 1945).[68] Visvesvaraya (the former Diwan) declared himself 'in general agreement' with it, while C.D. Deshmukh said: 'I welcome the second part of the Bombay Plan as an expression of the readiness of acknowledged leaders of industry and commerce to submit to much wider restraints on business in the interests of planning'.[69]

The Plan gave rise to a series of alternative plans: from the Indian Federation of Labour (under the influence of M.N. Roy), the All-India Manufacturers' Organisation and from Visvesvaraya himself. Industries left out of the Plan wanted to be included. M.A. Master and G.L. Mehta met with Tata in June 1944 'in regard to the omission of shipping from the 15-year Plan of the industrialists'. Tata admitted the oversight.

> Mr Master stated that the question of a mercantile marine for a country like India was of vital importance in any scheme of national planning, not merely from the economic point of view but also from the point of view of national defence... a proper freight policy could be evolved so as to encourage industries and develop export markets only if shipping was under national control.[70]

The British meanwhile, maintaining their hostility towards the capitalists, regarded the Plan as a conspiracy on their part to make money (once again, in peculiar agreement with sections of the Left). The

Intelligence Bureaus told the Government of India that the Plan was 'to the moderate benefit of India's millions and to the immense profit of Indian "Big Business"'.[71] The bellicose former Finance Member, now Secretary of State for War, Sir Percy Grigg, told the War Cabinet:

> This is a wild and chimerical scheme for spending thousands of non-existent crores [10s of millions of rupees] in no time on lines very similar to the Soviet 5-year plans, except that in India the industrialists and they alone are to be exempted from totalitarian control.[72]

Such a view was entirely mistaken. If the Plan was 'totalitarian' (which it was not), then the capitalists had declared their willingness to be placed under its 'totalitarian' controls. In fact, the Bombay Planners' extensive concessions to state intervention and a state-run economy simply demonstrated their alliance with (not their domination of) the future Congress state.

The view of the Bombay Plan and its authors put forward here is not universally accepted. For Vivek Chibber, it is an illusion and he takes issue with it in his account of Indian economic development, *Locked in Place*. Firstly, he says, the Bombay Plan was a 'maneuver' by the capitalists, panicked into action by the Quit India movement and designed to forestall socialism.[73] Secondly, the bourgeoisie were in fact against state control and only prepared to accept 'capitalist planning'.[74] Thirdly, the bourgeoisie retreated even from this position at top speed after 1947.[75] Finally, this position of the bourgeoisie inhibited the construction of a 'developmental state' (à la South Korea) in India after 1947.[76] Let me take each of these points in turn.

If the Bombay Plan was a mere ruse, it was certainly a most elaborate one – a charade played out as much between its authors as for the benefit of the mass movement. There is no hint of this in the notes, letters, memoranda and drafts preceding the Plan available in Indian archives. The Plan was not a reaction to the Quit India movement. The mass phase of that movement had been repressed 'within a period of six or seven weeks' of its commencement in August 1942.[77] The first meeting of the Planners' committee was at the end of the year (and there is no mention of Quit India in its proceedings). The first part of the Plan was published in January 1944. As I showed in the last chapter, the bourgeoisie was not unduly alarmed by the mass movement. They were concerned about the advance of 'socialism' – though what this could possibly have meant in Indian conditions remains unclear. At any rate, Chibber himself tells us that '[b]y 1945 the Old Guard [i.e. the Congress Right] was firmly and visibly in control of the party machinery again' – so why at this point the industrialists should be pretending to be state capitalists is a mystery.[78]

The evolution of the Indian bourgeoisie *in favour* of state intervention, planning, state control and the reasons for it has been the burden of this book. One hundred years of Indian business history – of calls for state intervention, acceptance of war economy, of agreement with Congress economic policy – stand against Chibber on this point. He argues that the bourgeoisie, while furiously resisting 'socialist planning', was prepared to accept 'capitalist planning'. It is hard to understand what is being discussed here. In Indian conditions, socialism was an impossibility. Capitalist (and state) planning was all that was on offer. Chibber says that the Bombay Plan was not 'a clarion call by a nationalistic bourgeoisie to its peers, exhorting them to join in the forward march of national progress'. On the contrary, he continues, it was 'a document . . . opening the way for *capitalist* planning'.[79] In India, in the late 1940s, these two things were one and the same.

Chibber produces very little evidence for the bourgeoisie's 'complete *volte-face* [against 'a disciplinary planning regime'] within a two-year period, between 1945 and 1947'.[80] Even then he admits, '[i]t is not clear if their [the Bombay Planners'] views regarding the necessity of some degree of control had veered to a contrary position'.[81] And in the end, 'the future direction of industrial development was still to be guided by the state'.[82] No doubt some sections of business reacted adversely when they realised the extent of the Congress state's economic control. But the relationship of the bourgeoisie to the new state would evolve slowly over the next four or five decades. It did not snap smoothly into a 'state versus capital' confrontation in 1947.[83]

The Government of India and planning

The Government of India responded to the capitalists' vision of the new Indian economy in two ways. Firstly, a Department of Planning and Development was set up, under a new government member, Ardeshir Dalal – one of the Bombay Plan's authors. Secondly, the government issued a *Statement of Government's Industrial Policy* in 1945. This echoed the main features of the Bombay Plan. Its aims were to increase national wealth, increase employment and better prepare India's defence. A list of no less than 20 major industries was put forward for '[c]entral control in the interests of co-ordinated development'. The government intended 'to encourage and promote the rapid industrialisation of the country to the fullest extent possible'. Government would license industrial undertakings and set regional industrial targets in order to prevent 'lopsided development', which resulted from 'a tendency for capitalists to go in for schemes which promise quick returns'. The statement warned: 'In a planned economy it is impossible to do without controls'.[84]

The statement did little to convince the bourgeoisie that the British were about to take up the question of industrialisation – having acted and argued against it throughout the war. Indeed, New Delhi's tentative proposals for industrialisation faced considerable opposition in London. Grigg told the India Committee of the War Cabinet in May 1945:

> These proposals were the result of pressure from a very small group of West Indian and Marwari industrialists hostile to this country, and anxious to establish their own exclusive control in the Indian industrial field... industrialisation would aggravate rather than cure India's troubles.[85]

The India Committee reported a few days later that 'the majority of us consider that these proposals are not in the interests of the Indian masses, and would merely entrench Indian "big business" in a position of monopoly'.[86]

The Indian bourgeoisie was not inclined to embrace the Government of India's proposals on industrialisation primarily because it had long since ceased to believe that that government would or could act in the interests of Indian economic development. In other words, while the bourgeoisie would accept state intervention, planning and control, it would only accept them from an Indian government, not a British one. Back in May 1940, Nehru had told the NPC:

> Obviously, when we refer to the State we mean a free and democratic India; we do not mean the present State in India, subordinate to and controlled by foreign authorities and interests. It would be absurd for the present State in India to interpret our recommendations in its own favour and thus add to its own political and economic power.[87]

Mehta told FICCI's annual meeting in March 1943, 'I cannot really see the reason for this sudden enthusiasm for nationalisation that is overtaking our Government at this time of day . . . before we think of nationalising our industries, we have to think of nationalising our Government'.[88]

The bourgeoisie versus partition

As was noted in the last chapter, the mainstream bourgeoisie was implacably hostile to the partitioning of India. Capitalists from Muslim backgrounds were largely indifferent to the issue until the Muslim League passed the Pakistan Resolution in March 1940. Non-Muslim industrialists maintained their opposition to the Pakistan demand.[89] FICCI's executive committee told the press in September 1942 that 'the communal problem has lent itself most to exploitation for impeding political advance' and called for 'an amicable settlement'.[90] Thakurdas told Sir Francis Low that he believed that the British Government would not partition and permanently weaken India and pointed to 'the danger of Pan-Islamism being encouraged in the North of India'.[91] Birla encouraged Thakurdas to meet with Jinnah 'to find out what exactly it is that he wants'. Thakurdas met first with Liaquat Ali Khan (December 1940) and concluded that 'it was not a question so much of pressing Pakistan . . . as to ensuring that the Mohammedans will get freedom from what the Muslims call "jabarjasti" [oppression] of the Hindus'. When he met with Jinnah, he discovered that for him, an agreement was only feasible along communal lines – 'only with this fundamental point of negotiation between a leader of Hindus [Gandhi] and a leader of Muslims [Jinnah]'.[92] M.C. Ghia told the Indian Merchants' Chamber in April 1941 that '[t]he idea of Pakistan is the most unfortunate idea, wrought with the gravest dangers to this country. Surely to talk of vivisecting India and bifurcating her in two or three portions, is a gospel of destruction'.[93]

As Pakistan became a more serious proposition, businessmen moved from general condemnation to a more serious analysis. In *An Alternative to Pakistan* (1943), Ardeshir Dalal argued that 'the day of the small independent sovereign state has passed . . . The tendency is towards the formation of larger and larger political units'. If partition were to take place, '"Pakistan" will emerge out of it a comparatively poor resource-less state'.[94] Homi Mody and John Mathai submitted a memorandum on Pakistan that was appended to the Sapru Committee Report in 1945.[95] Their purpose, they said, was 'to indicate what the economic consequences of separation are likely to be if it is decided upon for political reasons'. Perhaps surprisingly (or not, given the atmosphere arising from the war), the two businessmen identified defence as 'the crux of the problem' for Pakistan. They said that 'the revenue surpluses of Pakistan . . . will fall short of the requirements of defence by a large margin'.[96] In addition, economically, partition would break up 'an optimum unit [India] for economic development in terms of area, population and resources'. Both Pakistan and 'Hindustan' would suffer, but the former more so. They concluded that 'the division of India into separate sovereignties would spell stagnation and probable disaster'. Only close post-partition co-operation in both the economic and defence fields would make it workable at all.[97]

In a note to the Sapru Committee, Nalini Sarkar argued, somewhat prophetically, that if defence and economic co-operation (as advocated by Mody and Mathai) were possible after partition, he could 'see no reason why it should not be available in abundant measure within a united India . . . the act of separation itself will create further ill feelings, making co-operation difficult and impossible'.[98]

Industrialisation, he said, required economic unity and a sharing of the resources of Pakistan and 'Hindustan'. If India were divided, 'the Hindu area would have almost a monopoly of the mineral wealth. Consequently Pakistan would be placed at great disadvantage in respect of industrial development'. Divided India then 'would be condemned to a standard of living which may be even lower than what it is today'.[99] However, Sarkar pointed out that this kind of logic simply collapsed in the face of Jinnah's remarks to *The New York Times* in September 1942, when he said: 'If we are willing to live sensibly and poorly so long as we have freedom, why should the Hindus object? . . . The economy will take care of itself in time'.[100] Sarkar doubted whether Pakistan would have that time. But, he wrote, '[i]f the Muslims accept poverty as a badge of honour then we may conceivably have nothing to say'.[101]

If Pakistan were to be created on the basis of Muslim-majority districts rather than whole provinces,[102] it would contain very little industry. Jinnah was aware of this. He told the Muslim League Planning Committee in November 1944, 'Among the Mussalmans there are hardly any large concerns controlling really solid and big industry'.[103] Sir Reginald Coupland agreed: 'Indian industry, in fact, is located mainly in Hindu areas; it is financed and owned mainly by Hindu capitalists; it provides a livelihood mainly for Hindu labour'.[104] He calculated that in 1938, 'Pakistan' (Punjab, Sind, British Baluchistan and the North West Frontier Province – with no change in borders) contained just over 6 per cent of the industrial companies of British India.[105] 'West Pakistan' was overwhelmingly agrarian, while industry in 'East Pakistan' depended on the territory encompassing Calcutta.[106]

There were also few Muslim industrialists. At the time of partition there were less than 100 associations of Muslim businessmen in India, the overwhelming majority of these 'being of the single trade type' and very few located in the future Pakistan.[107] Jinnah had considerable difficulty finding suitable members for the Muslim League Planning Committee.[108] Various Muslim industrial families (the Ispahanis, Adamjees, Dadas, Habibs and others) eventually helped establish a number of 'nation-building' industries for Pakistan.[109] But the weakness of these industrialists was indicated by the fact that, according to Ispahani, Jinnah himself was the driving force behind these industries.[110] Their zeal for the cause was not as great as it might have been. They eventually moved to Pakistan – but

> it is important to remember that many of them had not initially intended to do so . . . many of these families had planned to carry out their business activities in both of the new independent states, while remaining in their original place of residence [i.e. in India].[111]

Pakistan too was headed towards a state-dominated economy.[112] This arose, however, not on the basis of a strong state allied to a strong bourgeoisie, but rather from the weakness of both.[113]

Thus partition certainly did not appear to be any kind of logical economic proposition. Why then did the Indian bourgeoisie eventually agree to it?

The acceptance of partition

For the kind of economy that they envisaged, the leaders of the bourgeoisie demanded the economic unity of all of India and a strong central government that was able to implement an economic plan. As Pakistan approached, the former was sacrificed in order to save the latter.[114]

The Bombay Plan stated that '[t]he maintenance of the economic unity of India' was 'an essential condition of any effective planning'. The kind of development that the Plan advocated was not feasible 'except on the basis of a central directing authority'.[115] Ramanathan Chettiar (South Indian Chamber of Commerce) told FICCI in March 1947 that '[t]he guidance and control of the Centre is most required to keep the different Provinces and States in the common fold'. Ramdas Kilachand (Bombay Seed Trades' Association) drew the meeting's attention to the disruptive rivalries and restrictions between provinces during the war. 'All these must now definitely end', he said, and 'for purposes of trade and communication, geographical India should be treated as a single unit'.[116] The Congress too remained committed to economic unity. 'This kind of development [the even spread of industry]', Nehru told the same meeting, 'will not take place if you look at the planning problem on a partial or parochial basis, or a provincial basis, or on a regional basis'.[117]

The British, however, pressured by the Muslim League, were moving in quite the opposite direction. If India was to remain as one, the League demanded that power should reside in the provinces, or groups of provinces, through which, in the majority-Muslim provinces, Muslim rights could be protected. Britain's successive plans followed this trajectory. The Cabinet Mission plan of 1946 was designed precisely to devolve power to provinces or groups thereof. Prime Minister Clement Attlee's February 1947 statement to Parliament announcing Britain's intention to leave in mid-1948 foresaw transferring power 'whether as a whole to some form of central Government for British India, or in some areas to the existing provincial Governments, or in such other ways as may seem most reasonable and in the best interests of the Indian people'.[118] The British schemes became more and more 'Balkanised' – that is, they envisaged a weaker and weaker centre – right up to the final (pre-partition) 'Plan Balkan' in May 1947. FICCI's 1947 annual meeting expressed great alarm at this trend of events.[119]

The only way, then, to preserve a centralised state, in the face of Muslim League demands for a devolved one, was to let the League have its Pakistan and to organise the Indian economy without it.[120] As *The Eastern Economist* remarked, '[w]hat is, therefore, politically practicable may not be economically satisfying or adequate'.[121]

India's non-Muslim industrialists therefore gradually came to accept that partition was the lesser of two evils. Ram had written to Thakurdas in August 1942 that

> we should not pay any price for Independence to the Muslims either in the way of Pakistan or increase in percentage of seats in the Centre or residual powers with the Provinces. If the Hindus made this mistake then it will be nothing short of suicide.[122]

Mody and Mathai said in their Note to the Sapru Committee Report 'Although in our opinion a division of the country is to be deplored, we should be prepared to consider it if there were no other basis for an agreed settlement'.[123] Medha Kudaisya concludes that 'by the mid-1940s the groundswell of opinion within big business was receptive to the idea of partition'.[124]

Birla was the businessman who had probably thought about the question the longest. He wrote later, 'I somehow or other not only believed in the inevitability of Partition but always considered this as a good way out of our difficulties'.[125] In December 1940 he told Thakurdas, 'I argued with him [Gandhi] that we could not object to Separation in case the Muslims really wanted it'.[126] When it seemed inevitable, he was firmly of the opinion that Muslim-majority districts, not whole provinces, had to be the basis for Pakistan.[127]

Thus it was done. The bourgeoisie, in partnership with the new state, wanted to get on with the economic job.[128] Master told FICCI in March 1948:

> [A]lthough politically separate, both the new States should, in their best interests, arrive at a friendly understanding regarding vital policies that they should adopt for building up their economic and industrial future... Once the partition was an accomplished fact, the country soon realised that the only way to overcome the terrible shock which it had received was to make immediately the best use of the independence it had secured.[129]

Although the immediate economic losses and disruption, especially in the border areas, were severe, 'the overall cost of partition to Indian big business was relatively small'.[130]

Economically, then, the bourgeoisie had calculated correctly. Pakistan apparently represented no irrevocable economic loss – and they got their interventionist state, replete with industrialisation, economic regulation and five-year plans. The point here is that by 1947, the bourgeoisie was so utterly committed to state intervention and planning that it was prepared to sacrifice Indian unity to get it. Economically, in the initial stages, this probably appeared to have been the right choice. Politically, however – and eventually economically too – there was a price to be paid.

CONCLUSION

One of the purposes of this account has been to answer the perceptive questions posed by an operative of the Government of India's Intelligence Bureau in March 1943:

> What exactly is the relationship between Congress and Big Business? If Congress is receiving the support of powerful businessmen, what is the real motive behind that support? Are they backing Congress for personal, local or national reasons? ... is Congress making use of Big Business for its own ends, or is Big Business using Congress as a tool to further possible schemes for an ultimate capitalist hegemony?[1]

The state and capital bring into being certain production arrangements (relations of production in Marxist terminology). They are different kinds of arrangements because their purposes are different. The state needs to produce sufficient war-making capacity to defend itself against, and to compete with, rival states. Capital needs to produce profit. At a certain point, capitalist production methods become necessary for efficient production to take place. Since the state requires efficient production for efficient war-making, it is often the state that encourages capitalism. This was the position that the British found themselves in during the First World War, though they decided to avoid promoting industrialisation in India by integrating its economy into an Imperial division of labour.

As capital becomes stronger, the two sets of production relations compete for resources – that is, they wrestle for domination. The

Indian bourgeoisie wrestled with the British state in this way until, as a result of the anti-colonial movement (of which the bourgeoisie was an integral part), that state was removed.

My account ends here, in 1947 (or thereabouts) because I would argue that something real and important happened in that year. The Indian struggle for independence was not a charade, or merely changing the colour of the rulers, or maintaining 'neo-colonial' domination. It was the beginning of the bourgeois revolution in India. It brought into being a new, independent state power, dominated by the Congress, with worked-out ideas on a new economic structure for India in which the state would figure strongly. It was aided in this venture by a politically conscious bourgeoisie prepared to accept a state-dominated economic structure.[2] It established national independence; the authority of a central state over (most of) India; a national market; and the conditions for reorganising the economy – most importantly, for our purposes, conditions in which Indian industry and Indian business could flourish.

It differed from the 'classical' bourgeois revolutions in that, while it enjoyed the support of a mass movement for 40 years or so, it was achieved by an alliance between the leadership of a new state and that of the bourgeoisie. Economically and numerically, the Indian bourgeoisie recognised its own weakness. A political leadership, capable of mobilising masses, and a new state, capable of organising the economy, were vital to its future. It found both these things in the Congress and therefore, as this account has tried to show, subordinated itself to the future Congress state.

That subordination did not lessen after independence. In fact, it increased and there were early signs that the capitalists realised that this was happening. Ghanshyamdas Birla told the secretary to the Cabinet Mission that '[h]e was afraid that the Congress would want to try Socialistic experiments which would be damaging'.[3] The FICCI president, Lala G. Lall, told the organisation's annual meeting in March 1947 of the Federation's 'severe disappointment and grave concern at the general attitude and the concrete proposals in the Budget Speech [of the Interim Government] regarding commerce and industry'. He singled out '[l]ack of any definite economic and financial policy, imposing unduly heavy burdens on industry and commerce ... coupled with threats of nationalisation'.[4] After Independence, Birla maintained that '[u]nwise speeches made by Ministers in the first rush of enthusiasm were scaring off both domestic and foreign capital alike'.[5] Homi Mody wanted to call a meeting of industrialists in January 1948 to consider the Congress Economic Programme Committee's decisions, 'in view of their extremely radical character', which would have 'disastrous reactions on the industrial structure of the country'.[6] When the new government issued its first Five-Year Plan in December 1951, it was roundly criticised by business on predictable grounds: 'anything that allowed for the expansion of Indian business was welcomed, but anything that led to the regulation or restriction of that sector was opposed'.[7]

But it was too late. Given events in the rest of the world, the state-directed path to development seemed overwhelmingly plausible, despite the whimpers of private enterprise. Post-independence euphoria, the towering popularity of the Congress and the widespread enthusiasm for planning and for the idea that the state should triumph over private interests were hard to beat. And, as we have seen, many of these sentiments existed within the bourgeoisie itself. The capitalists found themselves both dominated by, and profoundly entangled with, the new Congress state. The Indian state produced capitalism of a sort. But it was a capitalism subject to the state's political will, not one devoted to the pursuit of profit.

However, the re-emergence of capital's trend towards globalisation has fatally weakened the state-centric approach to economic development. Everywhere, capital as a production relation is becoming stronger at the expense of the state. This represents the continuation – and, in the advanced economies, the completion – of the bourgeois revolution as capital frees itself from the integuments of national states. That process resumed in India with the reforms of 1991.

I will leave the reader with that final thought. The final word I will leave, once again, to the Intelligence Bureau, which concluded its report to the Viceroy in 1944 in this way:

> The support given by Indian 'Big Business' to the Congress movement may be compared with that given by Russian "Big Business' to the Mensheviks before the Russian revolution and

that given by German 'Big Business' to the Nazis. In both instances, 'Big Business' failed conspicuously in the end to dominate the government which it had helped create and there is no reason to suppose that Indian 'Big Business' will prove any more successful in realizing any ambitions that it may have in this direction.[8]

NOTES

Introduction

1. For an explanation of why this happened at this time, see David Lockwood, *The Destruction of the Soviet Union: a Study in Globalization* (Macmillan: Houndmills, 2000).
2. Stanley A. Kochanek, 'Liberalisation and business lobbying in India', *Journal of Commonwealth and Comparative Politics* 34, 3 (November 1996), p.155.
3. Hilton L. Root, 'A Liberal India: the triumph of hope over experience', *Asian Survey* 38 (5) (May 1998), p.511; Kochanek, 'Liberalisation', p.158.
4. Stanley A. Kochanek, 'Briefcase politics in India: the Congress Party and the business elite', *Asian Survey* 27, 12 (December 1987), pp.1280–3; Kochanek, 'Liberalisation', p.155. Tripathi suggests that the term should really be applied 'to Indira Gandhi's tenure alone', Dwijendra Tripathi (ed.), *The Concise Oxford History of Indian Business* (New Delhi: Oxford University Press, 2007), p.183). The system certainly reached its height under her rule.
5. Root, 'Liberal India', p.526; Kochanek, 'Liberalisation', p.157.
6. Tripathi, *Concise History*, pp.185, 194, 197.
7. Kochanek, 'Liberalisation', p.158.
8. Gita Paramal & Margaret Herdeck claim that the regime now 'required business to take a permanent genuflected position before politicians, and vice versa' (Gita Paramal & Margaret Herdeck, *India's Industrialists* (Washington: Three Continents Press, 1985), p.385). Of one of the most famous success stories of this era, Dhirubhai Ambani's Reliance Industries, Tripathi says: 'It is widely believed that the Ambanis' success was to a large extent due to Dhirubhai's ability to manipulate, using fair and foul means

alike, the government machinery to his advantage' (Tripathis, *Concise History*, p.191).

9. Tripathi, *Concise History*, p.191.
10. Kochanek, 'Briefcase', pp.1283, 1300.
11. See Karl Marx, 'Preface' in *A Contribution to the Critique of Political Economy* (Moscow: Progress Publishers, 1970 [1859]). My account of historical materialism owes a great deal to G.A. Cohen, *Karl Marx's Theory of History* (Oxford: Clarendon, 1991).
12. Marx, *Preface*, p.21.
13. For an elaboration of this argument, see David Lockwood, 'Historical materialism and the state', *Critique* (June 2006), pp.163–78.
14. The distinction is made by Alex Callinicos, 'Bourgeois revolutions and historical materialism', *International Socialism*, 43 (1989), p.116.
15. Karl Marx & Frederick Engels, *Manifesto of the Communist Party* (Moscow: Progress Publishers, 1966), p.37.
16. Frederick Engels, 'Socialism: Utopian and scientific', in K. Marx & F. Engels (eds), *Selected Works* (Moscow: Progress Publishers, 1970), pp.384–5.
17. Callinicos, 'Bourgeois revolutions', p.124.
18. Robert Brenner, 'The social basis of economic development', in John Roemer (ed.), *Analytical Marxism* (ed.) (Cambridge: Cambridge University Press, 1986), p.32.
19. Engels, Afterword in 'Socialism: Utopian and scientific'.
20. 'At all events, I am sure the conservative people who have introduced capitalism into Russia, will be one day terribly astonished at the consequences of their own doings.' Engels to Danielson, 22 September 1892 (www.marxists.org/archive/marx/works/1892/letters/92_09_22.htm).

Chapter One Industry and Industrialists before 1914

1. To such an extent that *The Times of India* commented: 'It would seem that one of the dearest privileges of the Secretary of State for India is to go shopping on behalf of his dependencies' (12 September 1882, cited in Radhe Shyam Rungta, *The Rise of Business Corporations in India, 1851–1900* (Cambridge: Cambridge University Press, 1970), p.134. The president of the sixth Industrial Conference in Allahabad told his audience in December 1910, 'We should agitate for the abolition, or at best reduction, of the gigantic Store Department of the India Office in England.' (*The Leader* (Allahabad), 31 December 1910.
2. 'Industrial capitalism came to India as an unintended by-product of British economic penetration and political control' (Helen B. Lamb, 'The Indian

business communities and the evolution of an industrialist class', *Pacific Affairs* XXVIII 2 (June 1955), p.102.)

3. Karl Marx, 'The future results of the British rule in India', in Karl Marx and Frederick Engels (eds), *On Colonialism* (eds) (Moscow: Foreign Languages Publishing House, n.d [1853]).
4. Bhubanes Misra, *Evolution of the Indian Bourgeoisie – Part One* (Calcutta: Indian Institute of Management, n.d), pp.21–2; R.M. Lala, *For the Love of India: the Life and Times of Jamsetji Tata* (New Delhi: Penguin Portfolio, 2006), pp.99–100.
5. Shiva Chandra Jha, *Studies in the Development of Capitalism in India* (Calcutta: Firma KL Mukhopadhyay, 1963), p.178. The phenomenon of war as a driver of industrialisation will be a recurring one. The Tata family (of which, more below), having accumulated capital in the American Civil War, put it to good use during the Abyssinian War of 1868, in which they gained the contract to supply the British troops (see Jha, *Studies in the Development*, pp.174–5).
6. Jha, *Studies in the Development*, p.171.
7. Colin Simmons, 'Indigenous Enterprise in the Indian Coal Mining Industry c. 1835–1939', *Indian Economic and Social History Review* 13 (1976), p.195; Neil Charlesworth, *British Rule and the Indian Economy, 1800–1914* (London: Macmillan, 1982), p.36.
8. Amartya Kumar Sen, 'The pattern of British enterprise in India, 1854–1914: A causal analysis', in Rajat K. Ray (ed.), *Entrepreneurship and Industry in India, 1800–1947* (Delhi: Oxford University Press, 1992), p.110.
9. Morris D. Morris, 'Towards a reinterpretation of nineteenth-century Indian economic history', *Journal of Economic History* XXIII 4 (December 1963), pp.614–15.
10. Morris, 'Towards a reinterpretation', p.616.
11. Sunil Kumar Sen, *Studies in Industrial Policy and Development of India (1858–1914)* (Calcutta: Progressive Publishers, 1964), p.156.
12. *The Leader*, editorial, 12 November 1909.
13. Government of India, *Indian Industrial Commission 1916–1918, Report* (Calcutta: Superintendent of Government Printing, 1918), p.74.
14. Howard Cox, 'International business, the state and industrialisation in India: Early growth in the Indian cigarette industry, 1900–19', *Indian Economic and Social History Review* 27 3 (1990), p.297.
15. Advertisement in *The Leader*, 6 January 1910.
16. In particular the Bombay cotton manufacturers examined by A.P. Kannangara in 'Indian millowners and Indian nationalism before 1914', *Past and Present* 40 (July 1968), pp.147–64. Business sided with the

Moderates in Congress rather than the Extremists on the question of the boycott (p.156).

17. Indian National Congress, *The Madras Congress and Conferences 1908* (Madras: G.A. Natesan & Co., 1910), p.55.
18. M.P. Srivastava (ed.), *Constitutional and National Development in India (Montagu-Chelmsford Report)* (New Delhi: Ess Ess Publications, 1981), p.211.
19. Quoted in *Commerce*, reprinted in *The Leader*, 6 January 1912.
20. Sir John Hewett speaking on 1 December in *The Leader*, 3 December 1910; 'The exhibition', *The Leader*, 3 December 1910. Gokaran Nath Misra had told the Benares Industrial Conference in April 1910 that 'a vigorous policy of industrial development' would 'unite all classes and draw them through material progress along the paths of political peace'. (*The Leader*, 8 April 1910).
21. Srivastava, *Montagu-Chelmsford Report*, p.212. The Indian Industrial Commission thought this was the fault of government: 'Government was unfortunately not equipped to meet the tide of enthusiasm half-way; to guide it to success by expert aid and business advice; and to place the country on the path of sound industrial development by the provision of systematic technical and commercial education'. (*Indian Industrial Commission Report*, p.74.)
22. Cited in Kannangara, 'Indian millowners', p.151.
23. Quoted by Alfred Chatterton in 'The effect of protective tariffs', originally in *The Hindu*, reprinted in *The Leader*, 14 December 1910.
24. The biographer of Purshotamdas Thakurdas comments: 'In the context of present-day India [1957] with its Five-Year Plans, its river valley schemes and its power and irrigation projects, it is interesting to recall how even in those distant days, two decades before the outbreak of the second world war, the minds of progressive Indians were reaching out in similar if more modest directions.' (Frank Moraes, *Sir Purshotamdas Thakurdas* (Bombay: Asia Publishing House, 1957), p.26.)
25. Indian Industrial Conference, *The Congress and Conferences of 1905* (Madras: G.A. Natesan & Co., 1906), p.108.
26. Indian National Congress, *The Madras Congress and Conferences 1908*, pp. 91–2.
27. R.N. Mukherji, *Presidential Address* (Industrial Conference, Allahabad 1910) (Allahabad: Secretary of the Industrial Conference, 1910), p.5. See also the report on the Behar Industrial Conference in *The Leader*, 19 April 1910; A. Latifi, *The Industrial Punjab: a Survey of Facts, Conditions and Possibilities* (Bombay & Calcutta: Longman Green & Co., 1911), p.xix.
28. 'Notes on India', *The Leader*, 13 December 1909. In one of its regular appeals for state-sponsored education in and aid for industry, the newspaper further declared that the mining industry should not be run 'by men whose home

is not India, who carry away the product of their mines to foreign lands and reap enormous profits themselves'. (*The Leader*, 23 February 1910.)

29. Indian National Congress, *Report of the Proceedings of the Third Session of the Indian National Congress, 1887* (New York: Vintage Books, 1993 [1887]), p.65.
30. See Harkishen Lal's speech to the 1909 Industrial Conference, in which he called for a 'Sympathetic State' (*The Leader*, 6 January 1910); and Gangadhar Chitnavis in the Legislative Council on 17 March 1913, quoted in Roper Lethbridge, *The Indian Offer of Imperial Preference* (London: P.S. King & Sons, 1913), p.135.
31. *Indian Industrial Commission Report*, p.80. See also Latifi, *The Industrial Punjab*, p.xxvi.
32. Speech to 1st Industrial Conference 1905 in Indian Industrial Conference, *The Congress and Conferences of 1905*, p.108. Lethbridge wrote that up to the war, 'every year and throughout the year, the representatives of the Indian peoples ... have demanded, in season and out of season, the necessary protection for their industries'. (Lethbridge, *The Indian offer*, pp.4–5.)
33. Opening Address, 4th Industrial Conference Madras 1908 in Indian National Congress, *The Madras Congress and Conferences 1908*, p.4.
34. *The Leader*, 21 April 1910. See also 'India and protection', *The Leader*, 20 December 1910.
35. R.N. Mukherji, *Presidential Address*, p.4. See also the report of Madan Mohan Malaviya's opening address to the 6th Industrial Conference (1910) in Allahabad, *The Leader*, 31 December 1910.
36. Thomas M. Ainscough (HM Senior Trade Commissioner in India & Ceylon), *Report on the Conditions and Prospects of British Trade in India at the Close of the War* (London: HMSO, 1919), p.19; Srivastava, *Montagu-Chelmsford Report*, p.211; Molesworth at 1st Industrial Conference 1905 in Indian Industrial Conference, *The Congress and Conferences of 1905*, p.123 (emphasis in the original).
37. Letter of 10 March 1910 in Vinay Bahl, 'The emergence of large-scale steel industry in India under British colonial rule, 1880–1907', *Indian Economic and Social History Review* 31 4 (1994), p.444.
38. Indian Industrial Conference, *The Congress and Conferences of 1905*, p.108.
39. At the Bombay Millowners' AGM, April 1906, quoted in Kannangara, 'Indian millowners', pp.153–4.
40. Indian National Congress, *The Madras Congress and Conferences*, 1908, p.39.
41. *The Leader*, 23 April 1910.
42. It is therefore rather too simplistic to charge that the Government of India's pre-War industrial policies were entirely of the 'laissez faire' or 'night watchman' variety (Morris D. Morris, 'Indian industry and business in the age of

laissez-faire', in Divijendra Tripathi (ed.), *State and Business in India: A Historical Perspective* (New Delhi: Manohar, 1987), p.124; Morris, 'Towards a reinterpretation', p.615; Partha Sarathi Gupta, 'State and business in India in the age of discriminating protection', in Tripathi, *State and Business,* p.157), nor that it had 'no policy' for development (Krishan G. Saini, 'The economic aspects of India's participation in the First World War', in DeWitt C. Ellinwood & S.D.Pradhan (eds), *India and World War I*, (Delhi: Manohar, 1978), p.161), nor that its policy was one of 'neglect' (Misra, *Evolution of the Indian Bourgeoisie*, p.14) or 'unfriendliness' (Lovat Fraser, *Iron and Steel in India: A Chapter from the Life of Jamshedji N. Tata* (Bombay: The Times Press, 1919), p.6).

43. *Indian Industrial Commission Report*, p.75.
44. Cited in S. Ambirajan, *Classical Political Economy and British Policy in India* (Cambridge: Cambridge University Press, 1978), p.226.
45. Sen, *Studies in Industrial Policy and Development*, p.111.
46. Quoted in Sen, 'A causal analysis', p.119.
47. Stephen P. Cohen, 'Issue, role and personality: the Kitchener-Curzon dispute', *Comparative Studies in Society and History* X 3 (April 1968), p.341.
48. Fourth Budget speech to the Legislative Council, 26 March 1902 in George N. Curzon, *Lord Curzon in India, 1898–1905*, Thomas Raleigh (ed.) (London: Macmillan, 1906), p.103; Sixth Budget speech to the Legislative Council, 30 March 1904 in *Curzon in India*, p.138; Seventh Budget speech to the Legislative Council, 29 March 1905 in *Curzon in India*, pp.158–9.
49. Seventh Budget speech to the Legislative Council, 29 March 1905 in *Curzon in India*, p.159. The Indian Industrial Commission report noted, however, that, after Curzon's departure, 'it is believed that this department by no means took the form originally contemplated by Lord Curzon' (*Indian Industrial Commission Report*, pp.75–6).
50. Cox, 'Indian cigarette industry', p.299.
51. Curzon in 1903 in Sen, *Studies in Industrial Policy and Development*, p.99.
52. N.J. Shah, *A History of Indian Tariffs* (Bombay: Thacker & Company Ltd., 1924), pp.315–17. The India Office also rejected imperial preference at this time – but on the grounds that 'its adoption would give rise to demands for other changes in the fiscal system of the country'. (Shah, *History of Tariffs*, p.317.)
53. R.M. Lala, *The Creation of Wealth: the Tatas from the 19th to the 21st Century* (New Delhi: Penguin Portfolio, 2004), p.xxvi. When the Tata Iron and Steel Company was floated, the appeal for capital was made in Swadeshi-like terms (Sen, 'A causal analysis', p.125).
54. Bahl, 'The emergence of large-scale steel industry', p.431.
55. Resolution of the Finance Department in *Gazette of India*, 5 August 1882 in Rungta, *Rise of Business Corporations*, p.130.

56. 'Private enterprise in India – iron', *The Economist* (11 November 1882), pp.1400–01.
57. Bahl, 'The emergence of large-scale steel industry', p.432; Rungta, *Rise of Business Corporations*, p.132. But there was confusion in British ruling circles on this point. Only a few weeks later (between rejecting Ripon's proposals in November and ceasing to be Secretary of State on 16 December), Hartington told the Government of India that he agreed 'to the importance of development to the utmost of local industries and manufacturing, and of rendering India as independent as possible of home supplies'. (Bahl, 'The emergence of large-scale steel industry', p.429). Meanwhile, over at *The Economist*, while their India correspondent clearly approved of the Government of India's scheme, the editor gravely warned at the end of the article: 'So long as the Indian Government confines itself to the work of collecting and disseminating accurate information regarding the resources and requirement of the country, it will do good. When it goes beyond this it is travelling beyond its province' (*The Economist*, 11 November 1882:, p.1401).
58. Rajat K. Ray, *Industrialization in India: Growth and Conflict in the Private Corporate Sector, 1914–1947* (Delhi: Oxford University Press, 1979), p.240.
59. Sen, 'A causal analaysis', p.134.
60. Government of India to the Chamberlain enquiry, 1895 in Bahl, 'The emergence of large-scale steel industry', p.418. See also Sen, 'A causal analysis', p.124; Rungta, *Rise of Business Corporations*, p.134.
61. F.R. Harris, *Jamsetji Nusserwanji Tata: a Chronicle of his Life* (Bombay: Blackie & Son Ltd., 1953 [1924]), p.156.
62. Tata & Sons to Industry and Commerce Member, 18 February 1905 in Tata Central Archive File No. 108: TISCO 1904–16.
63. Miller continued, 'you must not make an appeal to us simply on the ground of benefit to India'. To which Dorabji Tata replied, 'No, not at all, it is only that India would benefit as a result'. (London meetings between Robert Miller, managing-director of the Bengal-Nagpur Railway Company and Tata Iron and Steel representatives, 1904–5, Tata Central Archives, File 108, TISCO 1904–16.)
64. Tata Central Archive File No. 108, TISCO 1904–16. So grateful was TISCO for state assistance in this and following years that in 1909, the company offered the Government of India a seat on the board 'in order that the Government may be fully acquainted with what is going on, and be able to control to a certain extent any apparent extravagance'. (TISCO management in Bahl, 'The emergence of large-scale steel industry', p.455.)

65. Padmini Swaminathan, 'State intervention in India: A case study of the Madras presidency', *Indian Economic and Social History Review* 29 (4) (1992), p.481.
66. Chatterton to A.G Cardew, secretary to the Madras Government, Revenue Department, 6 December 1908, in Swaminathan, 'State intervention in India', p.500.
67. Opening Address to the 4th Industrial Conference in Indian National Congress, *The Madras Congress and Conferences 1908*, pp.40–1.
68. *Indian Industrial Commission Report*, 107. See also Swaminathan, 'State intervention in India', p.491.
69. Swaminathan, 'State Intervention in India', 486 & 491.
70. Swaminathan notes 'the near unanimity amongst most of the officials in the [Madras] provincial government as regards the express need for state assistance in fostering indigenous industries and in helping in the encouragement/development of new industries'. (Swaminathan, 'State intervention in India', p.499.)
71. *The Leader*, 20 January 1910.
72. See the report on the Benares Industrial Conference in *The Leader*, 12 March 1910.
73. *Indian Industrial Commission Report*, p.76.
74. He did so because, according to Gokaran Naith Misra, 'in his opinion there could no longer be any doubt that the public eagerly desired a vigorous policy of industrial development' (speaking at the Benares Industrial Conference, reported in *The Leader*, 8 April 1910).
75. Government of India, *Papers relating to the Industrial Conference held at Ootacamund in September 1908* (Madras: Superintendent, Government Press, 1908), p.2.
76. Government of India, *Papers Relating to the Industrial Conference*, pp.80–4, 184–7, 194–7.
77. Note of dissent 19 September 1908 in Government of India, *Papers Relating to the Industrial Conference*, p.225. For other expressions of British dismay see 'Interpellations at the Viceroy's Council', *The Leader*, 4 January 1911.
78. Note by Chatterton 12 September 1908 in Government of India, *Papers Relating to the Industrial Conference*, p.188.
79. The recommendations of the Naini Tal Industrial Conference, although 'warmly recommended' by the United Provinces Lieutenant Governor and 'extended ... hearty support by the Government of India', were rejected by Lord Morley in early 1910. (*The Leader*, 26 February 1910; 29 March 1910.)
80. L/E/7/1302 Secretary of State Lord Morley to Viceroy, No. 50 Revenue, 29 July 1910.
81. *The Leader*, 4 January 1911. Swaminathan comments: 'when a provincial government [Madras] attempted to depart from the accepted norm of a passive

role of "night watchman" ... the attempt was soon aborted and the provincial government reprimanded for daring to address the Imperial authority to reconsider its decision'. (Swaminathan, 'State intervention in India', p.480.)

82. Conference resolution XI of 30 December 1910, reported in *The Leader,* 31 December 1910. See also 'The state and industry in India: Lord Morley's mistake', *Indian Daily News* (n.d.) reprinted in *The Leader,* 18 December 1910.
83. Swaminathan, 'State intervention in India', p.503.
84. *Indian Industrial Commission Report*, pp.79–80.
85. Neil Charlesworth, 'The problem of government financing in British India: Taxation, borrowing and allocation of resources in the inter-war period', *Modern Asian Studies* 19 3 (1985), pp.522–3; Cox, 'Indian cigarette industry', p.299.
86. L. Abrahams to the Secretary of State, 24 January 1910 in Cox, 'Indian cigarette industry', p.301. A compromise was reached between the two governments on this. The slightly higher duties had just the effects on the Indian tobacco industry that Abrahams had predicted. (Cox, 'Indian cigarette industry', p.310.)
87. Lethbridge, *India's Offer,* p.4.
88. Cox notes 'the intense disagreement between London and Calcutta on the question of tariff protection in the decade before the outbreak of World War I and the extent to which certain officials in Whitehall sought to obstruct the process of industrial development in India at this time'. (Cox, 'Indian cigarette industry', p.292.)
89. T.W. Holderness to the Secretary of State in Cox, 'Indian cigarette industry', p.306.
90. Lord Hardinge of Penshurst, *My Indian Years, 1910–1916* (London: John Murray, 1948), pp.3–4.
91. See for example Keith Jeffery, '"An English barrack in the oriental seas"? India in the aftermath of the First World War', *Modern Asian Studies*, XV (3) (1981), pp.369–72; John Gallagher & Anil Seal, 'Britain and India between the Wars', *Modern Asian Studies*, XV (3) (1981), pp.388–401; Brian R. Tomlinson, *The Political Economy of the Raj 1914–1947: The Economics of Decolonization in India* (London: Macmillan, 1979), pp.105–6, 179.
92. D.I. Macauley (Captain), 'India in Imperial defence', *Proceedings of the Central Asian Society* (London: Central Asian Society, 1910), p.3.
93. Ray, *Industrialization in India*, p.240.
94. French notes that late eighteenth-century classical economists 'did concede ... that the needs of national defence gave the state the right to overcome the dictates of economic freedom. The theory of *laissez-faire* never prevented the state from interfering in the economy for the sake of national defence' (David French, *British Economic and Strategic Planning, 1905–1915* (London: George Allen & Unwin, 1982), p.9.)

95. John McGuire, 'The world economy, the colonial state, and the establishment of the Indian National Congress', in Mike Shepperdson & Colin Simmons (eds), *The Indian National Congress and the Political Economy of India, 1885–1985* (Aldershot: Gower Publishing Company, 1992), p.48; Purshotamdas Thakkurdas papers, File No. 115, Nehru Memorial Museum and Library, New Delhi.
96. Note by Lord Roberts to the Committee on Imperial Defence 8 June 1891, p.11. Committee on Imperial Defence papers, Reel 1.
97. D. Chakrabarty & C. Bhattacharyya (eds), *Congress in Evolution: a collection of Congress Resolutions from 1885–1934* (Calcutta: The Book Company Ltd., 1935), pp.75, 80, 81, 110.
98. Hardinge, *My Indian Years*, p.32.
99. W.J. Macpherson, 'Investment in Indian railways, 1845–1875', *Economic History Review* 8 (2) (1955), p.179; Helen B. Lamb, 'The "state" and economic development in India', in Simon Kuznets et al. (eds), *Economic Growth: Brazil, India, Japan* (Durham NC: Duke University Press, 1955), p.476; Roopa Srinivasan, Manish Tiwari, Sandeep Silas (eds), *Our Indian Railway: Themes in India's Railway History* (New Delhi: Cambridge University Press (India), 2006). The prevention of famine was also a key consideration in the state development of railways. The 1880 Famine Commission urged state construction of railways and of industry in general (Sen, *Studies in Industrial Policy and Development*, p.102; Lamb, 'State and economic development', p.478). This can also be seen as a strategic consideration – to prevent a weakening of India's human resources and political unrest, both of which famine produced.
100. Lord Roberts, Note to the Committee of Imperial Defence, 8 June 1891, p.10. Committee of Imperial Defence papers, Reel 1.
101. *Report of a Committee appointed to consider the Military Defence of India*, 24 December 1901, recommendations 3–6. Committee of Imperial Defence papers, Reel 1.
102. Charlesworth, *British Rule and the Indian Economy*, p.58.
103. Sen, *Studies in Industrial Policy and Development*, pp.100–04. Sen calculates that 75 per cent of the railway track was state-owned by 1914.
104. Charlesworth, *British Rule and the Indian Economy*, p.59; S. Ambirajan, *Classical Political Economy and British Policy in India* (Cambridge: Cambridge University Press, 1978), p.227: Sen, *Studies in Industrial Policy and Development*, pp.105–13, 118–21.
105. *Indian Industrial Commission Report*, p.26; Sen, pp.123–5, 128; Charlesworth, *British Rule and the Indian Economy*, p.60.
106. *Indian Industrial Commission Report*, pp.25–6.

107. G.G. Jones, 'The state and economic development in India 1890–1947: The case of oil', *Modern Asian Studies* XIII (3) (1979), pp.359, 360, 368.
108. Charlesworth, *British Rule and the Indian Economy*, p.71.

Chapter Two The Great War

1. Reported in *The Leader* (Allahabad), 10 September 1914.
2. Government of India, *India's Contribution to the Great War* (Calcutta: Superintendent of Government Printing, 1923), pp.75–8, 102. Hardinge confirms these figures and adds 'enormous quantities' of tents, boots, clothing and saddlery, plus all the Indian planes and personnel of the Indian Air Force (Lord Hardinge of Penshurst, *My Indian Years, 1910–1916* (London: John Murray, 1948), p.103).
3. C.W.E. Cotton (Collector of Customs, Calcutta), *Handbook of Commercial Information for India* (Calcutta: Superintendent of Government Printing, 1919), p.101.
4. Stephen P. Cohen, *The Indian Army: its Contribution to the Development of a Nation* (Berkeley: University of California Press, 1971), p.69.
5. *The Leader*, 9 August 1914.
6. Reported in *The Leader*, 9 & 10 September 1914.
7. Government of India, *India's Contribution*, p.160.
8. The war gift and higher import duties are reported in *The Leader*, 3 March 1917. For background see Clive Dewey, 'The end of the imperialism of free trade: the eclipse of the Lancashire Lobby and the concession of fiscal autonomy to India', in Clive Dewey & A.G. Hopkins (eds), *The Imperial Impact: Studies in the Economic History of Africa and India* (London: The Athlone Press, 1978), p.42; Brian R. Tomlinson. 'India and the British Empire, 1880–1935', *Indian Economic and Social History Review* 12 (October-December 1975), pp.351–2.
9. Hardinge, *My Indian Years*, p.102. He went on: 'when India's need became pressing and requests were made for drafts [contingents of soldiers], machine-guns, aeroplanes, bombs etc., they were in almost every case refused'. This was a significant observation, considering the role that India would be expected to play as the war expanded.
10. Government of India, *India's Contribution*, pp.225–6.
11. Mesopotamia Commission, *Report of the Commission appointed by Act of Parliament* (Cd 8610, 1917). British Library, India Office Record: L/PS/20/257/1, p.10. The Mesopotamia Report continued: 'The Indian Army was thus suddenly and unexpectedly called upon to participate largely in an external warfare [sic] for which no preparation had been made, as the contingency of such a conflict had been assumed both by the Home and Indian Governments to be outside the sphere of reasonable probability.' (pp.10–11).

12. For the effects of this on the warring European societies, see David Lockwood, 'War, the state and the bourgeois revolution', *War & Society* 25 (2) (October 2006), p.53–78.
13. Despite Morris' contention that 'few of the wartime manufacturing novelties carried much weight and can be ignored here'. (Morris D. Morris, 'The growth of large-scale industry to 1947', in Dharma Kumar & Meghnad Desai (eds), *The Cambridge Economic History of India, Volume 2: c.1757–c.1970*, (Cambridge: Cambridge University Press, 1983), p.606.)
14. Government of India, *Defence of India Act of 1915* (Lahore: Superintendent of Government Printing, 1917), sections 2, 8 & 11. The Act was also designed for use against sabotage. John Keenan, manager of the Tata Steelworks, recalled: 'within an hour after we heard of the declaration of war, the Germans held a secret meeting and then refused in a body to make munitions for use against the Fatherland.' These Germans were interned under the Defence of India regulations in Ahmednagar. (John L. Keenan, *A Steel Man in India* (London: V. Gollancz Ltd, 1945), p.45.)
15. *The Leader*, 9, 11 & 12 August 1914.
16. Cotton, *Handbook of Commercial Information*, p.101.
17. Cotton, *Handbook of Commercial Information*, pp.220–2; Thomas M. Ainscough (HM Senior Trade Commissioner in India & Ceylon), *Report on the Conditions and Prospects of British Trade in India at the close of the War* (London: HMSO, 1919), p.109.
18. Government of India, *India's Contribution*, pp.109–10.
19. Government of India, *India's Contribution*, p.146.
20. British Library, India Office Record: Revenue & Statistics Department (War Trade) 1916, L/E/10/3; *The Leader*, 7 June 1916.
21. Reported in *The Leader*, 8 August 1914. The scope of acceptable state intervention also began to widen. The Government of India started to take an interest in, for example, health. This was sparked off by '[t]he high standards of comfort set in other parts of the Empire in the matter of the accommodation for sick and wounded'. (Government of India, *India's Contribution*, pp.161–2.)
22. In one instance, according to General Barrow (military secretary at the India Office), 'India asked [telegram from the Viceroy, 20 March 1915] for a supply of bombs to be sent ... The War Office replied [31 March] that they were sending out 59 bombs and suggested that India should manufacture its future requirements.' (British Library, Barrow Papers: MSS EUR E420/14. 'Statement showing demands in connection with operations in Mesopotamia and the steps taken to meet them', p.1.
23. British Library, India Office Record: Revenue & Statistics Department, 26 January 1916, L/E/7/855.

24. J.C.K. Peterson, 'Industrial development in Bengal', Indian Munitions Board (ed.), *Industrial Handbook 1919* (Calcutta: Superintendent of Government Printing, 1919), pp.17–18. See also Government of India, *India's Contribution*, pp.226, 231.
25. A telegram from the Viceroy to the Secretary of State on 24 September 1914 noted that 'Indians … strongly in favour of utilising present opportunity to encourage Indian industries and will not easily understand why we should be generous to hostile traders and thus neglect fundamental Indian interests'. (British Library, India Office Record: Revenue & Statistics Department (War Trade) 1916, L/E/10/2.)
26. *The Leader,* 30 December 1914.
27. *The Leader,* 28 August 1914.
28. *The Leader,* 20 September 1914.
29. *The Leader,* 17 November 1914.
30. *The Leader,* 29 December 1914.
31. See Tomlinson, 'India and the British Empire', pp.350–1.
32. British Library, India Office Record: Government of India, Commerce and Industries Department (Industries section) Revenue & Statistics 8417. Despatch Number 51 of 1915 to the Secretary of State. L/E/7/855, pp.9–10.
33. British Library, India Office Record: Telegram from the Secretary of State to the Government of India, Commerce & Industries Department, n.d. (likely January 1916). L/E/7/855; British Library, India Office Record: Resolution of the Government of India Number 3403, Revenue & Statistics 8417, 19 May 1916. L/E/7/855.
34. Pre-empting the commission's deliberations, *The Leader* editorialised in May that 'it is to be hoped that [the Commission] will not hesitate to recommend, and the Government of India and his Majesty's Government will not hesitate to accept the recommendation, to render substantial state aid to industries in all ways that may be found necessary or thought useful. Therein will be the economic salvation of the Indian people, at least in considerable measure' ('State aid to industries', *The Leader,* 12 May 1916.)
35. See British Library, India Office Record: Resolution of the Government of India Number 3403, Commerce & Industries Department (19 May 1916) L/E/7/855: 'the general fiscal relationship which exists between the various parts of the Empire and other countries must in the opinion of His Majesty's Government be reconsidered after the war … The same considerations apply with even greater force to any proposals involving the imposition of duties for the specific purpose of protecting Indian industries'.
36. Ainscough, *Trade in India at the Close of the War,* p.108; Partha Sarathi Gupta, 'State and business in India in the age of discriminating protection', in

Divijendra Tripathi (ed.), *State and Business in India: A Historical Perspective* (New Delhi: Manohar, 1987), pp.163–5. Chamberlain, in fact, encouraged the Government of India to take up the question through the IIC (See Gupta, 'Discriminating protection', p.168.

37. British Library, India Office Record: L.J. Kershaw, 'Encouragement of Indian industries', 3 January 1915 [should be 1916], Revenue & Statistics 8417, L/E/7/855.
38. British Library, India Office Record: T. Holland, 'Constitution of the proposed industrial committee' (Confidential Memorandum 26 February 1916 L/E/7/855).
39. An opinion mentioned in a telegram from Kershaw, at the India Office, to the Viceroy (British Library, India Office Record: Revenue & Statistics 1703, 1916 L/E/7/855).
40. Sir Dorabji Tata submitted a Note to the Commission 'on the lines, the scope and the details of inquiry by the Indian Industrial Commission', dated September 1916. In it, he suggested the '[e]xemption of the profits of new industrial undertakings for a certain period from income taxation' and retaining the reserves of the Government of India and the provincial governments in India 'for financing banking agencies assisting in the manufacture and marketing of indigenous products'. Tata Central Archive, Pune: 'Note by Sir Dorab Ji Tata on the lines, the scope and the details of inquiry by the Indian Industrial Commission', September 1916. Rack Number 73, Box Number 870.
41. Holland to Kershaw at the India Office, 2 October 1916 (British Library, India Office Record: Revenue & Statistics 4312, 1916, L/E/7/855; Meyer in Gupta, 'Discriminating protectionism', p.169; Hardinge, *My Indian Years*, p.129.
42. Government of India, *Indian Industrial Commission 1916–1918, Report* (Calcutta: Superintendent of Government Printing, 1918), pp.xv, 2, 4.
43. Government of India, *IIC Report*, p.1.
44. Government of India, *IIC Report*, p.235. The idea of provincial industry departments had been agreed at the India Office well before the commission produced its recommendations – see the communication from R.D. Bell, the commission's secretary to the Government of India's Commerce & Industries secretary, 30 November 1916 (British Library, India Office Record: Revenue & Statistics 513 (1917), L/E/7/855). Ainscough described this in 1919 as 'a system of State paternal guidance and control ... quite in keeping with the time-honoured spirit of Indian administration' (Ainscough, *Trade in India at the close of the War*, p.109).
45. Government of India, *IIC Report*, pp.234, 52, 2. The report went on that if this were not done, 'Indian capitalists will, in times of peace, be deprived

of a number of profitable enterprises whilst in the event of a war which renders sea transport impossible, India's all-important existing industries will be exposed to the risk of stoppage, her consumers to great hardship, and her armed forces to the gravest possible danger'. (Government of India, *IIC Report*, p.56.)

46. Government of India, *IIC Report*, pp.166, 234.
47. *Statement Exhibiting the Moral and Material Progress and Condition of India during the year 1919* (no author) (London: HMSO, 1920), pp.79–80.
48. British Library, India Office Record: Extracts from House of Lords debates, 4 March 1919, p.462. L/E/7/855.
49. M.N. Roy, *The Future of Indian Politics* (London: Dorrit Press Ltd., n.d), p.25.
50. Indian Munitions Board, *Industrial Handbook 1919*, 1.
51. British Library, India Office Record: Telegram from the Viceroy to Secretary of State, 3 February 1917. L/E/7/855.
52. 'Munition Board: Creation of new department', *The Leader*,18 February 1917.
53. Government of India, *IIC Report*, p.xvii.
54. *Moral and Material Progress 1919*, pp.83, 224; Indian Munitions Board, *Industrial Handbook 1919*, pp.2–9, 12; Cotton, *Handbook of Commercial Information 1919*, pp.102–3; Ainscough, *Trade in India at the Close of the War*, pp.18, 106–8; Government of India, *India's Contribution*, pp.105–7, 110–11, 130.
55. 'In India, as elsewhere, it has been found necessary to interfere frequently with the normal course of trade in pursuance of one of three aims – to satisfy the needs of the country; to satisfy the needs of the Empire and the Allies; and to hamper the enemy.' (T.W. Holdness (Permanent Under-Secretary of State for India), *Statement exhibiting the Moral and Material Progress and Condition of India during the Year 1917–18*, London: HMSO, 1919), p.91.)
56. *Moral and Material Progress 1917–1918*, p.9; Government of India, *Proceedings of the War Conference held at Delhi, 27th–29th April 1918* (Delhi: Superintendent of Government Printing, 1918), p.110.
57. 'Thus for the first time ... India was allowed to levy a protective tariff against Lancashire' (H.C.E. Zacharias, *Renascent India, from Rammohan Roy to Mohandas Gandhi* (London: George Allen & Unwin, 1933), p.169; D.V. Divekar, *The Future of Indian Fiscal Policy* (Madras: S. Ganesan, 1923), p.32.
58. ' ... the Government purchase of tea proved the salvation of the Indian tea industry in 1918' (*Moral and Material Progress 1917–1918*, p.103).
59. *Moral and Material Progress 1917–1918*, p.91.
60. *Moral and Material Progress 1917–1918*, pp.93–5.
61. For example, between December 1917 and January 1919, the Coal Controller placed restrictions on a number of 'second class collieries' (smaller mines), since it was thought that they drew labour away from larger producers,

thereby reducing the output of premier grade coal needed for the war effort (Colin Simmons, 'Indigenous enterprise in the Indian coal mining industry c. 1835–1939', *Indian Economic and Social History Review* 13 (1976), p.205).

62. '... the necessity for the measures adopted was generally recognised, and the coal industry, by its patriotic attitude, greatly assisted Government in relieving the situation'. (*Moral and Material Progress 1917–1918*, p.96.
63. Nehru Memorial Museum and Library (NMML), Purshotamdas Thakurdas papers: File Number 12, Cloth Control Committee I, February-October 1918.
64. NMML, M.A. Master Papers: Report to the Board meeting of the Indian Navigation and Railway Company (n.d.), Subject File 1/1, 1913, 'Scindia'. The company chairman, A. Simpson, had complained to the company's annual general meeting on 31 May 1916 that 'no rate of hire can compensate the Cos. for the disorganization of such services'. (NMML, M.A. Master Papers: Chairman's Report to the AGM of the Indian Navigation and Railway Company (31 May 1916), Subject File 1/1, 1913, 'Scindia'.
65. For the Committee's report see 'Price of cloth and raw cotton', *The Leader*, 6 April 1918; NMML, Purshotamdas Thakurdas papers: File Number 12, Cotton Control Committee I, February–October 1918.
66. *Cotton Cloth Act 1918* in NMML, Purshotamdas Thakurdas papers: File Number 14, Cloth Control Committee II, 1918–1919.
67. NMML, Purshotamdas Thakurdas papers: File Number 14, Cloth Control Committee II, 1918–19. The standard letter to cotton companies required them 'to manufacture ... standard cloth in the quantity and of the quality shown in the form attached to this letter'. Companies were given a deadline and instructed to deliver the cloth to a nominated railway station – where it would be inspected by the Assistant Controller. They were also reminded of the punitive sections of the Act 10 (1) (2): six months gaol and/or a fine.
68. N.B. Saklatwala (of Tata), speaking for the business members of the Cloth Control Committee, said that 'they would welcome, from the point of view of the mill-owners, the production of Standard Cloth as suggested'. The Bengal Chamber of Commerce (representing European interests), however, 'strongly deprecated Government interference with the normal course of trade' (Saklatwala in Proceedings of the second meeting of the Advisory Committee of the Controller of Cotton Cloth, 25 October 1918, NMML, Purshotamdas Thakurdas papers: File Number 14, Cloth Control Committee II, 1918–19); Bengal Chamber quoted in unidentified press cutting Calcutta, 25 February 1919 (NMML, Purshotamdas Thakurdas papers: File Number 14, Cloth Control Committee II, 1918–19).
69. Purshotamdas Thakurdas to *Times of India*, not dated, 1918; Purshotamdas Thakurdas to the Cloth Control Committee, 17 July 1918. Both in NMML,

Purshotamdas Thakurdas Papers: File Number 12, Cloth Control Committee I, February-October 1918.

70. Press Note from the Government of Bombay on regulation of prices, 15 February 1918 (NMML, Purshotamdas Thakurdas papers: File Number 12, Cloth Control Committee I, February-October 1918).
71. See *The Tribune* editorial, reprinted in *The Leader*, 15 December 1914; 'The Industrial Conference Address', *The Leader*, 27 December 1914; Manmohandas Ramji, 'Presidential Address' to the Madras Industrial Conference, *The Leader*, 27 December 1914; P. Chetty's speech to the Madras Industrial Conference, *The Leader*, 30 December 1914; Bhupendra Nath Basu's presidential address to the Madras Congress session, *The Leader*, 29 December 1914.
72. Madras Congress resolutions reported in *The Leader*, 8 January 1915.
73. D. Chakrabarty & C. Bhattacharyya (eds), *Congress in Evolution: a collection of Congress Resolutions from 1885–1934* (Calcutta: The Book Company Ltd., 1935), p.85. See also A.C. Mazumdar's list of things that the Government of India could do to help Indian industry, in his 'Presidential Address' to the 1916 Congress session (K.C. Sankarakrishna (ed.), *India's Demands: a Collection of the Speeches delivered on the platforms of the Indian National Congress and the All India Muslim League, 1916* (Madras: Sankarakrishna, 1917), p.47).
74. British Library, India Office Record: Government of India, Commerce and Industries Department (Industries section) Revenue & Statistics 8417. Despatch Number 51 of 1915 to the Secretary of State. L/E/7/855, p.1. A year later, the department reported that the government was still being reproached for 'the slow development of Indian industries'. It went on: 'nor can we deny that Government officers themselves had been brought up in a school which regarded industrial development as the particular attribute of private enterprise'. (British Library, India Office Record: Dispatch Number 17 of 1916 in 'The Goal of British Rule in India, Chelmsford Manuscript collection, MSS EUR E264 File Number 51, pp.315–16.)
75. British Library, India Office Record: Proceedings of the Indian Legislative Council, 21 March 1916, L/E/7/855, p.434. '[I]t is essentially necessary', said Sir Ibrahim, 'that the Government of India should have complete freedom in fiscal matters'. (p.437.)
76. British Library, India Office Record: Viceroy to Secretary of State, 26 January 1916. Revenue & Statistics 816, 1916. L/E/7/855.
77. See R.S.R. Bahadur, *Presidential Address of the Honourable Rai Sitanath Ray Bahadur at the Twelfth Session of the Indian Industrial Conference held at Lucknow, 1916* (Calcutta: B.M. Press, 1916), pp.15–16, 19.

78. V.P. Madhava Rao, *India's Industrial Problems* (Presidential Address to the Calcutta Industrial Conference, 1917) (Madras: printed by the Sons of India, 1918), p.17.
79. Jagat Narain (Chair, Reception Committee) to Lucknow Congress session in Sankarakrishna, *India's Demands*, pp.4–6.
80. Mazumdar drew a comparison with Japan in this regard at the Lucknow session (Sankarakrishna, *India's Demands*, p.47). V.P. Madhava Rao told the Calcutta Industrial Conference (over which he was presiding) in 1917, 'If the Indian people succeed in getting a representative form of Government... it is only then they can have a voice in the shaping of the fiscal policy of their country.' See Rao, *India's Industrial Problems*, p.12. M.N. Roy wrote a little later that 'as condition for India's full support to Britain in carrying the war to victory, the National bourgeoisie demanded self-government (within the Empire) and an immediate grant of fiscal autonomy'. (M.N. Roy, *The Future of Indian Politics* (London: Dorrit Press Ltd., n.d.), p.18.
81. Mazumdar in Sankarakrishna, *India's Demands*, p.49.
82. Copy of Sinha's speech in British Library, India Office Record: Despatch Number 17 of 1916 in 'The Goal of British Rule in India' MSS EUR E264/51, Appendix IV, p.395. The idea of winning the Government of India to Indian interests may not have been entirely misplaced. The Viceroy, Lord Hardinge, wrote, 'Considerations of Imperial policy, no less than a sense of appreciation of the services rendered by India during the war, make it imperative that we should convince the Indian people that their interests are our interests and that we govern India for the benefit of the people and without any underlying selfish motives.' (Lord Hardinge, *Memorandum by H.E. the Viceroy upon Questions Likely to Arise in India at the End of the War*, n.p., n.d. [1915], p.19.)
83. Cotton, *Handbook of Commercial Information*, p.100; *Moral and Material Progress 1919*, p.82. An estimated 60 per cent of India's total exports of raw hides were being sent to Germany and Austria before the war (Indian Munitions Board, *Industrial Handbook 1919*, p.18). Germany and her allies had supplied 9 per cent of India's imports in the five years before the war (Morris, 'The growth of large-scale industry to 1947', p.600).
84. Ainscough, *Trade in India at the close of the War*, p.11.
85. According to Chatterji, 'industrial investment, output and profits reached unprecedented levels during and shortly after the war'. (Basudev Chatterji, *Trade, Tariffs and Empire: Lancashire and British Policy in India, 1919–1939* (Delhi: Oxford University Press, 1992), p.90.)
86. *Madras Times* editorial reprinted in *The Leader*, 26 September 1914. In 1915, the Viceroy Lord Hardinge pointed out that, if not met, the demand for industrial development 'will certainly turn, and already shows signs of

turning, into an insistent request for a tariff penalising the import of all articles from abroad, whether British or foreign; and the demand for fiscal protection will inevitably be intensified'. (British Library, India Office Record: Government of India, Commerce and Industries Department (Industries section) Revenue & Statistics 8417. Despatch Number 51 of 1915 to the Secretary of State. L/E/7/855, p.2.) The following year, Hardinge apparently obtained an assurance from the British Government that once the war was over, 'the economic position of India would be reconsidered with a view to abolishing the excise duty on cotton'. (Hardinge, *My Indian Years,* p.140.)

87. B.P. Sitaramyya, *The History of the Indian National Congress, Volume 1 1885–1935* (Bombay: Padma Publishers, 1946 [1935]), p.158; Iqbal Singh, *The Indian National Congress: A Reconstruction, Volume One, 1885–1987* (New Delhi: Manohar, 1987), p.416.
88. It is interesting to note the role of Sir Thomas Holland (future chairman of the IIC and President of the Indian Munitions Board) in this: 'it was he who at the very initial stages of the investigation and the formation of the Company impressed upon the Government of India that by helping the Company the Government would be doing a great service to the country and creating a most useful industry under the most favourable conditions'. (Tata Central Archive (Pune), TISCO Board meeting minutes 15 August 1918. File Number 120, TISCO 1916–18.) It should also be remembered that the provision of state assistance was hesitant, to say the least. Pandit Malaviya pointed out in his 'Note' to the IIC report that if the government had assisted from the start, 'the industry would have been established in the country much earlier and the entire industrial prospect of the country would have been altered and improved'. (Madan Mohan Malaviya, 'Note' in Government of India, *Indian Industrial Commission 1916–1918, Report* (Calcutta: Superintendent of Government Printing, 1918), p.305.)
89. Government of India, *IIC Report*,p. 21.
90. R.M. Lala, *For the Love of India: the Life and Times of Jamsetji Tata* (New Delhi: Penguin Portfolio, 2006), p.154.
91. Tata Central Archive (Pune), Address to TISCO Board, 18 October 1917. File Number 120, TISCO 1916–18.
92. Lovat Fraser, *Iron and Steel in India: A Chapter from the Life of Jamshedji N. Tata* (Bombay: The Times Press, 1919), p.97.
93. Tata Central Archive (Pune), Minutes of TISCO Board meeting with Sir Thomas Holland, 19 September 1917. File Number 120, TISCO 1916–18.
94. F.R. Harris, *Jamsetji Nusserwanji Tata: a Chronicle of His Life* (Bombay: Blackie & Son Ltd., 1953 [1924]), pp.216–17.
95. Government of India, *India's Contribution*, p.129.

96. Tata Central Archive (Pune), TISCO Board meeting minutes, 7 November 1918. File Number 120, TISCO 1916–18. Some years later, Purshotamdas Thakurdas reminded the Viceroy: 'When the end of the war was not within sight Tata Steel Company agreed wholeheartedly with various suggestions and the recommendations of the Government of India … to extend their Works at rates for Machinery etcetera which today look a thoughtless enterprise' (NMML, Purshotamdas Thakurdas papers. Purshotamdas Thakurdas to Viceroy, 14 November 1924. File Number 41, Tata Iron and Steel Company 1923–30).
97. Tata Central Archive (Pune), TISCO Board meeting minutes, 7 November 1918. File Number 120 TISCO 1916–18; TISCO Board meeting minutes 10 April 1919. File Number 308, TISCO 1919–22. See also Fraser, *Iron and Steel in India*, pp.98–100.
98. Fraser, *Iron and Steel in India*, p.103.
99. Lala, *Love of India*, p.154.
100. R.M. Lala, *The Romance of Tata Steel* (New Delhi: Penguin/Viking, 2007), p.37.
101. Tata Central Archive (Pune), TISCO Board meeting minutes of 30 March 1916, 7 January 1918 and 31 July 1918. File Number 120, TISCO 1916–18.
102. Tata Central Archive (Pune), TISCO Board meeting minutes, 13 September 1917. File Number 120, TISCO 1916–18.
103. At the Board meeting of 10 August 1917, R.D. Tata reported that the British Government would support the Plate Mill but that the Government of India 'cannot consent to the proposals made by London'. On 12 September, however, he told the board that 'Government was prepared to incur such additional cost as would be involved in expediting the Plate Mill during War time'. (Tata Central Archive (Pune), R.D. Tata to TISCO Board meeting, 10 August 1917. File Number 120, TISCO 1916–18; TISCO Board meeting minutes, 12 September 1917. File Number 120, TISCO 1916–18.)
104. Tata Central Archive (Pune), TISCO Board meeting minutes, 15 August 1918. File Number 120, TISCO 1916–18.
105. Dwijendra Tripathi and Jyoti Jumani (eds), *The Concise Oxford History of Indian Business* (New Delhi: Oxford University Press, 2008), p.94; Lala, *Romance of Tata Steel*, p.39.
106. Tata Central Archives (Pune), TISCO Board meeting minutes, 7 April 1916. File Number 120, TISCO 1916–18.
107. Tata Central Archive (Pune), TISCO Board meeting minutes, 8 January 1918. File Number 120, TISCO 1916–18. *The Leader* was encouraging:

'The success of the Tata Steel Works opens up immense possibilities for the shipbuilding industry on a large scale to be carried on in India.' ('Shipbuilding in India', *The Leader*, 10 May 1916.)

108. Tata Central Archive (Pune), TISCO Board meeting minutes, 7 January 1918. File Number 120, TISCO 1916–18.
109. British Library, India Office Record: B.P. Padshah to Kershaw, 3 January 1918. L/E/10/14.
110. Tata Central Archive (Pune), TISCO Board meeting minutes, 7 November 1918. File Number 120, TISCO 1916–18.
111. Hardinge, *Questions Likely to Arise,* pp.31–3. Lord Willingdon, Governor of Bombay and Sir William Clark, Commerce and Industry Member agreed (Hardinge, *Questions Likely to Arise*, Appendix B, pp.6, 56). See also Kershaw's note on 'Encouragement of Indian industries', dated 3 January 1915 [but should be 1916]. British Library, India Office Record: Revenue and Statistics 8417, L/E/7/855.
112. Hardinge, *Questions Likely to Arise*, pp.14–19. In the Appendix B to this volume, there arises a chorus of hearty agreement to protection for Indian industries and abolition of the cotton excise duty from the men who ruled India: the Commander in Chief, the Lieutenant Governors of the Punjab and Burma, the Chief Commissioners of the Central Provinces and of Assam, and the Home and Finance Members of the Viceroy's Council.
113. Despatch Number 51 of 1915 to the Secretary of State. L/E/7/855, p.1.
114. Government of India, *IIC Report*, p.xix.
115. Government of India, *IIC Report*, p.234. In similar vein, Sir Thomas Holland told *The Leader* that the 'real object' of the industrial commission was 'the necessity for prompt and energetic action on a scale appropriate to the importance of India's premier position among the Dominions of the Empire'. (Interview with *The Leader*, 10 May 1916.)
116. British Library Chelmsford Correspondence 3 Viceroy to Secretary of State: 26 January 1917 (pp.17–18); 19 July 1917 (p.228); 8 September 1917 (pp.243–4).
117. Ainscough, *Trade in India at the Close of the War*, pp.107, 109.
118. Government of India, *India's Contribution*, p.231.
119. 'Prefatory Note to Conference, on studying foreign models of Government assistance to industry', (part of the 'Proceedings of the Third Conference of Departments of Industries, Simla 23–26 May 1921'), *Bulletins of Indian Industries and Labour* Number 18 (September 1921), p.114. See also *Moral and Material Progress 1919*, p.80. So confident was Sir Thomas Holland (the IIC chairman and IMB president) of ongoing state intervention and his role in it, that he sold his shares in, and resigned his directorship

of, the Eastern Chemical Company, in order to forestall a possible conflict of interest. At the India Office, Kershaw pointed out 'although the [Eastern Chemical] Company will probably never require State Aid, it might be affected by the encouragement of local chemical industries'. (British Library, India Office Record Kershaw to George Stapylton-Barnes (Board of Trade), 24 February 1916. Revenue and Statistics 1228, L/E/7/855.

120. T. Holland, 'Preface' (dated 24 March 1919) to *Industrial Handbook*, p.i.
121. Ainscough, *Trade in India at the Close of the War*, p.18; Government of India, *IIC Report*, p.56. See also Sir Thomas Holland's letter to Sir George Barnes (a member of the Viceroy's Council) 14 January 1917, Chelmsford 3, p.21.
122. Rajnarayan Chandravarkar, *Imperial Power and Popular Politics: Class, Resistance and the State in India, 1850–1950* (Cambridge: Cambridge University Press, 1998), p.49.
123. Ainscough, *Trade in India at the Close of the War*, p.18 – a phrase repeated on p.106. The authors of *India's Contribution* noted 'the growing demand for State assistance in industrial undertakings [which] must eventually result in India becoming to a very large extent economically selfsufficing' (Government of India, *India's Contribution*, p.108).
124. Viceroy to Secretary of State, 26 January 1917, Chelmsford 3, p.18.
125. British Library, India Office Record: Telegram from Department of Commerce and Industry, Government of India to Secretary of State, 29 June 1917. L/E/10/14.
126. British Library, India Office Record: Telegram from Department of Commerce and Industry, Government of India to Secretary of State, 30 June 1917. L/E/10/14.
127. British Library, India Office Record: Sir George Barnes (Commerce and Industry member, Government of India) to Sir Thomas Holderness (India Office), 6 October 1917. L/E/10/16.
128. British Library, India Office Record: Note by 'T.W.H.' [Holderness], 27 October 1917, Revenue and Statistics (War Trade). L/E/10/5.
129. Hardinge, *Questions Likely to Arise*, pp.39–40. The Viceroy advocated a relaxation of financial control and elected majorities in the Provincial Legislative Councils (p.21).
130. Hardinge, *Questions Likely to Arise*, p.32.
131. Hardinge, *Questions Likely to Arise*, Appendix B, p.19.
132. M.P. Srivastava (ed.), *Constitutional and National Development in India (Montagu-Chelmsford Report)* (New Delhi: Ess Ess Publications, 1981), pp.212–15.

133. Lloyd George to the Viceroy, April 1918 in Michael Howard, *The Continental Commitment: The Dilemma of British Defence Policy in the Era of the Two World Wars* (London: Ashfield Press, 1989), p.68.
134. Gupta, 'Discriminating protection', p.166.
135. See Tomlinson on 'the idea of creating an autarchic empire' in post-war conditions (Brian R. Tomlinson, *The Political Economy of the Raj 1914–1947: The Economics of Decolonization in India* (London: Macmillan, 1979), p.60).
136. Srivastava, *Montagu-Chelmsford Report*, p.213.
137. As noted above, it was possible that the British Government accepted responsibility for Tata's Plate Mill, despite the Government of India's misgivings. See note 103.
138. British Library, India Office Record: Imperial Institute (Committee for India), 'Report on Trade in Lac', 25 May 1917. Revenue and Statistics (War Trade) 4697, 1917. L/E/10/13.
139. British Library, India Office Record. 'Recommendations Respecting Foodstuffs and Raw Materials', marked 'before 1918'. Cabinet Document Number 99, L/E/10/17.
140. As Gallagher and Seal put it, 'Expenditure on field armies in France, the campaigns in Mesopotamia, the drives to Damascus and adventures in Persia and South Russia might be in defence of large imperial units, but they had little to do with Indian interests more narrowly construed' (John Gallagher & Anil Seal, 'Britain and India between the wars', *Modern Asian Studies* XV 3 (1981), pp.400–1.)
141. NMML, Purshotamdas Thakurdas papers: Cotton Cloth Act, 26 September 1918. File Number 14, Cloth Control Committee II, 1918–19.
142. NMML, Purshotamdas Thakurdas papers: Board of Trade memorandum to Economic Offensive Committee of Cabinet, 29 May 1918. File Number 14, Cloth Control Committee II, 1918–19.

Chapter Three Industrialisation Abandoned

1. L.L. Fermor, 'Thomas Henry Holland 1868–1947', *Obituary Notices of Fellows of the Royal Society*, VI (17) (November 1948), p.87.
2. Fermor, *Obituary*, p.87.
3. Fermor, *Obituary*, p.87.
4. For the case against this argument in post-WW1 Europe, see David Lockwood, 'War, the state and the bourgeois revolution', *War & Society* 25, 2 (October 2006), pp.75–7.

5. Thomas M. Ainscough (HM Senior Trade Commissioner in India & Ceylon), *Report on the Conditions and Prospects of British Trade in India at the Close of the War* (London: HMSO, 1919), p.109.
6. Brian R. Tomlinson, *The Political Economy of the Raj 1914–1947: The Economics of Decolonization in India* (London: Macmillan, 1979), p.60. For this argument see also Krishan G. Saini, 'The economic aspects of India's participation in the First World War', in *India and World War I*, DeWitt C. Ellinwood & S.D. Pradhan (eds) (Delhi: Manohar, 1978), p.173.
7. Vera Anstey, *The Economic Development of India* (London: Longmans, Green & Co., 1957 (first edition: 1929)), pp.220, 232.
8. Government of India, *Report of the Indian Retrenchment Committee, 1922–23* (London: HMSO 1923). British Library, India Office Record: L/MIL/17/5/1781, p.1.
9. Clive Dewey, 'The Government of India's "new industrial policy", 1900–1925: formation and failure', in K.N. Chaudhuri & Clive J. Dewey (eds), *Economy and Society: Essays in Indian Economic and Social History* (Delhi: Oxford University Press, 1979), pp.244, 246. Gupta agrees: Partha Sarathi Gupta, 'State and business in India in the age of discriminating protection', in Divijendra Tripathi (ed.), *State and Business in India: A Historical Perspective* (New Delhi: Manohar, 1987), p.180.
10. Dewey says, 'The chief culprit [for killing industrialization] was constitutional reform. The Montagu-Chelmsford reforms were what destroyed the new industrial policy by transferring control over industrialization to Indian minister in the provinces' (Dewey, 'new industrial policy', p.240). Chatterji agrees: 'The 1919 Act made industrial development a business of the provinces, and the provinces lacked the financial resources to do much about it.' Basudev Chatterji, *Trade, Tariffs and Empire: Lancashire and British Policy in India, 1919–1939* (Delhi: Oxford University Press, 1992), p.199). See also Anstey, *Economic Development*, p.219.
11. Gupta, 'age of discriminating protection', pp.159, 180.
12. Mesopotamia Commission, *Report of the Commission Appointed by Act of Parliament* (Cd 8610, 1917). British Library, India Office Record: L/PS/20/257/19, p.96.
13. See *The Leader*, 11 November 1914 and 'Basrah is under British occupation', *The Leader*, 26 November 1914.
14. The commission reported that from this point onwards, 'the initiative (except in regard to the security of the oil supply) no longer comes from London but from Sir John Nixon, obeying the general instructions of the Indian Government and sustained by their concurrence'. (Mesopotamia Commission, *Report*, p.16.) Lloyd George wrote later: 'This expedition ... was in respect of

its administration under the sole control and responsibility of the Indian Army authorities.' (David Lloyd George, *War Memoirs of David Lloyd George: Volume Two, 1915–1916* (Boston: Little and Brown, 1934), p.239).

15. Mesopotamia Commission, 36; Lord Hardinge of Penshurst, *My Indian Years, 1910–1916* (London: John Murray, 1948), 136. The British Government, however, was not fully in charge until July 1916 (Lloyd George, *War Memoirs*, p.242.)
16. Before the operation commenced, Hardinge told the Secretary of State, Lord Crewe, 'India has done her duty to the Empire'. (Paul K. Davis, *Ends and Means: the British Mesopotamian Campaign and Commission* (Cranbury, NJ: Associated University Presses, 1994), p.183.)
17. Mesopotamia Commission, *Report,* p.97. Though once operations began, the Government of India advocated 'forward movements' that the India Office was reluctant to accept. Davis is probably right to conclude: 'The Indian authorities seemed bent on proving that they could run the campaign and were equally determined not to hint [to the British Government] that they might not be doing everything possible.' (Davis, *Ends and Means,* p.199.)
18. Mesopotamia Commission, *Report,* p.41.
19. Mesopotamia Commission, *Report,* p.72. According to Lloyd George, the Indian forces in Mesopotamia 'were entirely in the hands of the reluctant and parsimonious authorities in Simla, and were stinted and starved of every kind of equipment and support' (Lloyd George, *War Memoirs,* p.244).
20. Mesopotamia Commission, *Report,* p.41. The commission commented: '[The need for] economy, as we have seen, engendered a disposition to reticence, and when this was reinforced by the natural tendency in all men to avoid censure, we fear that there grew up a dangerous habit of concealment' (Mesopotamia Commission, *Report,* p.74).
21. In Davis, *Ends and Means*, p.183.
22. Mesopotamia Commission, *Report,* pp.40, 49, 60.
23. Mesopotamia Commission, *Report,* p.38.
24. As Lloyd George put it, the Indian military authorities' 'neglect of medical equipment turned disaster into horror' (Lloyd George, *War Memoirs,* p.250). The treatment of Indian soldiers in Mesopotamia in fact reflected conditions for sick and wounded Indian soldiers in India (see Mesopotamia Commission, *Report,* p.95 forward; Lloyd George, *War Memoirs,* p.250).
25. In Davis, *Ends and Means,* p. 187.
26. See Mesopotamia Commission, *Report,* p.48.
27. Mesopotamia Commission, *Report,* p.116.

28. Josiah Wedgwood, 'Minority Report' in Mesopotamia Commission, *Report of the Commission appointed by Act of Parliament* (Cd 8610, 1917). British Library, India Office Record: L/PS/20/257/19, p.129. According to Davis, 'Hardinge ... claimed that since the expedition took place outside India, there was no obligation to consult the Council' (Davis, *Ends and Means*, p.200).
29. Mesopotamia Commission, *Report,* p.100. The commission also pointed out that since the Commander-in-Chief was also the Military Member of the Viceroy's Council, conflict of interest was bound to arise; 'This astounding system has only to be described to be condemned' (Mesopotamia Commission, *Report,* pp.98–9).
30. Mesopotamia Commission, *Report,* pp.82, 88.
31. Mesopotamia Commission, *Report,* p.105. See also Wedgwood on insufficient industrial mobilisation (Wedgwood, 'Minority Report', pp.128–9).
32. Wedgwood, 'Minority Report', p.123. Lloyd George commented: 'In the opening months of the war the Indian Government showed an extraordinary tardiness in rendering any help at all to the Empire in its struggle. Only under strong pressure would it send a single soldier to the front, and despite its enormous population it declared itself incapable of recruiting substantial additional forces.' (Lloyd George, *War Memoirs,* p.243.)
33. 'Mismanagement in Mesopotamia', *The Times*, 14 March 1916.
34. 'Absolootely Nootral', *The Morning Post*, 21 October 1916.
35. *The Leader*, 15 July 1917.
36. 'Mr Chamberlain Resigns', *The Times*, 13 July 1917.
37. Letter from Lord George Hamilton to *The Times*, 16 July 1917.
38. Secretary of State to Viceroy, 7 July 1917. British Library, India Office Record. *Papers of Viscount Chelmsford as Viceroy of India, 1916–21.* Mss Eur E264, Volume Three.
39. Viceroy to Secretary of State, 7 July 1917. British Library, India Office Record. *Papers of Viscount Chelmsford as Viceroy of India, 1916–21.* Mss Eur E264, Volume Three.
40. Mesopotamia Commission, *Report,* p.81.
41. General Duff to the commission (Mesopotamia Commission, *Report,* p.37).
42. '...the unpreparedness of the Indian army for its task in Mesopotamia was primarily due to a long standing policy of economy and restriction of military preparation to the needs of frontier warfare'. (Mesopotamia Commission, *Report,* p.37.)
43. Davis, *Ends and Means*, p.202.
44. Mesopotamia Commission, *Report,* p.37. On 14 September 1914, Kitchener asked the Viceroy: 'Can you manufacture any guns yourself?' Came the reply: 'Our manufacture of guns is negligible'. (in Wedgwood, 'Minority

Report', p.123.) *The Times* reported complaints 'about the defective quality of such of these munitions [bombs and hand grenades] as are manufactured in India'. (14 March 1916.)

45. Fifteen years or so later, Zacharias wrote, 'that wonderful system of government in India ... was proved to have failed, and to have failed utterly – not because it had been hampered or interfered with or otherwise thwarted, but on the contrary, because it had complete *carte blanche* to do or not to do, what in its own wisdom seemed good'. (H.C.E. Zacharias, *Renascent India, from Rammohan Roy to Mohandas Gandhi* (London: George Allen & Unwin, 1933), p.171.) Rudolf von Albertini suggests that the British Government was also pushed into reform by the Lucknow Pact of 1916 (Rudolf von Albertini, 'The impact of two world wars on the decline of colonialism', *Journal of Contemporary History* 4 1 (1969), p.22.
46. Parliamentary Debates, House of Lords, 12 July 1917 XXV (56) 973. British Library, India Office Record. L/MIL/7/18413.
47. Mesopotamia Commission, *Report,* p.116.
48. Wedgwood, 'Minority Report', p.132.
49. 'Montagu has moved for immediate action: With a view to the reorganization of the Executive Government of the Indian Empire in India and of the India Office', *The Times,* 11 July 1917.
50. Parliamentary Debates, House of Commons, 12 July 1917, 95 (93), p.2207.
51. Parliamentary Debates, House of Commons, 12 July 1917, 95 (93), pp.2203–4.
52. Parliamentary Debates, House of Commons, 12 July 1917, 95 (93), p.2208.
53. Wedgwood, 'Minority Report', p.121. Whereas politically Wedgwood recommended decentralization, in the military sphere he recommended that the Indian army should be controlled by the British War Office (Davis, *Ends and Means*, p.210).
54. Parliamentary Debates, House of Commons, 12 July 1917, 95 (93), pp.2209–9. See also 'The Mesopotamia debate', *The Leader,* 18 July 1917.
55. Viceroy's speech, 27 April 1918 in Government of India, *Proceedings of the War Conference held at Delhi, 27th–29th April 1918* (Delhi: Superintendent of Government Printing, 1918), p.13.
56. Letter from Sir Edward Gait to the Viceroy, 29 August 1916. British Library, India Office Record. *Papers of Viscount Chelmsford as Viceroy of India, 1916–21.* Mss Eur E264, Volume Fifty One, 'Goal of British Rule in India', p.153.
57. Note by Sir Syed Shams ul Huda, 20 August 1916, in Chelmsford, Goal of British Rule, p.135.
58. Edwin S. Montagu, *An Indian Diary* (London: William Heinemann Ltd, 1930), p.116.

59. M.P. Srivastava (ed.), *Constitutional and National Development in India (Montagu-Chelmsford Report)* (New Delhi: Ess Ess Publications, 1981), p.124.
60. Srivastava, *Montagu-Chelmsford Report*, p.220. See also Montagu in the House of Commons: Parliamentary Debates, House of Commons, 95 (93) 12 July 1917, p.2207; S.R. Mehrotra, 'The politics behind the Montagu Declaration of 1917', in C.H. Philips (ed.), *Politics and Society in India*, (London: George Allen & Unwin Ltd., 1963) pp.77–8, 85; John Gallagher & Anil Seal, 'Britain and India between the Wars', *Modern Asian Studies* XV (3) (1981), p.399.
61. Lord Hardinge of Penshurst, *Memorandum by H.E. the Viceroy upon Questions Likely to Arise in India at the End of the War* (Delhi: n.p., 1915), p.4, 38.
62. A fact duly noted by the Government of India. A copy of the Congress resolution (number XIX of December 1915) is included in Chelmsford, Goal of British Rule 26.
63. Edwin S. Montagu and Viscount Lord Chelmsford, *Report on Indian Constitutional Reforms* (London: HMSO, 1918), pp.266, 268.
64. Montagu and Chelmsford, *Report*, p.268.
65. Montagu and Chelmsford, *Report*, p.270. 'Political expediency' referred not only to calming nationalist passions but giving jobs to unemployed Bengali youth, thus keeping them out of political mischief.
66. Government of India, *Indian Industrial Commission 1916–1918, Report* (Calcutta: Superintendent of Government Printing, 1918), p.290.
67. Indo-British Association Ltd., *The Montagu-Chelmsford Report on Indian Constitutional Reform and the Future of Indo-British Commerce* (London: Merritt & Hutcher Ltd., n.d.), pp.4, 8. The Association claimed that European industries in India 'were founded by men who depended on their own resources and who did not seek financial assistance from the State . . . they did not wait for State aid' (p.5).
68. Montagu and Chelmsford, *Report*, p.283.
69. Srivastava, *Montagu-Chelmsford Report*, p.227; Shreegovind Mishra, *Constitutional Development and National Movement in India (1919–47)* (Patna: Janaki Prakashan, 1978), pp.9–10; R.N. Aggarwala, *National Movement and Constitutional Development of India (1857–1978)* (New Delhi: Metropolitan Book Company, 1978), pp.84, 107–8.
70. The Under Secretary of State, Lord Islington, told the Oxford Union in August 1917 that '[s]uch matters as Police, Education, Agriculture, Forestry, Public Works and Buildings, and questions regarding industrial enterprise might be handed over entirely to the larger of the Provincial Governments' (Chelmsford, Goal of British Rule, p.492). The Montagu-Chelmsford report included 'Industrial matters' in its 'Illustrative List I showing Provincial [Transferred] Subjects' (Montagu and Chelmsford, *Report*, p.294). See also

Government of India, *Statement Exhibiting the Moral and Material Progress and Condition of India during the Year 1919* (London: HMSO, 1920), pp.84–186.

71. As Daniel Buchanan wrote in 1934, 'the encouragement of industry requires a far-reaching unified government policy concerning not only raw materials and methods of production but markets as well. In fact, it must be associated with educational policy and almost every other great national interest. It is doubtful whether the mere provincial offices set up in India will have any considerable effect'. (Daniel H. Buchanan, *The Development of Capitalistic Enterprise in India* (London: Cass, 1966 [1934]), p.464.) At the India Office, Kershaw had written to the Financial Secretary in November 1920: '[F]ollowing the provincialisation of industries and the classification of the subject as "transferred" the functions of the Imperial Department will be much more restricted than was at first contemplated.' (British Library, India Office Record: L/E/7/1279.)
72. Helen B. Lamb, 'The "state" and economic development in India', in Simon Kuznets et al. (eds.), *Economic Growth: Brazil, India, Japan* (Durham NC: Duke University Press, 1955), p.483. On financial devolution to the provinces, see Montagu and Chelmsford, *Report*, pp.164–5.
73. Government of India, *Retrenchment Committee Report,* pp.131, 132, 212.
74. 'It is doubtful whether at that time sufficient regard was had to the fact that, under the Reforms Scheme, the development of industries had been classified as a provincial transferred subject.' (Government of India, *Retrenchment Committee Report*, p.131.)
75. Government of India, *Retrenchment Committee Report*, p.132. The former 'was, no doubt, useful during the war . . . but it is questionable whether it is now necessary to maintain an establishment on this scale for the purpose' (p.214).
76. Government of India, *Retrenchment Committee Report*, pp.133–4, 212, 216.
77. Government of India, *Retrenchment Committee Report*, p.292.
78. Government of India, *Retrenchment Committee Report*, pp.7–8, 50, 161.
79. 'Memorandum regarding Provincial Legislative Councils' and 'Memorandum on the Reforms Desirable in Respect of Provincial Legislative Councils', 20 July 1916 in Chelmsford, Goal of British rule, pp.18,40.
80. 'Conclusions in Council as regards Provisional Legislative Councils 31 August and 8 September 1916' in Chelmsford, Goal of British Rule, p.228. Much of the advice proffered to the Government of India was to this effect. The Home Member, Sir Reginald Craddock wrote, 'I do not believe in excessive provincial autonomy and in too great a withdrawal of the guidance of the Government of India' ('A Note Regarding a Formula', 12 September 1916 in Chelmsford, Goal of British Rule, p.230.) The Chief Commissioner of Ajmer-Merwara

suggested '[t]hat further progress along democratic lines of development such as the extension of the powers of Legislative Councils should be for the present discouraged'. (Sir Elliot Colvin, 'Note' in Chelmsford, Goal of British Rule, p.249). Some Indian members of the Imperial Legislative Council agreed. Speaking for a number of them, Sir C. Sankaram Nair reported, 'My colleagues are averse from the grant of further constitutional powers to the new [Provincial] Councils and assert their disinclination to see these develop into *quasi*-Parliaments'. (Draft Minute of Dissent, 25 October 1916 in Chelmsford, Goal of British Rule, p.285.) Another member, Nawab Zulfikar Ali Khan warned that the demand for provincial autonomy, as proposed by 'these noisy nationalists', was 'calculated to leave no controlling power in the hands of the British officials' (Letter to the Viceroy, 30 September 1916 in Chelmsford, Goal of British Rule, p.258).

81. Despatch Number 17 of [24 November] 1916 in Chelmsford, Goal of British Rule, p.328.
82. Mehrotra, 'Politics behind the Montagu Declaration', pp.88–9.
83. Viceroy's telegram to the Secretary of State, 18 May 1917 in Chelmsford, Goal of British Rule, p.426.
84. Montagu, *Indian Dairy*, p.42.
85. Tomlinson thinks this was the case: 'The Government of India . . . was convinced that it [the centralisation of industrial policy] was essential because no Indian minister in the provinces would have the time, the money, the authority or the will to implement the Industrial Commission's formidable list of proposals' (Brian R. Tomlinson, *The Political Economy of the Raj 1914–1947: The Economics of Decolonization in India* (London: Macmillan, 1979), p.59).
86. Robb suggests that the Government of India was not prepared 'to relinquish their paternalistic control over the universities and over industrial expansion, areas in which local and communal loyalties were thought likely to prove obstacles'. (P.G. Robb, *The Government of India and Reform: Policies towards Politics and the Constitution* (Oxford: Oxford University Press, 1976), p.107).
87. L.F. Rushbrook Williams, *Statement Exhibiting the Moral and Material Progress and Condition of India during the Year 1920* (London: HMSO, 1921), p.96.
88. A. Hirtzel (Deputy Under-Secretary of State for India), *Statement Exhibiting the Moral and Material Progress and Condition of India during the Year 1921* (London: HMSO, 1922), p.144; L.F. Rushbrook Williams, *Statement Exhibiting the Moral and Material Progress and Condition of India during the Year 1922–1923* (India: n.p., 1923), p.135; L.F. Rushbrook Williams, *Statement Exhibiting the Moral and Material Progress and Condition of India during the Year 1923–1924* (Calcutta: Government of India Central Publications Branch, 1924), p.150.

89. Rushbrook Williams, *Moral and Material Progress 1920*, p.97; Hirtzel, *Moral and Material Progress 1921*, p.145 & 147.
90. John Coatman, *Statement Exhibiting the Moral and Material Progress and Condition of India during the Year 1925–1926* (India: HMSO, 1927), p.317.
91. Montagu, *Indian Diary*, p.353.
92. 'Proceedings of the First Conference of Directors of Industries, Simla, 12–14 April 1920', *Bulletins of Indian Industries and Labour* Number 1 (1921), p.3.
93. 'Proceedings of the First Conference of Directors of Industries, Simla, 12–14 April 1920', *Bulletins of Indian Industries and Labour* Number 1 (1921), pp.56, 59.
94. 'Proceedings of the First Conference of Directors of Industries, Simla, 12–14 April 1920', *Bulletins of Indian Industries and Labour* Number 1 (1921), pp.4–10.
95. 'Proceedings of the [second] Conference of Directors of Industries, 1–4 November 1920', *Bulletins of Indian Industries and Labour* Number 5 (January 1921), p.3.
96. 'Proceedings of the [second] Conference of Directors of Industries, 1–4 November 1920', *Bulletins of Indian Industries and Labour* Number 5 (January 1921), pp.4, 20.
97. 'Proceedings of the [second] Conference of Directors of Industries, 1–4 November 1920', *Bulletins of Indian Industries and Labour* Number 5 (January 1921), pp.23–4.
98. 'Proceedings of the Third Conference of Departments of Industries, Simla 23–26 May 1921', *Bulletins of Indian Industries and Labour* Number 18 (September 1921), pp.3–4.
99. 'Proceedings of the Third Conference of Departments of Industries, Simla 23–26 May 1921', *Bulletins of Indian Industries and Labour* Number 18 (September 1921), p.4.
100. 'Proceedings of the Third Conference of Departments of Industries, Simla 23–26 May 1921', *Bulletins of Indian Industries and Labour* Number 18 (September 1921), p.108. It was reported that Holland told the conference: 'They were not industrially equipped. Ten years later they might be exposed to very serious dangers. If they did not get their chemical service into running order their chemical industries were not going to be fit to manufacture munitions.' (Bulletin Number 18, Third Conference, 107.) It was proposed that a fourth conference should be held in December 1922. However, with the exception of Punjab, Assam and Madras, none of the Provincial Ministers of Industries had anything they wished discussed. The conference was therefore postponed (National Archives of India. Government of India, Department of Industries – Industries Branch. File No. I – 214).

101. Holland's reply: 'The President said that those were both "munitions". The soldier's principal "munition" was his food.' (Bulletin Number 18, Third Conference, 107.)
102. Only Burma voted in favour of the Industrial Service and the Chemical Service; on the latter, Punjab and Madras did not vote. ('Proceedings of the Fourth Conference of Departments of Industries, Calcutta 17–19 April 1922', *Bulletins of Indian Industries and Labour* Number 27 (September 1922), pp.19–20, 21–4).
103. Government of India, *Statement Showing the Action Taken on the Recommendations of the Retrenchment Committee, 1927*. British Library, India office Record, IOR/V/27/300/12 1927, pp.1–32, 62, 95.
104. Government of India, *Statement Showing the Action Taken*, p.70.
105. Government of India, *Statement Showing the Action Taken*, p.63.
106. Government of India, *Statement Showing the Action Taken*, p.94.
107. Government of India, *Statement Showing the Action Taken*, p.97; Anstey, *Economic Development,* p.220.

Chapter Four Empire

1. Potter, for example writes: 'Colonialism refers to a relationship between an independent state and an area of land not an integral part of that state which, with its inhabitants, is entirely subject to the rule of that state through officials of that state physically present in the area.' (David C. Potter, 'Manpower shortage and the end of colonialism: the case of the Indian civil service', *Modern Asian Studies* 7 (1) 1973: 47.) In fact, unless modern imperialism is defined as colonialism, it is difficult to precisely define it as anything at all. As John Strachey put it, 'though exploitation and oppression are fully possible by these methods ["indirect forms of imperialism"], indirect imperialism is an unstable and transitory thing when compared to actual, direct, colonial possession. Colonialism is the hard core of imperialism: and colonialism is vanishing from the face of the earth'. John Strachey, *The End of Empire* (London: Victor Gollancz Ltd., 1959), p.144.
2. Oliver MacDonagh, 'The anti-imperialism of free trade', *Economic History Review* 14, 3 (1962), p.492.
3. Joseph Schumpeter, *Imperialism and Social Classes* (New York: A.M. Kelley, 1951 [1919]), p.122.
4. Schumpeter, *Imperialism and Social Classes*, p.83.
5. Schumpeter, *Imperialism and Social Classes*, pp.84–5, 122.

6. Schumpeter described such groups as 'a vigorous, idle aristocracy' (Ancient Rome); 'mercenary groups and bellicose adventurers' (Venice); and 'free-booter personalities' (India). (Schumpeter, *Imperialism and Social Classes*, p.97.) The Indian businessman, G.D. Birla, quoted James Stuart Mill on this question: '[W]hen a country holds another in subjection, the individuals of the ruling people who resort to the foreign country to make their fortunes, are of all others, those who most need to be held under powerful restraint.' (In G.D. Birla, *A statement on behalf of the Federation of Indian Chambers of Commerce and Industry in reply to the circular letter dated the 27th July 1929 issued by the Associated Chambers of Commerce of India and Ceylon to influence opinion in England against India's right to adapt her economic policy to her own needs* (Calcutta: Federation of Indian Chambers of Commerce and Industry, n.d.), p.5.
7. That Kautsky had similar views on imperialism to those of Schumpeter is demonstrated in John Kautsky's chapter 'J.A. Schumpeter and Karl Kautsky: parallel theories of imperialism', in John H. Kautsky, *Karl Kautsky: Marxism, Revolution and Democracy* (New Brunswick: Transaction Publishers, 1994).
8. J. Kautsky 'Schumpeter and Kautsky', p.140.
9. Ronald Robinson and John Gallagher with Alice Denny, *Africa and the Victorians: the Official Mind of Imperialism* (Houndmills: Macmillan Publishers Ltd., 1985 [1961]), pp.20–1.
10. Schumpeter, *Imperialism and Social Classes*, p.85.
11. 'Schumpeter has to grapple with the paradoxical problem, from his standpoint, of how it is that imperialist tendencies, which ought to have become progressively weaker, became, in the late nineteenth and early twentieth centuries, especially prominent' (Tom Kemp, *Theories of Imperialism* (London: Dobson Books Ltd., 1967), pp.94–5).
12. See J.A. Hobson, *Imperialism: a Study* (London: Allen & Unwin, 1938); V.I. Lenin, *Imperialism: the Highest Stage of Capitalism* (Moscow: Progress Publishers, 1970); N.I. Bukharin, *Imperialism and World Economy* (New York: H. Fertig, 1966).
13. Lenin, *Imperialism*, pp.73, 75.
14. Lenin, *Imperialism*, p.86.
15. 'The principle spheres of investment of British capital are the British colonies ... [But] French capital exports are invested mainly in Europe, primarily in Russia ... German capital invested abroad is divided almost evenly between Europe and America.' Lenin, *Imperialism*, pp.62–3.
16. See Cobden in MacDonagh, 'Anti-imperialism of free trade', p.498; '[I]t would be well to engraft our free trade agitation upon the peace movement. They are one and the same thing' (p.492).

17. Schumpeter wrote: '[I]t follows that capitalism is by nature anti-imperialist. Hence we cannot readily derive from it such imperialist tendencies as actually exist' (*Imperialism and Social Classes*, p.96). Kautsky said that 'exploitation colonies' (non-settler colonies) enriched those who exploited them through plunder and trade – not by territorial acquisition (Karl Kautsky, 'Socialism and colonial policy' (1907), www.marxists.org/archive/kautsky/1907/colonial/index.htm.)
18. D.K. Fieldhouse, *Economics and Empire 1830–1914* (London: Weidenfeld and Nicolson, 1973), p.476.
19. For a longer version of this argument and its relationship to Marxism, see my 'Historical materialism and the state', *Critique* 34, 2 (August 2006), pp.163–78; for its application to pre-revolutionary Russia, see *Cronies or Capitalists? The Russian Bourgeoisie and the Bourgeois Revolution from 1850 to 1917* (Newcastle upon Tyne: Cambridge Scholars Publishing, 2009); for its application to Europe in the First World War, see 'War, the state and the bourgeois revolution', *War & Society* 25, 2 (October 2006), pp.53–78.
20. '[T]he state, first, divides its subjects *according to territory* . . . This organisation of citizens according to locality is a feature common to all states.' (F. Engels, 'The origin of the family, private property and the state', in K. Marx and F. Engels, *Marx and Engels Selected Works* (Moscow: Progress Publishers, 1970 [1884]), p.576.)
21. According to Otto Hintze, 'All state organization was originally military organization, organization for war . . . Larger groups of people united in the more solid structure of the state, primarily for defensive and offensive purposes.' (Otto Hintze, *The Historical Essays of Otto Hintze*, F. Gilbert (ed.) (New York: Oxford University Press, 1975), p.181.)
22. See Nigel Harris, *Of Bread and Guns* (Harmondsworth: Penguin, 1983), pp.231–2. According to C.C. Wrigley, 'Marxists have of course generally treated the state as derivative from and subordinate to the power of capital, and have failed to see that government is independent in origin and that its personnel have interests which may often converge with those of the owners of capital but are not necessarily either identical or weaker' (C.C. Wrigley, 'Neo-mercantile policies and the new imperialism', in Clive Dewey & A.G. Hopkins (eds), *The Imperial Impact: Studies in the Economic History of Africa and India*, (London: The Athlone Press, 1978), p.22).
23. Kautsky wrote that capitalists investing in the developing world could avoid the dangers of rebellion and loss of capital 'if the agricultural territory to which they are exporting capital is under the state power of a country with a European capitalist culture, that is, if it loses its independence and becomes a colony'. Further: 'They want the state power of their own country to do

this' ('Socialism and colonial policy'). See also John Gallagher & Ronald Robinson, 'The imperialism of free trade', *Economic History Review*, second series, VI, 1 (1953), pp.6–7, 16; D.K. Fieldhouse: 'the ultimate explanation of formal annexation was that the original economic issue had to some degree become "politicized" and therefore required a political solution'. (*Economics and Empire*, p.476)

24. See, for example, Kidron's account of the apparent symbiosis of British capital and the British state in India (Michael Kidron, *Capitalism and Theory* (London: Pluto Press, 1974), p.145.
25. But as Schumpeter points out, the link affects both systems: 'Nationalism and militarism, while not creatures of capitalism, become "capitalized" and in the end draw their best energies from capitalism... And they, in turn, affect capitalism, cause it to deviate from the course it might have followed alone, support many of its interests.' (*Imperialism and Social Classes*, p.128.)
26. John Sender & Sheila Smith, *The Development of Capitalism in Africa* (London: Methuen, 1986), p.50.
27. Manali Chakrabarti, 'Why did Indian big business pursue a policy of economic nationalism in the inter-war years?' *Modern Asian Studies* 43, 4 (2009), pp.996, 998.
28. In Britain's case, MacDonagh dates this from 1846, with Lord Palmerston's return to the Foreign Office. Palmerston promised 'British pressure upon foreign governments whenever the folly of British investors threatened to prove particularly costly', sent out gunboats to protect 'British interests' in Portugal, intervened in Borneo, restarted the Kaffir war and (inevitably) raised defence expenditure (MacDonagh, 'Anti imperialism of free trade', 493). See also Leland H. Jenks, *The Migration of British Capital to 1875* (London: Nelson, 1971 [1927]), p.125.
29. Gallagher & Robinson, *Africa and the Victorians*, p.409. To illustrate their argument, they cite the case of British intervention in the Lower Niger in 1884: 'It was not the case that the merchants pressed the Crown to pacify and develop the Lower Niger for them. Most of the traders still wanted to operate in a *res nullius*, where there would be a fair field and no tariffs, without an imperial authority to tax them and get in their way. All they asked for was protection against the interference of foreign governments and help in breaking the power of the middle men.' (Gallagher & Robinson, *Africa and the Victorians*, p.177.)
30. As we know, Schumpeter's (and, to an extent, Kautsky's) identification of imperialism with atavistic elements led them to the conclusion that it would, with the development of capitalism, die out. In identifying its real origins in the national state, it becomes clear that in the late nineteenth and

early twentieth centuries, it was, on the contrary, on the rise. For a longer version of this argument, see David Lockwood, 'War, the state and the bourgeois revolution'.

31. The company's trading post in Surat was raided twice by Shivaji, the Maratha leader, in the 1660s (Barbara & Thomas Metcalfe, *A Concise History of India* (Cambridge: Cambridge University Press, 2002), p.46).
32. Marx wrote: 'The East India Company commenced by attempting merely to establish factories for their agents, and places of deposit for their goods. In order to protect them, they erected several forts.' (Karl Marx, 'The East India Company – its history and results' (11 July 1853) in *On Colonialism* by Karl Marx and Frederick Engels (Moscow: Foreign Languages Publishing House, n.d), p.48.)
33. Cited in Geoffrey Moorhouse, *India Britannica* (London: Paladin Books, 1984), pp.34–5. Moorhouse adds: 'This was a genuine cry from the pocket of men bent on commercial speculation and nothing but, and it was to be repeated time and again for at least another hundred years.'
34. Karl Marx, 'The Government of India' (20 July 1853) in *On Colonialism* by Karl Marx and Frederick Engels, p.64.
35. Nick Robins, *The Corporation that Changed the World: How the East India Company Shaped the Modern Multinational* (London: Pluto Press, 2006), p.67.
36. H.V. Bowen, *The Business of Empire: the East India Company and Imperial Britain, 1756–1833* (Cambridge: Cambridge University Press, 2007), pp.44–5. Company troops were sent to Ceylon (1795), Malacca (1795), the Cape (1795 & 1806), Egypt (1801), Mauritius (1810) and Java (1811). Bowen comments 'it was recognised [by the East India Company] that the lines of defence for British India were now being drawn several thousand miles from the subcontinent itself.' (pp.46–7)
37. Bowen, *Business of Empire*, p.47.
38. Karl Marx, 'The East India Company – its history and results', p.49.
39. Robins, *Corporation that Changed the World*, p.143. He adds that from the beginning of the nineteenth century 'as a free standing corporation, the Company's trajectory was remorselessly downhill, so that it became little more than an implementing agency for imperial expansion, its commercial character peeled away until it traded in little but paper'. At this stage, however, no British Government wanted to take on the responsibility of direct rule (see Bowen, *Business of Empire*, p.69; Robinson & Gallagher, *Africa and the Victorians*, p.10).
40. Robinson & Gallagher, *Africa and the Victorians*, p.13. They continue: 'it seemed imperative to make sure of the communications between the British Isles and India, if the spine of prosperity and security was not to be snapped'.

41. 'This revenue was large enough to support what must have been one of the largest standing armies in the world, and still leave a surplus of tribute. To maintain this army was to be the strongest power in the East' (C. Northcote Parkinson, *War in the Eastern Seas, 1793–1815* (London: George Allen and Unwin, 1954), p.47).
42. Gordon Johnson, 'Government and nationalism in India, 1880–1920', in Sugata Bose (ed.), *South Asia and World Capitalism*, (Delhi: Oxford University Press, 1990), p.238.
43. Robinson & Gallagher add: 'The growth of India's trade, and so of its revenue, nourished the military forces of the Indian government and this force in turn secured and promoted trade and investment throughout India, south-east Asia, and the Far East' (*Africa and the Victorians*, p.12).
44. Indian troops were sent to China (1839, 1856, 1859); Persia (1856); Afghanistan (1878); Egypt (1882); Burma (1885); Nyasaland (1893); Mombasa and Uganda (1896); and the Sudan (1896 and 1897). (Brian R. Tomlinson, 'India and the British Empire, 1880–1935', *Indian Economic and Social History Review* 12 (October-December 1974), p.342).
45. 'Appendix' (31 May 1901) in 'Military needs of the Empire in a war with France and Russia (12 August 1901), p.55. Committee of Imperial Defence, Papers 1888–1914 (Microform, Public Record Office, London), Reel 1.
46. Robinson & Gallagher, *Africa and the Victorians*, p.12. See also: David Washbrook, 'South Asia, the world system and world capitalism', in Sugata Bose (ed.) *South Asia and World Capitalism*, pp.43, 58; John Gallagher, *The Decline, Revival and Fall of the British Empire* (Cambridge: Cambridge University Press, 2004), p.78.
47. Mehrotra, writing on the 'Imperial federationists' in the 1890s, tells us 'more and more [Imperial] federation-enthusiasts, despairing of the prospect of a real federation, directed their attention to the more practical problems of imperials co-operation in defence and trade' (S.R. Mehrotra, 'Imperial federation and India, 1868–1917', *Journal of Commonwealth Political Studies* I, 1 (November 1961), p.32).
48. 'A Note on the Military Policy of India' (19 July 1905), cited in Philip Magnus, *Kitchener: Portrait of an Imperialist* (London: John Murray, 1958), p.230. See also Stephen P. Cohen, 'Issue, role and personality: the Kitchener-Curzon dispute', *Comparative Studies in Society and History* X, 3 (April 1968), p.342. It should be noted that from 1911, the Dominions were represented on the Committee of Imperial Defence, while India was represented by the Secretary of State (Franklyn A. Johnson, *Defence by Committee: the British Committee of Imperial Defence, 1885–1959* (London: Oxford University Press, 1960), pp.104, 109–11).

49. Committee of Imperial Defence minutes, 104th meeting, 19 August 1909, p.2. Committee of Imperial Defence, Papers 1888–1914 (Microform, Public Record Office, London), Reel 5.
50. Maurice Ollivier, compiler and editor, *The Colonial and Imperial Conferences from 1887 to 1937 – Volume Two* (Ottawa: Queen's Printer and Controller of Stationery, 1954), p.8.
51. Report of a sub-committee of the Committee of Imperial Defence to formulate Questions connected with Naval and Military Defence of the Empire for the Imperial Conference of 1911 (11 March 1911), p.2. Committee of Imperial Defence, Papers 1888–1914 (Microform, Public Record Office, London), Reel 6.
52. Michael Howard, *The Continental Commitment: The Dilemma of British Defence Policy in the Era of the Two World Wars* (London: Ashfield Press, 1989), p.62.
53. Tariff Commission [UK], *The Status of the Dominions and their Relations with Foreign Countries* (Westminster: P.S. King & Sons, 1920), pp.2, 10–11; S.R. Mehrotra, *India and the Commonwealth, 1885–1929* (London: George Allen & Unwin, 1965), p.83.
54. Tariff Commission, *Status of the Dominions*, p.11. See also Holland on 'the prominent role given to imperial reorganisation in the post-1918 reconstruction debate' as a way 'to stem political and economic decline after 1918'. (R.F. Holland, *Britain and the Commonwealth Alliance, 1918–1939* (London: Macmillan, 1981), p.24.)
55. According to Tomlinson, 'the idea of creating an autarchic empire, by substituting imperial preference for free trade, gained adherents in the Government of India and in the British Government' (Brian R. Tomlinson, *The Political Economy of the Raj 1914–1947: The Economics of Decolonization in India* (London: Macmillan, 1979), p.60). The idea appealed a great deal more to London than to Delhi, as we shall see. Balkrishna Madan adds: 'imperial military considerations lay behind the movement towards the economic co-ordination of the Empire through preferential trade' (Balkrishna Madan, *India and Imperial Preference: a Study in Commercial Policy* (Bombay: Oxford University Press, 1939), p.2).
56. See British Library, India Office Record. L/E/10/5.
57. Telegram from the Secretary of State for the Colonies, 8 May 1916 – by an oversight, the Government of India's copy was despatched several weeks later (British Library, India Office Record. L/E/10/6). See also *Leader*, 1 May 1916.
58. Resolution of the Economic Conference of the Allies, British Library, India Office Record. L/E/10/5. Reconstruction Committee, 'German Post-War Economic Policy', May 1917. British Library, India Office Record. L/E/10/13.

See also Secretary of State to Viceroy, n.d. (early December 1917), British Library, India Office Record. L/E/10/15; letter from N.N. Wadia to Kershaw (India Office) 6 December 1918, British Library, India Office Record. L/E/10/11.

59. Resolutions of the Economic Conference of the Allies, British Library, India Office Record. L/E/10/5.
60. The Paris Conference, BL IOR L/E/10/5.
61. Unsigned communication from the India Office to the Government of India. The Government of India urged the India Office that 'proper opportunity is given to India for expression of her views on any points affecting her interests'. (The Paris Conference, British Library, India Office Record. L/E/10/5).
62. Resolutions of the Imperial War Conference, British Library, India Office Record. L/E/10/5.
63. *Parliamentary Debates*, House of Commons, 2 August 1916, p.360.
64. British Library, India Office Record. L/E/10/13. Gupta writes that, with the end of the war and the Montagu-Chelmsford reforms on the way, 'It becomes necessary to get Indian external economic policy in line with Britain and the rest of the empire without delay' (Partha Sarathi Gupta, 'State and business in India in the age of discriminating protection', in Divijendra Tripathi (ed.), *State and Business in India: A Historical Perspective*, (New Delhi: Manohar, 1987), p.171).
65. Holland, *Britain and Commonwealth*, p.25.
66. Imperial War Conference, Proceedings (24 June 1918), British Library, India Office Record. L/E/10/17. A 'Memorandum on the Inter-Allied Control of Raw Materials after the War' ('before 1918') said that it was essential 'to set up within the Empire some arrangement for co-ordinating the action of [the Empire's] various parts' (War Cabinet Document 56. British Library, India Office Record. L/E/10/17). The Committee on the Trade Relations of the United Kingdom within the Empire stated in February 1918, 'The principle should be maintained that the Empire, in all bargaining as to raw materials, should act as a unit' (British Library, India Office Record. L/E/10/17).
67. Imperial War Cabinet minutes, 26 April 1917. British Library, India Office Record. L/E/10/11. See also resolution of the Imperial War Conference, 26 June 1918. British Library, India Office Record. L/E/10/17.
68. Balfour Committee resolution, 2 February 1917. British Library, India Office Record. L/E/10/11.
69. Minutes cited in Gupta, 'State and business in India', p.166. In its 'Interim Report on certain Essential Industries', the Balfour Committee stated, 'When using the word "Britain" in this Report we intend it to include the whole of the British Empire' (British Library, India Office Record. L/E/10/13).

70. Balfour Committee, Letter and Resolutions to Lloyd George, 2 February 1917. British Library, India Office Record. L/E/10/13.
71. Bonar Law, reporting to the House of Commons on the Imperial War Cabinet meeting, 27 April 1917. British Library, India Office Record. L/E/10/11.
72. Holland, *Britain and Commonwealth*, p.109.
73. Colonial Office, Memorandum on Economic Relations of the Colonies and Protectorates to the Empire (July 1923). British Library, India Office Record. L/E/7/1291.
74. Nor did the British Government expect it to be. A British cabinet document noted before 1918: 'After the war any proposals to control the resources of the Dominions, Colonies and Dependencies for the benefit of the Mothercountry will be invariably considered, as they were sometimes considered during the war, in a purely business spirit... Certainly Egypt and India will require strong inducements to make them give us control of their cotton and jute' ('General Considerations on Imperial Trade Policy', Cabinet Document 52 ('before 1918'). British Library, India Office Record. L/E/10/17).
75. See for example the comments by the Commander-in-Chief and the Lieutenant Governor of the Punjab in Lord Hardinge of Penshurst, *Memorandum by H.E. the Viceroy upon Questions Likely to Arise in India at the End of the War* (Delhi: n.p., 1915), Appendix B, pp.18, 36. See also the Government of India's response to the Balfour Committee in Gupta, 'State and business in India', p.172.
76. Kershaw, Aide-memoir for the Foreign Office in preparation for the Paris Conference (n.d.). British Library, India Office Record. L/E/10/5.
77. Telegram from Department of Commerce, Government of India to Secretary of State, 8 December 1922. British Library, India Office Record. L/E/7/1291/3720.
78. Imperial Conference, 1930, *Summary of Proceedings* (London: HMSO, 1930), pp.127, 130.
79. Gallagher, *Decline Revival and Fall*, p.87.
80. Keith Jeffery, 'The military defence of the British Empire, 1918–1922' (PhD diss., University of Cambridge, n.d.), p.3; John Gallagher, 'Nationalisms and the crisis of empire, 1919–1922', *Modern Asian Studies* 15, 3 (1981), p.358.
81. See Leo Amery's memorandum to the Imperial War Cabinet (March 1917) in which he argued that '[t]he retention of German East Africa, of Palestine and Mesopotamia, and of the German Pacific Colonies' was indispensible for the security of 'that great southern half of the British Empire, which lies in an irregular semi-circle around the Indian Ocean' ('A Note on the Possible Terms of Peace', 20 March1917 in Gallagher, 'Nationalisms and the crisis of empire', p.357.

82. See J.O. Rawson, 'The role of India in imperial defence beyond Indian frontiers and home waters, 1919–1939' (PhD diss, University of Oxford, 1976), p.148; Jeffery, 'Military defence of the British Empire', p.37.
83. Jeffery, 'Military defence of the British Empire', p.2.
84. Gallagher, 'Nationalisms and the crisis of empire', p.365. So great was the need for troops that the Secretary of State for War, Winston Churchill, proposed the retention of conscription in January 1919 – and got his way (Jeffery, 'Military defence of the British Empire', pp.28–9).
85. British Library, India Office Record. L/MIL/7/19323 in Keith Jeffery, '"An English barrack in the Oriental Seas"? India in the aftermath of the First World War', *Modern Asian Studies* XV 3 (1981), p.375. See also the Report of the Army in India Committee, which raised the possibility of an Imperial Cabinet, an Imperial General Staff, Imperial Naval and Air Staffs and an Imperial Foreign Office (British Library, India Office Record. L/MIL/17/5/1762. Report of the Army in India Committee, pp.3, 8).
86. '[A]fter 1918 the reader [of the documents of the Committee for Imperial Defence] becomes conscious of a new sound: the heavy and ominous breathing of a parsimonious and pacific electorate.' (Howard, *Continental Commitment*, p.79).
87. Howard, *Continental Commitment*, p.78.
88. Howard, *Continental Commitment*, p.63.
89. Tariff Commission (UK), *Status of the Dominions*, p.12.
90. Holland, *Britain and Commonwealth*, p.120.
91. BL IOR L/MIL/17/5/1761. Minutes of the Army in India Committee, First Meeting 28 July 1919.
92. BL IOR L/MIL/M/5/1761. Minutes of the Army in India Committee, First Meeting 28 July 1919. 'Appendix' by Lt. Gen. Sir H.V. Cox.
93. British Library, India Office Record. L/MIL/17/5.1762. Army in India Committee Report, p.1.
94. British Library, India Office Record. L/MIL/17/5/1761. Minutes of the Army in India Committee, Seventeenth Meeting, 23 October 1919. Another witness, Colonel Repington, told them that 'the [Imperial] General Staff should be the military link of the Empire' (Tenth Meeting, 14 October 1919). Field Marshal Allenby reminded them that 'the Indian Army are Imperial troops. In any case, he thought the War Office must control everything' (Twelfth Meeting, 16 October 1919).
95. British Library, India Office Record. L/MIL/17/5.1762. Army in India Committee Report, pp.7, 9.
96. In John Gallagher & Anil Seal, 'Britain and India between the wars', *Modern Asian Studies* 15, 3 (1981), p.401.

97. L.F. Rushbrook Williams, *Statement Exhibiting the Moral and Material Progress and Condition of India during the Year 1920* (London: HMSO, 1921), pp.17–18.
98. Esher had correctly predicted an adverse reaction from New Delhi. He wrote to Sir William Robertson on 14 August 1919, 'There will be great resistance by the Government of India to the principle that General Staff is one and indivisible, that its training and spirit are homogeneous, that war is its main objectives, and finally that war for an Empire like ours in whatever theatre cannot be treated as a local ailment but must be treated as a symptom'. (Reginald, Viscount Esher, *Journals and Letters of Reginald, Viscount Esher – Volume Four: 1916–1930*, Viscount Esher Oliver (ed.) (London: Ivor Nicholson & Watson Ltd., 1938), pp.241–2.
99. British Library, India Office Record. L/MIL/17/5/1761. Minutes of the Army in India Committee, Seventeenth Meeting, 7 February 1920.
100. British Library, India Office Record. L/MIL/17/5/1761. Minutes of the Army in India Committee, Seventeenth Meeting, 7 February 1920. Deshpande notes, however, that there were aspects of the Esher Report that did interest the Government of India – those concerning 'the connection between industrial development and military strength' (Anirudh Deshpande, *British Military Policy in India, 1900–1945: Colonial Constraints and Declining Power* (New Delhi: Manohar, 2005), p.61. See British Library, India Office Record. L/MIL/17/5/1762. The Army in India Committee Report, Part II, pp.7–8.
101. Jeffery, 'Military defence of the British Empire', p.43. And not only with its military plans. In March 1921 the Colonial Office and the Committee for Imperial Defence suggested 'A Common Imperial Policy in Foreign Affairs' – 'to avoid the Governments of the Empire drifting into divergent or even incompatible positions'. The Government of India objected, since it had no real voice in formulating imperial policy and, in any case, its advice was 'too often ignored' (British Library, India Office Record. L/E/7/1206. Colonial Office memorandum for the Committee for Imperial Defence, 'A Common Imperial Policy in Foreign Affairs' (March 1921) and the Government of India's response). The India Office was at pains to hide the disagreement from the rest of the Empire: 'both in regard to this question and any other matter of policy in which the G. of I. and H.M.G. may be at variance, it is desirable that, if it can possibly be avoided, the difference of view should not be revealed in an Imperial Cabinet meeting' (British Library, India Office Record. L/E/7/1206. India Office on the Government of India's response to 'A Common Imperial Policy', May 1921).

102. British Library, India Office Record. L/MIL/17/5/1761. Minutes of the Army in India Committee, Seventeenth Meeting, 7 February 1920.
103. See A. Hirtzel (Deputy Under-Secretary of State for India), *Statement Exhibiting the Moral and Material Progress and Condition of India during the Year 1921* (London: HMSO, 1922), pp.14–16; Pradeep Barua, 'Strategies and doctrines of imperial defence: Britain and India, 1919–45', *Journal of Imperial and Commonwealth History* 25, 2 (May 1997), pp.243–4.
104. D. Chakrabarty and C. Bhattacharyya (eds), *Congress in Evolution: a Collection of Congress Resolutions from 1885–1934* (Calcutta: The Book Company Ltd.), pp.193, 114.
105. Barua, 'Strategies and doctrines of imperial defence', p.244. Gallagher and Seal imply that, under the combined pressure of the India Office and the Government of India, the British Government rather let the notion of India's imperial strategic role lapse. This seems unlikely (on the following page, they list four areas in which Indian troops were deployed over the next decade) (Gallagher & Seal, 'Britain and India between the wars', pp.402–3). There were ongoing disputes as to which government would foot the bill.
106. Indian Statutory Commission, *Report of the Indian Statutory Commission, Volume II* (London: HMSO, 1930), paras 202–9 (pp.171–5).
107. Helmut Mejcher, 'British Middle East policy 1917–1921: The inter-departmental level', *Journal of Contemporary History* 8, 4 (1973), pp.83–5. London's fears and New Delhi's hopes of what an independent Indian military machine was capable of were played out in Waziristan from 1919 to 1920. There, acting more or less independently, the Government of India rushed into a punitive campaign on the Frontier, brought the Indian Army nearly to defeat, provoked an open insurrection in Waziristan (not to mention a serious cholera outbreak) and would have used poison gas on its opponents if Britain had not stopped it. It disagreed with London on peace terms and proceeded to sign a peace treaty with the approval of neither the Secretary of State nor the Cabinet (Brian Robson, *Crisis on the Frontier: the Third Afghan War and the Campaign in Waziristan, 1919–1920* (Strud: Spellmount, 2007); see also British Library, India Office Record. L/MIL/17/5/1761. Minutes of the Army in India Committee, Second Meeting, 29 July 1919). Britain did not object primarily to the morality or methods of the operation. Control was the essential principle at work.
108. The imperial scheme necessitated state intervention but not state industrialisation. The emphasis here was on imperial state control of raw materials: 'we do not see how the State can avoid interfering with the distribution of certain

supplies to manufacturers' (British Library, India Office Record. L/E/10/17. 'Memorandum on the Inter-Allied Control of Raw Materials after the War' ('before 1918')). Balfour, writing to Lloyd George, suggested that 'some kind of Government assistance or encouragement' be provided to ensure raw materials production 'for the economic or military security of the Empire' (British Library, India Office Record. L/E/10/12. Balfour to Lloyd George, 4 May 1917). An Interim Report from his Committee stated that '[i]t is desirable also that the Government of India should be urged to undertake control of supplies of Jute and Cotton' (British Library, India Office Record. L/E/10/11. Balfour Committee, Interim Report on the Treatment of Exports from the UK and British Overseas Possessions, 1917).

109. Barua writes, 'the British colonial establishment in India as represented by the bureaucracy and the Indian army had developed into an independent institution with only nominal control from Whitehall... Their actions, though rarely pro-Indian from the perspective of the Indian nationalists, nevertheless followed a more independent route than Whitehall would have preferred' (Barua, 'Strategies and doctrines of imperial defence', p.261). Sir George Schuster, the Finance Member from 1928, put the position as follows: 'I myself felt that it was my duty as a member of the Government of India to work for Indian interests and that if at any point there was a conflict between British and Indian interests I must fight for the latter... In short, I felt that I was a responsible member of the Government of India and not in any sense a Whitehall Civil Servant' (Sir George Schuster, *Private Work and Public Causes: A Personal Record 1881–1978* (Cowbridge: D. Brown and Sons, 1979), pp.90–1). The rest of his chapter on India is almost entirely a record of conflict between the Government of India and the British Government. See also Gupta, 'State and business in India', p.161; Gallagher and Seal, 'Britain and India between the wars', pp.391–401 – though the last two authors see this conflict as primarily a question of revenue.

Chapter Five Protection and Development: State and Bourgeoisie in the Inter-War Period

1. See Shiva Chandra Jha, *Studies in the Development of Capitalism in India* (Calcutta: Firma KL Mukhopadhyay, 1963), pp.179–83.
2. Aditya Mukherjee, *Imperialism, Nationalism and the Making of the Indian Capitalist Class, 1920–1947* (New Delhi: Sage Publications, 2002), p.31.
3. See Sumit Sarkar, *Modern India, 1885–1947* (Madras: Macmillan India Ltd., 1983), p.327; Basudev Chatterji, *Trade, Tariffs and Empire: Lancashire and British Policy in India, 1919–1939* (Delhi: Oxford University Press, 1992), p.320.

4. As Chakrabarti says, 'the interests of diverse groups may converge unexpectedly when there are overriding economic reasons for it. And under such compelling circumstances... [the] big business group in colonial India seemed to display an apparently homogeneous class consciousness... the factor which most comprehensively influenced the class consciousness of big business class in colonial India was its converging economic interests'. (Manali Chakrabarti, 'Why did Indian big business pursue a policy of economic nationalism in the inter-war years?' *Modern Asian Studies* 43, 4 (2009), p.103.) The importance of struggle in cohering a class interest is noted by Marx and Engels: 'The separate individuals [within the bourgeoisie] form a class only insofar as they have to carry on a battle against another class; otherwise they are on hostile terms with each other as competitors' (Karl Marx & Frederick Engels. *The German Ideology*. New York: International Publishers, 1973 [1845], p.82.)
5. Mukherjee, *Imperialism, Nationalism,* p.19.
6. Mody to the Fifth Plenary Session, First Round Table Conference, 20 November 1930. In Indian Round Table Conference, 12 November 1930–19 January 1931 *Proceedings* (London: HMSO, 1931), p.155. A representative of the Indian Merchants' Chamber was reported as saying that contemporary India was 'not the India of the Moghuls or of the I.C.S. but the India of Mahatma Gandhi and the Congress, the commercial India of a Sir Purshotamdas, a B.F. Madon, a Subedar and a Prof. Shah' (*Times of India*, 30 October 1928. Nehru Memorial Museum and Library (henceforward NMML): Papers of Sir Purshotamdas Thakurdas (henceforward PT Papers), File No. 40 Part 4.
7. Mukherjee, *Imperialism, Nationalism*, p.19.
8. Claude Markovits, *Indian Business and Nationalist Politics, 1931–1939: The Indigenous Capitalist Class and the Rise of the Congress Party* (Cambridge: Cambridge University Press, 1985), pp.27, 29. There is a useful summary of both sides of this debate in Chakrabarti, 'Why did Indian big business pursue?'.
9. Markovits characterises the Indian capitalists as integrated into an economy over which they had no control and as separated from the necessary political power to do anything about it. My conclusion from this is that, in order to advance economically, they had to advance politically.
10. Chakrabarti writes: '[I]t was not the formation of nation state that moulded the national big bourgeoisie, but instead in the possibility of its formation this class saw an opportunity for furthering its own interest.' (Chakrabarti, 'Why did Indian big business pursue?' p.1026.) Chakrabarti's article demonstrates how economic position determined political position for European

business interests in Kanpur – they 'realised that their economic interests were in line with Indian big business' (Chakrabarti, 'Why did Indian big business pursue?' p.1015).

11. By Sarkar, among others. See Sarkar, *Modern India*, pp.279–80.
12. Bipan Chandra, *Nationalism and Colonialism in Modern India* (New Delhi: Orient Longman, 1979), p.158.
13. Chandra, *Nationalism and Colonialism*, p.162.
14. '... the capitalists, while putting forward their own positions, took extreme care to project these positions as geared not merely to their own class interests but those of the society or the Indian nation as a whole' (Mukherjee, *Imperialism, Nationalism*, p.79).
15. Marx & Engels, *German Ideology*, pp.65–6. It should be noted that this passage appears as part of the argument against ideas having an independent existence and determining the course of history.
16. Marx & Engels, *German Ideology*, p.66. On the role of the bourgeoisie as a revolutionary class, taking society forward, see Karl Marx & Frederick Engels, *Manifesto of the Communist Party* (Moscow: Progress Publishers, 1966), pp.43–7.
17. As encapsulated by the Federation of Indian Chambers of Commerce and Industry (FICCI) at its annual meeting in April 1933: 'that India should have the fullest liberty to become self-subsistent as regards all articles needed for the consumption of the masses and to develop all industries that can be developed in the conditions of India' (Resolution, FICCI 6th Annual Meeting, Delhi 15–16 April 1933. NMML: PT Papers, File No. 126, Part II). The Federation of Indian Chambers of Commerce and Industry (FICCI) was founded in 1927 as an all-India business organisation. It became the dominant organisation of the Indian bourgeoisie. See Mukherjee, *Imperialism, Nationalism*, pp.35–8; Medha M. Kudaisya, *The Life and Times of G.D. Birla* (New Delhi: Oxford University Press, 2003), pp.115–16.
18. According to Morris, 'It was the politically hot issue, a major manifestation of the conflict between nationalist and imperial objectives' (Morris D. Morris, 'The growth of large-scale industry to 1947' in Dharma Kumar & Meghnad Desai (eds), *The Cambridge Economic History of India, Volume 2: c.1757–c.1970* (Cambridge University Press, Cambridge 1983), p.625). Birla identified it as a national, not a class, issue. Speaking to FICCI's 3rd annual meeting, he said: 'It may be easy to misrepresent the motive of the capitalist when he advocates protection and to depict him as the arch-enemy of the consumer. But what about the Indian National Congress which is certainly not a capitalist organisation?... What does the popular propaganda for a

boycott of foreign goods mean if not protection to the indigenous industry?' (Kudaisya, *The Life and Times of G.D. Birla*, p.150).

19. Edwin S. Montagu and Viscount Lord Chelmsford, *Report on Indian Constitutional Reforms* (London: HMSO, 1918), p.216.
20. T.W. Holdness (Under Secretary of State for India), *Statement Exhibiting the Moral and Material Progress and Condition of India during the Year 1917–18* (London: HMSO, 1919), p.26.
21. See Krishan G. Saini, 'The economic aspects of India's participation in the First World War', in DeWitt C. Ellinwood & S.D. Pradhan (eds), *India and World War I* (Delhi: Manohar, 1978), p.166.
22. See Kershaw, 'Memorandum on the present position of the Tariff Question', 9 April 1917. British Library, India Office Record: L/E/10/13, War Trade 1917.
23. Department of Commerce and Industries, Government of India. Despatch No. 18 of 1917, 5 October 1917. British Library, India Office Record: L/E/10/11 Revenue and Statistics, War Trade 6302 1917.
24. Sir Geoffrey Corbett told the Imperial Conference in 1930, on behalf of the Indian delegation that, in the previous seven years, four industries had received protection: steel, the bamboo paper industry, the match industry and cotton textiles (Imperial Conference, 1930, *Summary of Proceedings* (London: HMSO, 1930), pp.81–2). For further detail on protected industries up to 1939, see B.N. Andarkar, *Studies in Indian Economics issued by the Office of the Economic Adviser. First Series. Aspects of the Indian Tariff, No. 2: The History of the Indian Tariff, 1924–39* (Delhi: Government of India Press, 1940), pp.6–65.
25. Presidential speech in FICCI, *Proceedings of the Sixth Annual Meeting held at Delhi on the 15th and 16th April, 1933* (Calcutta: n.p. 1933), p.13.
26. FICCI, *Note on Ottawa Scheme of Preferences* (Cawnpore: The Job Press, 1936), p.1.
27. Gupta suggests that, in the Indian case, the internal situation was important: after the Lucknow Pact (December 1916) and the Government of India statement on reform (January 1917), '[i]t becomes necessary to get Indian external economic policy in line with Britain and the rest of the empire without delay' (Partha Sarathi Gupta, 'State and business in India in the age of discriminating protection', in Divijendra Tripathi (ed.), *State and Business in India: A Historical Perspective* (New Delhi: Manohar, 1987), p.171).
28. FICCI, *Note on Ottawa Scheme*, p.1. Gallagher identifies British domestic pressure to this end. In June 1930, the Trades Union Congress suggested to the government that the Empire become an economic bloc. By September, the Federation of British Industry had joined the TUC in sponsoring the

policy (John Gallagher, *The Decline, Revival and Fall of the British Empire* (Cambridge: Cambridge University Press, 2004), p.116). Holland adds that 'it was natural that the discarding of the gold standard should have put the aspirations for imperial autarky back in the political picture' (R.F. Holland, *Britain and the Commonwealth Alliance, 1918–1939* (London: Macmillan, 1981), p.128).

29. Stanley Baldwin (24 May 1932) in Report of the Indian Delegation to the Ottawa Conference. NMML: PT Papers, File No. 127.
30. Legislative Assembly debates, 6 December 1932 VII (7) 2992. British Library, India Office Record: L/E/9/1123.
31. FICCI, *Note on Ottawa Scheme*, p.73. Gadgil wrote in 1932: 'The Empire is to be converted into a closed economic system and . . . once the policy is adopted the system will become more and more closed' (D.R. Gadgil, *Imperial Preference for India: the Ottawa Agreement Examined* (Poona: Gokhale Institute of Politics and Economics, 1932), p.ii.)
32. The Committee's report quoted in Government of India, *Statement Exhibiting the Moral and Material Progress and Condition of India during the Year 1919* (London: HMSO, 1920), p.228.
33. See Indian Fiscal Commission, *Report of the Indian Fiscal Commission, 1921–22* (Simla: Government Central Press, 1922), p.4.
34. Chatterji, *Trade, Tariffs and Empire*, p.91. However, Wagle points out that fiscal autonomy may have been the 'thin end of the wedge'. Viceroys were henceforward under pressure not to stand with 'the imperial interest against the explicit wishes of the Legislature'. And fiscal autonomy led on to the Fiscal Commission (opposed by the Viceroy and his government) which gave rise to 'discriminating protection', various Tariff Boards and some tariff protection (Dileep M. Wagle, 'Imperial preference and the Indian steel industry, 1924–39', *Economic History Review* 34, 1 (February 1981), pp.126, 130.)
35. Gupta, *State and Business in India*, p.175.
36. Indian Fiscal Commission, *Report of the Indian Fiscal Commission, 1921–22* (Simla: Government Central Press, 1922), pp.23–4, 28. The Commission had support for this idea from no less a person than the Prince of Wales, who told a meeting during his visit in November 1921, 'It is to the industries of India . . . that I look for the moral and material development of India that we wish for the people of that great land'. (Quoted by Vehkatareddi Nayadu in the Legislative Assembly, 14 November 1922. British Library, India Office Record: L/E/7/1302.)
37. Indian Fiscal Commission, *Report*, p.37.
38. Militarily valuable industries that deserved special consideration were steel and iron, leather and leather goods, copper, zinc, sulphur, ammonia, refined

glycerine, mineral jelly and rubber goods. See Indian Fiscal Commission, *Report*, pp.59–60.

39. Indian Fiscal Commission, *Report*, pp.xvi, 31, 51. Woods comments, 'the recommended "discriminating protection" represented the sort of line that the Government of India preferred and which followed the kind of mildly interventionist policy towards encouragement of Indian industry that Chelmsford favoured' (Philip Woods, *Roots of Parliamentary Democracy in India: Montagu Chelmsford Reforms, 1917–1923* (Delhi: Chanakya Publications, 1996), p.191).
40. Clive Dewey, 'The end of the imperialism of free trade: the eclipse of the Lancashire Lobby and the concession of fiscal autonomy to India', in Clive Dewey & A.G. Hopkins (eds), *The Imperial Impact: Studies in the Economic History of Africa and India* (London: The Athlone Press, 1978), pp.48–9. See also Mukherjee, *Imperialism, Nationalism*, pp.188, 191–4.
41. Minute of Dissent in Indian Fiscal Commission, *Report of the Indian Fiscal Commission, 1921–22* (Simla: Government Central Press, 1922), pp.176–9.
42. Minute of Dissent in Indian Fiscal Commission, *Report*, pp.177–8. The dissenters dangled something of an imperial carrot in front of the British. Sufficient industrialisation, they said, would 'enable India to maintain in Indian waters a navy sufficient for the defence of India, officered and manned by Indians. It will also prove a valuable Imperial asset'. (Minute of Dissent in Indian Fiscal Commission, *Report*, p.197.)
43. ' ... the Government of India are endeavouring to steer a course which, without rejecting in so many terms the recommendations of the [Fiscal Commission] Report, will reduce to a minimum the risk of any evil results that would, I think, follow from the adoption of the more thoroughgoing plan advocated by the Minute of Dissent' (C.H. Kisch (18 January 1923) in Basudev Chatterji, 'The political economy of "discriminating protection": the case of textiles in the 1920s', *Indian Economic and Social History Review* 20, 3 (1983), p.250).
44. On imperial preference before the Fiscal Commission, see Gadgil, *Imperial Preference for India*, pp.1–2.
45. Indian Fiscal Commission, *Report*, p.123. The commission's report declared: 'We do not forget that the United Kingdom is the heart of the Empire, that on its strength depends the strength and cohesion of the Empire, and that its strength is bound up with the prosperity of its export trade, which has enabled a small island to find the resources which bind together Nations known as the British Empire. Unless the United Kingdom maintains its export trade the heart of the Empire will weaken, and this is a contingency to which no part of the Empire can be indifferent'. (Indian Fiscal Commission, *Report*, p.142.)

46. Indian Fiscal Commission, *Report*, pp.142–3.
47. Department of Commerce and Industry, Government of India, Despatch No. 18, 5 October 1917. British Library, India Office Record: L/E/10/11, Revenue and Statistics, War Trade 6302. The tone of this communication was such that the India Office appointed a special committee to consider it. The committee spotted that the Government of India was attempting to set conditions on its acquiescence to imperial preference. But imperial preference, declared the committee, 'is no longer an open question' (Report of the Special Committee appointed to consider Letter No. 18 from the Government of India on Imperial Preference, 4 March 1918. British Library, India Office Record: L/E/10/11). See also the correspondence between the Commerce and Industries Department and the India Office on 2 March and 6 March 1917 (British Library, India Office Record: L/E/10/11 Revenue and Statistics, War Trade 1618/1917).
48. Department of Commerce, Government of India to Secretary of State, 8 December 1922. British Library, India Office Record: L/E/7/1291 3720.
49. Imperial Economic Conference (October–November 1923), *Record of Proceedings and Documents* (London: HMSO, 1924), p.197. The Indian delegation did in fact vote for closer empire economic co-operation, causing some consternation in the Viceroy's Executive Council (Brian R. Tomlinson, *The Political Economy of the Raj 1914–1947: The Economics of Decolonization in India* (London: Macmillan, 1979), p.120).
50. Minute of Dissent in Indian Fiscal Commission, *Report*, p.193.
51. Presidential speech to the Maharashtra Chamber of Commerce, 8 May 1929. NMML: PT Papers, File No. 42 Part II.
52. Gadgil, *Imperial Preference*, p.ii.
53. Balkrishna Madan, *India and Imperial Preference: a Study in Commercial Policy* (Bombay: Oxford University Press, 1939), pp.3–4.
54. Mukherjee, *Imperialism, Nationalism*, pp.209–10; Chatterji, *Trade, Tariffs and Empire*, pp.371–2. The exclusion of FICCI prompted Birla to remark, in May 1932, 'the Ottawa Conference has more or less been given a burial from its very inception'. (G.D. Birla, *In the Shadow of the Mahatma: a Personal Memoir* (Bombay: Orient Longmans Ltd., 1955), p.55.
55. Letter from Lala Shri Ram to Secretary of State, Private Secretary to the Viceroy and Secretary of the Commerce Department, 16 September 1930. NMML: Walchand Hirachand Archive, File No. 8 Part II.
56. Imperial Economic Conference at Ottawa, 1932, *Summary of Proceedings and Copies of Trade Agreements* (London: HMSO, 1932), p.17.
57. Indian Delegation to the Imperial Economic Conference (Ottawa 1932), *Report of the Indian Delegation* (Simla: Government of India Press, 1932), p.46. British Library, India Office record: L/E/9/1124.

58. Indian Delegation to the Imperial Economic Conference (Ottawa 1932), *Report of the Indian Delegation* (Simla: Government of India Press, 1932), NMML: PT Papers, File No. 127. Hirachand told the FICCI annual meeting in 1933 that 'the Government of India, controlled as it is from London, had no choice but to acquiesce in the policy enunciated by the British Government' (FICCI, *Proceedings of the Sixth Annual Meeting*, p.4). See also B. Sitarama Raju's Minute of Dissent to the report of the Committee appointed by the Legislative Assembly to examine a report on the working of the scheme of mutual preferences between India and the United Kingdom arising from the Ottawa Trade Agreement (British Library, India Office record: L/E/9/1122).
59. NMML: PT Papers, File No. 127.
60. NMML: PT Papers, File No. 127. For a detailed critique of the Ottawa Agreement from the Indian capitalists' point of view see Mukherjee, *Imperialism, Nationalism*, pp.208–77.
61. Lord Willingdon (13 November 1932) in Chatterji, *Trade, Tariffs and Empire*, p.373.
62. Abdur Rahim, Sitarama Raju and Har Bilas Sarda noted in an 'Explanatory Note', 'Our colleagues evidently attach no importance to the fact that such expert and business opinion as we received was adverse to the Ottawa Scheme of Tariffs' (Report of the Special Committee on the Ottawa Agreement, British Library, India office record: L/E/9/1123). See also Mukherjee, *Imperialism, Nationalism*, p.216.
63. Speech in FICCI, *Proceedings of the Sixth Annual Meeting*, p.8.
64. Chatterji, *Trade, Tariffs and Empire*, p.406; Federation of Indian Chambers of Commerce and Industry, *Note on Ottawa Scheme of Preferences* (Cawnpore: The Job Press, 1936), p.72.
65. FICCI, *Note on Ottawa Scheme of Preferences* (Cawnpore: The Job Press, 1936), p.5. In fact, according to FICCI, France and Italy, in response to the Ottawa Agreement, had adopted 'a policy of developing their colonial possessions on lines similar to the British scheme' (pp.68–9).
66. FICCI Executive Committee 1934 in Mukherjee, *Imperialism, Nationalism*, p.212. The pro-British journal *Capital* commented in November 1934 that 'underlying all [FICCI's] ideas is a bitter hatred of Great Britain and everything British. It is conclusive proof, if proof were needed, that commercial safeguards for the British in India are essential . . . to protect them from *a few* Indians who constantly use the national cry in furtherance of their own interests'. (*Capital*, 22 November 1934. British Library, India Office record: L/E/9/1122.
67. Dorab Tata, Address to General Meeting, 25 October 1923. Tata Central Archive (henceforward TCA), File No. 308 (a), TISCO 1923–24.

68. TCA, File No. 308, TISCO 1919–1922.
69. John Peterson to G. Rainy, Chief Secretary, Political department, 13 January 1923. TCA File No. 308(a), TISCO 1923–24.
70. Memorandum from TISCO to Government of India, 13 October 1923. TCA File No. 308(a), TISCO 1923–4. Peterson defended the expansion plans, drawing attention to the government's changing attitude: 'If the Steel Company were short-sighted in adopting [the plans], their short-sightedness was certainly shared in by all the Government Authorities responsible for the prosecution of the War.' (Peterson to Chadwick, 13 November 1923. TCA, File No. 308(a), TISCO 1923–4.
71. Memorandum for TISCO to Government of India, 13 October 1923. TCA, File No. 308(a), TISCO 1923–4.
72. Peterson to Sir Charles Innes, 13 January 1924. TCA, File No. 308(a), TISCO 1923–4.
73. At this stage, the help sought was confined to advance purchases and loans rather than protection. Peterson alluded to one reason for this in a memorandum concerning Tata lobbying around the 1921–2 Budget: 'I think it would be a good policy not to raise the question of higher import duties till at least all our Greater Extensions Material and the material for subsidiaries in which we are interested has come in, because any rise in the Import Duty would affect the cost of our extensions and the subsidiaries.' Memorandum: Re Jamshedpur Proposals, 8 March 1921. TCA, File No. 308, TISCO 1919–22.
74. R.M. Lala, *The Romance of Tata Steel* (New Delhi: Penguin/Viking, 2007), p.44.
75. TCA Steel Industry debates Part 1 Legislative Assembly, 27 May 1924, 2348; 4 June 1924, 2574.
76. Both sides would probably have agreed with Sir Thomas Holland: 'Without steel manufactures on a large scale and, therefore, for the near future at least, without the Tata Steel Company, there can be no National India, and all political reforms must be non-productive . . . the Tata Steel Co. is as much a National necessity as the Telegraph Department or the Army. That it is the product of private enterprise does not alter the fact' (Quoted by Sir Dorab Tata, TISCO General Meeting, 25 October 1923. TCA, File No. 308(a), TISCO 1923–4).
77. Indian Tariff Board, *Report of the Indian Tariff Board regarding the Grant of Protection to the Steel Industry* (Calcutta: Superintendent of Government Printing, 1924), p.178.
78. TCA, Legislative Assembly, 27 May 1924. Steel Industry Debates Part 1. In fact, the Bill represented the last gasp of an old policy, rather than the dawn of a new one.

79. TCA, Legislative Assembly, 27 May 1924. Steel Industry Debates Part 1.
80. TCA, Legislative Assembly, 27 May 1924. Steel Industry Debates Part 1. Business activists also gave support outside the Assembly. On hearing the news that the Bengal Chamber of Commerce (a European body) would come out against steel industry protection, a host of Indian industrialists refused the invitation to attend the opening session of the Association of Chambers of Commerce of India and Ceylon in November 1923 (NMML: PT Papers, File No. 42).
81. TCA, Steel Industry Debates Part 1.
82. See the speeches of W.S.J. Wilson and Sir Charles Innes, Legislative Assembly 27 May 1924 (TCA, Steel Industry Debates Part 1). In fact, the Bombay Chamber of Commerce (European) committee, noting that 'the Tata Iron and Steel Company rendered very material help in supplying the needs of the armies in Mesopotamia during the recent war', resolved that 'a very limited amount of protection would probably, if carefully applied, be to the good of the country, for it might assist in the development of a basic iron and steel industry which, although not essential to an agricultural country such as India, would probably further its commercial development (Bombay Chamber of Commerce, Excerpts from the Proceedings of the Committee, October 1923. NMML PT Papers File No. 42 (p.iv)).
83. 'Re-Organization of the capital of the Tata Iron and Steel Company' (Circular to shareholders), 6 November 1924. TCA, File No. 308(a), TISCO 1923–24.
84. Tata's desperate search for further state funds is detailed in NMML: PT Papers File No. 41, TISCO 1923–30.
85. John L. Keenan, *A Steel Man in India* (London: V. Gollancz Ltd, 1945), p.163.
86. Indian Tariff Board, *Report of the Indian Tariff Board Regarding the Increase of Duties on Steel* (Bombay: Government Central Press, 1924), p.45.
87. NMML: PT Papers, File No. 41, TISCO 1923–30.
88. Minutes of TISCO Committee meeting, 5 November 1924 in NMML: PT Papers, File No. 41, TISCO 1923–30; TISCO Board meeting, 6 November 1924, TCA File No. 308(a) TISCO 1923–24.
89. Indian Tariff Board, *Report Regarding the Increase of Duties on Steel*, pp.7, 46.
90. Indian Tariff Board, *Report Regarding the Increase of Duties on Steel*, pp.28–31.
91. See Sir Charles Innes' (Commerce and Railways Member) speech introducing the Bill, 26 January 1927. TCA Steel Industry Debates Part 2.
92. Das, 18 February 1927. TCA Steel Industry Debates Part 2. As R.K. Shanmukham Chetty had pointed out though, 'In so far as the policy of Imperial Preference is based merely on Empire sentiment, I think it has been abandoned by every Dominion in the British Empire' (Chetty, 14 February 1927. TCA Steel Industry Debates Part 2).

93. Gavin-Jones and Moore on 14 February 1927. TCA Steel Industry Debates Part 2.
94. The Indian Merchants' Chamber, the Calcutta Iron Merchants' Association and a meeting of 'trades people, small industrialists and consumers of steel products' in Delhi were among those who protested (TCA Steel Industry Debates Part 2).
95. Mehta on 14 February 1927. TCA Steel Industry Debates Part 2.
96. Chatterji, *Trade, Tariffs and Empire,* p.239.
97. See the Viceroy on the subject: Lord Hardinge of Penshurst, *Memorandum by H.E. the Viceroy upon Questions Likely to Arise in India at the End of the War* (Delhi: n.p., 1915), p.19; and similar statements by an array of British Indian officials in Appendix B.
98. The Viceroy, Lord Chelmsford, *The Goal of British Rule in India.* British Library, India Office record: MSS EUR E264/51, 314–315; Department of Commerce and Industry to Secretary of State, 13 January 1919. National Archives of India: Government of India, Department of Commerce and Industry Proceedings, February 1919; Indian Fiscal Commission Report 1921–22.
99. Chatterji, *Trade, Tarrifs and Empire*, pp.239–59.
100. Chatterji, 'The political economy of discriminating protection ', p.267.
101. Claude Markovits, *Indian Business and Nationalist Politics, 1931–1939: The Indigenous Capitalist Class and the Rise of the Congress Party* (Cambridge: Cambridge University Press, 1985), p.69. According to the *Indian National Herald*, 'Mr H.P. Mody [the Bombay mill owners' representative] . . . carries the palm for his inextinguishable faith in the indispensability of British patronage . . . Not all the rebuffs the mill-owners have suffered have weakened Mr Mody's optimism in the ultimate beneficence of Government towards the industry' (30 June 1927). NMML, HP Mody Papers: V Bound Press Clippings File No. 1, 1901–27.
102. Chatterji, *Trade, Tariffs and Empire*, p.276. The British were also wary of the Japanese. See Kershaw's (India Office) and Chamberlain's (Secretary of State) comments on Japan's attendance at the Paris Economic Conference (British Library, India Office record: L/E/10/5). A British businessman from the Madura district (Madras Presidency) wrote to the government, 'should they [the Japanese] be permitted to capture the Cotton Ginning Industry of this Presidency, they will be infinitely more difficult to deal with than ever the Germans were. They have no Commercial Morality' (J.C. Harvey, 11 May 1917. British Library, India Office record: L/E/10/13 Revenue and Statistics War Trade 4529 1917).
103. The Commerce Member, Sir Charles Innes, was at pains not to give the 'impression that they [the Bombay mill owners] must square the Swaraj

Party before we pay attention to them' (Chatterji, *Trade, Tariffs and Empire*, p.248).

104. Chatterji, *Trade, Tariffs and Empire*, p.251.
105. Report in *Bombay Chronicle*, 24 August 1924. NMML: H.P. Mody Papers, V(i) Bound Press Clippings File No. 1 1901–27.
106. Cited in Indian Tariff Board, *Report of the Indian Tariff Board (Cotton Textile Industry Enquiry), 1927* (Bombay: Government Central Press, 1927), p.2.
107. Chatterji, 'Political economy of discriminatory protection', pp.260–4.
108. Reported in the *Evening News*, 7 June 1927. NMML, H.P. Mody Papers: V(i) Bound Press Clippings File No. 1 1901–27. Chatterji tells us, 'Naturally the millowners of Lancashire were overjoyed' (Chatterji, 'Political economy of discriminatory protection', p.265).
109. Indian Tariff Board, *Cotton Textiles 1932*, p.3.
110. Mukherjee, *Imperialism, Nationalism*, pp.200–2. Birla rejected the measure in the Legislative Assembly on 'the ground that the wider interest of the country demand[ed] that Imperial Preference could not be accepted' (Mukherjee, *Imperialism, Nationalism*, p.202).
111. See Brian R. Tomlinson, 'India and the British Empire, 1880–1935', *Indian Economic and Social History Review* 12 (October–December 1974), p.308; Mukherjee, *Imperialism, Nationalism*, p.233.
112. Presidental speech, 31 March 1934 in Mukherjee, *Imperialism, Nationalism*, p.235.The rest of Sarkar's speech was highly critical of the agreement.
113. Mukherjee, *Imperialism, Nationalism*, p.233.
114. Chatterji, *Trade, Tariffs and Empire*, pp.384–9.
115. Birla, letter to Kasturbhai Lalbhai enclosed in a letter to Purshotamdas Thakurdas, 14 November 1934. NMML: PT Papers, File No. 126 Part 1.
116. Birla, letter to Kasturbhai Lalbhai enclosed in a letter to Purshotamdas Thakurdas, 14 November 1934. NMML: PT Papers, File No. 126 Part 1.
117. Lalbhai to Sir Joseph Bhore, 5 November 1934. NMML: PT Papers, File No. 126 Part 1.
118. Mukherjee, *Imperialism, Nationalism*, pp.249–51.
119. See, for example, Chatterji on Mody's 'Progressive Party' in *Trade, Tariffs and Empire*, p.437.
120. See Gallagher, *Decline, Revival and Fall*, pp.121–2; Tomlinson, India and the British Empire I, 366–7.
121. G.D. Birla, *A Statement on behalf of the Federation of Indian Chambers of Commerce and Industry in reply to the circular letter dated the 27th July 1929 issued by the Associated Chambers of Commerce of India and Ceylon to influence opinion in England against India's right to adapt her economic policy to her own needs* (Calcutta: Federation of Indian Chambers of Commerce and Industry, n.d), p.5.

122. The Minute of Dissent to the Report of the Indian Fiscal Commission declared that '[t]he Indian people . . . will not be satisfied by a policy which is likely to make them concentrate their efforts for many years to come on the manufacture of simpler forms of goods' (Minute of Dissent in Indian Fiscal Commission, *Report*, p.211). See also Chandra, *Nationalism and Colonialism*, p.151.
123. Sarkar, *Modern India*, p.360.
124. Chandra, *Nationalism and Colonialism*, p.149. See the Legislative Assembly resolution (16 February 1923) pointing out 'that the fiscal policy of the Government of India may legitimately be directed towards fostering the development of industry in India' (Indian Tariff Board, *Report regarding the Grant of Protection to the Steel Industry*, p.1).
125. Indian Fiscal Commission, *Report*, p.57.
126. The imagined scope of such industries expanded rapidly. The Director-General of Ordnance declared in August 1922, that 'In the wider sense all industries are of importance from the military point of view'. The Secretary of the Army Department stated that there was 'no known machine-manufactured' article in India 'which would not be utilised in war'. The Secretary of the Industries Department went even further, citing Sir Thomas Holland to the effect that 'every kind of commodity utilized by an army, including foodstuffs, was a munition of war, and that it was the object of the Industries Department to render the country self-supporting in respect of every possible class of goods'. (National Archives of India: Department of Industries – Industries Branch File No. I–211 Proceedings August 1922 Part B.)
127. As Sarkar points out, 'the more far-sighted sections of the bourgeoisie in an under-developed country would be quite ready to accept a measure of state regulation, planning, public investments in basic industries to create a favourable infra-structure for their own growth' (Sarkar, *Modern India*, p.360).
128. Presidential speech to the FICCI 6th annual meeting, 15 April 1933. NMML: Walchand Hirachand Archives, File Number 6 (a) I.
129. FICCI, *Proceedings of the Seventh Annual Meeting held at Delhi on the 31st March and 1st April, 1934* (Ahmedabad: n.p. 1934), pp.21, 23. Sarkar distanced himself from 'the extreme type of State Socialism and economic regimentation that have been enforced in Russia' (p.25) and stressed that the purpose of his scheme was to *avoid* revolution (p.67).
130. See NMML, PT Papers: File Number 25, 1920–21. See also Report of the Railway Industries Committee, n.d. British Library, India Office record: L/E/7/1279.

131. He said, 'I am averse to company management, even by Indian companies under the present circumstances' (Frank Moraes, *Sir Purshotamdas Thakurdas* (Bombay: Asia Publishing House, 1957), p.35). Such a view pre-dated the Railway Committee. In 1916 the Congress president, Ambica Charan Mazumdar, told the Congress session that once a national government was formed, 'the railways owned by the State and controlled by the State will then be conducted upon national lines and will be the hand-maid of the national industries by offering facilities for their growth and development' (K.C. Sankarakrishna (ed.), *India's Demands: a Collection of the Speeches delivered on the platforms of the Indian National Congress and the All India Muslim League, 1916* (Madras: Sankarakrishna, 1917), p.48). In the same year, *The Leader* editorialised that 'Indian opinion is strongly in favour of the State undertaking management of railways at present under Company management' ('State *versus* Company Management', 10 May 1916).
132. Press report cited in Moraes, *Sir Purshotamdas Thakurdas*, p.35.
133. NMML, M.A. Master Papers: Subject File 1, File Number 13.
134. *Report on the System of Management to be Adopted in India* (by the Committee chairman plus four others, including Thakurdas, 22 July 1921) and *Summary of Recommendations.* NMML, PT Papers: File No. 27, 1921.
135. Proceedings of the Indian Legislative Council, 14 March 1918 in NMML, M.A. Master Papers: Subject File E. File Number 777, 1918–46.
136. Cited in Baman Chandra Das, *Financial Autonomy for India* (Calcutta: B.C. Das, 1919), p.50.
137. Dwijendra Tripathi (ed.), *The Concise Oxford History of Indian Business* (New Delhi: Oxford University Press, 2007), pp.99–100.
138. See Surendra Nath Bannerjea's speech in Proceedings of the Indian Legislative Council, 22 March 1918. NMML, M.A. Master Papers: Subject File E. File Number 777, 1918–46.
139. Chairman's speech to Scindia's fourth ordinary general meeting, 19 December 1923. NMML, Walchand Hirachand Archives: File No. 326, I.H.P. Mody told the Indian Shipping Conference (on which, more below) 'the satisfaction of the national aspiration of the people in the domain of shipping . . . would help in satisfying the national aspirations of the country'. (Proceedings of the Mercantile Marine Conference, 3–4 January 1930. NMML, M.A. Master Papers: Subject File A Scindia File No. 64, 1929–30.
140. See NMML, M.A. Master Papers: Subject File I File No. 48.
141. Morarjee at Scindia's seventh ordinary general meeting, 30 October 1926. NMML, Walchand Hirachand Archives: File No. 326, I.

142. Morarjee at Scindia's fourth ordinary general meeting, 19 December 1923. NMML, Walchand Hirachand Archives: File No. 326, I.
143. Morarjee complained in 1922: 'There is absolutely no direct encouragement for building up and developing Indian Merchant Marine. No subsidies. No bounties. No cheap loans. No special railway rates. No discrimination of tonnage dues. No reservation of Coastal Trade'. Morarjee at Scindia's third ordinary general meeting, 31 October 1922. NMML, Walchand Hirachand Archives: File No. 326, I.
144. NMML, M.A. Master Papers: Subject File I, File No. 44 1929.
145. Reporting on an interview with the India Office's Sir Louis Kershaw, Morarjee wrote 'Sir Louis said the Government would never reserve Indian coastal trade for India and that we could never expect either subsidies or bounties' (NMML, M.A. Master Papers: Subject File I, File No. 48 1929).
146. Morarjee at Scindia's third ordinary general meeting, 31 October 1922. NMML, Walchand Hirachand Archives: File No. 326, I.
147. J.A. Woodward to Scindia directors, 5 December 1929. NMML, M.A. Master Papers: Subject File No. 64.
148. Haji, 'Note on conversation regarding Indian Shipping during the Delhi session'. NMML, M.A. Master Papers: Subject Files, Scindia File No. 53, 1929.
149. Viceroy to the annual session of the Associated Chambers of Commerce, Calcutta 17 December 1928. NMML, M.A. Master Papers: Subject File I, File No. 48.
150. Reported in a cable from Master to Narottam Morarjee, 5 September 1929. NMML, M.A. Master Papers: Subject File 69.
151. Proceedings of the Merchant Marine Conference, New Delhi, 3–4 January 1930. NMML, M.A. Master Papers: Subject File 64, 1930. In fact, Master's copy of the Proceedings is marked throughout by points of agreement with the Viceroy's views.
152. See Hirachand's Note on conversations with Sir Joseph Bhore (Commerce Member), 3 August 1932. NMML, M.A. Master Papers: Subject File 79, 1932; Bhore's letter to Hirachand, 17 January 1933. NMML, M.A. Master Papers: Subject File 95, 1933.
153. NMML, M.A. Master Papers: Subject File A, Scindia File Number 53, 1929.
154. Master wrote to the Indian Merchants' Chamber in Bombay (21 April 1931) that 'it will be clear that whatever promises might have been made and whatever hopes might have been created . . . the Government were not prepared to do anything to carry out the undertaking of direct financial assistance as the Government had no funds' (NMML, M.A. Master Papers: Subject File 69).
155. Legislative Assembly debates, 2 March 1922, II (39), p.2698. British Library, India Office Record: L/E/7/1279.

156. See NMML, M.A. Master Papers: Subject File I File No. 44, 1929; NMML, Walchand Hirachand Archives: File No. 587.
157. Statement on Indian Shipping on behalf of Indian Shipowners. NMML, M.A. Master Papers: Subject File A Scindia File No. 64, 1929–30 (emphasis in original).
158. Legislative Assembly, 26 January 1931. NMML, M.A. Master Papers: Subject File No. 64, 1930.
159. Addressing the annual meeting of FICCI, 14–16 February 1930, cited in Kudaisya, *Birla*, p.151.
160. See Narottam Morarjee (13 July 1928) in NMML, M.A. Master Papers: Subject File I File No. 48, 1929; Hirachand to FICCI 6th annual meeting, 15 April 1933 in NMML, Walchand Hirachand Archives: File No. 6 (a) I. See also Gupta, *State and Business in India*, p.202.
161. FICCI, *Proceedings of the Seventh Annual Meeting*, p.25. C.D. Deshmukh told the Central Provinces Legislative Council in January 1935: 'Planned economy in a nation implies certain pre-requisites, and those are complete self-sufficiency of the nation... and freedom from economic dependence in any form on any foreign country' (NMML, C.D. Deshmukh Papers: Speeches and Writings (Unpublished), 1932–37. File No. 1 Series No. 46.
162. Presidential speech in FICCI, *Proceedings of the Sixth Annual Meeting*, p.4.
163. Mukherjee, *Imperialism, Nationalism*, pp.253–7, 287–95; Chatterji, *Trade, Tariffs and Empire*, p.434.
164. Presidential speech to FICCI 6th Annual Meeting 1933, pp.9–10. The meeting resolved that India should be represented at the International Economic Conference 'only by Indians enjoying the confidence of the Indian commercial community' (p.120). See also the remarks of D.P. Khaitan from the Indian Chamber of Commerce (p.124).
165. Cited in Mukherjee, *Imperialism, Nationalism*, p.218.
166. The Indian bourgeoisie would not have been surprised at Ray's assertion that 'only savage, single-minded determination and will-power, that brooked no obstacle or resistance, that did not quail at any sight of privation and suffering, could have carried the Indian economy forward at a pace comparable to that of Japan or Russia during the inter-war period. Such a procedure needed, above all, a national will' (Rajat K. Ray, *Industrialization in India: Growth and Conflict in the Private Corporate Sector, 1914–1947* (Delhi: Oxford University Press, 1979), p.234).
167. Nalini Sarkar commented: 'The events of 1933 have clearly shown that the trend of economic thought and policy is towards the intensification of economic nationalism, in some cases on the basis of a conscious plan... There is a distinct bias in favour of a policy of economic

autarchy.' (Nalini Sarkar, Presidential speech, FICCI 7th annual meeting, 1934, p.5).

168. See Chandra, *Nationalism and Colonialism*, pp.154–5.
169. Frederick Engels, *Anti-Duhring* (Moscow: Progress Publishers, 1969), p.219.

Chapter Six Congress and the Bourgeoisie: Inter-War Politics

1. 'With the rise of indigenous industrial capital went also an increasing demand for indigenous control of a nation-state, whose services, in every area from tariff protection to budgetary subvention to the repression of labour, were as essential for its progress here as in every other second-phase industrialization' (David Washbrook, 'South Asia, the world system and world capitalism', in *South Asia and World Capitalism*, ed. Sugata Bose (Delhi: Oxford University Press, 1990), p.75. See also Government of India, *Despatch on Proposals for Constitutional Reform* (Simla: Government of India Press, 1930), pp.4–5: 'the trading classes, which as a whole used in the past to be content to occupy themselves with their business, have been taking a more and more active share in politics'.
2. Frank Moraes, *Sir Purshotamdas Thakurdas* (Bombay: Asia Publishing House, 1957), p.213.
3. Businessmen were also pushed into politics by the fact that in both the Montagu-Chelmsford and 1935 schemes business ('Commerce and Industry') had reserved seats in both the Central and Provincial legislatures. They were elected by Chambers of Commerce and similar institutions. Thakurdas, for example, represented the Bombay cotton trade in the post-Montagu-Chelmsford Bombay Legislative Assembly (Philip Woods, *Roots of Parliamentary Democracy in India: Montagu Chelmsford Reforms, 1917–1923* (Delhi: Chanakya Publications, 1996), pp.252, 274, 286; House of Commons, *Proposals for Indian Constitutional Reform* (London: HMSO, 1933), Appendix II, pp.89–93; Moraes, *Thakurdas*, p.29).
4. For example, in D. Chakrabarty & C. Bhattacharyya (eds), *Congress in Evolution: a collection of Congress Resolutions from 1885–1934* (Calcutta: The Book Company Ltd., 1935), no resolutions on economic matters appear between the session of 1915 and that of 1920. In Indian National Congress, *Resolutions on Economic Policy and Programme, 1924–54* (New Delhi: All-India Congress Committee, 1954), there is a further gap between the Faizpore Congress' Agrarian Programme (December 1936) and the Congress Working Committee's Election Manifesto (December 1945).

5. *The Leader*, 7 January 1912. The article also pointed out that the industrialists were only allowed to use the Congress' *pandal* for one day – from 10.30 am to 1.30 pm.
6. Indian National Congress, *Report of the Proceedings of the Third Session of the Indian National Congress, 1887* (New York: Vintage Books, 1993 [1887]), p.65.
7. Indian National Congress, *All-India Congress Committee 1926* (Madras: General Secretary of the AICC, 1927), pp.77, 84.
8. Indian National Congress, *Resolutions on Economic Policy and Programme, 1924–54* (New Delhi: All-India Congress Committee, 1954), pp.6–9; D. Chakrabarty & C. Bhattacharyya (eds), *Congress in Evolution: a collection of Congress Resolutions from 1885–1934* (Calcutta: The Book Company Ltd., 1935), p.29; National Planning Committee, *Abstract of Proceedings, Number 1* (Bombay: National Planning Committee, n.d. [1939]), p.3; J.B. Kripilani, *The Indian National Congress, 1930–1934* (Allahabad: All-India Congress Committee, n.d.), p.68.
9. Jawaharlal Nehru, *Nehru: The First Sixty Years, Volume 1*, Dorothy Norman (ed.) (London: The Bodley Head, 1965), p.248. He added: 'Perhaps [the Government of India] even pictured, with their usual perspicacity, the red gold of the Bolsheviks stealing its way into Karachi and corrupting the Congress leaders'.
10. Mohandas K. Gandhi, *The Collected Works of Mahatma Gandhi* (Delhi: Publications Division, Ministry of Information and Broadcasting, 1958–94), Volume 42, pp.308–9.
11. Presidential address, December 1936 in Nehru, *First Sixty Years, I*, p.472.
12. Nehru, *First Sixty Years, I*, p.692.
13. Congress Working Committee Election Manifesto, December 1945 in Indian National Congress, *Resolutions on Economic Policy*, pp.16–18.
14. Akshayakumar R. Desai, *Social Background of Indian Nationalism* (Bombay: Popular Prakashan, 1966 [1948]), p.179.
15. Before the Non-Cooperation Movement, says Krishna, 'The Congress was still composed largely of those who had taken to the new professions of law, journalism, teaching and Western medicine' (Gopal Krishna, 'The development of the Indian National Congress as a mass organization, 1918–1923', *Journal of Asian Studies* 25, 3 (May 1966), p.423).
16. Krishna, 'Development as mass organisation', p.424.
17. Figures extracted from Krishna, 'Development as mass organisation', p.424. After the Non-Cooperation movement, Congress made attempts to expand its mass base, which accounts for the reduction after 1921.
18. 'Perhaps the most important element in the early years was the emergence of a new class of professional politicians who called themselves public workers

and became completely identified with the Congress cause. They did not make their appearance until the first civil disobedience campaign [1920], but thereafter their number increased rapidly' (Stanley A. Kochanek, *The Congress Party of India: the Dynamics of a One-Party Democracy* (Princeton: Princeton University Press, 1968), p.365).

19. Desai, *Social Background*, pp.197, 198.
20. 'Political discontent born of the economic suffering due to unemployment among the educated middle class was an important factor in the growth of the political current of militant nationalism' (Desai, *Social Background*, p.199).
21. Later on, much the same could be said of the Muslim League. Sayeed tells us: 'Muslim educated classes were not so much concerned about their religious and cultural rights as they were about their share in the government of the country. The tremendous following Jinnah had among these classes lay in the fact that he offered them political power under a new Muslim State' (Khalid B. Sayeed, *Pakistan: the Formative Phase, 1857–1948* (London: Oxford University Press, 1968), p.179).
22. J.C. Scott, *Seeing Like a State: How Certain Schemes to Improve the Human Condition Have Failed* (New Haven: Yale University Press: 1998), p.88.
23. Peter Holquist, *Making War, Forging Revolution: Russia's Continuum of Crisis, 1914–1921* (Cambridge: Harvard University Press, 2002), p.136. See also David Lockwood, *Cronies or Capitalists? The Russian Bourgeoisie and the Bourgeois Revolution from 1850 to 1917* (Newcastle upon Tyne: Cambridge Scholars Publishing, 2009), pp.131–6.
24. Tony Cliff, *Deflected Permanent Revolution* (London: Socialist Workers Party, 1990 [1963]), p.24.
25. Markovits and Chatterji detect a division between Tata and the Bombay mill owners, on the one hand, and FICCI (including Birla and Thakurdas) and the Ahmedabad mill owners, on the other – with the former closer to the British and the latter closer to Congress (Claude Markovits, *Indian Business and Nationalist Politics, 1931–1939: The Indigenous Capitalist Class and the Rise of the Congress Party* (Cambridge: Cambridge University Press, 1985); Basudev Chatterji, *Trade, Tariffs and Empire: Lancashire and British Policy in India, 1919–1939* (Delhi: Oxford University Press, 1992), pp.320–1). Gordon, more specifically in Bombay, divides business between 'industrialists' and 'marketeers', with the latter as the partisans of nationalism (A.D.D. Gordon, *Businessmen and Politics: Rising Nationalism and a Modernising Economy in Bombay, 1918–1933* (New Delhi: Manohar, 1978).)
26. Birla to Thakurdas, 28 June 1932. Nehru Memorial Museum and Library: Purshotamdas Thakurdas Papers (henceforward, NMML: PT Papers), File Number 107, Part 1.

27. Mukherjee brings out this point in his review of Gordon: 'The point Gordon misses is that unlike [the Indian landlords and princes], the industrialists' basic long-term interests were not tied up with colonialism; on the contrary, their industrial growth was possible only with the overthrow of colonialism' (Aditya Mukherjee, 'Business and politics in Bombay', *Indian Historical Review* 9, 1–2 (1981), p.217).
28. Gordon concedes: 'The activities of the industrialists [at this stage, with the "marketeers" behind them] had, by 1929, created a series of inter-linking arguments... [which] taken together, stood as a complete doctrine of economic nationalism' (Gordon, *Businessmen and Politics*, p.199).
29. Rudolf von Albertini, 'The impact of two world wars on the decline of colonialism', *Journal of Contemporary History* 4, 1 (1969), p.21.
30. Thakurdas to Deviprasad Khaitain, 9 September 1927. NMML: PT Papers, File Number 42, III 1923–34.
31. See Chatterji, *Trade, Tariffs and Empire*, p.320; Gordon, *Businessmen and Politics*, pp.174, 179; Aditya Mukherjee, *Imperialism, Nationalism and the Making of the Indian Capitalist Class, 1920–1947* (New Delhi: Sage Publications, 2002), pp.276–7; Manali Chakrabarti, 'Why did Indian big business pursue a policy of economic nationalism in the inter-war years?' *Modern Asian Studies* 43, 4 (2009), p.1025.
32. Medha M. Kudaisya, *The Life and Times of G.D. Birla* (New Delhi: Oxford University Press, 2003), pp.120–1.
33. Mukherjee comments that this 'lent weight to their assertion that they were taking positions not based on narrow class interests but national interests' (Mukherjee, *Imperialism, Nationalism*, p.276).
34. Most importantly Birla and Thakurdas. Businessmen who actually joined the Congress included Jamnalal Bajaj, Vodilal Lallubhai Mehta, Samuel Aaron and Lala Shankar Lal.
35. Ratan Tata to Gokhale, 29 November 1909 and 8 July 1910. Tata Central Archive: Important Correspondence. Rack Number 73, Box 870. See also, 'Mr Ratan Tata's Patriotism', *The Leader*, 11 December 1909.
36. John L. Keenan, *A Steel Man in India* (London: V. Gollancz Ltd, 1945), p.217.
37. Geoffrey Jones, 'Jamnalal Bajaj, Mahatma Gandhi, and the struggle for Indian Independence', Harvard Business School, 12 October 2007: www.hbs.edu/businesshistory/pdf/struggleforindianind.pdf, pp.12–13.
38. Kudaisya, *Birla*, p.113.
39. Birla to N.M. Mazamdar (for Dorab Tata), 7 June 1929. NMML: PT Papers, File Number 42 Part II.
40. Moraes, *Thakurdas*, p.38.

41. Mukherjee, *Imperialism, Nationalism*, p.55.
42. Motilal Nehru to Purshotamdas Thakurdas, 29 May 1930. NMML: PT Papers, File Number 91, Part II 1929–30.
43. Thakurdas to Motilal Nehru, 22 September 1930. NMML: PT Papers, File Number 104. Thakurdas was invited to attend the Congress session in Delhi in 1932. An anonymous Congress supporter urged him to take up the leadership of the Bombay Congress in August 1930 (NMML: Invitation (20 April 1932) – PT Papers, File Number 107 Part III; Anonymous letter (2 August 1930) – PT Papers, File Number 100 1930).
44. Thakurdas (December 1929) in G.D. Birla, *A Statement on behalf of the Federation of Indian Chambers of Commerce and Industry in reply to the circular letter dated the 27th July 1929 issued by the Associated Chambers of Commerce of India and Ceylon to influence opinion in England against India's right to adapt her economic policy to her own needs* (Calcutta: Federation of Indian Chambers of Commerce and Industry, n.d.).
45. Kudaisya, *Birla*, p.121.
46. Kudaisya, *Birla*, pp.122–3.
47. On the Round Table Conference: 'it was decided [by the FICCI Executive Committee] that the representatives of the Federation on the Round Table Conference should work under the political leadership of Mahatma Gandhi' (FICCI letter to Thakurdas, 27 July 1931. NMML: PT Papers, File Number 104). On the reformed constitution: 'Our readiness to go to the Councils cannot be of any avail unless the country [i.e. the Congress] also decides upon such a policy' (Nalini Sarkar, presidential speech in Federation of Indian Chambers of Commerce and Industry, *Proceedings of the Seventh Annual Meeting held at Delhi on the 31st March and 1st April, 1934* (Ahmedabad: n.p. 1934), p.72).
48. See Markovits, *Indian Business*, p.187; Sumit Sarkar, *Modern India, 1885–1947* (Madras: Macmillan India Ltd., 1983), pp.327, 359; Rajat K. Ray, 'Review of Claude Markovitz [sic], *Indian Business and Politics, 1937–1939*', *Indian Economic and Social History Review* 25 (1988), p.392; Chakrabarti, *Why Did Indian?* pp.986, 1025.
49. Mukherjee, *Imperialism, Nationalism*, p.67.
50. In Basudev Chatterji, 'The political economy of "discriminating protection": the case of textiles in the 1920s', *Indian Economic and Social History Review* 20, 3 (1983), p.269. See also Gandhi, 'More of Millowners Greed', *Young India*, 10 May 1928, *Collected Works*, Volume 36.
51. Kudaisya, *Birla*, pp.133–6.
52. Mukherjee, *Imperialism, Nationalism*, pp.66, 274–6.
53. Chatterji, *Trade, Tariffs and Empire*, p.322.
54. Mukherjee, *Imperialism, Nationalism*, p.547.
55. Chatterji, *Trade, Tariffs and Empire*, p.355.

56. He described his efforts to Birla, 16 September 1930. NMML: PT Papers, File Number 104.
57. FICCI Executive Committee minutes, 16 May 1930. NMML: PT Papers, File Number 104. Having adopted a radical boycott stance, both Thakurdas and the Executive Committee gave some thought as to whether Thakurdas should attend as a private individual – given that 'every party and every interest will be represented at the [Round Table] Conference except the Congress and the organised Indian Commerce and Industry... questions concerning economic India will be left entirely to the mercy of the representatives of the European vested interests' (FICCI Executive Committee to Thakurdas, 12 September 1930. NMML: PT Papers, File Number 104). It was decided to maintain the boycott; Thakurdas did not attend (see also Thakurdas to Sir Joseph Bhore, 10 September, 1930; Birla to Sarabhai, 6 September 1930; Sarabhai to Birla, 10 September 1930. NMML: PT Papers, File Number 104).
58. FICCI, *Representation submitted to H.E. the Viceroy by the Committee of the Federation on the present political situation in India* (Delhi: Oxford Printing Works, 1930), pp.6–7.
59. Not before Lord Irwin attempted (eventually unsuccessfully) to exclude Birla from the business delegation. See NMML: PT Papers, File Number 104.
60. Birla to Lord Lothian (Under Secretary of State), 4 August 1932. NMML: PT Papers, File Number 126, Part II. The point was also made by Thakurdas to the Third Round Table Conference: 'so long as you have Mr Gandhi in gaol you will find that the people of India will not seriously consider Constitution making' (Indian Round Table Conference, November–December 1932. *Sub-Committees' Reports; Summaries of Discussions and the Secretary of State's Statement* (Calcutta: Government of India Publications branch, 1933), p.104).
61. Letter from the Chamber to Governor of Bengal, 16 January 1932. NMML: PT Papers. File Number 107 Part III.
62. Indian Merchants' Chamber to Home Department, Government of India, 10 May 1930. NMML: PT Papers, File Number 91, Part III 1929–30.
63. FICCI resolution at 6th Annual meeting, 15–16 April 1933. NMML: PT Papers, File Number 126, Part II.
64. See House of Commons, *Proposals for Indian Constitutional Reform* (London: HMSO, 1933).
65. FICCI, *Constitutional Reforms for India* (Ahmedabad: Indian Printing Works, 1935).
66. FICCI, *Proceedings of the Sixth Annual Meeting held at Delhi on the 15th and 16th April, 1933* (Calcutta: n.p. 1933), pp.106, 114.
67. Chandra tells us: 'Again and again Birla, and through him, though virtually silently, Gandhi assured British statesmen and officials that even the

otherwise condemned reforms could be worked if the "personal touch" between the two sides was established' (Bipan Chandra, *Nationalism and Colonialism in Modern India* (New Delhi: Orient Longman, 1979), pp.179, 190). See also Kudaisya, *Birla*, p.166.

68. Chandra comments: 'once the Congress postponed the decision on acceptance of office and refused to commit itself to office rejection, the battle was half-won by the ministerialists' (Chandra, *Nationalism and Colonialism*, p.191).
69. P.N. Chopra (ed.), *Towards Freedom, 1937: Experiments with Provincial Autonomy* (New Delhi: Oxford University Press, 1985), pp.237–40.
70. See Sarkar, *Modern India*, p.358; Mukherjee, *Imperialism, Nationalism*, p.71.
71. G.D. Birla, *In the Shadow of the Mahatma: A Personal Memoir* (Bombay: Orient Longmans Ltd., 1955), pp.196, 208.
72. Mukherjee notes, 'The bourgeoisie's understandable inclination to remain within the bourgeois framework, has surprisingly been often misunderstood . . . for a desire to remain in the imperial framework' (Aditya Mukherjee, 'The Workers' and Peasants' Parties, 1926–30: an aspect of Communism in India', *Studies in History* III, 1 & 2 (1981), p.31. See also Mukherjee, *Imperialism, Nationalism*, pp.52–3; Mukherjee, 'Business and politics in Bombay', p.218).
73. Sarkar, *Modern India*, p.132.
74. Thakurdas to Thomas Holland, 16 October 1920 in Chatterji, *Trade, Tariffs and Empire*, p.320.
75. Sarkar, *Modern India*, p.208; Markovits, *Indian Business*, p.37. He was joined by Jamnadan Dawarkadas, Cowasji Jehangir, Pheroze Sethna and Setalvad.
76. Kudaisya, *Birla*, p.63.
77. Chatterji, *Trade, Tariffs and Empire*, p.357. See also Gordon on the pro-nationalist sentiments of Marwari and Gujarati merchants: *Businessmen and Politics*, p.159.
78. Sarkar, *Modern India*, p.207.
79. Birla in Markovits, *Indian Business*, p.69.
80. Thakurdad to Motilal Nehru, 1 May 1928. NMML: PT Papers, File Number 40 Part 4. What those quarters were remains unclear.
81. Kudaisya, *Birla*, p.124.
82. Lalji Naranji to Thakurdas, 20 March 1930. NMML: Pt Papers, File Number 91 Part III, 1929–30.
83. *Times of India*, 25 May 1930. NMML: PT Papers, File Number 91 Part II, 1929–30.
84. Mody at the fifth plenary, 20 November 1930. Indian Round Table Conference, 12 November 1930–19 January 1931, *Proceedings* (London: HMSO, 1931), p.156.
85. Sarkar, *Modern India*, p.292; Kudaisya, *Birla*, p.126.

86. NMML: PT Papers, File Number 100, 1930. The sub-committee included Birla, Thakurdas, Chunilal V. Mehta, Ambulal Sarabahi, Kasturbhai Lalbhai and Lalji Naranji.
87. It was reported that Thakurdas took part in salt agitation demonstrations in Bombay (NMML: PT Papers, File Number 91, Part II, 1929–30). For business support in the early stages of the campaign see also Chatterji, *Trade, Tariffs and Empire*, p.323; Sarkar, *Modern India*, p.292.
88. Gordon, *Businessmen and Politics*, p.201. Chatterji agrees: 'From the start Bombay millowners had no time for Civil Disobedience' (*Trade, Tariffs and Empire*, p.327).
89. Gordon, *Businessmen and Politics*, p.232.
90. Cited by the Viceroy to the Secretary of State, 24 April 1930 in Sarkar, *Modern India*, p.292. It is doubtful whether the governor differentiated between 'industrialists' and 'merchants' as Gordon does.
91. Government of India, *Despatch on Proposals for Constitutional Reform* (Simla: Government of India Press, 1930), p.4.
92. See Thakurdas to Motilal Nehru, 4 June 1930. NMML: PT Papers, File Number 91 Part III 1929–30.
93. Lalji Naranji to Thakurdas, 28 March 1930. NMML: PT Papers, File Number 91 Part II 1929–30.
94. Thakurdas to Sarabhai, 18 November 1930. NMML: PT Papers, File Number 42 (VII) 1923–34.
95. See his letters to the Viceroy (28 April and 12 May 1930); to George Schuster (30 May 1930); and to the Viceroy again (10 June 1930). NMML PT Papers: to the Viceroy – File Number 99 Part II 1930; to Schuster – File Number 91 Part II 1929–30.
96. It seems to me that Gordon rather overstates the case when he suggests that 'the industrialists were persuaded that their best interests lay in actively seeking to destroy civil disobedience, or, failing this, in seeking peace between Congress and the government' (Gordon, *Businessmen and Politics*, p.221). These are two very different things. The bourgeoisie still supported the aims of the campaign. They sought to use the power that the campaign had demonstrated to extract a compromise agreement from the British. If the civil disobedience movement was 'destroyed' (rather than toned down or suspended), it would weaken their negotiating position – and would weaken the Congress, which was not their objective at all (see Mukherjee, 'Business and politics in Bombay', p.219). This is, to an extent, confirmed by Markovits, who writes that at the end of the campaign, 'once the Congress had been decisively weakened they [FICCI] had no way of influencing the government at all' (Markovits, *Indian Business*, p.180).

97. Birla to Thakurdas, 16 January 1931 in Kudaisya, *Birla*, p.128. The Congress leadership at least was willing to give the bourgeoisie the benefit of the doubt regarding its position. Nehru told the Lucknow session in 1936 that the bourgeoisie's lack of ardour in the later stages of the campaign was due to the fact that they 'were hit hard by the Government's drastic policy of seizure and confiscations of money and properties' (Nehru, *The First Sixty Years, I,* p.431).
98. Thakurdas to the Viceroy, 20 September 1930; Viceroy to Thakurdas, 29 September 1930. NMML: PT Papers, File Number 99 Part 1.
99. Birla to Thakurdas, 16 January 1931. NMML: PT Papers, File Number 42 Part VII.
100. See Sarkar, *Modern India*, p.311; Chatterji, *Trade, Tariffs and Empire*, p.325.
101. Kudaisya, *Birla*, p.129.
102. They were only dissuaded from doing so when the Executive Committee threatened to resign *en masse* (Kudaisya, *Birla*, pp.137–8).
103. Birla, *In the Shadow*, p.183.
104. Nehru at Lahore Congress, 29 December 1929 in Nehru, *The First Sixty Years, I,* pp.203–4.
105. Nehru, *The First Sixty Years, I*, p.315.
106. Nehru at Lucknow, April 1936 in Nehru, *The First Sixty Years, I,* p.434.
107. Jawaharlal Nehru, *An Autobiography: with Musings on Recent Events in India* (Bombay: Allied Publishers, 1962 [1936], p.523.
108. Hira Lal Seth, *The Red Star of the East* (Lahore: Hero Publications, 1943), p.1.
109. Congress Working Committee resolution, 18 June 1934 in Indian National Congress, *Resolutions on Economic Policy,* p.10.
110. *Bombay Congress Bulletin*, 'For the Emergency Council, B.P.C.C.', 19 July 1932 and 10 October 1932. NMML: PT Papers, File Number 107 Part 1 and File Number 100, 1930. Thakurdas had commented earlier to Birla, 'With all the Congress leaders in jail, the Congress activities are in the hands of irresponsible people, who pose as Congress. My apprehension is that these men are not very discreet and they will, sooner or later, lose the sympathy of the commercial community'. (Thakurdas to Birla, 25 June 1932. NMML: PT Papers, File Number 107 Part II.)
111. NMML: PT Papers, File Number 42 Part V, 1923–30.
112. Birla to Thakurdas, 28 June 1932. NMML: PT Papers, File Number 107, Part 1.
113. Kudaisya, *Birla*, p.166.
114. 'A Bombay manifesto of twenty-one businessmen', *Times of India*, 20 May 1936 in Markovits, *Indian Business*, p.206.

115. *Times of India*, 11 June 1936 in Chandra, *Nationalism and Colonialism*, pp.188–9.
116. NMML: PT Papers, File Number 42 Part V 1923–34.
117. He wrote to Hirachand (who sent on a copy to Thakurdas) on 26 May 1936, 'I feel that your manifesto, far from helping, has done positive harm to the capitalistic system'. Thakurdas replied (29 May) that his object in signing was 'to make it quite clear that the somewhat aggressive manner in which Jawaharlal was preaching socialism, verging on communism, can do no good to the country' (NMML: PT Papers, File Number 177, 1936–43. See also Chandra, *Nationalism and Colonialism*, p.192).
118. 'Vallabhbhai [Patel], Rajaji [Chakravarthi Rajagopalachari] and Rajendra [Prasad] Babu are all fighting Communism and Socialism. It is therefore necessary that some of us who represent the healthy Capitalism should help Gandhiji as far as possible and work with a common objective' (Birla to Thakurdas, 3 August 1934 in Sarkar, *Modern India*, p.331).
119. Birla to Sir Samual Hoare, 14 March 1932, *In The Shadow*, p.48.
120. Chakrabarti argues that 'the socialist group in the Congress . . . had a definite place for big industries, [on] which the big business wanted to capitalise'. (Chakrabarti, *Why Did Indian?* p.1026.)
121. Ambalal Sarabhai, Draft Notes on the Swaraj government programme, 6 October 1931. NMML: Walchand Hirachand Archive, File Number 8 Part II.
122. NMML: H.P. Mody Papers III (a) Speeches and Writings, File Number 12/17 1936.
123. R.M. Lala, *The Romance of Tata Steel* (New Delhi: Penguin/Viking, 2007), pp.49–50.
124. NMML: PT Papers, File Number 42 Part I 1923–34; see also Markovits, *Indian Business*, p.181.

Chapter Seven The Second World War

1. Linlithgow (3 September 1939) in Victor A.J.H. Linlithgow, *Speeches and Statements* (New Delhi: Government of India (Bureau of Public Information), 1945), pp.199–200.
2. 'In spite of the constitutional folderols of the nineteen-twenties, the imperial crisis of the late nineteen-thirties was so terrible that the British had to cut constitutional corners in India' (John Gallagher & Anil Seal, 'Britain and India between the wars', *Modern Asian Studies* 15, 3 (1981), p.412.)

3. See, for example, Brian R. Tomlinson, 'India and the British Empire, 1935–1947', *Indian Economic and Social History Review* 13 (1976), p.332; Gallagher & Seal, 'Between wars', pp.402–3.
4. Bisheshwar Prasad, *Official History of the Indian Armed Forces in the Second World War 1939–45, Volume 12: Defence of India – Policy and Plans* (New Delhi: Combined Inter-Services Historical Section: India and Pakistan, 1963), p.53; Nandan Prasad, *Official History of the Indian Armed Forces in the Second World War 1939–45, Volume 4: Expansion of the Armed Forces and Defence Organisation, 1939–45* (New Delhi: Combined Inter-Services Historical Section: India and Pakistan, 1956), p.9.
5. See Martin A. Wainwright, *Inheritance of Empire: Britain, India and the Balance of Power in Asia, 1938–1955* (Westport: Praeger, 1994), pp.13–14.
6. Garran Report in J.O. Rawson, 'The role of India in imperial defence beyond Indian frontiers and home waters, 1919–1939' (PhD diss., University of Oxford, 1976), p.280. See also Keith Jeffery, 'The military defence of the British Empire, 1918–1922' (PhD diss., University of Cambridge, n.d.), p.298; Pradeep Barua, 'Strategies and doctrines of imperial defence: Britain and India, 1919–45,' *Journal of Imperial and Commonwealth History* Volume 25 Number 2 (May 1997), p.245.
7. Prasad, *Expansion of the Armed Forces*, pp.10–11. These commitments were kept secret by the Government of India 'since it ran counter to the publicly accepted defence policy of India'.
8. Wainwright, *Inheritance*, pp.16–17.
9. Brian Bond, *British Military Policy between the Two World Wars* (Oxford: Clarendon Press, 1980), p.120; Wainwright, *Inheritance*, pp.17–18.
10. Report of the Indian Defence Committee 1938–39. British Library (henceforward BL): India office record (henceforward IOR), L/MIL/17/5/1802. In his evidence to the committee, General Sir William Bartholomew said that the Indian army had been 'deprived of the equipment necessary for modern warfare . . . in recent years he had felt that the Indian Army was in danger of degenerating into a militia'. (Minutes of the Seventh Meeting of the Indian Defence Committee, 13 October 1938. BL: IOR, L/MIL/5/887.)
11. As a result, some of Chatfield's recommended preparations had also to be carried out in secret. The Secretary of State for India reported to the Secretary of State for War the Viceroy's view that 'public opinion would react very violently to any suggestion that the [proposed 'Imperial Reserve'] Division to be equipped with the aid of His Majesty's Government was to be at the beck and call of the authorities here; and he asks me to let you know that he hopes that you will not refer to it in public as the Imperial

Reserve Division' (Zetland to Hore-Belisha, 24 September 1938. BL: IOR, L/WS/1/154.

12. See Linlithgow's statement on 18 October 1939 in *Speeches and Statements*, pp.204–11.
13. N.C. Sinha & P.N. Khera (eds), *Official History of the Indian Armed Forces in the Second World War 1939–45, Volume 14: Indian War Economy (Supply, Industry and Finance)* (New Delhi: Combined Inter-Services Historical Section: India and Pakistan, 1962), p.58.
14. Chatfield Committee report, pp.51–4. BL, IOR: L/MIL/17/5/1802. Sinha concludes that the Chatfield committee 'found itself compelled not to recommend any large or advanced project of munitions production' (Sinha & Khera, *War Economy*, pp.140, 148).
15. See Bishwa Mohan Prasad, *Second World War and Indian Industry, 1939–45: a Case Study of the Coal Industry in Bengal and Bihar* (Delhi: Anamika Prakashan, 1992), p.66; R.F. Holland, *Britain and the Commonwealth Alliance, 1918–1939* (London: Macmillan, 1981), p.194 (writing on the Dominions, but with conclusions that apply to India).
16. 'India as Arsenal of the East', *The Statesman*, 9 March 1942. See also 'War and Indian industry', *The Hindu*, 10 March 1942: 'vested interests...see in the building up of new Indian industries the rearing of a potential trade rival, who would compete with them in the post-war period'. Both in Nehru Memorial Museum and Library (henceforward NMML): Purshotamdas Thakurdas Papers (henceforward PT papers), File Number 279 Part 1.
17. Reported by M.C. Ghia to a general meeting of the Indian Merchants' Chamber, 12 November 1941. Indian Merchants' Chamber. *Annual Report of the Indian Merchants' Chamber for the year 1941* (Bombay: J.K. Mehta, 1942), p.596.
18. Letter from Wavell to Mody, 5 June 1942. NMML: H.P. Mody Papers, Subject File Number 14.
19. It was attended by delegations from India, Rhodesia, Australia, East Africa, South Africa, the Federated Malay States, Ceylon, Burma and others.
20. Linlithgow 25 October 1940, in *Speeches and Statements*, p.258.
21. In the end, some non-official advisers were invited by the government – but packed off ('they were given a parting send-off like unwelcome guests') before sessions began. See Federation of Indian Chambers of Commerce and Industry, *Correspondence and relevant documents relating to important questions dealt with by the Federation during the year 1940–41* (New Delhi: n.p. 1941), pp.164, 175; C.B. Mehta's presidential address to the 33rd annual general meeting of the Indian Merchants' Chamber, 29 January 1941. Indian Merchants' Chamber, *Annual Report 1941*, p.xlii.

22. Ghia at general meeting of the Indian Merchants' Chamber, 30 April 1941 in Indian Merchants' Chamber, *Annual Report 1941*, p.550.
23. C.B. Mehta's presidential address to the 33rd annual general meeting of the Indian Merchants' Chamber, 29 January 1941. Indian Merchants' Chamber *Annual Report 1941*, pp.xli–xlii.
24. 'Regarding East Group Conference', letter from FICCI to Government of India, 12 November 1940 in FICCI *Correspondence 1940–41*, p.174. This letter, although marked 'Secret', was published in *The Hindustan Times*, 19 November 1940.
25. See Sinha & Khera, *War Economy*, pp.33–4; Prasad, *Second World War and Indian History*, p.65.
26. Reported in 'War and Indian industry', *The Hindu*, 10 March 1942.
27. FICCI Executive Committee, March 1942 in Federation of Indian Chambers of Commerce and Industry, *Report of the Proceedings of the Executive Committee for the year 1942–43* (New Delhi: India Print Works, 1943), pp.46–7.
28. See Wainwright, *Inheritance*.
29. Sinha & Khera, *War Economy*, p.50. See also 'India's Industrial Problems', *The Hindustan Standard*, 11 March 1942 in NMML: PT Papers, File Number 279 Part 1.
30. Wainwright, *Inheritance*, p.37.
31. Reported in *The Hindustan Times* 9 March 1942 in NMML: PT Papers File Number 279 Part 1.
32. 'No Scorching in India', *National Herald* 14 March 1942 in NMML: PT Papers, File Number 279 Part 1.
33. See FICCI president to Viceroy (probably March 1942) in NMML: PT Papers, File Number 279 Part 1; FICCI Executive Committee, *Report of the Proceedings 1942–43*, pp.54–5. On Scorched Earth see editorials in *Hindustan Times* 21 March 1942; *Bombay Chronicle* 23 March 1942; *The Hindu* 2 April 1942, all in NMML: PT Papers, File Number 279 Part 1.
34. *The Statesman*, 16 & 18 March 1942 in NMML: PT Papers, File Number 279 Part 1; 23 March 1942 in NMML: PT Papers, File Number 279 Part 2.
35. Statement by the FICCI president, G.L. Mehta, 25 March 1942 in NMML: PT Papers, File Number 279 Part 2. The FICCI secretary suggested that Thakurdas and Birla should make a statement to the press along these lines (FICCI secretary to president, 20 March 1942 in NMML: PT Papers, File Number 279 Part 1).
36. Reported in *The Hindustan Standard*, 3 April 1942. A similar statement was made in the Council of State by General Sir Alan Hartley. Both in NMML: PT Papers, File Number 279 Part 2.

37. 'All strands of British policy became subsumed in the immediate end of obtaining the greatest amount of Indian support for the Imperial war effort... the tactic of producing a consensus of Indian and British interests was now irrelevant.' (Tomlinson, 'India and the British Empire 1935–1947', p.341.) See also Wainwright, *Inheritance*, p.12.
38. Chatfield Report, p.8. BL: IOR, L/MIL/17/5/1802.
39. B.M. Birla (Ghanshyamdas' younger brother) told G.W. Tyson (who reported it to the Governor of Bengal) that 'the Cripps mission was regarded as a hurried last minute attempt to strike a bargain when we found we were in a jamb [sic] with the Japanese'. Letter from G.W. Tyson to the Governor of Bengal, n.d. BL: IOR, L/PJ/8/618A.
40. Linlithgow, 8 August 1940 in *Speeches and Statements*, pp.250–2. The Executive Council was eventually expanded to include (among others) two businessmen, H.P. Mody (Supply) and Nalini Sarkar (Education, Health and Lands). See Viceroy's invitation to Mody to serve (19 June 1941) and Mody's acceptance (5 July 1941). NMML: Papers of H.P. Mody, Subject File Number 13.
41. Birla to Viceroy via his Private Secretary, J.G. Laithwaite, 28 August 1940. NMML: PT Papers, File Number 239 Part 1.
42. M.C. Ghia, presidential address to the Indian Merchants' Chamber general meeting, 30 July 1941 in Indian Merchants' Chamber, *Annual Report 1941*, pp.574–5.
43. Indian Merchants' Chamber telegram to Congress, 31 March 1942. NMML: PT Papers, File Number 239 Part 1.
44. Tomlinson, 'India and the British Empire 1935–1947', p.342.
45. Francis G. Hutchins, *Spontaneous Revolution: the Quit India Movement* (Delhi: Manohar, 1971), p.183. See also Sumit Sarkar, *Modern India, 1885–1947* (Madras: Macmillan India Ltd., 1983), p.376.
46. Hutchins, *Spontaneous Revolution*, pp.188–90. At the Internal Affairs Committee (of the Executive Council) on 8 December 1943, it was agreed that 'an economic warfare against Congress was the approved policy'. H.P. Mody dissented (Partha Sarathi Gupta (ed.), *Towards Freedom: Documents on the Movement for Independence in India: 1943–1944, Part 3* (New Delhi: Indian Council of Historical Research, 1997), p.2444).
47. Wainwright suggests that at this point 'the potential existed for Whitehall to court the favour of the Indian business community by involving its most prominent representatives at the highest levels [in] its expansion of the country's defense infrastructure' (Wainwright, *Inheritance*, pp.36–7). The reason for the British not seizing this opportunity lay in the fact that the Empire's interest and that of business – the one strategic, the other

developmental – were at loggerheads. Conflict between them was endemic, rather than a matter of policy choice.

48. Sir John Herbert to the Viceroy, 25 January 1943. Gupta, *Towards Freedom 1943–4* Part III, p.2437.
49. Sir Henry Twynan to the Viceroy, 15 May 1943. BL: IOR, L/PJ/8/618A.
50. Sir Andrew Clow to the Viceroy, 10 November 1942. BL: IOR, L/PJ/8/618A.
51. Private secretary to the Viceroy to private secretary to the Secretary of State, 16 March 1943. BL: IOR, L/PJ/8/618A.
52. Text of the EPT Act 1940 in *The Gazette of India*, 27 January 1940. NMML: PT Papers, File Number 35. See also, Prasad, *Second World War and Indian Industry*, p.128.
53. NMML: PT Papers, File Number 35.
54. Indian Merchants' Chamber, *Views of the Committee on the Excess Profits Tax Bill* (Bombay: n.p., 7 February 1940), p.2. See also FICCI statement on EPT Bill, 29 January 1940. NMML: PT Papers, File Number 35; FICCI Executive Committee press communiqué, 3 March 1941 in FICCI, *Correspondence 1940–41*, p.349.
55. Report submitted to the Committee of the Federation by the E.P.T. Bill Sub-Committee in FICCI, *Correspondence 1940–41*, p.37. See also NMML: PT Papers, File Number 35.
56. Aditya Mukherjee, *Imperialism, Nationalism and the Making of the Indian Capitalist Class, 1920–1947* (New Delhi: Sage Publications, 2002), p.313.
57. See Sir Henry Twynan's notes for the Viceroy, 26 July 1943 in Nicholas Mansergh & Penderel Moon (eds), *The Transfer of Power, 1942–7. Volume 4: The Bengal Famine and the New Viceroyalty, 15 June 1943 – 31 August 1944* (London: HMSO, 1973), pp.118, 122; Amery to the Viceroy Lord Wavell, 7 December 1944 in Mansergh & Moon, *Transfer of Power* Volume 4, p.291. On the Left see Aditya Mukherjee, 'The Workers' and Peasants' Parties, 1926–30: An aspect of Communism in India', *Studies in History* III, 1 & 2 (1981), pp.1–44.
58. Churchill's statement to Parliament, 10 September 1942 in Hindustan Times, *India Unreconciled: A Documented History of Indian Political Events from the Crisis of August 1942 to October 1943* (New Delhi: Hindustan Times Press, 1943), p.42.
59. At the onset of the Quit India campaign, the Indian Section of the Eastern Service of the BBC (which employed, among others, George Orwell) was instructed to focus on Gandhi, 'who should be gradually built up as a backward pacifist and Pétainist (in this connexion his associations with prominent Indian industrialists such as Mr Birla could usefully be stressed) who has become a dangerous obstacle to the defence of India, and whose policies

in fact if not in design play straight into Japanese hands'. (cited in W.J. West's, Introduction of George Orwell's *The War Commentaries*, ed. W.J. West (Harmondsworth: Penguin, 1987), p.19.)

60. It is around this letter, the replies to it and the Intelligence Bureau's assessments that the Government of India file, 'The Role of Big Business' (BL: IOR, L/PJ/8/618A) is built.
61. Viceroy's letter to the Governors, 2 November 1942. BL: IOR, L/PJ/8/618A. It should be said that some of the Governors, as well as the Intelligence Bureau, expressed some scepticism towards these ideas.
62. Medha M. Kudaisya, *The Life and Times of G.D. Birla* (New Delhi: Oxford University Press, 2003), p.197. Even three years later Birla went so far as to tell Thakurdas: 'Calcutta may be bombed but that is nothing. After all, India cannot keep herself aloof from the war experience' (Birla to Thakurdas, 30 October 1942. NMML: PT Papers, File Number 239 Part 4).
63. Lala Shri Ram to Amritlal Ojha 17 May 1940. NMML: PT Papers, File Number 239 Part 1. In terms of 'selfish interests', the extent to which the war was a windfall for Indian business remains unclear. Prasad believes that '[p]rofits easily made during the war led to the development of unhealthy tendencies among industrialists for making undue profits' (Prasad, *Second World War and Indian Industry*, p.68). Kudaisya says that '[i]n overall terms, Indian industry made immense profits from the wartime expansion of the economy' (Kudaisya, *Birla*, p.207). Tomlinson, though, says that much of the increased industrial production was 'siphoned off by a system of military requisitions' (Tomlinson, 'India and the British Empire 1935–47', p.340) – at government-controlled prices. Homi Mody told the Bombay Rotary Club in June 1941, 'No fortunes are being made by legitimate means as in the last war' (Homi Mody, *Reflections, Wise and Otherwise* (Bombay: Asia Publishing House, 1961), p.63).
64. Kudaisya, *Birla*, p.197.
65. Extract from Churchill's speech at the Mansion House, 10 November 1942. NMML: PT Papers File Number 240.
66. FICCI, *Report of the Proceedings* p.68.
67. Draft FICCI manifesto, August 1939 in Mushiral Hasan (ed.), *Towards Freedom: Documents on the Movement for Independence in India: 1939, Part 1* (New Delhi: Indian Council of Historical Research, 2008), p.276.
68. FICCI press communiqué 13 September 1942. NMML: PT Papers File Number 267. See also M.C. Ghia at the Indian Merchants' Chamber 29 January 1942 in Indian Merchants' Chamber, *Annual Report of the Indian Merchants' Chamber for the year 1942* (Bombay: J.K. Mehta, 1943), p.iv;

Thakurdas at the East Indian Cotton Association AGM, 12 December 1942 reported in *The Hindu* 13 December 1940 and Press statement by the India Merchants' Association 4 July 1942 in NMML: PT Papers File Number 239 Part 3.

69. Speech at Bombay town hall meeting 10 June 1940. NMML: PT Papers, File Number 240.
70. V.K. Dhage to FICCI in 1941; R.M. Gandhi to FICCI, 1940 both in Mukherjee, *Imperialism, Nationalism,* pp.301, 304.
71. Speech at Bombay town hall meeting 10 June 1940. NMML: PT Papers, File Number 240.
72. Presidential speech to the Indian Merchants' Chamber AGM in Indian Merchants' Chamber, *Annual Report of the Indian Merchants' Chamber for the Year 1940* (Bombay: J.K. Mehta, 1941), p.xxxix.
73. FICCI resolution for the 12th Industries Conference 14 November 1940 in FICCI, *Correspondence 1940–41*, p.301.
74. Ghia to the Indian Merchants' Chamber 12 November 1941 in Indian Merchants' Chamber, *Annual Report 1942*, p.596. See also the resolution on 'Establishment of Key and Defence Industries' at FICCI's annual session 7–8 March 1942 in NMML: PT Papers, File Number 367.
75. According to *The Hindustan Times* 9 March 1942 in NMML: PT Papers, File Number 279 Part 1.
76. See Ghia at the Indian Merchants' Chamber general meeting 30 April 1941 in Indian Merchants' Chamber, *Annual Report 1942*, p.553.
77. FICCI press communiqué 3 March 1941 in FICCI, *Correspondence 1940–41*, p.347.
78. Mody, 'India and the war', speech at the Bombay Rotary Club, 24 June 1941. NMML: Papers of H.P. Mody, III: Speeches and Writings, File Number 29.
79. FICCI Press communiqué on 'Budget Proposals of the Government of India for the Year 1944–45', 3 March 1944 in Federation of Indian Chambers of Commerce and Industry, *Correspondence and relevant documents relating to important questions dealt with by the Federation during the year 1944* (Bombay: India Printing Works, 1945), p.40.
80. FICCI Press communiqué on 'Supplementary Budget proposals of the Government of India' 10 November 1940 in FICCI, *Correspondence 1940–41*, p.186.
81. Press statement by the Indian Merchants' Chamber 4 July 1942. NMML: PT Papers, File Number 239 Part 3.
82. The Secretary of State, Leo Amery, complained to the Viceroy: 'If only the big industrialists in India could realise... that their interest now lies

in stable evolution and in a policy of industrial development' (Amery to Viceroy 28 June 1943 in Mansergh & Moon, *Transfer of Power* Volume 4, p.36). The Indian capitalists realised exactly that – the problem was that the British were offering no such evolution nor any such policy.

83. Indian Chamber of Commerce, comments on speech by Mudaliar, 17 March 1941. NMML: PT Papers File Number 240.
84. FICCI Press communiqué, 3 March 1941 in FICCI, *Correspondence 1940–41*, p.348. See also FICCI's resolutions for the Industries Conference in FICCI, *Correspondence 1940–41*, pp.258–9; FICCI, *Report of the Proceedings*, p.53.
85. Birla to Thakurdas 25 June 1940. NMML: PT Papers, File Number 239 Part 1.
86. *The Hindu,* 10 March 1942 NMML: PT Papers, File Number 279 Part 1; *The Hindustan Standard*, 23 March 1941 NMML: PT Papers, File 240.
87. FICCI Press communiqué 13 September 1942. NMML: PT Papers, File Number 267.
88. Thakurdas to Sir Stanley Reed 20 January 1943.NMML: PT Papers, File Number 239 Part 5.
89. Ghia to IMC general meeting 30 July 1941. Indian Merchants' Chamber, *Annual Report 1942*, p.573.
90. Sir John Herbert to Viceroy 1 March 1943. BL: IOR, L/PJ/8/618A. See also the assessment of the Intelligence Bureau: 'the Congress movement, both overt and underground, has received substantial support from Indian "Big Business"'. BL: IOR, 'Role of Big Business', L/PJ/8/618A.
91. Those named were Messrs Bachraj & Co., the Tata Group, the Birla brothers, the Dalmia-Jain group, Hirachand Walchand, G.L. Mehta and the Indian Chamber of Commerce (Calcutta) (BL: IOR, 'Role of Big Business', L/PJ/8/618A).
92. Mehta in FICCI *Report of the Proceedings*, p.67.
93. C.P. Ramaswami Aiyar to Viceroy 6 August 1942 in Nicholas Mansergh & Penderel Moon (eds), *The Transfer of Power, 1942–7. Volume 2: 'Quit India', 30 April–21 September 1942* (London: HMSO, 1971), p.592. Even Chandra suggests that the industrialists 'failed to give the Quit India Movement of 1942 the type of strong backing they had given to the Civil Disobedience Campaigns of 1920 and 1930' (Bipan Chandra, *Nationalism and Colonialism in Modern India* (New Delhi: Orient Longman, 1979), p.157).
94. Cited in Government of India Intelligence Bureau, 'Congress and "Big Business"' 28 February 1944. BL IOR: L/PJ/8/618A. For an indication of Left opinion see the socialist leaflet 'The Freedom Struggle Front' (December 1942) in Sarkar, *Modern India*, pp.397–8.

95. Sir Henry Twynan (Governor of Central Provinces and Berar) wrote to the Viceroy (25 May 1942) that the 'new line' of opposition to the war and renewed civil disobedience was 'developed by Gandhi's capitalist friends' (Mansergh & Moon, *Transfer of Power* Volume 2, p.119). The Intelligence Bureau, on the other hand, reported that 'the underground leaders are by no means satisfied with the part played by "Big Business" and are far from being a subservient instrument of the big industrialists' ('Congress and "Big Business"' 28 February 1944. BL: IOR, L/PJ/8/618A).
96. Kudaisya, *Birla*, pp.198–9.
97. Birla to Thakurdas 11 September 1940. NMML: PT Papers, File Number 239 Part 1.
98. Thakurdas to Birla 7 November 1942. NMML: PT Papers, File Number 239 Part 4.
99. Ghia to IMC general meeting 12 November 1941 in Indian Merchants' Chamber, *Annual Report 1942*, p.592.
100. Sarkar, 'The way out', *Amrita Bazar Patrika* n.d. (probably May–June 1943). NMML: PT Papers, File Number 239 Part 6.
101. On Nehru's 'severe and ... vindictive sentence' see FICCI president to Viceroy 10 November 1940 in FICCI, *Correspondence 1940–41*, p.337.
102. Kudaisya, *Birla*, p.200.
103. Thakurdas, Tata and Birla to Viceroy 5 August 1942. NMML: PT Papers, File Number 239 Part 4.
104. 'Congress and "Big Business"' 28 February 1944. BL: IOR, L/PJ/8/618A. Sarkar, somewhat begrudgingly, concedes that 'it is not impossible that sections of Indian business for a brief while tended to give some covert support to a movement (even if violent) which might quickly push out the British' (Sarkar, *Modern India*, p.393). As will be seen, my belief is that capitalist support was rather more substantial than that. Sarkar himself indicates that business support for Quit India was 'considerable' in Bombay (p.397). Vivek Chibber argues that 'such evidence as we do have' indicates that the bourgeoisie did not support the movement (Vivek Chibber, *Locked in Place: State-Building and Late Industrialization in India* (Princeton: Princeton University Press, 2006), p.93). He relies for this assertion on the Intelligence Bureau report, cited above. But the purpose of that report was to ascertain whether "Big Business" was *the moving force* behind Quit India – something which the Bureau had no trouble in disproving.
105. NMML: PT Papers, File Number 239 Part 4.
106. Mehta to Viceroy August 1942 in FICCI, *Report of the Proceedings*, p.66.
107. Executive Committee meeting 12 September 1942, FICCI, *Report of the Proceedings*, p.67.

108. The Bureau reported large donations by the Ahmedabad Maskati Cloth Market Mahajan, by Kasturbhai Lalbhai and by other mill owners (Intelligence Bureau Report 17 September 1942. BL: IOR, L/PJ/8/618A). The Diwan of Baroda told the Viceroy that 'he had no doubt whatever that the Ahmedabad mill-owners were helping to keep the agitation going' (Reported by the Viceroy to the Secretary of State 21 November 1942. Nicholas Mansergh & Penderel Moon (eds), *The Transfer of Power, 1942–7. Volume 3: Reassertion of Authority, 21 September 1942–12 June 1943* (London: HMSO, 1971), p.290). Financial donations from business were 'laundered' through various channels – see Kudaisya, *Birla*, p.206.
109. Executive Committee 12 September 1942 in FICCI *Report of the Proceedings*, p.67.
110. Lala Shri Ram to Thakurdas 31 August 1942. NMML: PT Papers, File Number 239 Part 4.
111. Intelligence Bureau Report, 17 September 1942. BL: IOR, L/PJ/8/618A. See also Government of Bihar report February 1943 in Gupta, *Towards Freedom 1943–44* Part III, p.2453.
112. Central Intelligence Office (Bengal) Report 4 September 1943 in Gupta, *Towards Freedom 1943–44* Part III, p.2466; Intelligence Bureau Report 17 September 1942. BL: IOR, L/PJ/8/618A; Kudaisya, *Birla*, p.206.
113. Mehta to Viceroy 11 February 1943; see also Thakurdas to Viceroy on behalf of the East India Cotton Association 13 February 1943. NMML: PT Papers, File Number 239 Part 5.
114. Press communiqué 13 February 1942. NMML: PT Papers File Number 267.
115. G.D. Birla, *In the Shadow of the Mahatma: A Personal Memoir* (Bombay: Orient Longmans Ltd., 1955), p.222; NMML: PT Papers, File Number 239 Part 5.
116. Statement by H.P. Mody on the resignations 7 July 1944; Statement accompanying the resignations 17 February 1943. NMML: Papers of H.P. Mody, Subject File Number 14.
117. Bipan Chandra, *Communalism in Modern India* (New Delhi: Vikas Publishing House, 1984), p.75.
118. Chandra, *Communalism in Modern India*, p.65.
119. Chandra, *Communalism in Modern India*, p.73. Markovits agrees that 'there is no hard evidence that . . . Muslim businessmen were systematically barred from entry into industry by entrenched Hindu interests' (Claude Markovits, *Merchants, Traders, Entrepreneurs: Indian Business in the Colonial Era* (Basingstoke: Palgrave Macmillan, 2008), p.82). Supporters of Pakistan, like M.A.H. Ispahani, claim: 'Most of the industries and almost the entire

internal trade ... were in the hands of the Hindus. Muslims only subsisted on the crumbs which were swept off these monopolists' tables ... In view of these conditions, the conviction grew among the Muslims that, with the passing of power into the hands of the Hindus, they would be crushed beyond repair ... reduced to the status of the depressed classes and even worse. Without a doubt this would have happened' (Mirza Abol Hassan Ispahani, 'Factors leading to the Partition of British India' in C.H. Philips & Mary D. Wainwright (eds), *The Partition of India: Policies and Perspectives, 1935–1947* (Cambridge, Massachusetts: MIT Press, 1970), pp.356–9).

120. Chandra, *Communalism in Modern India*, pp.72–3.
121. Chandra, *Communalism in Modern India*, p.73. See also Mushirul Hasan, *Legacy of a Divided Nation: India's Muslims since Independence* (London: C. Hurst & Co., 1997), p.76.
122. Markovits, *Merchants, Traders*, p.81; Hasan, *Legacy*, p.70; Kenneth McPherson, *The Muslim Microcosm: Calcutta, 1918 to 1935* (Wiesbaden: Franz Steiner Verlag, 1974), pp.120–1.
123. Brijmohan Birla to Thakurdas 28 August 1942. NMML: PT Papers, File Number 239 Part 4.
124. Ispahani to Jinnah 18 March 1944 in Mahomed Ali Jinnah & Mirza Abol Hassan Ispahani, *M.A. Jinnah – Ispahani Correspondence, 1936–1948,* ed. Z.H. Zaidi (Karachi: Forward Publications Trust, 1976), p.409.
125. See Federation of Indian Chambers of Commerce and Industry, *Proceedings of the Twentieth Annual Meeting held at New Delhi on 3rd and 4th March 1947* (New Delhi: FICCI, 1947); Federation of Indian Chambers of Commerce and Industry, *Proceedings of the Twenty-First Annual Meeting held at New Delhi on 28th and 29th March 1948* (New Delhi: FICCI, 1948).
126. Birla to Thakurdas 9 May 1929. NMML: PT Papers File Number 42 Part 3.
127. NMML: PT Papers, File Number 91 Part 3 1929–30. Thakurdas tended to blame communal tensions on the British – see his letter to Birla 16 April 1934. NMML: PT Papers, File Number 126 Part 1.
128. C.B. Mehta at IMC general meeting 4 May 1940 in Indian Merchants' Chamber, *Annual Report 1940*, p.504.
129. See Ispahani to Jinnah 27 March 1944 and 3 April 1944, Jinnah& Ispahani, *Correspondence*, pp.412–15.
130. Ispahani to Jinnah 24 October 1944, Jinnah &Ispahani, *Correspondence*, p.433.
131. Jinnah to Ispahani 15 April 1945, Jinnah & Ispahani, *Correspondence*, p.444.
132. Mirza Abol Hassan Ispahani, *Qaid-E-Azam Jinnah As I knew Him* (Karachi: Forward Publications Trust, 1967), p.129.

133. Ispahani, *Qaid-E-Azam Jinnah As I knew Him*, pp.129–30.
134. In Chaudhri Muhammad Ali, *The Emergence of Pakistan* (New York: Columbia University Press, 1967), p.38.
135. Jinnah, Speech at the Lahore Session in Mahomed Ali Jinnah, *Some Recent Speeches and Writings of Mr Jinnah*, collected and edited by Jamil-ud-din Ahmad (Lahore: Sh. Muhammad Ashraf, 1942), pp.138–56. The League would go on to reject the Cripps proposals because they did not unequivocally concede the Pakistan demand (Ali, *Emergence*, p.440).
136. As Chandra puts it, they saw 'the objective possibilities of using Muslim communalism, which was already there, *which they did not create*, which was getting whole-hearted support from the colonial state, and which was beginning to grow rapidly, for advancing their own interests' (Chandra, *Communalism in Modern India*, p.73).
137. Chandra, *Communalism in Modern India*, p.75.

Chapter Eight Planning and Partition

1. Tomlinson writes that 'Britain's imperial interests, in so far as they directly affected India, dictated an early withdrawal in good order' (Brian R. Tomlinson, 'India and the British Empire, 1935–1947', *Indian Economic and Social History Review* 13 (1976), p.347). Chandra et al. suggest that, with all due respect to the post-war upheaval in India, this was 'a result of their realization that their legitimacy to rule had been irrevocably eroded over the years' (Bipan Chandra et al., *India's Struggle for Independence, 1857–1947* (New Delhi: Penguin, 1989), p.483).
2. Christopher Bayly & Tim Harper, *Forgotten Wars: The End of Britain's Asian Empire* (London: Allen Lane, 2007), pp.10–11.
3. Bayly & Harper, *Forgotten Wars*, p.137.
4. Bayly & Harper, *Forgotten Wars*, p.98.
5. Bayly & Harper, *Forgotten Wars*, p.137.
6. Tomlinson, 'India and the British Empire, 1935–1947', p.343.
7. N.C. Sinha & P.N. Khera (eds), *Official History of the Indian Armed Forces in the Second World War 1939–45, Volume 14: Indian War Economy (Supply, Industry and Finance)* (New Delhi: Combined Inter-Services Historical Section: India and Pakistan, 1962), p.33.
8. Bishwa Mohan Prasad, *Second World War and Indian Industry, 1939–45: a Case Study of the Coal Industry in Bengal and Bihar* (Delhi: Anamika Prakashan, 1992), p.97.
9. Medha M. Kudaisya, *The Life and Times of G.D. Birla* (New Delhi: Oxford University Press, 2003), p.223.

10. Prasad, *Second World War and Indian Industry*, pp.10, 71–4. The Order was repealed in December 1945 in order to make it more rigorous. Controls on coal continued after the war under the Essential Supplies (Temporary Powers) Act of 1946.
11. C.D. Deshmukh, Reserve Bank governor and future Finance Minister, remarked, 'War uproots traditional ways of thinking, accustoms men to regulation, makes people technical-minded, forces the growth of new concepts and promotes adaptability to new conditions. Planning calls for heavy sacrifices, even as much as war demands' (Speech at the Poona Rotary Club, 25 February 1945. Nehru Memorial Museum and Library (henceforward NMML), C.D. Deshmukh Papers, Speeches and Writings (Unpublished), Series Number 43 File Number 2).
12. K.B. Krishna, *Plan for Economic Development of India (A Critical and Historical Survey)* (Bombay: Padma Publications, 1945), pp.69–70.
13. Government of India, Reconstruction Committee of Council. *Record of the First Meeting of the General Policy Committee* (New Delhi: n.p., January 1944), p.v.
14. Government of India, Reconstruction Committee, *First Meeting*, p.3. At the same meeting, the representative of the princely state of Travancore (Sir C.P. Ramaswami Aiyar) 'emphasised the absolute importance of central planning, central direction and central stimulus... it would always be necessary that the economy, the financial and the planning policy of India should be directed from the centre' (Government of India, Reconstruction Committee, *First Meeting*, p.21).
15. Government of India, Reconstruction Committee of Council. *Second Report on Reconstruction Planning* (New Delhi: n.p., 23 October 1944), pp.1–3, 8, 9.
16. Point seven of the Mission's Report in Sinha and Khera, *Indian War Economy*, p.44. In the Government of Bombay's pamphlet on reconstruction, the only mention of industry is section IV: 'Industries (Small scale)' (Government of Bombay, *Post-War Reconstruction – Bombay Province* (Bombay: Government Central Press, n.d.), pp.25–8).
17. Sir M. Visvesvaraya, *Reconstruction in Post-War India: a Plan of Development All Round* (Bombay: The All-India Manufacturers' Organisation, September 1944), pp.39–41.
18. Visvesvaraya, *Reconstruction in Post War India*, pp.11–12. See also the even more detailed list on page 40.
19. Basudev Chatterji (ed.), *Towards Freedom: Documents on the Movement for Independence in India, 1938: Part 1* (New Delhi: Oxford University Press, 1999), pp.857–60.

20. Resolutions of the Conference of Ministers of Industries 2–3 October 1930 in National Planning Committee, *Abstract of Proceedings, Number 1* (Bombay: National Planning Committee, n.d. [1939]), p.9.
21. Report on the NPC's first meeting 17 December 1938. NMML: Papers of J.C. Kumarappa, Subject File Number 11: National Planning Committee.
22. Chairman's Memorandum 4 June 1939, NPC, *Abstract Number 1*, p.73; Note for the Guidance of Sub-Committees of the NPC, NPC, *Abstract Number 1*, p.79.
23. Chairman's Memorandum 4 June 1939, NPC, *Abstract Number 1*, p.74.
24. Note by the Chairman for the 5th NPC session 30 August 1940, National Planning Committee, *Abstract of Proceedings, Number 4* (Bombay: National Planning Committee, October 1940), p.5.
25. Note by the Chairman for the 5th NPC session 30 August 1940, NPC, *Abstract Number 4*, p.7.
26. Note for the Guidance of Sub-Committees of the NPC, NPC, *Abstract Number 1*, p.81; Chairman's Memorandum to all members of the NPC and chairmen and secretaries of all Sub-Committees 12 February 1940, National Planning Committee, *Abstract of Proceedings, Number 2* (Bombay: National Planning Committee, May 1940), p.7.
27. Key industries were: power, fuel, metals, machine tools, machinery and machining parts, heavy engineering industries (ships, locomotives, automobiles, aircraft etc.), instruments and apparatus and chemicals (List of Defence Industries, Key Industries and Public Utilities, NPC, *Abstract Number 1*, p.102).
28. Chairman's Memorandum to all members of the NPC and chairmen and secretaries of all Sub-Committees 12 February 1940, NPC, *Abstract Number 2*, p.7.
29. NPC Resolutions on Engineering Industry in K.T. Shah, *Handbook of National Planning Committee* (Bombay: Vora & Co., 1946), pp.75–7. National workshop: Report of the Sub-committee on Engineering, NPC, *Abstract Number 2*, p.39.
30. Resolutions on Manufacturing Industries, Shah, *NPC Handbook*, p.80.
31. Shah, *NPC Handbook*, pp.77–9, 93–4, 100–02.
32. Shah, *NPC Handbook*, pp.95, 139.
33. Jawaharlal Nehru, *Nehru: The First Sixty Years, Volume 1*, ed. Dorothy Norman (London: The Bodley Head, 1965), p.693.
34. Chairman to NPC members and chairmen and secretaries of all Sub-Committees 27 September 1939. NMML: Purshotamdas Thakurdas Papers (henceforward PT Papers), File Number 220 Part 1.
35. Nehru, *First Sixty years I*, pp.695–6. The attitude of the businessmen concerned will be considered in more detail later in the chapter.

36. Secretary of the Government of the United Provinces to General Secretary of the NPC 6 March 1941. NMML: PT Papers, File Number 220, Part 2.The death-throes of this version of the NPC are covered in Parts 2 and 3 of this file.
37. Such remarks would not have been considered particularly unusual when, as Talbot points out, 'The Muslim League's Economic Planning Committee thus emerged in an intellectual climate which had rejected traditional laissez-faire beliefs' (Ian Talbot, 'Planning for Pakistan: the Planning Committee of the All-India Muslim League, 1943–46'. *Modern Asian Studies* 28 (4) 1994, pp.876, 881).
38. Krishna, *Plan for Economic Development of India*, p.79.
39. Talbot, *Planning for Pakistan*, pp.880–7.
40. David C. Potter, 'Manpower Shortage and the End of Colonialism: the Case of the Indian Civil Service' *Modern Asian Studies* 7 (1) 1973, pp.68, 73.
41. See Chandra et al., *India's Struggle*, pp.488–9, 491.
42. Chairman's notes on Congress policy, NPC, *Abstract Number 1*, p.66.
43. See Aditya Mukherjee, *Imperialism, Nationalism and the Making of the Indian Capitalist Class, 1920–1947* (New Delhi: Sage Publications, 2002), pp.417–20.
44. '... the men who are primarily interested in planning are the industrialists. Their interest in planning is interest in industrialisation' (Krishna, *Plan for Economic Development of India*, p.35).
45. G.D. Birla, *Principles of Economic Planning* (New Delhi: East Economist Ltd., 1943), pp.3, 52–3.
46. Birla, *Principles of Planning*, pp.50–2.
47. Mody told the Bombay Rotary Club in June 1941 that, after the war, '[w]e may also need to have a sort of National Development Corporation, financed partly by the State and partly be industrialists to undertake essential industries' (Homi Mody, *Reflections, Wise and Otherwise* (Bombay: Asia Publishing House, 1961), p.64). In his papers, Thakurdas marked and preserved: an article in *The Times of India* (2 December 1942) on the Beveridge Report in Britain; the paper's editorial on the same subject, calling for 'colossal and unremitting effort by the State' (3 December 1942); and an editorial in *The Hindu* (11 January 1945) quoting the labour organiser and sociologist, Jerome Davis, then touring the Soviet Union: 'Reconstruction, he points out, is "part of a centralised planned economy for the entire nation"' (NMML: Pt Papers, File Number 239 Part 7).
48. Federation of Indian Chambers of Commerce and Industry, *Correspondence and relevant documents relating to important questions dealt with by the Federation during the year 1941–42* (Bombay: India Printing Works, 1942),

pp.140–3; Government of India, Reconstruction Committee, *First meeting*, p.28.

49. Master to Hirachand 18 October 1938 in Chatterji, *Towards Freedom 1938 Part 1*, p.866.
50. Nehru, *First 60 years I*, p.690.
51. Nehru, *First 60 years I*, p.693. Vivek Chibber suggests that bourgeois opposition to state control and intervention on the NPC was much more trenchant and this 'played an important part in the demise of that body', with the bourgeoisie withdrawing funds (Vivek Chibber, *Locked in Place: State-Building and Late Industrialization in India* (Princeton: Princeton University Press, 2006), pp.87, 90). In fact, business opposition was not strong enough to make them leave the committee and their objections to general nationalisation were hardly surprising. However, their opposition was by no means absolute. The NPC sub-committee on Manufacturing Industries recommended total state ownership or control (see above) – despite the fact that it was chaired by Ambilal Sarabhai, a leading industrialist (Chibber, *Locked in Place*, note 13, p.276). As noted earlier, the NPC stopped functioning at the outbreak of the war partly as a result of Nehru's arrest and partly as a result of the resignation of the Congress ministries, which also provided funds and facilities – not because of capitalist intransigence. The business community was eager to send along representatives when NPC meetings restarted in September 1945. I will deal with Chibber's more general propositions on the relationship between state and capital in India later in this chapter.
52. NMML: PT Papers, File Number 291, Part 1. Lala says that Ardeshir Dalal was also there (R.M. Lala, *The Joy of Achievement: Conversations with J.R.D. Tata* (New Delhi: Penguin, 1997), pp.76–7).
53. Baldev Raj Nayar, 'Business attitudes toward economic planning in India', *Asian Survey* 11 (9) 1971, p.855.
54. Baldev Raj Nayar: 'the national struggle led even the business and managerial elite in its planning venture to a conception of the national and public interest which seemed to override group interests' (Nayar, 'Business attitudes', p.855).
55. R.M. Lala, *Beyond the Last Blue Mountain: a Life of J.R.D. Tata* (New Delhi: Penguin, 1993), p.221.
56. John Mathai, 'General Note for the first Post-War Economic Development Committee meeting', 8 December 1942. NMML: PT Papers, File Number 291 Part 1.
57. Proceedings of the first Post-War Economic Development Committee meeting, 11 December 1942. NMML: PT Papers, File Number 291 Part 1.

58. Purshotamdas Thakurdas, J.R.D. Tata, G.D. Birla, Ardeshir Dalal, Shri Ram, Kasturbhai Lalbhai, A.D. Shroff & John Matthai, *Memorandum Outlining a Plan of Economic Development for India, Parts One and Two* (Harmondsworth: Penguin, 1945) henceforward Bombay Plan, pp.66, 92.
59. G.D. Birla, *The Plan Explained* (speech at the Annual Meeting of FICCI, 4 March 1944). 1944: n.p., n.d.), p.11.
60. On independence see Mathai, 'General Note'; Bombay Plan, pp.8, 51; press interview by Plan authors, *Bombay Chronicle* 18 January 1945 in Bimal Prasad (ed.), *Towards Freedom: Documents on the Movement for Independence in India: 1945* (New Delhi: Indian Council of Historical Research, 2008), p.98. On economic unity: 'Final Draft of the Committee's Report' 20 December 1945 in NMML: PT Papers, File Number 291, Part 1; Bombay Plan, p.8.
61. Bombay Plan, pp.9, 65–8. Birla wrote, '[I]t will be a great disservice to the country if a plan is made to make the rich richer and the poor poorer. After all, a plan has no meaning if it cannot give relief to the most depressed' (Birla, *Plan Explained*, p.10). State control and state ownership, the Plan said, 'will also tend to diminish inequalities of income' (Bombay Plan, p.69).
62. Bombay Plan, pp.9, 31, 58.
63. Although the issue of 'INDUSTRY: (i) State ownership and/or control' was first on the 'List of Subjects for the Committee's first meeting', it did not appear in the first part of the Plan and was obviously the subject of intense discussion before being covered in the second part. See 'Papers for first Post-War Economic Development Committee' 8 December 1943; 'Final Draft of the Economic Committee's report', c. 30 December 1943; and the report by Tata's Statistics Department (21 July 1943), which concluded that 'on the whole a cautious attitude is desirable' (NMML: PT Papers File Number 291 Part 1).
64. Bombay Plan, pp.90, 98–9. See also Mathai, 'General Note', 8 December 1942 and Proceedings of the First Committee 11 December 1942. NMML: PT Papers, File Number 291 Part 1.
65. Bombay Plan, pp.94–6.
66. Bombay Plan, pp.39–40, 82.
67. FICCI, Press statement on the Plan, n.d. NMML: PT Papers, File Number 291 Part 1.
68. All in Prasad, *Towards Freedom 1945*, pp.983–93. Since the layman had no real idea of the Plan's implications, Birla noted, '[t]he enthusiasm displayed, therefore, may be taken only as a sign of impulsive sympathy' (Birla, *Plan Explained*, p.1).
69. Visvesvaraya, *Reconstruction in Post War India*, p.11; Deshmukh at the Poona Rotary Club 25 February 1945. NMML: C.D. Deshmukh Papers, Speeches and Writings (Unpublished), Series Number 43 File Number 2.

70. Tata enquired whether Master's company, Scindia, would monopolise the shipping industry and added, perhaps as a threat, that 'if Scindia monopolised all shipping in the future there would be a demand for nationalisation of shipping since it was a key industry'. There followed a snappish sort of exchange with Tata apparently threatening to enter the shipping industry as Scindia 'had thought it fit to intrude in aviation' (Notes [presumably by Master] on meeting between M.A. Master, G.L. Mehta and J.R.D. Tata 14 June 1944. NMML: M.A. Master Papers, Subject File 164, 1944).
71. British Library (henceforward BL): India Office Record (henceforward IOR), L/PJ/8/618A.
72. Sir Percy Grigg, 'India: Constitutional Position' 11 July 1945 in Nicholas Mansergh & Penderel Moon (eds), *The Transfer of Power, 1942–7. Volume 5: The Simla Conference, 1 September 1944 – 28 July 1945* (London: HMSO, 1974), p.1232.
73. Chibber, *Locked in Place*, pp.86, 98.
74. Chibber, *Locked in Place*, pp.86, 89, 97.
75. Chibber, *Locked in Place*, pp.86, 105–8.
76. Chibber, *Locked in Place*, pp.29, 32, 85.
77. Chandra et al., *India's Struggle*, p.463.
78. Chibber, *Locked in Place*, p.107.
79. Chibber, *Locked in Place*, p.97.
80. Chibber, *Locked in Place*, p.86. He seems to rely on a statement by Mehta (March 1945) and a memorandum by the Indian Chamber of Commerce (September 1945) (Chibber, *Locked in Place*, pp.165–6).
81. Chibber, *Locked in Place*, p.108.
82. Chibber, *Locked in Place*, p.136.
83. Chibber's final point concerns his over-arching thesis on developmental states and their relationship to the bourgeoisie in South Korea and India. Space prevents me from dealing with it adequately here (for a treatment of the issues in a different context see David Lockwood, *The Destruction of the Soviet Union: a Study in Globalization* (Macmillan: Houndmills, 2000). He argues that the Indian bourgeoisie 'blocked the building of a successful developmental state' by resisting it and thereby ensuring that India remained committed to 'Import-Substituting Industrialization' rather than 'Export-Led Industrialization' (Chibber, *Locked in Place*, pp.29, 85). The commitment to the latter, he says, was the reason for South Korea's success. However, following the Korean War, the South Korean military state did not set boldly out on the road to exports. The state, strong because the war had crippled other domestic actors and because the threat from the north remained, set out instead on the path of militarised autarky. It was only later, due to

the changes in the global economy (from the 1960s) that the state changed course, adopted export-led industrialisation and forced South Korean capitalists to follow it (see Lockwood, *Destruction of the Soviet Union*, pp.164–8; Alice H. Amsden, *Asia's Next Giant: South Korea and Late Industrialization* (New York: Oxford University Press, 1989), p.72). It was the state that engineered the change in strategy, not the South Korean bourgeoisie. In India, it was the state that clung to import-substituting industrialisation – not because of, but despite, the Indian bourgeoisie.

84. Government of India, Planning and Development Department, *Statement of Government's Industrial Policy* (New Delhi: Press of the Private Secretary to the Viceroy, 1945), pp.1–4, 6–8.
85. Grigg at the India Committee of the War Cabinet, 14 May 1945. Mansergh & Moon, *Transfer of Power, Volume 5*, pp.1031–2.
86. India Committee report on Government of India's proposals, 19 May 1945. Mansergh & Moon, *Transfer of Power Volume 5*, p.1052. British Government thinking was not unanimous on this point. Ernest Bevin (Minister for Labour and National Service) had warned Leo Amery (Secretary of State) in 1942: 'I doubt very much whether whole-hearted co-operation in the industrialisation of India is sufficiently in [the British Government's] mind. In fact, there may well be opposition to it by those who look upon India only as a customer and think that assistance towards her industrialists would be harmful to this country's interests' (Bevin to Amery 21 September 1942 in Nicholas Mansergh & Penderel Moon (eds), *The Transfer of Power, 1942–7. Volume 3: Reassertion of Authority, 21 September 1942–12 June 1943* (London: HMSO, 1971), p.8). Amery reported to the Viceroy that when the proposals were being discussed, it was asserted 'that I was only concerned in selling up four hundred million Indians to a handful of greedy Hindu industrialists' (by Sir Percy Grigg of course. Amery to Wavell, 11 July 1945 in Mansergh & Moon, *Transfer of Power Volume 5,* p.1229). However, it was Amery's view that India's industrialists were 'the ablest and most enterprising [group]. I cannot see anything very much wrong in enabling them to do for India today what men of the same type did for this country a hundred years ago' (Amery to Wavell, 19 July 1945 in Mansergh & Moon, *Transfer of Power Volume 5,* p.1282). See also the Cabinet discussion of the Government of India's proposals, 30 May 1945 in Mansergh & Moon, *Transfer of Power Volume 5*, pp.1065–9; Grigg's memorandum, 'India: Constitutional Position', 11 July 1945, Mansergh & Moon, *Transfer of Power Volume 5*, p.1231; Tomlinson, 'India and the British Empire 1935–47', p.344.
87. Chairman's Opening Address on the first day, NPC 3rd session, May 1940. NPC, *Abstract Number 2*, p.33.

88. G.L. Mehta to FICCI annual meeting, 4 March 1943 in Prasad, *Towards Freedom 1945*, pp.1010–11.
89. In a paper, 'Regional Development of Industries', prepared for the Post-War Economic Development Committee by the Tata statistics department in July 1943, there is no mention of the possibility of Pakistan – just as there is none in the Bombay Plan itself. NMML: PT Papers, File Number 291 Part 1.
90. Press statement 12 September 1942, Federation of Indian Chambers of Commerce and Industry, *Report of the Proceedings of the Executive Committee for the Year 1942–43* (New Delhi: India Print Works, 1943), p.67.
91. Thakurdas to Low 1 June 1945. NMML: PT Papers File Number 239 Part 7.
92. Birla to Thakurdas 18 December 1940; Thakurdas to Birla 19 December 1940; Birla to Thakurdas 22 December 1940; Note on meeting with Jinnah 1 January 1941. NMML: PT Papers, File 177 1936–43.
93. Ghia at IMC general meeting 30 April 1941. Indian Merchants' Chamber, *Annual Report of the Indian Merchants' Chamber for the year 1942* (Bombay: J.K. Mehta, 1943), p.560.
94. Ardeshir R. Dalal, *An Alternative to Pakistan* (Bombay: 16 February 1943, n.p.), pp.3–5. This point was also made by Nehru in *The Discovery of India* (London: Meridian Books, 1947), p.457.
95. The Sapru Committee was charged with examining the communal question in a judicial framework.
96. Homi Mody & John Mathai, *A Memorandum on the Economic and Financial Aspects of Pakistan* (Bombay: Commercial Printing Press, 1945), pp.1, 19–20.
97. Mody & Mathai, *Memorandum*, pp.26–7.
98. N.R. Sarkar, 'Mr N.R. Sarkar's Note on the Economic Implications of Pakistan' in Sir Taj Bahadur Sapru, M.R. Jayakar, N.G. Ayyangar & Jagdish Prasad (eds), *Constitutional Proposals of The Sapru Committee* (Bombay: Secretary, Sapru Committee, 1945), p.xxi.
99. Sarkar, *Note in Sapru Committee*, pp.xvii–xviii.
100. Quoted in Sarkar, *Note in Sapru Committee*, p.xix.
101. Sarkar, *Note in Sapru Committee*, p.xx. In predicting the collapse of Pakistan without close co-operation with India, none of these writers could have foreseen the forthcoming Cold War and the consequent amounts of US aid channelled to the new state (see Tariq Ali, *Can Pakistan Survive? The Death of a State* (Harmondsworth: Penguin Books, 1983), pp.52–3).
102. As it eventually was – and this, Sarkar argued, was the only way it could have been: 'Pakistan on the basis of contingent districts is the only logical

basis on the principle of religious division' (Sarkar, *Note in Sapru Committee*, p.xx).

103. Quoted in Talbot, *Planning for Pakistan*, p.878.
104. Reginald Coupland, *The Future of India: the Third Part of a Report on the Constitutional Problem in India submitted to the Warden and Fellows of Nuffield College, Oxford* (London: Oxford University Press, 1943), p.79.
105. Coupland, *Future of India*, p.190.
106. Coupland, *Future of India*, p.78.
107. Hanna Papanek, 'Pakistan's big businessmen: Muslim separatism, entrepreneurship, and partial modernization', *Economic Development and Cultural Change* 21 (1) October 1972, p.11.
108. Talbot, *Planning for Pakistan*, p.877.
109. Kenneth McPherson, *The Muslim Microcosm: Calcutta, 1918 to 1935* (Wiesbaden: Franz Steiner Verlag, 1974), p.151.
110. Mirza Abol Hassan Ispahani, *Qaid-E-Azam Jinnah As I Knew Him* (Karachi: Forward Publications Trust, 1967), pp.130–3.
111. Papanek, 'Pakistan's big businessmen', p.13.
112. See Resolution II of the Muslim League Karachi session 24–26 December 1943 in Syed S. Pirzada (ed.), *Foundations of Pakistan. All-India Muslim League Documents. Volume Two, 1924–1947* (Karachi & Dacca: National Publishing House, 1970), pp.466–70. The Viceroy reported to Amery in March 1945 that 'The Muslim League, and Muslims generally, will probably press for State ownership or at least State participation on a large scale' (Wavell to Amery 6 March 1945, Mansergh & Moon, *Transfer of Power Volume 5*, p.662).
113. Papanek argues that the Pakistani economy did not end up dominated by the state because 'the economy was in chaos and the very small number of available government officials were needed for tasks other than the management of state enterprises' (Papanek, 'Pakistan's big businessmen', p.10).
114. See Claude Markovits, *Merchants, Traders, Entrepreneurs: Indian Business in the Colonial Era* (Basingstoke: Palgrave Macmillan, 2008); Kudaisya, *Birla*, chapter 9.
115. Bombay Plan, p.8.
116. Federation of Indian Chambers of Commerce and Industry, *Proceedings of the Twentieth Annual Meeting held at New Delhi on 3rd and 4th March 1947* (New Delhi: FICCI, 1947), pp.85, 88.
117. FICCI, *Proceedings 20th annual meeting 1947*, p.24. Asim Roy points out: 'The unqualified commitment of the Congress to a strong centre stemmed from its vision of a strong, united and modernized India'. This was 'inseparable

from the need and demand for India's reconstruction, based on centralized planning' (Asim Roy, 'The high politics of India's partition: The revisionist perspective' in Mushirul Hasan (ed.), *India's Partition: Process, Strategy and Moblization* (New Delhi: Oxford University Press, 2001), p.123).

118. Quoted in Sumit Sarkar, *Modern India, 1885–1947* (Madras: Macmillan India Ltd., 1983), p.446.
119. See the resolution on 'Powers and Policies of the Indian Union Government' in FICCI, *Proceedings 20th annual meeting*, p.139. See also the May 1946 articles in *The Eastern Economist* cited in Kudaisya, *Birla*, p.239.
120. See Markovits, *Merchants, Traders*, pp.90–1.
121. Quoted in Kudaisya, *Birla*, p.235. Roy says that the Congress too, from 1930, sought 'an answer to the Muslim Question that made no demand on its "sacred cow", that is the strong centre' – but ultimately failed to find one (Roy, 'High politics' in Hasan, *India's Partition*, p.125).
122. Ram to Thakurdas 29 September 1942. NMML: PT Papers, File Number 239 Part 4.
123. NMML: Papers of H.P. Mody, Subject File Number 16.
124. Kudaisya, *Birla*, p.234. This presents another problem for the analysis of Chibber (see above). If the Indian bourgeoisie was *really* (though secretly) opposed to centralisation and planning, then their way was clear. They simply had to accept British and Muslim League proposals for a weak central authority. They knew from their experience after the First World War that central planning on a provincial basis was impossible. The bourgeoisie, however, did the exact opposite.
125. G.D. Birla, *In the Shadow of the Mahatma: A Personal Memoir* (Bombay: Orient Longmans Ltd., 1955), p.267.
126. Birla to Thakurdas 18 December 1940. NMML: PT Papers, File Number 177 1936–43.
127. He wrote to Cripps in December 1946 that 'it should be made clear . . . they [Muslims] can have their own constitution only in the places where they are in a majority; which means not the whole of the Punjab nor the whole of Bengal' (Birla, *In the Shadow*, p.271). He was not totally confident that this position would win through. Sir John Colville, Governor of Bombay, met Birla and reported to the Secretary of State: 'he also made the interesting remark that he was proposing to develop his businesses in Bombay rather than in Calcutta, because he though some form of Pakistan would come about' (Colville to Pethwick-Lawrence 18 December 1946. Nicholas Mansergh & Penderel Moon (eds), *The Transfer of Power, 1942–7. Volume 9: The Fixing of a Time Limit, 4 November 1946–22 March 1947* (London: HMSO, 1980), p.381).

128. Birla had written to Cripps in October 1946: 'But more than politics the present poverty of our people needs serious attention from our Government. It has not been possible, however, for the Government to tackle economics. They are busy with politics which at present means only Jinnah!' (Birla, *In the Shadow*, p.268).
129. M.A. Master 28 March 1948 in Federation of Indian Chambers of Commerce and Industry, *Proceedings of the Twenty-First Annual Meeting held at New Delhi on 28th and 29th March 1948* (New Delhi: FICCI, 1948), p.78. Hirachand tried to put the friendly understanding into practice by inviting Pakistan's Governor-General (Jinnah) and Prime Minister (Liaquat Ali Khan) to send a message of support for the launching of Scindia's third Haj ship in September 1947. He urged the unity of Indian and Pakistani shipping against the British (NMML: M.A. Master Papers, Subject File 216 1947).
130. Kudaisya, *Birla*, p.245. On economic losses see K.L. Luthra, *Impact of Partition on Industries in Border Districts of East Punjab* (New Delhi: Board of Economic Inquiry, East Punjab), p.1949.

Conclusion

1. Intelligence Bureau report (18 March 1943), Home Department, Government of India. British Library (henceforward BL), India Office Record (henceforward IOR): L/PJ/8/618A.
2. According to the Intelligence Bureau, 'the available evidence does not appear to justify any assumption that "Big Business" has secretly been using Congress as an unsuspecting instrument towards the achievement of its own ends . . . the two have been working together in a partnership of convenience with no illusions on either side' (Intelligence Bureau report, (28 February 1944), Home Department, Government of India. BL: IOR, L/PJ/8/618A).
3. As reported by F.F. Turnbull to the Viceroy, 6 June 1946. Nicholas Mansergh & Penderel Moon (eds), *The Transfer of Power, 1942–7. Volume 7: The Cabinet Mission, 23 March – 29 June 1946* (London: HMSO, 1977), p.825.
4. Federation of Indian Chambers of Commerce and Industry, *Proceedings of the Twentieth Annual Meeting held at New Delhi on 3rd and 4th March 1947* (New Delhi: FICCI, 1947), p.16. These sentiments were embodied in a resolution passed on the same day (pp.65–6). It should be noted that the Budget to which FICCI objected (which included a wealth tax, a capital gains tax and an increase in general taxation) was put forward by Liaquat Ali Khan, the Muslim League Finance Minister in the Interim Government.

5. G.D. Birla, *In the Shadow of the Mahatma: A Personal Memoir* (Bombay: Orient Longmans Ltd., 1955), p.276.
6. Mody to M.A. Master 28 January 1948. Nehru Memorial Museum and Library: M.A. Master Papers, Subject File H, number 1060.
7. Baldev Raj Nayar, 'Business attitudes toward economic planning in India', *Asian Survey* 11 (9) 1971, pp.855–6.
8. Intelligence Bureau report (28 February 1944), Home Department, Government of India. BL: IOR, L/PJ/8/618A.

BIBLIOGRAPHY

Aggarwala, R.N. *National Movement and Constitutional Development of India (1857–1978)*, New Delhi: Metropolitan Book Company, 1978.

Ainscough, Thomas M. (HM Senior Trade Commissioner in India & Ceylon). *Report on the Conditions and Prospects of British Trade in India at the Close of the War*, London: HMSO, 1919.

Ali, Chaudhri Muhammad. *The Emergence of Pakistan*, New York: Columbia University Press, 1967.

Ali, Tariq. *Can Pakistan Survive? The Death of a State,* Harmondsworth: Penguin Books, 1983.

Ambirajan, S. *Classical Political Economy and British Policy in India*, Cambridge: Cambridge University Press, 1978.

Amsden, Alice H. *Asia's Next Giant: South Korea and Late Industrialization*, New York: Oxford University Press, 1989.

Andarkar, B.N. *Studies in Indian Economics issued by the Office of the Economic Adviser. First Series. Aspects of the Indian Tariff, No. 2: The History of the Indian Tariff, 1924–39,* Delhi: Government of India Press, 1940.

Anstey, Vera. *The Economic Development of India*, London: Longmans, Green & Co., 1957 [1929].

Bahadur, R.S.R. *Presidential Address of the Honourable Rai Sitanath Ray Bahadur at the Twelfth Session of the Indian Industrial Conference held at Lucknow, 1916*, B.M. Press, Calcutta 1916.

Bahl, Vinay. 'The emergence of large-scale steel industry in India under British colonial rule, 1880–1907', *Indian Economic and Social History Review,* 31, 4 (1994), 413–60.

Barua, Pradeep. 'Strategies and doctrines of imperial defence: Britain and India, 1919–45', *Journal of Imperial and Commonwealth History,* 25, 2 (May 1997), 240–66.

Bayly, Christopher and Harper, Tim. *Forgotten Wars: The End of Britain's Asian Empire*, London: Allen Lane, 2007.

Birla, G.D. *A Statement on behalf of the Federation of Indian Chambers of Commerce and Industry in reply to the circular letter dated the 27th July 1929 issued by the Associated Chambers of Commerce of India and Ceylon to influence opinion in England against India's right to adapt her economic policy to her own needs*, Calcutta: Federation of Indian Chambers of Commerce and Industry, n.d.

—— *Principles of Economic Planning*, New Delhi: East Economist Ltd., 1943.

—— *The Plan Explained* (speech at the Annual Meeting of FICCI, 4 March 1944). 1944: n.p., n.d.

—— *In the Shadow of the Mahatma: A Personal Memoir*, Bombay: Orient Longmans Ltd., 1955.

Bond, Brian. *British Military Policy between the Two World Wars*, Oxford: Clarendon Press, 1980.

Bose, Sugata. *South Asia and World Capitalism*, Delhi: Oxford University Press, 1990.

Bowen, H.V. *The Business of Empire: the East India Company and Imperial Britain, 1756–1833*, Cambridge: Cambridge University Press, 2007.

Brenner, Robert. 'The social basis of economic development', in John Roemer (ed.), *Analytical Marxism*, Cambridge: Cambridge University Press, 1986.

Buchanan, Daniel H. *The Development of Capitalistic Enterprise in India*, London: Cass, 1966 [1934].

Bukharin, Nikolai Ivanovich. *Imperialism and World Economy*, New York: H. Fertig, 1966.

'Proceedings of the First Conference of Directors of Industries, Simla, 12–14 April 1920', *Bulletins of Indian Industries and Labour*, Number 1 (1921).

'Proceedings of the [second] Conference of Directors of Industries, 1–4 November 1920', *Bulletins of Indian Industries and Labour*, Number 5 (January 1921).

'Proceedings of the Third Conference of Departments of Industries, Simla 23–26 May 1921', *Bulletins of Indian Industries and Labour*, Number 18 (September 1921).

'Proceedings of the Fourth Conference of Departments of Industries, Calcutta 17–19 April 1922', *Bulletins of Indian Industries and Labour*, Number 27 (September 1922).

Busch, Briton Cooper. *Britain, India, and the Arabs, 1914–1921*, Berkeley: University of California Press, 1971.

Callinicos, Alex. 'Bourgeois revolutions and historical materialism', *International Socialism*, 43 (1989).

Chakrabarti, Manali. 'Why did Indian big business pursue a policy of economic nationalism in the interwar years?' *Modern Asian Studies*, 43, 4 (2009), 979–1038.

Chakrabarty, D. and Bhattacharyya, C. (eds). *Congress in Evolution: a collection of Congress Resolutions from 1885–1934*, Calcutta: The Book Company Ltd., 1935.

Chamberlain, Austen. 'Introduction', in Roper Lethbridge, *The Indian Offer of Imperial Preference*, London: PS King & Son, 1913.

Chandavarkar, Rajnarayan. *Imperial Power and Popular Politics: Class, Resistance and the State in India, 1850–1950*, Cambridge University Press, Cambridge 1998.

Chandra, Bipan. *Nationalism and Colonialism in Modern India*, New Delhi: Orient Longman, 1979.

—— *Communalism in Modern India*, New Delhi: Vikas Publishing House, 1984.

Chandra, Bipan et al. *India's Struggle for Independence, 1857–1947,* New Delhi: Penguin, 1989.

Charlesworth, Neil. *British Rule and the Indian Economy, 1800–1914*, London: Macmillan, 1982.

—— 'The problem of government financing in British India: taxation, borrowing and allocation of resources in the inter-war period', *Modern Asian Studies,* 19, 3 (1985).

Chatterji, Basudev. 'The political economy of "discriminating protection": the case of textiles in the 1920s', *Indian Economic and Social History Review,* 20, 3 (1983), 239–75.

—— *Trade, Tariffs and Empire: Lancashire and British Policy in India, 1919–1939*, Delhi: Oxford University Press, 1992.

—— (ed.). *Towards Freedom: Documents on the Movement for Independence in India, 1938: Part 1*, New Delhi: Oxford University Press, 1999.

Chatterton, Alfred. 'The war and Indian industries', in Ganapathi A. Natesan (ed.), *All About the War: The India Review War Book*, Madras: G.A. Natesan & Co., 1915.

Chaudhuri, K.N. 'Economic problems and Indian Independence', in C.H. Philips and Mary D. Wainwright (eds), *The Partition of India: Policies and Perspectives, 1935–1947,* Cambridge, Massachusetts: M.I.T. Press, 1970.

Chaudhuri, K.N. and Dewey, Clive J. (eds). *Economy and Society: Essays in Indian Economic and Social History*, Delhi: Oxford University Press, 1979.

Chibber, Vivek. *Locked in Place: State-Building and Late Industrialization in India*, Princeton: Princeton University Press, 2006.

Chopra, P.N. (ed.). *Towards Freedom, 1937: Experiments with Provincial Autonomy*, New Delhi: Oxford University Press, 1985.

Cliff, Tony. *Deflected Permanent Revolution*, London: Socialist Workers Party, 1990 [1963].

Coatman, John. *Statement Exhibiting the Moral and Material Progress and Condition of India during the Year 1925–1926*, India: HMSO, 1927.

Cobden, Richard. *The Political Writings of Richard Cobden*, New York: Kraus, 1969 [1903].

Cohen, G.A. *Karl Marx's Theory of History: A Defence*, Oxford: Clarendon, 1991.

Cohen, Stephen P. 'Issue, Role and Personality: the Kitchener-Curzon Dispute', *Comparative Studies in Society and History,* X, 3 (April 1968), 337–55.

—— *The Indian Army: its Contribution to the Development of a Nation*, Berkeley: University of California Press, 1971.

Cotton, C.W.E. (Collector of Customs, Calcutta). *Handbook of Commercial Information for India*, Calcutta: Superintendent of Government Printing, 1919.

Coupland, Reginald. *The Future of India: the Third Part of a Report on the Constitutional Problem in India submitted to the Warden and Fellows of Nuffield College, Oxford*, London: Oxford University Press, 1943.

Cox, Howard. 'International business, the state and industrialisation in India: Early growth in the Indian cigarette industry, 1900–19', *Indian Economic and Social History Review*, 27, 3 (1990), 289–312.

Curtis, L. (ed.). *Papers relating to the Application of the principle of Dyarchy to the Government of India*, Oxford: Clarendon Press, 1920.

Curzon, George N. *Lord Curzon in India, 1898–1905,* edited by Thomas Raleigh, London: Macmillan, 1906.

Dalal, Ardeshir R. *An Alternative to Pakistan*, Bombay: 16 February 1943, n.p.

Das, Baman Chandra. *Financial Autonomy for India*, Calcutta: B.C. Das, 1919.

Davis, Paul K. *Ends and Means: the British Mesopotamian Campaign and Commission*, Cranbury N.J.: Associated University Presses, 1994.

Desai, Akshayakumar R. *Social Background of Indian Nationalism*, Bombay: Popular Prakashan, 1966 [1948].

Deshpande, Anirudh. *British Military Policy in India, 1900–1945: Colonial Constraints and Declining Power*, New Delhi: Manohar, 2005.

Dewey, Clive. 'The end of the Imperialism of free trade: the eclipse of the Lancashire Lobby and the concession of fiscal autonomy to India', in Clive Dewey and AG Hopkins (eds), *The Imperial Impact: Studies in the Economic History of Africa and India,* London: The Athlone Press, 1978.

—— 'The Government of India's "New Industrial Policy", 1900–1925: Formation and failure', in K.N. Chaudhuri and Clive J. Dewey (eds), *Economy and Society: Essays in Indian Economic and Social History*, Delhi: Oxford University Press, 1979.

Dewey, Clive and Hopkins, A.G. (eds). *The Imperial Impact: Studies in the Economic History of Africa and India*, London: The Athlone Press, 1978.

Divekar, D.V. *The Future of Indian Fiscal Policy*, Madras: S. Ganesan, 1923.

Dockrill, Michael L. *British Documents on Foreign Affairs – Reports and Papers from the Foreign Office Confidential Print. Part II, From the First to the Second World War. Series 1: the Paris Peace Conference of 1919. Volume 13: Minutes of the Supreme Economic Council,* Frederick, Md: University Publications of America, 1991.

Ellinwood, DeWitt C. and Pradhan, S.D. (eds). *India and World War 1*, Delhi: Manohar, 1978.

Engels, Frederick. 'The origin of the family, private property and the state', in K. Marx and F. Engels (eds), *Selected Works*, Moscow: Progress Publishers, 1970.

—— 'Socialism: utopian and scientific', in K. Marx & F. Engels (eds), *Selected Works*, Moscow: Progress Publishers, 1970.

Esher, Reginald, Viscount. *Journals and Letters of Reginald, Viscount Esher – Volume Four: 1916–1930*, edited by Oliver, Viscount Esher, London: Ivor Nicholson & Watson Ltd., 1938.

Federation of Indian Chambers of Commerce and Industry. *Representation submitted to H.E. the Viceroy by the Committee of the Federation on the present political situation in India*, Delhi: Oxford Printing Works, 1930.

—— *Proceedings of the Sixth Annual Meeting held at Delhi on the 15th and 16th April, 1933*, Calcutta: n.p. 1933.

—— *Proceedings of the Seventh Annual Meeting held at Delhi on the 31st March and 1st April, 1934*, Ahmedabad: n.p. 1934.

—— *Constitutional Reforms for India*, Ahmedabad: Indian Printing Works, 1935.

—— *Note on Ottawa Scheme of Preferences*, Cawnpore: The Job Press, 1936.

——*Correspondence and relevant documents relating to important questions dealt with by the Federation during the year 1940–41*, New Delhi: n.p. 1941.

—— *Correspondence and relevant documents relating to important questions dealt with by the federation during the year 1941–42*, Bombay: India Printing Works, 1942.

—— *Report of the Proceedings of the Executive Committee for the year 1942–43*, New Delhi: India Print Works, 1943.

—— *Correspondence and relevant documents relating to important questions dealt with by the Federation during the year 1944*, Bombay: India Printing Works, 1945.

—— *Correspondence and relevant documents relating to important questions dealt with by the Federation during the year 1945*, New Delhi: FICCI, 1946.

—— *Proceedings of the Twentieth Annual Meeting held at New Delhi on 3rd and 4th March 1947*, New Delhi: FICCI, 1947.

—— *Proceedings of the Twenty-First Annual Meeting held at New Delhi on 28th and 29th March 1948*, New Delhi: FICCI, 1948.

Fermor, L.L. 'Thomas Henry Holland 1868–1947', *Obituary Notices of Fellows of the Royal Society*, VI, 17 (November 1948), 83–114.

Fieldhouse, D.K. *Economics and Empire 1830–1914*, London: Weidenfeld and Nicolson, 1973.

Fraser, Lovat. *Iron and Steel in India: A Chapter from the Life of Jamshedji N. Tata*, Bombay: The Times Press, 1919.

French, David. *British Economic and Strategic Planning, 1905–1915*, London: George Allen & Unwin, 1982.

Gadgil, D.R. *Imperial Preference for India: the Ottawa Agreement Examined*, Poona: Gokhale Institute of Politics and Economics, 1932.

—— *The Industrial Evolution of India in Recent Times, 1860–1939*, Bombay: Oxford University Press, 1971 [1924].

Gallagher, John. 'Nationalisms and the crisis of empire, 1919–1922', *Modern Asian Studies*, 15, 3 (1981), 355–68.

—— *The Decline, Revival and Fall of the British Empire*, Cambridge: Cambridge University Press, 2004.

Gallagher, John and Robinson, Ronald. 'The imperialism of free trade', *Economic History Review*, second series, VI, 1 (1953), 1–15.

Gallagher, John and Seal, Anil. 'Britain and India between the wars', *Modern Asian Studies,* 15, 3 (1981), 387–414.

Gandhi, Mohandas K. *The Collected Works of Mahatma Gandhi*, Delhi: Publications Division, Ministry of Information and Broadcasting, 1958–94.

Gordon, A.D.D. *Businessmen and Politics: Rising Nationalism and a Modernising Economy in Bombay, 1918–1933*, New Delhi: Manohar, 1978.

Government of Bombay. *Post-War Reconstruction – Bombay Province*, Bombay: Government Central Press, n.d.

Government of India. *Papers relating to the Industrial conference held at Ootacamund in September 1908*, Madras: Superintendent, Government Press, 1908.

—— *Defence of India Act, 1915.*

—— *Indian Industrial Commission 1916–1918, Report*, Calcutta: Superintendent of Government Printing, 1918.

—— *Proceedings of the War Conference held at Delhi, 27th–29th April 1918*, Delhi: Superintendent of Government Printing, 1918.

—— *Statement Exhibiting the Moral and Material Progress and Condition of India during the year 1919*, London: HMSO, 1920.

—— *Report of the Indian Fiscal Commission, 1921–22*, Simla: Government Central Press, 1922.

—— *India's Contribution to the Great War*, Calcutta: Superintendent of Government Printing, 1923.

—— *Report of the Indian Retrenchment Committee, 1922–23*, London: HMSO 1923. British Library, India Office Record: L/MIL/17/5/1781.

—— *Despatch on Proposals for Constitutional Reform*, Simla: Government of India Press, 1930.

—— *Report of the Indian Delegation to the Imperial Economic Conference, Ottawa 1932,* Calcutta: Central Publications Branch, 1932.

—— Reconstruction Committee of Council. *Record of the First Meeting of the General Policy Committee*, New Delhi: n.p., January 1944.

—— Reconstruction Committee of Council. *Second Report on Reconstruction Planning*, New Delhi: n.p., 23 October 1944.

—— Planning and Development Department. *Statement of Government's Industrial Policy*, New Delhi: Press of the Private Secretary to the Viceroy, 1945.

Gupta, Partha Sarathi. 'State and business in India in the age of discriminating protection', in Divijendra Tripathi (ed.), *State and Business in India: A Historical Perspective*, New Delhi: Manohar, 1987.

—— (ed.). *Towards Freedom: Documents on the Movement for Independence in India: 1943–1944, Part 3*, New Delhi: Indian Council of Historical Research, 1997.

Habib, Irfan. *Essays in Indian History: Towards a Marxist Perspective*, New Delhi: Tulika Books, 1997.

Hardinge of Penshurst, Lord. *Memorandum by H.E. the Viceroy upon Questions Likely to Arise in India at the End of the War*, Delhi: n.p., 1915.

—— *My Indian Years, 1910–1916*, London: John Murray, 1948.

Harnetty, Peter. *Imperialism and Free trade: Lancashire and India in the Mid-Nineteenth Century*, Hong Kong: University of British Columbia Press, 1972.

Harris, F.R. *Jamsetji Nusserwanji Tata: a Chronicle of His life*, Bombay: Blackie & Son Ltd., 1953 [1924].

Harris, Nigel. *Of Bread and Guns*, Harmondsworth: Penguin, 1983.

Hasan, Mushirul. *Legacy of a Divided Nation: India's Muslims since Independence*, London: C. Hurst & Co., 1997.

—— (ed.). *India's Partition: Process, Strategy and Moblization*, New Delhi: Oxford University Press, 2001.

—— *Making Sense of History: Society, Culture and Politics*, New Delhi: Manohar, 2003.

—— (ed.). *Towards Freedom: Documents on the Movement for Independence in India: 1939, Part 1*, New Delhi: Indian Council of Historical Research, 2008.

—— (ed.). *Towards Freedom: Documents on the Movement for Independence in India: 1939, Part 2*, New Delhi: Indian Council of Historical Research, 2008.

Hindustan Times. *India Unreconciled: A Documented History of Indian Political Events from the Crisis of August 1942 to October 1943*, New Delhi: Hindustan Times Press, 1943.

Hintze, Otto. *The Historical Essays of Otto Hintze*, edited by F. Gilbert, New York: Oxford University Press, 1975.

Hirtzel, A. (Deputy Under-Secretary of State for India). *Statement Exhibiting the Moral and Material Progress and Condition of India during the Year 1921*, London: HMSO, 1922.

Hobson, John A. *Imperialism: a Study*, London: Allen & Unwin, 1938.

Holdness, T.W. (Under Secretary of State for India). *Statement Exhibiting the Moral and Material Progress and Condition of India during the Year 1917–18*, London: HMSO, 1919.

Holland, R.F. *Britain and the Commonwealth Alliance, 1918–1939,* London: Macmillan, 1981.

House of Commons. *Proposals for Indian Constitutional Reform*, London: HMSO, 1933.

Holquist, Peter. *Making War, Forging Revolution: Russia's Continuum of Crisis, 1914–1921*, Cambridge: Harvard University Press, 2002.

Howard, Michael. *The Continental Commitment: The Dilemma of British Defence Policy in the Era of the Two World Wars*, London: Ashfield Press, 1989.

Hutchins, Francis G. *Spontaneous Revolution: the Quit India Movement*, Delhi: Manohar, 1971.

Imperial Conference, 1930. *Summary of Proceedings*, London: HMSO, 1930.

Imperial Economic Conference (October-November 1923). *Record of Proceedings and Documents*, London: HMSO, 1924.

Imperial Economic Conference, 1923. *Summary of Conclusions*, Cape Town: Cape Times Ltd., 1924.

Imperial Economic Conference at Ottawa, 1932. *Summary of Proceedings and Copies of Trade Agreements*, London: HMSO, 1932.

Indian Fiscal Commission. *Report of the Indian Fiscal Commission, 1921–22*, Simla: Government Central Press, 1922.

—— *Statement of Witness No. 161* (P.C. Dutt, Barrister and President of the Jubbulpore Municipal Committee), Anjuman Islamia Press, Jubbulpore 1916.

Indian Industrial Conference. *The Congress and Conferences of 1905*, Madras: G.A. Natesan & Co., 1906.

—— *India's Annual Conference. Being a collection of papers read to the 2nd Industrial Conference in Calcutta, December 1906*, Madras: Srinivasa Varadacheri & Co., 1907.

Indian Merchants' Chamber. *Views of the Committee on the Excess Profits Tax Bill*, Bombay: n.p., 7 February 1940.

—— *Annual Report of the Indian Merchants' Chamber for the year 1940*, Bombay: J.K. Mehta, 1941.

—— *Annual Report of the Indian Merchants' Chamber for the year 1941,* Bombay: J.K. Mehta, 1942.

—— *Annual Report of the Indian Merchants' Chamber for the year 1942,* Bombay: J.K. Mehta, 1943.

—— *Annual Report of the Indian Merchants' Chamber for the year 1943,* Bombay: J.K. Mehta, 1944.

Indian Munitions Board, *Industrial Handbook 1919*, Calcutta: Superintendent of Government Printing, 1919.

Indian National Congress. *Report of the Proceedings of the Third Session of the Indian National Congress, 1887*, New York: Vintage Books, 1993 [1887].

—— *The Madras Congress and Conferences 1908*, Madras: G.A. Natesan & Co., 1910.

—— *All-India Congress Committee 1926*, Madras: General Secretary of the AICC, 1927.

—— *Resolutions on Economic Policy and Programme, 1924–54*, New Delhi: All-India Congress Committee, 1954.

Indian Round Table Conference, 12 November 1930–19 January 1931. *Proceedings*, London: HMSO, 1931.

Indian Round Table Conference, November–December 1932. *Sub-Committees' Reports; Summaries of Discussions and the Secretary of State's Statement*, Calcutta: Government of India Publications branch, 1933.

Indian Statutory Commission. *Report of the Indian Statutory Commission, Volumes I and II*, London: HMSO, 1930.

Indian Tariff Board. *Report of the Indian Tariff Board regarding the Grant of Protection to the Steel Industry*, Calcutta: Superintendent of Government Printing, 1924.

—— *Report of the Indian Tariff Board Regarding the Increase of Duties on Steel*, Bombay: Government Central Press, 1924.

—— *Report of the Indian Tariff Board Regarding the Grant of Protection to the Ship-Building Industry*, Calcutta: Government of India Central Publications Branch, 1926.

—— *Report of the Indian Tariff Board (Cotton Textile Industry Enquiry), 1927*, Bombay: Government Central Press, 1927.

—— *Report of the Indian Tariff Board Regarding the Grant of Protection to the Cotton Textile Industry*, Calcutta: Government of India Central Publications Branch, 1932.

—— *Report of the Indian Tariff Board on the Iron and Steel Industry*, Delhi: Manager of Publications, 1934.

Indo-British Association Ltd. *The Montagu-Chelmsford Report on Indian Constitutional Reform and the Future of Indo-British Commerce*, London: Merritt & Hutcher Ltd., n.d.

Ispahani, Mirza Abol Hassan. *Qaid-E-Azam Jinnah As I Knew Him*, Karachi: Forward Publications Trust, 1967.

—— 'Factors leading to the Partition of British India', in C.H. Philips and Mary D. Wainwright (eds), *The Partition of India: Policies and Perspectives, 1935–1947*, Cambridge, Massachusetts: MIT Press, 1970.

Jeffery, Keith. 'The military defence of the British Empire, 1918–1922', PhD diss., University of Cambridge, n.d.

—— '"An English barrack in the Oriental Seas"? India in the aftermath of the First World War', *Modern Asian Studies,* XV, 3 (1981), 369–86.

—— *The British Army and the Crisis of Empire, 1918–22*, Manchester: Manchester University Press, 1984.

Jenks, Leland H. *The Migration of British Capital to 1875*, London: Nelson, 1971 [1927]).

Jha, Shiva Chandra. *Studies in the Development of Capitalism in India*, Calcutta: Firma KL Mukhopadhyay, 1963.

Jinnah, Mahomed Ali. *Some Recent Speeches and Writings of Mr Jinnah*, collected and edited by Jamil-ud-din Ahmad, Lahore: Sh. Muhammad Ashraf, 1942.

Jinnah, Mahomed Ali and Ispahani, Mirza Abol Hassan. *M.A. Jinnah–Ispahani Correspondence, 1936–1948*, Z.H. Zaidi (ed.), Karachi: Forward Publications Trust, 1976.

Johnson, Franklyn A. *Defence by Committee: the British Committee of Imperial Defence, 1885–1959*, London: Oxford University Press, 1960.

Johnson, Gordon. 'Government and Nationalism in India, 1880–1920', in Sugata Bose (ed.), *South Asia and World Capitalism*, Delhi: Oxford University Press, 1990.

Jones, Geoffrey. 'Jamnalal Bajaj, Mahatma Gandhi, and the struggle for Indian Independence', Harvard Business School, 12 October 2007: www.hbs.edu/businesshistory/pdf/struggleforindianind.pdf.

Jones, G.G. 'The state and economic development in India 1890–1947: the case of oil', *Modern Asian Studies,* XIII, 3 (1979), 353–75.

Joshi, Arun. *Lala Shri Ram: a Study in Entrepreneurship and Industrial Management*, New Delhi: Orient Longman, 1975.

Kale, Vaman G. 'The war and Indian trade', in Ganapathi A. Natesan (ed.), *All About the War: The India Review War Book,* Madras: G.A. Natesan & Co., 1915.

Kannangara, A.P. 'Indian millowners and Indian nationalism before 1914', *Past and Present,* 40 (July 1968), 147–64.

Kautsky, John H. *Karl Kautsky: Marxism, Revolution and Democracy*, New Brunswick: Transaction Publishers, 1994.

Kautsky, Karl. 'Socialism and colonial policy' (1907). www.marxists.org/archive/kautsky/1907/colonial/index.htm.

—— 'Imperialism and war' (September 1914). www.marxists.org/archive/kautsky/1914/09/war.htm.

Keenan, John L. *A Steel Man in India*, London: V. Gollancz Ltd, 1945.

Kemp, Tom. *Theories of Imperialism*, London: Dobson Books Ltd., 1967.

Khanolkar, G.D. *Walchand Hirachand: Man, His Time and Achievements*, Bombay: Walchand & Co., 1969.

Kidron, Michael. *Capitalism and Theory*, London: Pluto Press, 1974.

Kochanek, Stanley A. *The Congress Party of India: the Dynamics of a One-Party Democracy*, Princeton: Princeton University Press, 1968.

—— 'Briefcase politics in India: the Congress Party and the business elite', *Asian Survey,* 27, 12 (December 1987), 1278–301.

—— 'The transformation of interest politics in India', *Pacific Affairs,* 68, 4 (Winter 1995–96), 529–50.

—— 'Liberalisation and business lobbying in India', *Journal of Commonwealth and Comparative Politics,* 34, 3 (November 1996), 155–73.

Kripilani, J.B. *The Indian National Congress, 1930–1934*, Allahabad: All-India Congress Committee, n.d.

Krishna, Gopal. 'The development of the Indian National Congress as a mass organization, 1918–1923', *Journal of Asian Studies,* 25, 3 (May 1966), 413–30.

Krishna, K.B. *Plan for Economic Development of India (A Critical and Historical Survey)*, Bombay: Padma Publications, 1945.

Kudaisya, Medha M. *The Life and Times of G.D. Birla*, New Delhi: Oxford University Press, 2003.

Kumar, Dharma and Desai, Meghnad (eds), *The Cambridge Economic History of India, Volume 2: c.1757–c.1970*, Cambridge University Press, Cambridge 1983.

Kuznets, Simon et al. (eds), *Economic Growth: Brazil, India, Japan*, Durham NC: Duke University Press, 1955.

Lala, R.M. *Beyond the Last Blue Mountain: a Life of J.R.D. Tata*, New Delhi: Penguin, 1993.

—— *The Joy of Achievement: Conversations with J.R.D. Tata*, New Delhi: Penguin, 1997.

—— *For the Love of India: the Life and Times of Jamsetji Tata*, New Delhi: Penguin Portfolio, 2006.

—— *The Creation of Wealth: the Tatas from the 19th to the 21st Century*, New Delhi: Penguin Portfolio, 2004.

—— *The Romance of Tata Steel*, New Delhi: Penguin/Viking, 2007.

Lamb, Helen B. 'The Indian business communities and the evolution of an industrialist class', *Pacific Affairs,* XXVIII, 2 (June 1955), 101–16.

—— 'The "state" and economic development in India', in Simon Kuznets et al. (eds), *Economic Growth: Brazil, India, Japan,* Durham NC: Duke University Press, 1955.

Latifi, A. *The Industrial Punjab: a Survey of Facts, Conditions and Possibilities*, Bombay & Calcutta: Longman Green & Co., 1911.

Lenin, Vladimir Ilyich. *Imperialism: the Highest Stage of Capitalism*, Moscow: Progress Publishers, 1970.

Leaders' Conference. *An Authentic Account of the Leaders' Conference held at new Delhi on 19th and 20th February 1943 in respect of Mahatma Gandhi's Fast*, New Delhi: The Convenors of the Conference, 1943.

Lethbridge, Roper. *The Indian Offer of Imperial Preference*, London: P.S. King & Sons, 1913.

—— 'Indian industrial expansion after the war', in Ganapathi A. Natesan (ed.), *All About the War: The India Review War Book*, Madras: G.A. Natesan & Co., 1915.

Linlithgow, Victor A.J.H. *Speeches and Statements*, New Delhi: Government of India (Bureau of Public Information), 1945.

Lloyd George, David. *War Memoirs of David Lloyd George: Volume Two, 1915–1916*, Boston: Little and Brown, 1934.

Lloyd-Greame, Philip. *The Imperial Economic Conference*, Westminster: National Unionist Association, n.d. [1923?]

Lockwood, David. *The Destruction of the Soviet Union: a Study in Globalization*, Macmillan: Houndmills, 2000.

—— 'Historical materialism and the state', *Critique,* 34, 2 (August 2006), 163–78.

—— 'War, the state and the bourgeois revolution', *War & Society,* 25, 2 (October 2006), 53–78.

—— *Cronies or Capitalists? The Russian Bourgeoisie and the Bourgeois Revolution from 1850 to 1917*, Newcastle upon Tyne: Cambridge Scholars Publishing, 2009.

Luthra, K.L. *Impact of Partition on Industries in Border Districts of East Punjab*, New Delhi: Board of Economic Inquiry, East Punjab, 1949.

Macauley (Captain), D.I. 'India in Imperial defence', *Proceedings of the Central Asian Society*, London: Central Asian Society, 1910.

MacDonagh, Oliver. 'The anti-imperialism of free trade', *Economic History Review*, 14, 3 (1962), 489–501.

Macpherson, W.J. 'Investment in Indian railways, 1845–1875', *Economic History Review,* 8, 2 (1955), 177–86.

Madan, Balkrishna. *India and Imperial Preference: a Study in Commercial Policy*, Bombay: Oxford University Press, 1939.

Magnus, Philip. *Kitchener: Portrait of an Imperialist*, London: John Murray, 1958.

Malaviya, Madan Moham. 'Note' in Government of India, *Indian Industrial Commission 1916–1918, Report*, Calcutta: Superintendent of Government Printing, 1918.

Mansergh, Nicholas and Moon, Penderel (eds). *The Transfer of Power, 1942–7. Volume 2: 'Quit India', 30 April – 21 September 1942*, London: HMSO, 1971.

—— (eds). *The Transfer of Power, 1942–7. Volume 3: Reassertion of Authority, 21 September 1942 – 12 June 1943*, London: HMSO, 1971.

—— (eds). *The Transfer of Power, 1942–7. Volume 4: The Bengal Famine and the New Viceroyalty, 15 June 1943 – 31 August 1944*, London: HMSO, 1973.

—— (eds). *The Transfer of Power, 1942–7. Volume 5: The Simla Conference, 1 September 1944 – 28 July 1945*, London: HMSO, 1974.

—— (eds). *The Transfer of Power, 1942–7. Volume 7: The Cabinet Mission, 23 March –29 June 1946*, London: HMSO, 1977.

—— (eds). *The Transfer of Power, 1942–7. Volume 9: The Fixing of a Time Limit, 4 November 1946–22 March 1947*, London: HMSO, 1980.

Markovits, Claude. *Indian Business and Nationalist Politics, 1931–1939: The Indigenous Capitalist Class and the Rise of the Congress Party*, Cambridge: Cambridge University Press, 1985.

—— *Merchants, Traders, Entrepreneurs: Indian Business in the Colonial Era*, Basingstoke: Palgrave Macmillan, 2008.

Marx, Karl. 'The East India Company – its history and results', (11 July 1853), in Karl Marx and Frederick Engels (eds), *On Colonialism,* Moscow: Foreign Languages Publishing House, n.d.

—— 'The Government of India', (20 July 1853), in Karl Marx and Frederick Engels (eds), *On Colonialism,* Moscow: Foreign Languages Publishing House, n.d.

—— 'The future results of the British rule in India', (8 August 1853), in Karl Marx and Frederick Engels (eds), *On Colonialism,* Moscow: Foreign Languages Publishing House, n.d.

—— *A Contribution to the Critique of Political Economy*, Moscow: Progress Publishers, 1970 [1859].

Marx, Karl and Engels, Frederick. *The German Ideology*, New York: International Publishers, 1973 [1845].

—— *Manifesto of the Communist Party*, Moscow: Progress Publishers, 1966 [1848].

—— *On Colonialism*, Moscow: Foreign Languages Publishing House, n.d.

—— *Karl Marx on India. From the New York Daily Tribune (including Articles by Frederick Engels) and Extracts from Marx-Engels Correspondence 1853–1862*, edited by Iqbal Husain, New Delhi: Tulika Books, 2008.

—— (eds). *Selected Works*, Moscow: Progress Publishers, 1970.

Masani, Minoo. *Picture of a Plan*, Bombay: Oxford University Press, 1945.

McGuire, John. 'The world economy, the colonial state, and the establishment of the Indian National Congress', in Mike Shepperdson and Colin Simmons (eds), *The Indian National Congress and the Political Economy of India, 1885–1985*, Aldershot: Gower Publishing Company, 1992.

McPherson, Kenneth. *The Muslim Microcosm: Calcutta, 1918 to 1935*, Wiesbaden: Franz Steiner Verlag, 1974.

Mehrotra, S.R. 'Imperial Federation and India, 1868–1917', *Journal of Commonwealth Political Studies,* I, 1 (November 1961).

—— 'The politics behind the Montagu Declaration of 1917', in C.H. Philips (ed.), *Politics and Society in India*, London: George Allen & Unwin Ltd., 1963.

—— *India and the Commonwealth, 1885–1929*, London: George Allen & Unwin, 1965.

Mejcher, Helmut. 'British Middle East policy 1917–1921: The inter-departmental level', *Journal of Contemporary History,* 8, 4 (1973), 81–101.

Metcalfe, Barbara and Thomas. *A Concise History of India*, Cambridge: Cambridge University Press, 2002.

Mishra, Shreegovind. *Constitutional Development and National Movement in India (1919–47)*, Patna: Janaki Prakashan, 1978.

Misra, Bhubanes. *Evolution of the Indian Bourgeoisie – Part One*, Calcutta: Indian Institute of Management, n.d.

Mody, Homi. *Reflections, Wise and Otherwise*, Bombay: Asia Publishing House, 1961.

Mody, Homi and Mathai, John. *A Memorandum on the Economic and Financial Aspects of Pakistan*, Bombay: Commercial Printing Press, 1945.

Montagu, Edwin S. *An Indian Diary*, London: William Heinemann Ltd, 1930.

Montagu, Edwin S. and Chelmsford, Viscount Lord. *Report on Indian Constitutional Reforms*, London: HMSO, 1918.

Moorhouse, Geoffrey. *India Britannica*, London: Paladin Books, 1984.

Moraes, Frank. *Sir Purshotamdas Thakurdas*, Bombay: Asia Publishing House, 1957.

Morris, Morris D. 'Towards a reinterpretation of nineteenth-century Indian economic history', *Journal of Economic History,* XXIII, 4 (December 1963), 606–18.

—— 'The growth of large-scale industry to 1947' in Dharma Kumar and Meghnad Desai (eds), *The Cambridge Economic History of India, Volume 2: c.1757–c.1970*, Cambridge: Cambridge University Press, 1983.

—— 'Indian industry and business in the age of *laissez-faire*', in Divijendra Tripathi (ed.), *State and Business in India: A Historical Perspective*, New Delhi: Manohar, 1987.

Mukherjee, Aditya. 'Business and politics in Bombay', *Indian Historical Review,* 9, 1–2 (1981), 214–22.

—— 'The Workers' and Peasants' Parties, 1926–30: an aspect of Communism in India', *Studies in History,* III, 1 & 2 (1981), 1–44.

—— *Imperialism, Nationalism and the Making of the Indian Capitalist Class, 1920–1947*, New Delhi: Sage Publications, 2002.

Mukherjee, S. 'Emergence of Bengalee entrepreneurship in tea plantation in a Bengal District, 1879–1933', *Indian Economic and Social History Review,* 13, 4 (1976), 487–505.

Mukherji, R.N. *Presidential Address* (Industrial Conference, Allahabad 1910), Allahabad: Secretary of the Industrial Conference, 1910.

Muldoon, Andrew. *Empire, Politics and the Creation of the 1935 India Act: Last Act of the Raj*, Furnham: Ashgate, 2009.

Murti, S. Satya. *The Montagu-Chelmsford Reform Proposals*, Madras: T.S. Joshi, 1918.

Naidu, M. [V.S.S. Shastri]. 'The Bombay Plan', *Workers' International News,* 5, 7 (December 1944). www.marxists.org/history/etol/newspape/win/vol05a/no07a/naidu.htm.

Natesan, Ganapathi A. (ed.). *All About the War: The India Review War Book*, Madras: G.A. Natesan & Co., 1915.

—— (ed.). *India's Goal. Constructive Criticisms by Leading Indians on the Montagu-Chelmsford Scheme*, Madras: G.A. Natesan & Co., 1919.

National Planning Committee. *Abstract of Proceedings, Number 1*, Bombay: National Planning Committee, n.d. [1939].

—— *Abstract of Proceedings, Number 2*, Bombay: National Planning Committee, May 1940.

—— *Abstract of Proceedings, Number 3*, Bombay: National Planning Committee, July 1940.

—— *Abstract of Proceedings, Number 4*, Bombay: National Planning Committee, October 1940.

Nayar, Baldev Raj. 'Business attitudes toward economic planning in India', *Asian Survey,* 11, 9 (1971), 850–65.

Nehru, Jawaharlal. *An Autobiography: with Musings on Recent Events in India*, Bombay: Allied Publishers, 1962 [1936].

—— *The Discovery of India*, London: Meridian Books, 1947.

—— *Nehru: The First Sixty Years, Volumes 1 and 2*, Dorothy Norman (ed.), London: The Bodley Head, 1965.

Ollivier, Maurice (compiler and editor). *The Colonial and Imperial Conferences from 1887 to 1937 – Volumes One to Three*, Ottawa: Queen's Printer and Controller of Stationery, 1954.

Orwell, George. *The War Commentaries*, W.J. West (ed.), Harmondsworth: Penguin, 1987.

Papanek, Hanna. 'Pakistan's big businessmen: Muslim separatism, entrepreneurship, and partial modernization', *Economic Development and Cultural Change,* 21, 1 (October 1972), 1–32.

Paramal, Gita and Herdeck, Margaret. *India's Industrialists*, Washington: Three Continents Press, 1985.

Parkinson, C. Northcote. *War in the Eastern Seas, 1793–1815*, London: George Allen and Unwin, 1954.

Pavlov, V.I. *The Indian Capitalist Class: a Historical Study*, Delhi: People's Publishing House, 1964.

Pedersen, Jorgen Dige. 'Explaining economic liberalization in India: state and society perspectives', *World Development,* 28, 2 (2000), 265–82.

Philips, C.H. (ed.). *Politics and Society in India*, London: George Allen & Unwin Ltd., 1963.

Philips, C.H. and Wainwright, Mary D. (eds). *The Partition of India: Policies and Perspectives, 1935–1947*, Cambridge, Massachusetts: MIT Press, 1970.

Pirzada, Syed S. (ed.). *Foundations of Pakistan. All-India Muslim League Documents. Volume Two, 1924–1947*, Karachi & Dacca: National Publishing House, 1970.

Potter, David C. 'Manpower shortage and the end of colonialism: the case of the Indian Civil Service', *Modern Asian Studies,* 7, 1 (1973), 47–73.

Prasad, Bimal (ed.). *Towards Freedom: Documents on the Movement for Independence in India: 1945*, New Delhi: Indian Council of Historical Research, 2008.

Prasad, Bisheshwar. *Official History of the Indian Armed Forces in the Second World War 1939–45, Volume 12: Defence of India – Policy and Plans*, New Delhi: Combined Inter-Services Historical Section: India and Pakistan, 1963.

Prasad, Bishwa Mohan. *Second World War and Indian Industry, 1939–45: a Case Study of the Coal Industry in Bengal and Bihar*, Delhi: Anamika Prakashan, 1992.

Prasad, Nandan. *Official History of the Indian Armed Forces in the Second World War 1939–45, Volume 4: Expansion of the Armed Forces and Defence Organisation, 1939–45*, New Delhi: Combined Inter-Services Historical Section: India and Pakistan, 1956.

Raghavan, S.R.S. *Planned Economic Development for India*, Allahabad: Kitabistan, 1944.

Rahimtulla, Ibrahim, Ayyar, T.V. Seshagiri, Birla, G.D., Dwarkadas, Jamnadas and Morarjee, Narottam. 'Minute of Dissent' in Indian Fiscal Commission, *Report of the Indian Fiscal Commission, 1921–22*, Simla: Government Central Press, 1922.

Rao, V.P. Madhava. *India's Industrial Problems (Presidential Address to the Calcutta Industrial Conference, 1917)*, Madras: Sons of India, 1918.

Rawson, J.O. 'The role of India in imperial defence beyond Indian frontiers and home waters, 1919–1939', PhD diss., University of Oxford, 1976.

Ray, Rajat K. *Industrialization in India: Growth and Conflict in the Private Corporate Sector, 1914–1947*, Delhi: Oxford University Press, 1979.

—— 'Review of Claude Markovitz [sic], *Indian Business and Politics, 1937–1939*', *Indian Economic and Social History Review,* 25 (1988), 391–4.

—— (ed.). *Entrepreneurship and Industry in India, 1800–1947*, Delhi: Oxford University Press, 1992.

Robb, P.G. *The Government of India and Reform: Policies towards Politics and the Constitution*, Oxford: Oxford University Press, 1976.

Robins, Nick. *The Corporation that Changed the World: How the East India Company Shaped the Modern Multinational,* London: Pluto Press, 2006.

Robinson, Ronald and Gallagher, John with Alice Denny. *Africa and the Victorians: the Official Mind of Imperialism*, Houndmills: Macmillan Publishers Ltd., 1985 [1961].

Robson, Brian. *Crisis on the Frontier: the Third Afghan War and the Campaign in Waziristan, 1919–1920*, Strud: Spellmount, 2007.

Roemer, John (ed.). *Analytical Marxism*, Cambridge: Cambridge University Press, 1986.

Root, Hilton L. 'A Liberal India: the triumph of hope over experience', *Asian Survey,* 38, 5 (May 1998), 510–34.

Roy, Asim. 'The high politics of India's Partition: the revisionist perspective', *India's Partition: Process, Strategy and Moblization,* edited by Mushirul Hasan, New Delhi: Oxford University Press, 2001.

Roy, M.N. *The Future of Indian Politics*, London: Dorrit Press Ltd., n.d.

Rumbold, Algernon. *Watershed in India, 1914–1922*, London: Athlone Press, 1979.

Rungta, Radhe Shyam. *The Rise of Business Corporations in India, 1851–1900*, Cambridge: Cambridge University Press, 1970.

Rushbrook Williams, L.F. *Statement exhibiting the Moral and Material Progress and Condition of India during the Year 1920*, London: HMSO, 1921.

—— *Statement exhibiting the Moral and Material Progress and Condition of India during the Year 1922–1923*, India: n.p., 1923.

—— *Statement exhibiting the Moral and Material Progress and Condition of India during the Year 1923–1924*, Calcutta: Government of India Central Publications Branch, 1924.

Saini, Krishan G. 'The economic aspects of India's participation in the First World War', in DeWitt C. Ellinwood and S.D. Pradhan (eds), *India and World War I*, Delhi: Manohar, 1978.

Sankarakrishna, K.C. (ed.). *India's Demands: a Collection of the Speeches delivered on the platforms of the Indian National Congress and the All India Muslim League, 1916*, Madras: Sankarakrishna, 1917.

Sarkar, N.R. 'Mr N.R. Sarkar's Note on the economic implications of Pakistan', in Sir Taj Bahadur Sapru, M.R. Jayakar, N.G. Ayyangar and Jagdish Prasad (eds), *Constitutional Proposals of The Sapru Committee*, xvi–xxi, Bombay: Secretary, Sapru Committee, 1945.

Sarkar, Sumit. *Modern India, 1885–1947*, Madras: Macmillan India Ltd., 1983.

Sayeed, Khalid B. *Pakistan: the Formative Phase, 1857–1948*, London: Oxford University Press, 1968.

Schumpeter, Joseph. *Imperialism and Social Classes*, New York: A.M. Kelley, 1951 [1919].

Schuster, Sir George. *Private Work and Public Causes: A Personal Record 1881–1978*, Cowbridge: D. Brown and Sons, 1979.

Scott, J.C. *Seeing Like a State: How Certain Schemes to Improve the Human Condition Have Failed*, New Haven: Yale University Press, 1998.

Sen, Amartya Kumar. 'The pattern of British enterprise in India, 1854–1914: A causal analysis', in Rajat K. Ray (ed.), *Entrepreneurship and Industry in India, 1800–1947*, Delhi: Oxford University Press, 1992.

—— *Studies in Industrial Policy and Development of India (1858–1914)*, Calcutta: Progressive Publishers, 1964.

Sender, John and Smith, Sheila. *The Development of Capitalism in Africa*, London: Methuen, 1986.

Seth, Hira Lal. *The Red Sun of the East: A Biographical Study of Jawaharlal Nehru*, Lahore: Hero Publications, 1943.

Shah, K.T. *Handbook of National Planning Committee*, Bombay: Vora & Co., 1946.

Shah, N.J. *A History of Indian Tariffs*, Bombay: Thacker & Company Ltd., 1924.

Shepperdson, Mike and Simmons, Colin (eds). *The Indian National Congress and the Political Economy of India, 1885–1985*, Aldershot: Gower Publishing Company, 1992.

Simmons, Colin. 'Indigenous enterprise in the Indian coal mining industry c. 1835–1939', *Indian Economic and Social History Review*, 13 (1976), 189–217.

—— '"De-industrialization", Industrialization and the Indian Economy, c. 1850–1947', *Modern Asian Studies*, 19, 3 (1985).

Singh, Iqbal. *The Indian National Congress: A Reconstruction, Volume One, 1885–1987*, New Delhi: Manohar, 1987.

Sinha, N.C. and Khera, P.N. (eds). *Official History of the Indian Armed Forces in the Second World War 1939–45, Volume 14: Indian War Economy (Supply, Industry and Finance)*, New Delhi: Combined Inter-Services Historical Section: India and Pakistan, 1962.

Srinivasan, Roopa, Tiwari, Manish, and Silas, Sandeep (eds). *Our Indian Railway: Themes in India's Railway History*, New Delhi: Cambridge University Press (India), 2006.

Srivastava, M.P. (ed.). *Constitutional and National Development in India (Montagu-Chelmsford Report)*, New Delhi: Ess Ess Publications, 1981.

Strachey, John. *The End of Empire*, London: Victor Gollancz Ltd., 1959.

Swaminathan, Padmini. 'State intervention in India: a case study of the Madras presidency', *Indian Economic and Social History Review*, 29, 4 (1992), 479–506.

Talbot, Ian. 'Planning for Pakistan: the Planning Committee of the All-India Muslim League, 1943–46', *Modern Asian Studies*, 28, 4 (1994), 875–89.

Tariff Commission [UK]. *The Status of the Dominions and their Relations with Foreign Countries*, Westminster: P.S. King & Sons, 1920.

Tata, J.R.D. *Letters*, edited by Arvind Mambro, New Delhi: Rupa & Co., 2004.

Thakurdas, Purshotamdas, Tata, J.R.D., Birla, G.D., Dalal, Ardeshir, Ram, Shri, Lalbhai, Kasturbhai, Shroff, A.D. and Matthai, John. *Memorandum Outlining a Plan of Economic Development for India, Parts One and Two*, Harmondsworth: Penguin, 1945.

Thakurta, Paranjoy G. 'Bombay Plan and mixed-up economy', *Businessline,* 7 September 2004.

Tinker, Hugh. 'India in the First World War and after', *Journal of Contemporary History*, III, 4, (October 1968), 89–107.

Tomlinson, Brian R. 'India and the British Empire, 1880–1935', *Indian Economic and Social History Review,* 12 (October–December 1974), 337–80.

—— 'India and the British Empire, 1935–1947', *Indian Economic and Social History Review,* 13 (1976), 331–49.

—— *The Political Economy of the Raj 1914–1947: The Economics of Decolonization in India*, London: Macmillan, 1979.

Tripathi, Dwijendra. *The Dynamics of a Tradition: Kastubhai Lalbhai and his Entrepreneurship*, New Delhi: Manohar, 1981.

—— (ed.). *State and Business in India: A Historical Perspective*, New Delhi: Manohar, 1987.

—— (ed.). *The Concise Oxford History of Indian Business*, New Delhi: Oxford University Press, 2007.

Visvesvaraya, Sir M. *Reconstruction in Post-War India: a Plan of Development All Round*, Bombay: The All-India Manufacturers' Organisation, September 1944.

von Albertini, Rudolf. 'The impact of two world wars on the decline of colonialism', *Journal of Contemporary History,* 4, 1 (1969), 17–35.

Wagle, Dileep M. 'Imperial preference and the Indian steel industry, 1924–39', *Economic History Review,* 34, 1 (February 1981), 120–31.

Wainwright, Martin A. *Inheritance of Empire: Britain, India and the Balance of Power in Asia, 1938–1955*, Westport: Praeger, 1994.

Washbrook, David. 'South Asia, the world system and world capitalism', in Sugata Bose (ed.), *South Asia and World Capitalism*, Delhi: Oxford University Press, 1990.

Woods, Philip. *Roots of Parliamentary Democracy in India: Montagu Chelmsford Reforms, 1917–1923*, Delhi: Chanakya Publications, 1996.

Wrigley, C.C. 'Neo-mercantile policies and the new imperialism', in Clive Dewey and A.G. Hopkins (eds), *The Imperial Impact: Studies in the Economic History of Africa and India,* London: The Athlone Press, 1978.

Zacharias, H.C.E. *Renascent India, from Rammohan Roy to Mohandas Gandhi*, London: George Allen & Unwin 1933.

INDEX

A

Abrahams, Lionel (Financial Secretary India Office) 24
Abyssinian War Second (1868) 16
Afghan War Third (1919) 53
Ainscough, Thomas (British Trade Commissioner) 14, 41, 46, 47, 53
All India Congress Committee 129, 131–32, 134, 136, 138, 143–44, 158–60, 165–67, 169, 174, 177, 179–82, 187, 195–96
All-India Chemical Service 71
All-India Industrial Service 70–71
America 33, 41, 85, 106, 152, 155
American Civil War 8, 16
American Technical Mission 1942 (Grady Mission) 154, 176
Amery, Leo (Secretary of State) 152
Anstey, Vera 54
Australia 153–54
Austria 84

B

Babtie, Sir William 57
Bajaj, Jamnalal 132
Baldwin, Stanley (Prime Minister) 98, 110
Balfour, Lord 85
Belgium 106, 109
Benares Congress 26
Besant, Annie 131
Bhore, Sir Joseph 115
Birla, Ghanshyamdas 100, 103, 105, 113–16, 131, 133–44, 146–48, 156–57, 159, 161–62, 165–68, 171, 181–82, 184, 189, 194, 196, 197
Blackett, Sir Basil 108
BMOA *See* Bombay Mill Owners Association
Bombay Mill Owners Association (BMOA) 14, 112–14, 135
Bombay Plan 182, 185–88, 192
Bombay Seed Trades' Association 192
Bose, Subhas Chandra 128, 145, 148, 177
Bourgeois Revolution 5
Bourgeoisie
  Class 3
  Economy 122, 132, 161, 182
  Indian Beginings 28, 93
  Political 3, 11, 124
Bright, John 74
British
  Empire 3, 8, 15–16, 23, 25–30, 34, 37, 42, 46–47, 49–51, 53–55, 62–65, 72–73, 78, 80–88, 91–93, 98, 101–105, 110, 116, 119, 123–24, 140, 150–155, 162, 175

State 4–8, 12, 33, 51, 78–81, 85, 87, 89, 92, 94–95, 115–117, 122, 124, 126, 150, 157, 169, 196
British India Navigation Company 32, 80, 118, 121, 191
Buchanan, Sir George 58

C

Capitalism 5–6, 8, 74–76, 130, 170, 178, 181, 183, 185, 195, 197
Capitalists 2, 4
Caste System 9
Cecil, Lord (Under-Secretary of State and Foreign Affairs) 85
Central Department of Industries 69
Chamberlain, Austen (Secretary of State) 34, 36, 40, 60–61, 63, 83
Chatfield
  Committee 156
  Report 152
Chatterton, Alfred 19–22
Chelmsford, Lord (Secretary of State/Viceroy) 11, 43, 46–47, 64–65, 67
Churchill, Winston 158, 160–62, 166
Civil Disobedience 95, 103, 133–34, 136–37, 139–42, 144, 146, 158, 165–67
Coastal Traffic Reservation Bill 120–21, 141
Cobden, Richard 74
Colliery Control Order (1944) 175
Colonialism 7, 73–77, 93–95, 126, 131
Compagnie des Indes 79
Congress Socialist Party 145–46
Corbett, Sir Geoffrey 87
Cotton Textile Industry (Protection) Bill (1930) 113
Crewe, Lord (Secretary of State for India) 23, 28
Cripps Mission (1942) 157–58
Currimbhoy, Fazilbhoy 35
Curzon, Lord (Viceroy) 15–19, 23, 25, 28–29

D

Dalal, Ardeshir 188, 190
Defence of India Act (1915) 31–32
Department of Commerce and Industry 16
Duff, Sir Harry 'Beauchamp' 58, 60

E

East India Company 78–79
Eastern Group Conference (1940) 153–54
Engels, Frederick 5–6, 74, 96, 125
Esher, Lord 89–91
Excess Profits Tax (1940) 159

F

Faizpur Congress (1936) 128
Federation of Indian Chambers of Commerce and Industry (FICCI) 97–98, 103–06, 112–14, 116–17, 122–24, 127, 134–38, 142, 144, 152, 154–56, 160–69, 171, 181, 184–85, 189, 192–94, 196
First World War 6, 9, 15, 23, 30, 33–34, 40–41, 43, 45–46, 55, 69–70, 73, 78, 81, 84, 93, 96, 98, 130, 150, 176, 195
France 5, 13, 30, 79
French Economic Conference 5–6, 79, 82

G

Gallagher, John 74
Gandhi
  Indira 1, 3

Gandhi (*Contd*)
  Mohandas 2, 128, 132–33, 135–38, 140–44, 147, 159, 161, 166–69, 190, 194
  Sanjay 1
Garran Tribunal 150
Germany 13, 20, 32–33, 77, 83–84, 124, 128, 150, 159, 181
Ghia, M.C. 153, 157, 190
Government of India Act 80, 138, 149, 161
Grady Mission *See* American Technical Mission
Grigg, Sir Percy 186, 188

H

Hamilton, Lord (Secretary of State) 18
Hardinge, Lord (Viceroy) 25, 30–31, 34–36, 40, 46–48, 57, 64
Hartington, Lord (Secretary of State) 17
Harvey, W.L. 19
Herbert, Sir John 156
Hewett, Sir John 11, 20
Holderness, Thomas 24, 34, 48, 57, 84
Holland 78, 79
Holland, Sir Thomas 35, 37, 42, 44, 47, 52–53, 69–71, 99, 140

I

IIC *See* Indian Industrial Commission
Imam, Syed Hasan 13
Imperial Conference
  1911 81
  1921 87
  1923 102
  1930 87, 89
Imperial Economic Conference (Ottowa 1932) 98, 103–05
Imperial War Conference
  1917 82, 84
  1918 85
Imperialism 25, 74–75, 77, 114, 130, 170
Import Duties Act (1932) 103
Inchcape, Lord (James L. Mackay) 118–20
Indian Army 30–31, 53, 60, 89, 91, 150–51, 162, 180
Indian Civil Service (ICS) 180
Indian Expeditionary Force 30, 56
Indian Fiscal Commission (1921) 112
Indian Independence 184
Indian Industrial Commission (IIC) 13, 15, 20, 27, 34, 36–37, 42, 47, 53, 70
Indian Merchant Marine 118–21
Indian Merchants' Chamber 118, 137, 141, 157, 160, 163–64, 190
Indian Munitions Board 36–37, 45–46, 52, 69, 118
Indian National Congress 3, 5–6, 10, 13, 64
Indian Nationalism 107–08, 120, 133, 166
Indian Retrenchment Committee 66, 69, 71
Indian Self-Governance 41
Indian Tariff Board 100
India's Strategic Position 25
Indo-British Association 65
Indo-British Trade Agreement (1935) 115, 123
Industrialisation 3–4, 9, 20, 49, 65, 152, 164, 177, 188, 191
Industry
  Automobile 1, 153, 164–65
  Cigarette and Tabacco 16, 24
  Coal 9, 32, 176
  Cotton 8–9, 15–16, 19, 31, 37–38, 46, 50–51, 84, 93, 111–16, 120, 128, 152, 175
  Iron and Steel 9, 15–18, 24, 27, 34, 107, 109–11
  Jute 8–9, 30, 32, 37, 50, 93, 133

Lead and Zinc 48
Leather 20, 37
Munitions 33, 36–37, 45–46, 52, 61, 69–70, 118, 152, 154
Salt 38–39, 141
Ship Building 119, 164, 177
Shipping 127, 185
State Control of 175–76, 178–79, 184
Tea 8, 38
Irwin, Lord (Viceroy) 120–21, 135–36, 140, 144
Islington, Lord (Under Secretary of State for India) 34, 36
Italy 77, 124, 128, 150

J

Japan 13, 33, 41, 85, 112–14, 119, 124, 128, 150, 156, 160–62, 167, 169
Jinnah, Muhammad Ali 170–73, 180, 189–91
Joshi, N.M. 107

K

Karachi Congress (1931) 127, 147, 178
Kautsky, Karl 74, 76
Keenan, John 109, 132
Kershaw, L.J. 34, 45, 84, 86
Kisch, C.H. 100
Krishna, Gopal 129

L

Laissez-faire 15, 28, 41, 46, 53, 69
Lal, Chaman 71, 103, 107
Law, Bonar (Secretary of State for the Colonies) 50
Lawley, Sir Arthur 21
Lenin, Vladimir 75–77
Linlithgow, Lord (Viceroy) 139, 149, 157, 161
Lloyd George, David 49, 82, 87

M

Macauley, Captain D.I. 25
Madras Agriculture Committee 15
Malaviya, Madan Mohan 35, 108, 134
Marta, Vishnawath Prasad 14
Marx, Karl 5, 8, 79, 96
Mehta, Chunilal 111, 154, 163, 166–67, 171, 185, 189
Mehta, G.L. 162
Mesopotamia 42–43, 53, 55–63, 88, 89
Mesopotamia Commission 55, 58, 60–63
Meston, Sir James 49
Meyer, William 35
Miller, Robert 18
Milner, Lord 81
Minto, Lord (Viceroy) 14
Mody, Homi 94, 113–15, 122, 142, 146, 148, 163–64, 169, 190, 193, 197
Mody-Lees Pact 114–15
Molesworth, Sir Guilford 14
Montagu, Edwin (Under Secretary of State and Minister for Munitions) 61–65, 68–69
Montagu-Chelmsford Report 14, 49–50, 53–54, 64–65, 68–69, 90, 96, 99
Morarjee, Narottam 100, 118–19
Morley, Lord (Secretary of State for India) 14, 22–23, 28, 32
Mountbatten, Lord 175
Mudaliar, Ramaswami A. 164
Mughal Empire 78
Mukherjee, R.N. 35
Mukherji, R.N. 13–14
Muslim League 168, 170, 172–73, 180, 189, 191, 193

N

Narain, Jagat 40
Narayan, Jayaprakash 145
Nath, Lala Baij 12–14, 71, 107, 161, 196

Nehru
  Jawaharlal 127–28, 140, 145–46, 167, 178–79, 180–82, 189, 192
  Motilal 133–34
Nicolson Commission 60
Non-Cooperation Movement (1921) 106, 167

O

Opium 24
Ottoman Empire 55

P

Padshah, Burjorji 44–45
Pakistan 170, 172–73, 180, 189–94
Pakistan Resolution (1940) 189
Partition 170, 189, 194
Patel, V.J. 107, 135, 168
Perin, Charles 44
Poland 149
Privatisation 1
Public Safety Bill (1928) 134

Q

Quit India Movement 159–60, 162, 166–68, 171, 186–87

R

Rahimtulla, Ibrahim 100
Railways 9, 14–15, 17–19, 25–27, 37, 42–43, 80, 106, 117–118, 121, 127, 153–54, 171, 175
Ram, Lal Shri 103, 161, 168, 182, 193
Ranade, Mahadev Govind 12
Ripon, Lord (Viceroy) 17–18
Roberts, Lord 26
Robinson, Ronald 74
Roger Mission 154
Roger, Sir Alexander 154
Royal Indian Navy
  Revolt in 180
Rudman, F.R. (Department of Munitions and Industry) 70

S

Sapru Committee 190, 193
Sarabhai, Ambalal 136, 143, 147
Sarkar, Nalini R. 114, 117, 122, 138–39, 167, 169, 190–91
Schumpeter, Joseph 74–76
Scindia Steam Navigation Company 100, 118–21
Scorched Earth Policy 155
Scramble for Africa 75, 78
Second World War 6–7, 134, 149–50, 161–62, 164, 169
Seven Years' War (1756–1763) 79
Simon Commission (1930) 91, 140
Simons, Sir John 84
Soviet Union (USSR) 1, 124, 128, 130, 155, 181, 186
Spain 79
Steel Protection Bill 108, 110
Swadeshi Movement 10–12, 14, 142, 146
Swaraj Party 108, 127, 134
Sykes, Sir Frederick 142

T

Tata
  Dorabji 35, 42–43, 45, 106, 133, 146
  Jamsetji 16, 18–19, 168, 182–83, 185
  Jehnagir Ratanji Dadabhoy 167, 182
  Ratanji Dadabhoy 109
Tata Iron and Steel Company (TISCO) 18–19, 37, 42–45, 105–11, 131–32, 148, 152, 182
Ten Year Rule 88

Thakurdas, Purshotamdas 39, 108, 117–18, 126, 131, 133–36, 140–43, 146–47, 155, 162–63, 165, 167–68, 171, 178, 182, 189, 193–94
Trades Disputes Bill (1929) 134

V

Visvesvaraya, Sir Mokshagundam 177, 185

W

War of the Austrian Succession (1740–1748) 79
War of the Spanish Succession (1701–1714) 79
Wedgwood, Josiah 58–59, 61–62
Willingdon, Lord (Viceroy) 103
WWI *See* First World War
WWII *See* Second World War